A PRACTITIONER'S GUIDE TO INHERITANCE ACT CLAIMS

A PRACTITIONER'S GUIDE TO INHERITANCE ACT CLAIMS

Fourth edition

Nasreen Pearce

WS &H

Wildy, Simmonds & Hill Publishing

ISBN: 978-0-85490-298-9

British Library Cataloguing in Publication Data

A catalogue record for this book is available from the British Library

Third edition 2017

This edition published in 2023 by

Wildy, Simmonds & Hill Publishing
Wildy & Sons Ltd
Lincoln's Inn Archway
Carey Street
London WC2A 2JD
www.wildy.com

Typeset by Heather Jones, North Petherton, Somerset.
Printed in Great Britain by CPI Antony Rowe, Chippenham, Wiltshire.

Contents

Table of Cases

References are to page numbers

Table of Statutes

References are to page numbers

Table of Statutory Instruments

References are to page numbers

Table of Guides and Codes of Practice

References are to page numbers

Table of International Materials

References are to page numbers

Chapter 1

Introduction

1.1 BACKGROUND

It has long been a characteristic of English law that, provided a person has testamentary capacity and complies with the formalities relating to the making of a valid will, they may, in their will, make provision for the disposal of their entire estate on death as they choose, and their estate will devolve in accordance with the terms of the will. If a person dies without having made a will, or if they leave a will which in law is not valid, the law relating to intestacy operates and the estate will devolve in accordance with that law. If the provisions made in the will do not dispose of the entirety of the estate, then the property will devolve in part in accordance with the terms of the will, and the remainder will pass under the law of intestacy. In many legal systems, and especially those based on Roman law, immediate family members and other defined persons enjoy fixed rights of inheritance to the estate of the deceased irrespective of the deceased's wishes and thus complete freedom of testation is unknown.

Statutes and, consequently, case law have, however, made inroads into this freedom in order to meet progressive thinking, social and economic needs and pressures, and scientific changes that have occurred since the First and Second World Wars. The ratification by the United Kingdom in 1951 of the European Convention for the Protection of Human Rights and Fundamental Freedoms 1950 (Human Rights Convention), which came into force in 1953, and its subsequent incorporation into UK law in the Human Rights Act 1998 have also impacted on domestic legislation and its interpretation. In order to be Convention-compliant and to deal with the impact of these changes, courts have interpreted statutory provisions and confronted the particular circumstances of the case that they are faced with in order to fill the lacuna in legislation and to meet with the justice of the case. For example, in relation to cohabitants, constructive trust law has been relied on to establish beneficial interests; and with regard to those on state benefits, courts have arrived at a decision which meets some of the needs of the claimant while enabling the person to continue receiving some, if not all, of the benefits. The case of *Ilott v The Blue Cross and Others* [2017] UKSC 17 is an example of the court's jurisdiction to depart from the testator's will so as to meet with the justice of the case and the needs of the claimant on state benefits (for the overruled decisions of the Court of Appeal, see *Ilott v Mitson* [2011] EWCA Civ 346, [2012] 2 FLR 170 and [2015] EWCA Civ 797). This approach has led some to suggest that the principle of testamentary freedom has been undermined and that the purpose of the legislation is being ignored. This perception is misconceived because Lord Hughes' judgment in *Ilott v The Blue Cross and Others* [2017] UKSC 17 begins with a recognition of the individual's testamentary freedom and the specific limitations of the provisions in the Inheritance (Provisions for Family and Dependants) Act 1975 (I(PFD)A 1975) (at [1]–[2]). When dealing with the historical background to the current law, Lord Hughes again referred to the significance attached by English law to testamentary freedom. Similarly, regarding the decision in relation to the express wishes of the testatrix, Lord Hughes pointed out (at [47]) that:

> it was not correct to say of the wishes of the deceased that because Parliament has provided for claims by those qualified under section 1 it follows that that by itself strikes the balance between testamentary wishes and such claim. It is not the case that once there is a qualified claimant and a demonstrated need for maintenance, the testator's wishes cease to be of any weight. They may of course be overridden, but they are part of the circumstances of the case and fall to be assessed in the round together with all other relevant factors.

(See, also, Lady Hale's judgment at [50]–[66].)

However, the courts are having to face the challenges presented to them as a result of social changes, in order to find a just and fair solution, which they have been doing for centuries and will continue to do so until the government of the day has the will and is persuaded to deal with the issues, and the slow wheels of the legislature get round to making the appropriate changes.

The first statutory provision to make inroads into testamentary freedom was the Inheritance (Family Provision) Act 1938 (I(FP)A 1938). It applied to the estates of persons dying after 13 July 1939 who were domiciled in England and Wales. It introduced into English law the concept of reasonable testamentary provision and provided for the maintenance of dependants out of the deceased's estate. The Intestates' Estates Act 1952 amended the I(FP)A 1938. The most important change was the extension of the I(FP)A 1938 to cases where the deceased was intestate. It also permitted the court to award to a surviving spouse the whole of the income of the net estate; increased the amount of the lump sum order which could be made; provided for the extension of the 6-month time limit within which claims had to be brought in certain circumstances; and made provisions for the protection of personal representatives.

Matrimonial Causes Act 1965, ss 26–28 made provisions for a former spouse to apply for an order for maintenance from the deceased's estate on the ground that the deceased had not made reasonable provision for the survivor's maintenance after the deceased's death. The Family Provision Act 1966 further amended the I(FP)A 1938, most importantly by extending the court's jurisdiction to hear such claims to the county courts where the value of the net estate did not exceed £5,000.

The I(PFD)A 1975, which came into force on 1 April 1976, repealed the previous enactments and made comprehensive provisions for a limited class of persons identified in s 1(1) of the Act (as subsequently amended) to make a claim against the estate of the deceased on the ground that the disposition of an estate (whether effected by will, by the intestacy rules or by the combination of the two) has failed to make reasonable financial provision for what is needed for their maintenance and for the court to make orders out of the estate of a deceased in their favour. This still remains the Act under which a claim against the estate of a deceased person may be made, although it has been amended over the years to meet the needs of an ever-changing modern global society, the varied forms of family and the extension of non-traditional family. For example, I(PFD)A 1975, s 15 was extended by the Matrimonial and Family Proceedings Act 1984 (MFPA 1984) to give the court power, when dealing with a claim under the MFPA 1984 for financial relief after an overseas divorce, annulment of marriage or legal separation order, to make an order disentitling one or both of the parties from making any claims for an order under the I(PFD)A 1975. Civil Partnership Act 2004 (CPA 2004), s 71, Sch 4, Part 2, para 21 inserted an additional s 15ZA to extend the restriction to civil partnerships (see, further, para 7.11.1).

The Law Reform (Succession) Act 1995 amended the I(PFD)A 1975 by extending the class of persons who can apply for financial provision, to include any person (not the spouse or a former spouse of the deceased) who, during the 2 years immediately preceding the death of the deceased, had been living with the deceased in the same household as the deceased as the husband or wife of the deceased.

In the meantime, the struggle for the rights of those in same sex relationships had continued since the decriminalisation of such relationships as a result of the enactment of the Sexual Offences Act 1967. The impact of this legislation in relation to the inheritance rights of those in same sex relationships and claims under the I(PFD)A 1975, observations made in the judgments in the Court of Appeal and the House of Lords (now the Supreme Court) in *Fitzpatrick v Sterling Housing Association Ltd* [1998] Ch 304 and the decision in *Mendoza v Ghaidan* [2002] EWCA Civ 1533, [2003] 1 FLR 468, led the way to the court applying the same principle in a claim made by the survivor of a couple in a same sex relationship under the I(PFD)A 1975 in *Saunders v Garrett* [2005] WTLR 749.

Although the CPA 2004 had received Royal Assent on 18 November 2004, it did not come into force until 5 December 2005 and therefore it could not be applied to the case.

The CPA 2004 led to further amendments to the I(PFD)A 1975 so that certain persons in same sex relationships were included within the class of persons eligible to make a claim under the Act. The CPA 2004 initially made provision to enable same sex couples to make a formal commitment to each other by registering their civil partnership. This is done by both individuals signing a civil partnership document in the presence of each other, the registrar and two witnesses. The civil partnership document must then also be signed by the registrar and the witnesses. Once the partnership has been registered, the couple's relationship is treated in the same way as a marriage. In order to take account of the provisions set out in the CPA 2004, the I(PFD)A 1975 was amended by CPA 2004, Sch 4, paras 15–27, to give same sex couples who have entered into a civil partnership the same rights as those enjoyed by married opposite sex couples. With effect from 5 December 2005, a surviving civil partner of the deceased has had the right to apply for financial provision on the same basis as a surviving spouse. Where the same sex couple have not entered into a civil partnership, on the death of one of them, the survivor may claim as a cohabitant of the deceased provided the conditions set out in CPA 2004, s 1(B) are met. A surviving civil partner may also apply for, and be granted, probate and letters of administration (CPA 2004, Sch 4, para 6). Amendments made to the Administration of Estates Act 1925, the Intestates' Estates Act 1952 and the Family Provisions Act 1966 have resulted in a surviving civil partner having the same status as a surviving spouse. A surviving civil partner now also has the same rights on intestacy as a surviving spouse and rights as a spouse to acquire the family home when their partner dies intestate. Civil partnership, like marriage, amounts to valuable consideration for the purposes of the Administration of Estates Act 1925 (CPA 2004, Sch 4, paras 7–14).

The right to enter into a civil partnership was then not available to opposite sex couples. In *Steinfeld & Keidan v Secretary of State for Education* [2017] EWCA Civ 81, the couple, who were of the opposite sex, appealed against the dismissal of their case for judicial review. All three judges of the Court of Appeal recognised that the current legal position whereby civil partnership was available only to same sex couples was open to criticism, but by a majority of 2:1 concluded that the government should be given more time to undertake a proper assessment of the best way forward, including the extension of civil partnership to opposite sex couples. Arden LJ, however, considered that the potential violation of the appellants' rights was not justified by the government's current policy of 'wait and see', which she considered to be open-ended in time, focused solely on the reduction of civil partnership, and not addressing the wider issues. On further appeal to the Supreme Court, the court exercised its power under Human Rights Act 1998, s 4 to make a declaration that 'sections 1 and 3 of CPA (to the extent that they preclude an opposite sex couple from entering into a civil partnership) are incompatible with article 14 of ECHR taken in conjunction with article 8 of the Convention' (*R (Steinfeld and Keidan) v Secretary of State for International Development (in substitution for the Home Secretary and the Education Secretary)* [2018] UKSC 32, [62]).

In the meantime, Tim Loughton MP introduced a Private Members' Bill – the Civil Partnership Act 2004 (Amendment) Bill 2016–17. The Bill proposed an amendment to the CPA 2004 to remove its limitation to 'same sex couples' and thus provide that couples in same sex and opposite sex relationships may enter into a civil partnership with the same rights.

It had its second reading on 13 January 2017, but the debate was adjourned until 12 May 2017. With the announcement of the General Election and dissolution of Parliament on 3 May 2017, the Bill failed. Subsequently, the issue was dealt with pursuant to the Civil Partnership Marriages and Deaths (Registration etc) Act 2019, under the Civil Partnership (Opposite-sex Couples) Regulations 2019 (SI 2019/1458). Consequently, as from 31 December 2019, opposite sex couples are now able to enter into a civil partnership with all the rights enjoyed by same sex partners set out in the CPA 2004.

The situation of cohabiting couples whether in same sex or opposite sex relationships remains in limbo. Notwithstanding the recommendations made by the Law Commission in its report, *Cohabitation: The Financial Consequences of Relationship Breakdown*, Law Com No 307 (TSO, 2007), for the extension of rights to cohabiting couples and the fact that the Family Law (Scotland) Act 2006 has given rights and remedies to separating cohabitants including rights on death, the government has been reluctant to introduce legislation to do so in England and Wales. The government's initial response was that the research on the Scottish legislation needed to be reviewed, and that the family justice system was undergoing major reforms. Time has passed and, to date, nothing has been done to correct this injustice and discrimination.

The Law Commission in its report published on 14 December 2011, *Intestacy and Family Provision Claims on Death*, Law Com No 331 (TSO, 2011), made further recommendations in relation to claims made under the I(PFD)A 1975, which included giving inheritance rights to certain categories of cohabitants. The Law Commission set out its recommendation in two draft Bills – the draft Inheritance and Trustees' Powers Bill and the draft Inheritance (Cohabitants) Bill. The provisions set out in the Law Commission's draft Inheritance and Trustees' Powers Bill included provisions to:

- ensure that where a couple are married or in a civil partnership, assets pass on intestacy to the surviving spouse/civil partner in all cases where there are no children or other descendants;
- simplify the sharing of assets on intestacy where the deceased was survived by a spouse and children or other descendants;
- protect children who suffer the death of a parent from the risk of losing an inheritance from that parent in the event that they are adopted after death;
- amend the legal rules which currently disadvantage unmarried fathers when a child dies intestate;
- remove arbitrary obstacles to family provision claims by dependants of the deceased and anyone treated by the deceased as a child of their family outside the context of a marriage/civil partnership;
- permit a claim for family provision in certain circumstances where the deceased died 'domiciled outside England and Wales but left property and family members and dependants here'; and
- reform trustees' statutory powers to use income and capital for the benefit of trust beneficiaries (subject to any express provision in the trust instrument).

These provisions were incorporated into the Inheritance and Trustees' Powers Act 2014, which received Royal Assent on 14 May 2014 and came into force on 1 October 2014. The Act includes reforms to intestate succession and amendments to the I(PFD)A 1975 as set out in Inheritance and Trustees' Powers Act 2014, Sch 2. These, and the impact of the reforms on intestacy, are dealt with later in the text where appropriate.

The draft Inheritance (Cohabitants) Bill has not as yet been implemented.

In 2012, the Supreme Court in *Gow (FC) v Grant* [2012] UKSC 29 considered the lead up to, and developments since, the Law Commission's *Cohabitation* report and the rights set out in the Family Law (Scotland) Act 2006. In her judgment, Lady Hale stated:

> 55. ... Thus, it seems to me, the flexibility inherent in the Scottish provisions is preferable to the Law Commission's proposal that the losses should be shared between them. On the other hand, the Law Commission's proposed list of factors to be taken into account in the exercise of the court's discretion might be a useful addition to the Scottish law, as also might the power to make a periodical payments order in those rare cases where it is not practicable to make an order that a capital sum be paid by instalments.
>
> 56. The main lesson from this case, as also from the research so far, is that a remedy such as this is both practicable and fair. It does not impose upon unmarried couples the responsibilities of marriage but redresses the gains and losses flowing from their relationship. As the researchers comment, 'The Act has

> undoubtedly achieved a lot for Scottish cohabitants and their children'. English and Welsh cohabitants and their children deserve no less.

See, further, [45]–[56] of the judgment.

The Cohabitation Rights Bill 2019–21 was first introduced in the House of Lords in October 2013 but did not progress beyond the first reading. Since then, it has been introduced annually with some revisions, the last occasion being on 6 February 2020. The Bill proposes to safeguard the rights of persons who live together or have lived together as a couple, and to address the economic benefits that one party has derived and the economic contribution of the other, including the non-financial contribution made by another so as to provide a just and fair result and to make provisions for a cohabitant or former cohabitant on the death of one of the parties to the relationship. The current long title of the Bill states that it is 'A bill to provide certain protections for persons who live together or have lived together as a couple; to make provision about property of deceased persons survived by a cohabitant and for connected purposes'.

Meanwhile, a report, *The rights of cohabiting partners*, published on 4 August 2022 by the Women and Equalities Committee (a cross-party group of MPs) (available at https://publications.parliament.uk/pa/cm5803/cmselect/cmwomeq/92/report.html) recommends a pragmatic approach for reforming cohabitation law to protect cohabiting couples and the need for legislation to be introduced in the next parliamentary session in line with the recommendation made in the Law Commission's report. In particular, the report stresses the fact that there are now 3.6 million cohabitants (one in five couples) living together in the United Kingdom. In relation to inheritance rights, the committee recommends that cohabitants must have the right to inherit the family home after the death of a partner and without the obligation of paying an inheritance tax bill. It also recommends that the government must implement the recommendations made by the Law Commission in 2011, which would provide cohabitants with the right to inherit under the intestacy rules; review the inheritance tax scheme so that cohabiting partners are placed on an equal footing to married couples and civil partners; and that clear guidelines should be published, setting out how pension schemes should treat surviving cohabiting partners. For further information, see https://committees.parliament.uk/committee/328/women-and-equalities-committee/news/172666/myth-of-common-law-marriage-leaves-disadvantaged-groups-disproportionately-at-risk/.

Resolution, too, has urged that the legal limbo for cohabiting couples should be ended to ensure that cohabiting couples have better legal protection.

The government in its response received on 4 October 2022 has rejected the Committee's recommendations. It has taken the view that:

> ... reform of inheritance and family provision rights for cohabitees needs to be considered as part of the wider approach to reform of the law on cohabitation rights, so that a consistent approach is taken. As the Law Commission commented in its 2011 report, 'this issue has the potential to be divisive and contentious', for example the recommended reform would have the effect of promoting the interests of cohabitees over family members of the deceased, potentially including their children. As a result, the Government intends to take a cautious approach in this area and would want to consult ahead of pursuing any reforms.
>
> In the meantime, the principle of freedom of testamentary capacity means that anyone is able to make a will which ensures a cohabiting partner is made a beneficiary to their estate, and the extent to which they are. It is therefore open to individuals to set their affairs in order in a way that ensures provision is made for a cohabiting partner.

The full text of the government's response is available on the UK Parliament website, at https://publications.parliament.uk/pa/cm5803/cmselect/cmwomeq/766/report.html#:~:text=Appendix%3A%20Government%20Response,-Recommendation%201%3A%20The&text=We%20partially%20accept%20this%20recommendation,and%20living%20together%20as%20cohabitants.

The Marriage (Same Sex Couples) Act 2013 came into force on 29 March 2014 and makes marriage between same sex couples lawful. Consequently, in all existing legislation in England and Wales, a reference to 'marriage' includes marriage between same sex couples; a reference to 'married couples' is to be read as including married same sex couples; and a reference to a 'married person' includes a person who is married to a person of the same sex.

Consequently, reference to cohabitants who are living together or have formerly lived together as a married couple includes those who are in a same sex relationship. Expressions such as 'husband' includes a man who is married to another man; 'wife' includes a woman who is married to another woman; 'widower' includes a man whose spouse has died; and 'widow' includes a woman whose marriage has ended with the death of the other party to that marriage (see Marriage (Same Sex Couples) Act 2013, Schs 1 and 2).

The I(PFD)A 1975, as amended, governs claims by specified dependants of a deceased person against the estate of the deceased who died domiciled in England and Wales, on the ground that the disposition of the deceased's estate effected by their will or the law of intestacy, or the combination of their will and that law, is not such as to make reasonable financial provision for the claimant (see Chapter 4). Thus a claim arises only if it can be established that:

(1) the deceased died domiciled in England and Wales;
(2) the claimant is one of the restricted classes of person, set out in s 1(1), as amended, who has a right to make a claim (see Chapter 4); and

(3) the deceased failed to make reasonable financial provision for the claimant.

A claim for an order for financial provision under I(PFD)A 1975, s 2 must be made within 6 months from the date on which representation with respect to the estate of the deceased is first taken out, but nothing prevents the making of the application before such representation is taken out. A general discretion, however, is conferred by s 4 on the court to extend that time limit (see Chapter 3).

In the definition of 'financial provision', the I(PFD)A 1975 makes a distinction between a surviving spouse and civil partner of the deceased and other claimants. In the case of a surviving spouse/surviving civil partner, it means such financial provision as it would be reasonable in all the circumstances of the case for the surviving spouse/surviving civil partner to receive, whether or not that provision is required for their maintenance. In respect of all other claimants, it means such financial provision as it would be reasonable for the claimant to receive for their maintenance (s 1(2)). It is thus for the claimant to establish whether the deceased's disposition considered *objectively* makes or fails to make reasonable provision for the claimant in all the circumstances of the case. The claimant is not entitled to any relief simply because the deceased acted unreasonably or that the disposition or lack of it 'produces an unreasonable result in that it does not make any or any greater provision for the applicant' (see *Re Coventry* [1980] Ch 461, 474–475). The issue therefore is whether the provision or lack of provision made by the deceased is reasonable and not whether the deceased acted unreasonably, unfairly or unjustly.

If the court finds that the deceased has not made reasonable financial provision for the claimant, then, in determining whether and in what manner the court should exercise its powers under the I(PFD)A 1975, there is a mandatory duty on the court to have regard to each of the matters set out in s 3, as amended (see Chapter 7).

The orders which the court may make are set out in I(PFD)A 1975, s 2. The court also has powers to vary, discharge or suspend orders made for periodical payments under s 2(1)(a) and a limited power to vary a lump sum order. Secured periodical payments orders made under the Matrimonial Causes Act 1973 and maintenance agreements may also be varied or discharged (see para 8.12).

The orders made by the court under the I(PFD)A 1975 may be met only out of the net estate of the deceased as defined by s 25(1). Sections 8 and 9 make further provisions for property disposed of by way of a gift in contemplation of death but not to take effect until death, provision made to a nominated person and property held on a joint tenancy to be regarded as part of the net estate of the deceased.

Formerly, where the claimant intended to apply under s 9 for the deceased's severable share of property held on a joint tenancy to be included as part of the net estate, the application had to be made within 6 months from the date on which representation with respect to the deceased's estate was first taken out and the court did not have any discretion to extend the time limit. This provision has now been amended by the Inheritance and Trustees' Powers Act 2014 to remove the time limit, but any application under I(PFD)A 1975, s 9 should be made within the substantive application and within the time limits set out in I(PFD)A 1975, s 4 (see Chapter 9).

The court also has powers under I(PFD)A 1975, ss 10 and 11 in relation to transactions entered into by the deceased with the intention of defeating a claim for financial provision under the Act where it would facilitate the making of financial provision for the claimant (see Chapter 10).

Lastly, a claim under the I(PFD)A 1975 is personal to the claimant, so that if the claimant dies during the course of the proceedings, the claim comes to an end and is not enforceable by the personal representatives of the claimant. Only where an order has been made upon a claim is there an enforceable cause of action, which can continue to subsist for the benefit of one estate against the other (see *Whyte v Ticehurst* [1986] Fam 64 and *Re R* (1986) 14 Fam Law 58).

With the European Union's policy of free movement, it was recognised that there was need for co-operation and a single code for jurisdiction, applicable law, recognition and enforcement of decisions and legislation between Member States in most areas of the law. This having been achieved in most areas of civil, family and matrimonial law, the need for similar provisions in relation to succession rights was considered necessary. The Committee on Legal Affairs on Succession and Wills in its report dated 16 October 2006 set out its recommendations for consideration by the European Parliament. These recommendations were subsequently embodied in Regulation (EU) No 650/2012 of the European Parliament and of the Council of 4 July 2012 on jurisdiction, applicable law, recognition and enforcement of decisions and acceptance and enforcement of authentic instruments in matters of succession and on the creation of a European Certificate of Succession [2012] OJ L201/107 (EU Regulation 650/2012; also known as Brussels IV), which came into effect on 17 August 2015. Although the Regulation does not apply to the United Kingdom, where a citizen of an EU Member State has assets in the United Kingdom and elsewhere in the European Union, the provisions set out in the Regulation may have an impact where a possible claim under the I(PFD)A 1975 is being considered. An overview of the provisions contained in the Regulation is set out in Chapter 9.

1.2 URGENT NEED FOR LAW REFORM

As indicated above, the Law Commission has recommended reform in the law relating to cohabiting couples since 2006. Data for 2021 released by the Office for National Statistics (ONS) on 9 March 2022 indicates that the population of cohabiting couples has increased by 22.9% over the last decade to 3.6 million (see www.ons.gov.uk/peoplepopulationandcommunity/birthsdeathsandmarriages /families/bulletins/familiesandhouseholds/2021#toc). In 2020, 13.1% of the population aged 16 and over were cohabiting compared with 11.3% in 2010. The majority of people aged 55 and over who are cohabiting has also increased in the last decade. Cohabiting couples make up the fastest growing type of family group, with over 3.4 million couples in England and Wales. An academic report on cohabitation by Dr Esmée Hanna and Dr David Grainger of Leeds University, which was published to coincide with the creation of the Cooperative Law Service, also suggested an increase. The Economic and Social Research Council's report of February 2015, *Cohabitation trends and patterns in the UK*, by Ann Berrington and Juliet Stone, also documents the increase in cohabiting couples in the United Kingdom. The Chairman of Resolution has drawn attention to this growing trend when stating that this is a feature of our modern society; that unfortunately current cohabitation law is failing to provide this family group with the rights that some of them mistakenly think they have and that lawmakers should introduce legislation that will provide legal protection and fair outcomes at the time of a couple's separation.

All the reports, including the House of Commons Briefing Paper, *"Common law marriage" and cohabitation* of 9 February 2016 and the most recent report, *The rights of cohabiting partners*, published on 4 August 2022 by the Women and Equalities Committee (a cross-party group of MPs), confirm the disadvantages in law experienced by cohabiting couples. These reports also confirm that a high percentage of cohabiting couples (51% according to the British Social Attitudes survey) believe that they have a 'common law marriage', which gives them the same rights as those enjoyed by married couples. This is, of course, incorrect. It is only when separation occurs that the shock of their real status emerges.

The need for reform in this area of the law has been outstanding for over a decade, during which the government has found the time and will to bring about reforms relating to the status of same sex couples so that they now have the choice of entering into either a civil partnership or marriage, which, in both cases, gives them the same rights as those enjoyed by married couples. Yet the government of the day has shown little support to give effect to the Law Commission's recommendation as set out in its draft Inheritance and Trustees' Powers Bill or the Cohabitation Rights Bill. Although the Bill has been introduced in the House of Lords, there also appears to be opposition to the reforms by some members of the House of Lords.

The urgent need for reform in this area of the law is evident. While it is acknowledged that any reform of the law must be well researched, there is now more than adequate research and review of reports prepared over the years. What is required is support from the government to progress the Cohabitation Rights Bill through in order to provide this family group with the same rights and protection, fairness, justice and equal status as those who are married or in civil partnership relationships.

Chapter 2

Proof of Death and Domicile

2.1 INTRODUCTION

An application for financial provision may only be brought against the estate of a deceased person who was domiciled in England and Wales at the time of their death (I(PFD)A 1975, s 1(1)). Proof of death and domicile of the deceased in England and Wales are thus the first two pre-conditions which a claimant must establish when applying for financial provision under the Act. These are issues which may be raised as preliminary issues by a defendant who intends to resist the claimant's application. If the deceased died domiciled elsewhere than in England and Wales, a claim under the Act cannot be entertained by the court. The Act does not extend to Scotland and Northern Ireland, the Isle of Man or the Channel Islands (s 1(1)).

2.2 PROOF OF DEATH

The Births and Deaths Registration Act 1953 and the Registration of Births and Deaths Regulations 1987 (SI 1987/2088) as amended by the Registration of Births and Death (Amendment) (England and Wales) Regulations 2021 (SI 2021/1436) which came into force on 21 December 2021 govern the registration of births and deaths. Death is proved by the production of a certified copy of the death certificate, which may be obtained from the registrar for the sub-district in which the death occurred or the body was found, on payment of a fee of £11. If the certificate is required urgently, a priority service is available at a cost of about £35. It can be ordered online at www.gov.uk/order-copy-birth-death-marriage-certificate. The application form to order a death certificate can be obtained at www.gov.uk/government/publications/death-certificate-application-form.

The applicant will need to provide the deceased's full name, status, i.e. whether married/divorced/in a civil partnership, occupation, date of birth, place and date of death and the last known address of the deceased if different from the place of death. If 12 months have elapsed since the death of the deceased, the application for the death certificate should be made to the General Register Office at Smedley Hydro, Trafalgar Road, Birkdale, Southport PR8 2HH, and may be made online or by post at PO Box 2, Southport PR8 2JD. Enquiries: certificate.services@gro.gov.uk. Tel: 0300 123 1837. Further information is available on the website: www.gov.uk/general-register-office.

There is a different process for obtaining a certificate in Scotland and Northern Ireland. For Northern Ireland, see www.nidirect.gov.uk/services/order-death-certificate-online. For Scotland, see www.scottishcertificates.org.uk.

Where the death has occurred overseas, the death must be registered according to the local law in the country where the person died. Death can also be registered at a British Consulate or the British High Commissioner and the Overseas Registration Unit of the Foreign, Commonwealth and Development Office. The death will first have to be registered in accordance with the registration procedure in the country where the person died and a local certificate of death obtained. This local death certificate will be accepted in the United Kingdom provided it is accompanied by a certified translation if the document is not in English. To register the death with the Overseas Registration Unit of the Foreign, Commonwealth and Development Office, it will be necessary to provide the following documents and payment:

- the original local death certificate with a translation;
- a photocopy of the photo page of the deceased's passport and, if this is not available, then the original full UK birth certificate, naturalisation or registration certificate and written permission of the next of kin or executor if the applicant is not the next of kin or the deceased's executor;
- payment of the registration fee of £150 and £50 per copy. Payment may be made online by emailing Overseas.RegistrationUnit@fcdo.gov.uk. The reference number provided, together with the registration form and the above documents, should be sent to Overseas Registration Unit, Foreign Commonwealth and Development Unit, Hanslope Park, Hanslope Milton Keynes MK19 7BH.

A death certificate of a person who has died in active service with the armed forces is issued by the Ministry of Defence. This will be in the form of a notification of death or presumed death. The Registrar General of Shipping and Seamen is responsible for providing a certificate of evidence of death of a merchant seaman.

Where death has occurred in unusual circumstances, such as an accident or air crash, a post-mortem or coroner's inquest may be held, especially where there is reason to believe that 'a violent unnatural or sudden death has occurred and the body is irrecoverable or destroyed (see the Coroners and Justice Act 2009 and the Coroners (Investigations) Regulations 2013 (SI 2013/1629)). The coroner may make a report to the Secretary of State, who may then direct that an inquest be held. When a coroner's inquest is opened and the investigation is ongoing, an interim certificate of the fact of death will be issued by the coroner. A final certificate is issued at the conclusion of the inquest. If the inquest is delayed, application should be made to obtain a limited grant *ad litem* (see 3.2.3) or commencing an application before grant pursuant to Inheritance and Trustees' Powers Act 2014, Sch 2, para 6 (see 3.3.1) or seek permission to swear death under Non-Contentious Probate Rules 1987 (SI 1987/2024), r 53. Similarly, where the fact of death is known, but not the date when the deceased died, an application may be made for permission to swear death, and the affidavit in support should set out the circumstances in which the deceased was last seen or their body was found. Where a disaster such as a plane crash or the tsunami in December 2004 has occurred, the Principal Registry of the Family Division will be supplied with a list or details of the persons involved in the case of a crash, or it should be provided with evidence that the person was in the region of the disaster. The Principal Registry and/or the Ministry of Justice will usually issue a circular listing the names of those who have died or other directions on how an application for permission to swear death and/or for a grant should be made.

Where two or more persons die together as a result of an accident or disaster, entitlement under a will or on intestacy may depend on who died first. Pursuant to Law of Property Act 1925, s 184, the younger of the two or more persons is deemed to have survived the older ones.

In the case of missing persons, under common law a presumption of death will arise if the person has been missing for a continuous period of 7 years and there is no evidence of that person having been seen alive during that period. A declaration under common law is limited in scope, which has now been rectified to some extent by the Presumption of Death Act 2013, which came into force on 1 October 2015. The Act applies to England and Wales. The Presumption of Death (Northern Ireland) Act 2009 and the Presumption of Death (Scotland) Act 1977, respectively, apply to Northern Ireland and Scotland.

The Presumption of Death Act 2013 enables any person to apply to the High Court for a declaration, provided it can be established that the missing person is thought to be dead or has not been known to be alive for a period of at least 7 years. If a declaration is made, it will be served on the Registrar General for England and Wales for registration, and once registered will serve as 'conclusive proof of the missing person's death and the date and time of death'. Certified copies of entries in the register issued by the Registrar General will be treated as evidence of the missing person's death. The declaration is also 'effective against all persons and for purposes including for the purposes of the acquisition of an interest in any property and the ending of a marriage or civil partnership' (s 3). The missing person's property will pass to others in the same way as if the missing person had died. When making the declaration, the court has power to determine any issue relating to an interest in any property and the domicile of the missing person at the time of their presumed death (s 7). The Guardianship (Missing Persons) Act 2017, which received Royal Assent on 27 April 2017, makes provision for application also to be made for the court to appoint a guardian to deal with the missing person's property and financial affairs, i.e. a 'guardianship order'.

2.3 DOMICILE

Domicile is a legal concept of law which is not easily defined. It is based on where a person has their permanent home and is relevant in many situations where it is necessary to establish which legal system should be applied, particularly relating to issues of personal status. It is not the same as a person's ordinary residence or habitual residence.

Domicile as a pre-condition to any claim under the I(PFD)A 1975 has been the subject of criticism, particularly given the social and political changes which have occurred since the commencement of the Act. As a result of the European Union, globalisation and the ability and freedom to move freely between countries, people now live, work and have homes and businesses in countries other than the country of their nationality. It is therefore not surprising that there are many who take the view that 'habitual residence' of the deceased immediately before their death should be the basis on which a claim should be brought against the estate of the deceased.

In *Cyganik v Agulian* [2006] EWCA Civ 129, [2006] 1 FCR 406, Longmore LJ observed at [58] that:

> I find it rather surprising that the somewhat antiquated notion of domicile should govern the question whether the estate of a person who was, on any view, habitually resident in England should make provision for his dependants. Now that many family matters are decided by reference to habitual residence there may, perhaps, be something to be said for reconsidering the terms of s1 of the Inheritance (Provision for Family and Dependants) Act 1975. As Dr JHC Morris observed of the concept of domicile in the last (3rd) edition of his *Conflict of Laws* (1984), which he wrote before he died,
>
>> 'Originally it was a good idea; but the once simple concept has been so overloaded by a multitude of cases that it has been transmuted into something further and further removed from the practicalities of life.'

The Law Commission in its report published in May 2011 disapproved of this view. The Inheritance and Trustees' Powers Bill initially introduced habitual residence to form the basis of a claim under the Act. This was rejected during the Bill's progress through the House of Lords, and it remained omitted from the Bill and from the Inheritance and Trustees' Powers Act 2014.

There are three types of domicile, namely: domicile of origin, domicile of dependency and domicile of choice.

2.4 DOMICILE OF ORIGIN

A person acquires a domicile of origin at birth from their parents and retains that domicile until it is changed by choice. The general principles which apply to determine domicile of origin were set out by Arden LJ in *Barlow Clowes International Ltd (In liquidation) v Hemwood* [2008] EWCA Civ 577 by reference to Dicey and Morris, *The Conflict of Laws* (Sweet & Maxwell, 14th edn, 2006) as follows (at [8]):

> (i) A person is, in general, domiciled in the country in which he is considered by English law to have his permanent home. A person may sometimes be domiciled in a country although he does not have his permanent home in it (Dicey, pages 122 to 126).
> (ii) No person can be without a domicile (Dicey, page 126).
> (iii) No person can at the same time for the same purpose have more than one domicile (Dicey, pages 126 to 128).
> (iv) An existing domicile is presumed to continue until it is proved that a new domicile has been acquired (Dicey, pages 128 to 129).[1]

The place where a child is born is immaterial (see *Re Flynn, Flynn v Flynn* [1968] 1 All ER 49, 52). A domicile of origin is capable of persisting during the lifetime of a person.

This is best illustrated by reference to *Olafisoye v Olafisoye (Jurisdiction)* [2010] EWHC 3539 (Fam), [2011] 2 FLR 553 and *Cyganik v Agulian* [2006] EWCA Civ 129, [2006] 1 FCR 406. *Olafisoye* was a family case where the husband was not domiciled or habitually resident in England. The wife was born in Scotland to parents who had settled in England and acquired a domicile of choice. She thus acquired her father's domicile, but while she was still a minor her father returned to live in Nigeria, therefore reviving his domicile of origin. She thus acquired his Nigerian domicile and this continued into her adulthood without her acquiring a new domicile elsewhere.

---

1 In the latest edition, domicile is dealt with in Chapter 6, see Dicey and Morris, *The Conflict of Laws* (Sweet & Maxwell, 16th edn, 2022).

The deceased in *Cyganik v Agulian* was a Greek Cypriot born in Cyprus. Although he had lived in England for about 34 years, he continued his close links with his family in Cyprus and owned property there. In 1972, he returned to Cyprus with the intention of permanently living there, but in 1974, when Northern Cyprus was occupied by Turkey, he returned to England. His intention to return to Cyprus remained. Having considered all the events in his life, his emotional attachments to the land of his birth and his identity, the Court of Appeal ruled that these factors outweighed all the other evidence which had been adduced to prove the contrary. The two elements of '*animo et facto*' and 'intention' to found a change of domicile had not been established.

In *CC v DD (Parental Order: Domicile)* [2014] EWHC 1307 (Fam), applying the principles set out in *Barlow Clowes International Ltd (In liquidation) v Hemwood* to the facts in the case, Theis J stated at [24], 'It is very much a question of fact based on the circumstances of each case. The court needs to consider the broad canvas of evidence in order to establish the intention of the relevant person'.

The domicile of origin of a legitimate child born during the lifetime of their father is that of the child's father. If the father dies before the child's birth, the child acquires the domicile of the mother (see *Urquhart v Butterfield* (1887) 37 Ch D 357, 377).

An illegitimate child acquires the domicile of their mother at birth (see Dicey and Morris, *The Conflict of Laws* (Sweet & Maxwell, 16th edn, September 2022)).

A child's domicile thereafter will change if and when the parent(s) change their domicile.

Once a child attains the age of 16, they are able to acquire a domicile of choice independently of their parents (Domicile and Matrimonial Proceedings Act 1973, s 3).

A foundling's domicile of origin is that of the country where the child is found.

The domicile of an adopted child will be that of the child's adopters because once an adoption order is made the adopted child is regarded in law as if they had been born to the adopters (Adoption and Children Act 2002, s 67(1)). As from the date of the adoption, the adopted child is treated as the legitimate child of their adopter(s) if adopted by a couple or by one of a couple (s 51(2)).

The domicile of origin of a child who has been the subject of a parental order will be that of the applicants in whose favour the parental order was made because, as in the case of adoption, the effect of a parental order is that the child is treated in law as the child of the applicants (Human Fertilisation and Embryology Act 2008 (HFEA 2008), ss 54(1) and 55).

2.5 DOMICILE OF DEPENDENCY

A child aged under 16 or a person who lacks mental capacity has a domicile of dependency which is that of their parents. Where the parents are married and living together, the domicile is that of the father. Where the parents are separated, the child's domicile or the domicile of the person lacking capacity is that of the parent with whom they have their home to the exclusion of the other; for example, if the child lives with their mother and does not have a home with the father, they take their mother's domicile or if having acquired the mother's domicile by living with her and being in her sole care and has not thereafter had a home with their father (Domicile and Matrimonial Proceedings Act 1973, s 4). Once a child attains the age of 16, they are able to acquire a domicile of choice independently of their parents, but until then their domicile will remain that which the person acquired from their parents (see *Olafisoye v Olafisoye (Jurisdiction)* [2010] EWHC 3539 (Fam), [2011] 2 FLR 553 and *Sekhri v Ray* [2013] EWHC 2290 (Fam) (see para 2.6.5)).

2.6 DOMICILE OF CHOICE

A domicile of choice is acquired when a person leaves their domicile of origin and lives in a country of their choice with the intention of permanently or indefinitely living there. There are therefore two elements which must both be satisfied before a domicile of choice is acquired, i.e.: (1) actual residence in the country of choice; and (2) the intention to live there permanently. The circumstances which led the person to leave their original domicile are immaterial. The test is whether the person intended to make their home in the new country until the end of their days or until something happens to change their mind (see *IRC v Bullock* [1976] 1 WLR 1178):

> Domicile of choice is a conclusion or inference which the law derives from the fact of a man fixing voluntarily his sole or chief residence in a particular place with the intention of continuing to reside there for an unlimited time. This is a description of the circumstances which create or constitute a domicile and not a definition of the term. There must be a residence freely chosen, and not prescribed or dictated by any external necessity, such as the duties of office, the demands of creditors, or the relief from illness; and it must be residence fixed not for a limited period or particular purpose, but general and indefinite in its future contemplation. It is true that residence originally temporary, or intended for a limited period, may afterwards become general and unlimited, and in such a case so soon as the change of purpose, or *animus manendi*,

can be inferred the fact of domicile is established (per Lord Westbury in *Udny v Udny* (1869) 1 LR Sc & Div 441).

In *Barlow Clowes International Ltd (In liquidation) v Hemwood* [2008] EWCA Civ 577, these two elements were elaborated upon as follows (at [8]):

(vi) Every independent person can acquire a domicile of choice by the combination of residence and an intention of permanent or indefinite residence, but not otherwise (Dicey, pages 133 to 138).
(vii) Any circumstance that is evidence of a person's residence, or of his intention to reside permanently or indefinitely in a country, must be considered in determining whether he has acquired a domicile of choice (Dicey, pages 138 to 143).
(viii) In determining whether a person intends to reside permanently or indefinitely, the court may have regard to the motive for which residence was taken up, the fact that residence was not freely chosen, and the fact that residence was precarious (Dicey, pages 144 to 151).
(ix) A person abandons a domicile of choice in a country by ceasing to reside there and by ceasing to intend to reside there permanently, or indefinitely, and not otherwise (Dicey, pages 151 to 153).
(x) When a domicile of choice is abandoned, a new domicile of choice may be acquired, but, if it is not acquired, the domicile of origin revives (Dicey, pages 151 to 153).[2]

If that person subsequently abandons that domicile and fails to acquire another domicile of choice, their domicile of origin reverts.

2.6.1 Residence

It is essential for the person who intends to change their domicile of origin to live in the country of their choice. The duration of the residence or the motive for so doing is immaterial, provided that it is accompanied by the necessary intention to live in that country permanently or indefinitely. The intention of residence must be fixed and must be for the indefinite future. It is not enough, for instance, that at any given point in time its length has not been determined. The duration of the residence is immaterial so long as it was for a settled purpose and not for other reasons, such as for health reasons alone, unless it is accompanied by cogent evidence of intention to make that country their permanent home.

A domicile of choice may be acquired by living in a country unlawfully in breach of immigration law. In *Mark v Mark* [2005] UKHL 42, [2005] 2 FLR 1193, a Nigerian woman established a home in England and obtained leave to remain

---

2 In the latest edition, domicile is dealt with in Chapter 6, see Dicey and Morris, *The Conflict of Laws* (Sweet & Maxwell, 16th edn, 2022).

in England until a specific date. Thereafter, she did not apply for an extension of her stay and she remained in England in breach of immigration law as an overstayer. In due course, she petitioned for divorce and applied for ancillary relief relying on her habitual residence. She also claimed that she had acquired a domicile of choice in England. Her husband opposed the proceedings on the ground that the English courts did not have jurisdiction because the wife's stay in England was unlawful. She succeeded in her claim both at first instance and before the Court of Appeal. The husband appealed to the House of Lords (now the Supreme Court). Baroness Hale in her judgment ruled that residence for the purpose of Domicile and Matrimonial Proceedings Act 1973, s 5(2) need not be lawful residence. The question of whether the residence is habitual is a factual one which should be answered by applying the test derived from tax cases. Her Ladyship said (at [36]):

> It is possible that the legality of a person's residence here might be relevant to the factual question of whether that residence is 'habitual'. A person who was on the run after a deportation order or removal directions might find it hard to establish a habitual residence here. But such cases will be rare compared with the large numbers of people who have remained here leading perfectly ordinary lives here for long periods, despite having no permission to do so. There will, however, be other statutory provisions, in particular those conferring entitlement to some benefit from the state, where it would be proper to imply a requirement that the residence be lawful.

In relation to whether an unlawful presence in England will prevent a person acquiring a domicile of choice, Her Ladyship said that there is no reason in principle why a person whose presence here is unlawful cannot acquire a domicile of choice in this country because although the person's presence may amount to the commission of a criminal offence, it could not be said with any certainty that the person would be required to leave the country if they were discovered. If the person has chosen to make their home in a new country for an indefinite period, it would be appropriate that the person should be connected to the system of law for purposes where domicile was relevant. The legality of a person's presence in a country may be relevant to establish the required intention. The issue is one of fact and dependent on the court scrutinising the evidence produced to establish the necessary intention that the person intended to live in the country of choice permanently despite the unlawfulness. It is not a question of law nor is it a matter on which the court has discretion. It is for the court to decide on the facts whether or not a person unlawfully in the country has acquired a domicile of choice. If on the facts the person has acquired a domicile of choice in this country, the person cannot be denied it because the court considers the person's case to be unmeritorious or tainted with 'moral or legal turpitude'. If the evidence does not establish the acquisition of domicile of choice by the person, the court does not have the power to grant it because it considers the person's case a deserving one. (Note that the decision in *Mark v Mark* overruled many of the decisions referred to in the judgment of Baroness Hale that had been cited previously as indicating that the person's presence in a country unlawfully would prevent that person acquiring a domicile of choice in that country, and differed from the proposition of law that had hitherto been stated by Dicey and Morris.)

If it can be established that a domicile of choice was acquired although the presence in England was unlawful, it will be unaffected by a subsequent deportation order (see *Cruh v Cruh* [1945] 2 All ER 545).

In the case of those who are refugees or seeking asylum from persecution or by reason of other forced circumstances, a change of domicile will not occur unless there is strong evidence which indicates that a domicile of choice has been acquired (see *Re Lloyd Evans, National Provincial Bank v Evans* [1947] Ch 695).

Where a person takes up residence in a country for reasons of health, the residence alone will not suffice to lead to a change of domicile. The issue of whether a domicile of choice has been acquired in such circumstances will depend on the person's state of mind.

2.6.2 Intention

In addition to living in the country of choice, it must be established that the deceased had the intention of making England their permanent home. This will require an evaluation of all the facts over the person's life. The case of *Cyganik v Agulian* [2006] EWCA Civ 129, [2006] 1 FCR 406 (see para 2.3) best illustrates this point. See, also, the cases referred to at para 2.6.5.

An intention to live in England for a fixed period or until the occurrence of a specific event, for example until the person's health improves, or for the purposes of employment (see *Irvin v Irvin* [2001] 1 FLR 178), or if their country becomes independent (see *Pletinka v Pletinka (Boucher cited)* (1964) 109 Sol Jo 72) will not suffice.

2.6.3 Burden of proof

It will be observed, therefore, that the presumption is against a change of domicile by an individual. Where the question of whether or not the deceased died domiciled in England is in issue or is likely to be raised, it is for the applicant to establish the deceased's domicile on clear and credible evidence based on all the circumstances relating to the deceased's life.

2.6.4 Standard of proof

It is for the applicant to establish that the deceased was domiciled in England and Wales on the civil standard of proof, i.e. on the balance of probabilities, but since it is a serious issue, the court is unlikely to infer it from slight indications or casual words. The claimant will have to provide convincing evidence of that fact. The evidence must be clear, cogent and convincing (see *Re Fuld's Estate (No 3), Hartley v Fuld* [1968] P 675).

2.6.5 Evidence

It is for the claimant to establish that the deceased died domiciled in England and Wales. Cogent and clear evidence is needed to show that the balance of probabilities has been tipped, and this is true whether the issue is the acquisition or loss of a domicile of choice (see, also, *Irvin v Irvin* [2001] 1 FLR 178). The burden of proof remains throughout on the claimant.

Where there is or may be any doubt of the deceased's domicile, the evidence on which it is intended to rely to establish domicile should be stated in the sworn statement in support of the claim. Application for a grant of probate will require a sworn statement confirming where the deceased died. This will provide *prima facie* evidence of the deceased's domicile at the time of their death, but it is not conclusive proof and may be challenged. If a claim under the I(PFD)A 1975 is made, the issue of domicile may become pertinent particularly where the evidence filed raises doubts.

If the statement on the grant states that the deceased had a domicile in a country other than England and Wales, the claimant will need to disprove that statement. Where there is or may be any doubt about the deceased's domicile, the evidence upon which it is intended to rely to establish domicile should be stated in the sworn statement in support of the claim.

In determining the issue of a change of domicile, particularly a change of domicile of origin, the court has to consider all the circumstances and factors from which the deceased's intention to change their domicile of origin can be ascertained. This will include looking back at the whole of the deceased's life, at what they did, experienced and endured during their life, and what were their inferred intentions in order to determine whether the deceased had acquired a domicile of choice in England by the date of their death. The deceased's age, religion, language, family and business ties and commitments, ownership of property, length of time the deceased remained in a country, their nationality, whether or not they changed that nationality or citizenship, whether they had made a will and if so the form and content of that will, the degree of their assimilation in the new country, will all be relevant factors.

There is no end to the evidence that may be adduced; the whole of a person's life and all that they said and did, however trivial, may be relied upon to determine what the person's intention was at any given moment of time (see *Cyganik v Agulian* [2006] EWCA Civ 129, [2006] 1 FCR 406 and *Re Flynn* [1968] 1 WLR 103).

Statements or declarations made by the deceased during their lifetime are not conclusive. Nor does any one factor override other relevant factors. The following examples of cases demonstrate the scrutiny with which the court will consider the issue of domicile.

In *Re Evans (Deceased), National Provincial Bank v Evans* [1947] 1 Ch 695, the deceased had been born in Wales. He eventually settled in Belgium, but in 1940, during the Second World War, he moved to the south of France and wrote a statement in which he confirmed that he was domiciled in Belgium. The document was accepted as providing evidence that the deceased had not abandoned his domicile of choice in Belgium.

In *Re Liddell-Grainger's Will Trusts* [1936] 3 All ER 173, an Englishman had moved to Scotland. He lived there for almost 40 years before his death. In his will, he asserted that he had not abandoned his domicile of origin. It was, however, contended that the statement in the will had been made to avoid the effect of the law in Scotland, which restricted a testator's right to dispose of property. The court held that the deceased's actions during his life and his continued residence in Scotland were strong evidence of his having acquired a domicile of choice in Scotland.

In *Mastaka v Midland Bank Executors and Trustees Co Ltd* [1941] Ch 192, the deceased testatrix had married a Russian in England. As the law then stood, the testatrix, on marriage, acquired the domicile of her husband. His whereabouts at the time of the deceased's death were not known. There was no direct evidence either that he was dead or that he had acquired a domicile of choice in England. In the absence of evidence to the contrary, the deceased was held not to be domiciled in England and Wales.

In *Bheekhun v Williams* [1999] 2 FLR 229, a couple from Mauritius set up home in England. They retained their British nationality when Mauritius became independent. The husband had business interests and property in both England and Mauritius. The couple separated and the wife obtained a decree nisi (now a conditional divorce order), but before decree absolute (now a final divorce order) and the resolution of her claim for financial relief, the husband died leaving his entire estate to his niece. It was contended by the personal representatives that the deceased had retained his domicile of origin and had not acquired a domicile of choice in England. It was held that evidence of the deceased's actions during his lifetime, and taking into consideration his British nationality, the length of his residency in England, and statements that he had made during the divorce proceedings, clearly indicated that the deceased had considered England his domicile of choice.

Cyganik v Agulian [2006] EWCA Civ 129, [2006] 1 FCR 406 is a case where the deceased's domicile of origin was Cyprus where he was born and where he lived until he was 14 years of age. He then came to England, where he lived for the next 34 years, but maintained close links with Cyprus and owned property there. In 1974, he returned to Cyprus with the intention of living there permanently. When the Turks invaded Northern Cyprus he left and came back to England, but his links with Cyprus continued, with him making clear express statements of his intention to return to live in Cyprus permanently. In 1993, he formed a relationship with the claimant and became engaged to her in 1999. He executed a will in 1995. In a claim brought under the I(PFD)A 1975, it was maintained by the claimant that the deceased had died domiciled in England. The court at first instance found on the facts that the deceased had not had the intention before 1995 of living permanently in England although he had resided here for 34 years and had established a substantial business. However, the court, relying on the development of the relationship between the deceased and the claimant, found that between 1995 when he made his will including the claimant as a beneficiary, and 1999 when he became engaged to her, the deceased acquired a domicile of choice in England. On appeal, the Court of Appeal ruled that the inference made by the trial judge of the deceased's change of intention was wrong. The court held that although it was appropriate and helpful to trace the deceased's life events, special care had to be taken in the analysis of the evidence about isolating individual factors from all the other factors present over time and treating a particular factor as decisive. On the facts, it was clear that apart from the commencement of the relationship with the claimant, his engagement to her and his expressed intention to marry her, nothing else in his life had altered and, therefore, the fact of his relationship with the claimant had to be examined carefully. The court held that:

(1) the adhesiveness of the domicile of origin, the incidence of the burden of proof and the level of the standard of proof all require the person contending for a domicile of choice to establish a clear case that the deceased intended to live permanently or indefinitely in England;
(2) the matrimonial factor, although relevant, was not determinative or conclusive in establishing the necessary intention;
(3) in order to determine the issue of 'intention' of a change of domicile of origin, it is necessary for the court to consider the whole of the

deceased's life in retrospect to see whether an inference could be made that he intended to make his home permanently or indefinitely in England; the evidence has to be sufficiently 'cogent and convincing' to establish a change, and the cumulative effect of the preponderance of the factors must 'clearly and unequivocally' point to an intention to change the domicile of origin. The evidence in this case had not been so clear. On the contrary, the evidence had 're-inforced the enduring character of the deceased's domicile of origin'.

In *Morgan v Cilento and Others; Re Shaffer* [2004] EWHC 188 (Ch), the claimant, who was the deceased's lover, sought to prove that the deceased had not lost his English domicile when he left to live in Australia and, alternatively, that he reacquired it when he left Australia and returned to England.

In *Dellar v Zivy* [2007] EWHC 2266 (Ch), a case which did not directly concern the deceased's domicile, the issue was whether English or French law applied to the interpretation of the deceased's will. In deciding that English law applied, the court had regard to the fact that the will had been made in England, written in English by English solicitors, who were appointed executors of the will, and by his will he had created a trust for sale. The will also expressly declared that the deceased was domiciled in England.

In *Kearly v Kearly* [2009] EWHC 1876 (Fam), [2010] 1 FLR 619, the issue of domicile arose in divorce proceedings to establish the court's jurisdiction to hear the application for divorce. The wife was Australian and living in Australia. The husband was English, but currently living in France where he worked. The wife issued divorce proceedings in England relying on the husband's English domicile of origin to establish jurisdiction. The husband belatedly sought to challenge the court's jurisdiction, contending that he was domiciled in Australia. The evidence established that the husband's address for tax purposes was that of his parents in England. He had not declared himself domiciled in Australia on Australian family application forms but had claimed to be simply resident there. He had not taken up Australian citizenship despite having had the opportunity to do so on two occasions. He had sought to liquidate his Australian assets. In dismissing the husband's case on the facts and referring to the evidence necessary to displace domicile of origin, Ryder J said, 'The hurdle is relatively high. Domicile of choice has to be established on clear, cogent evidence. A mere assertion as to being Australian is hardly sufficient.'

In *Holliday v Musa* [2010] EWCA Civ 335, [2010] 2 FLR 702, the deceased was of Turkish Cypriot origin and was born in Cyprus. He had emigrated to England in 1958 with his wife and children. He owned properties in Cyprus and England and visited Cyprus regularly with his family. In 1980, he and his wife separated, and in 1998 he commenced a relationship and had a child. For tax purposes, he claimed non-domiciled status. He died in Cyprus, but his body was brought to England for burial. In a claim made by his partner under the I(PFD)A 1975, the deceased's adult children contested the claim on the basis that the deceased had not lost his domicile of origin and, therefore, the court had no jurisdiction to hear the claim brought under the Act. In dismissing their appeal against the decision at first instance, the Court of Appeal followed the case of *Cyganik v Agulian* [2006] EWCA Civ 129, [2006] 1 FCR 406 and the principles laid down in *Re Fuld's Estate (No 3), Hartley v Fuld* [1968] P 675. The court, as its starting point, took account of the fact that the deceased had been resident in England and that it was the home of his family, and balanced it against all the evidence relating to his connection with Cyprus. It also took account of the fact that the deceased had not chosen to retire to Cyprus despite expressing an intention to do so. On the evidence, the court concluded that the deceased had continued to have his permanent home in England where he wished to spend the rest of his life and be buried in England.

In *Morris v Davies* [2011] EWHC 1773 (Ch), the deceased was English and lived in England until he was 38 years of age when his employment took him to Belgium, where he formed a relationship with and became engaged to a Belgian woman. She worked in France, so he moved there, but continued to visit Belgium at weekends and England annually. It was held that he had retained his domicile of origin.

In *Pedroni v Curati* [2011] EWHC 3442 (Ch), the issue of the deceased's domicile was relevant to determine under which of two wills that the deceased, who was Italian, had executed, should the deceased's estate be distributed. Notwithstanding substantial and significant evidence in support of the retention of his Italian domicile of origin, the court ruled that the deceased had formed an intention to live in England indefinitely and had thus acquired a domicile of choice and gave effect to the English will.

In *Sekhri v Ray* [2013] EWHC 2290 (Fam), the husband and wife were both of Indian origin. The wife was born in India and the husband in England. After their marriage, they moved to Singapore. On the breakdown of their marriage 2 years later, the wife returned to England with their only child. In proceedings for divorce, the issue of domicile was raised as a preliminary issue. The court held that although the standard of proof was the balance of probabilities, the issue of domicile of origin was more enduring and adhesive than a domicile of choice. It concluded that the husband's father was domiciled in England when the husband was born and, accordingly, that also was the husband's domicile of origin which he had retained. The wife had acquired an English domicile of choice before the family moved to Singapore. She had been living in England permanently and had formed a distinctive relationship with this country, where she wanted to become a consultant at a leading hospital. When she moved to Singapore, she did not abandon her English domicile of choice.

Z v C [2011] EWHC 3181 (Fam) was a case where an Israeli same sex couple entered the United Kingdom and, while here, entered into a surrogacy arrangement in India through an Israeli agency, resulting in the birth of twins. When the twins were born, the couple obtained an Israeli passport for the twins and took them to Israel. Subsequently, the couple were granted entry clearance to bring the twins to the United Kingdom. The couple applied for a parental order under the HFEA 2008. It was necessary for the couple to prove that at least one of them was domiciled in England and Wales. The couple's actions and connections with Israel before and after the twins were born were considered against the fact that Z had family links in the United Kingdom; both partners had resigned from their employment; on relocating to the United Kingdom, the couple had established a home and business in England; and the convincing evidence that, as a gay couple, they had faced, and would continue to face, discrimination in Israel and hostility from their family. In finding that Z had acquired a domicile of choice in England, the court took into account the reasons for the relocation to England and the steps taken to establish a home and business in England, and was satisfied of Z's intention to establish a permanent home in England with his partner and children.

In *Divall v Divall* [2014] EWHC 95 (Fam), the court was concerned with whether the English court had jurisdiction to entertain divorce proceedings issued by the husband. The husband was born in England and the wife in China. They met when the wife visited the United Kingdom as a tourist. They married and, initially, their intention was to live and work in Amsterdam, but because the wife had difficulties in obtaining a visa from the Dutch authorities, they decided to live in England so that the wife could obtain residency rights which would then allow her to live and work in Europe. They lived in England between 2002 and 2008, during which the wife obtained British citizenship and relinquished her Chinese nationality. In 2008 they relocated to Amsterdam where they both obtained employment and later bought a house. The marriage broke down when the wife left the husband and moved in with a Dutch man. The husband issued proceedings for divorce in England relying on both parties' English domicile. The wife challenged this assertion. On dismissing the husband's application, Moor J declined to make a finding on whether the wife had acquired a domicile of choice in England and Wales, indicating that it was possible that she never intended to settle in England permanently because the initial move to England had been to enable the wife to have free access of movement within the European Union. Alternatively, if she had, she had not retained it after she left England with her family to live in the Netherlands, and by the time the proceedings were issued she had no intention of returning to England. Moor J applied the principle that domicile of choice was less adhesive than domicile of origin and can be abandoned by a person by ceasing to live there and intending not to live there permanently. The wife had left England on a permanent basis to live in the Netherlands permanently. By the time the marriage broke down, the wife had no intention of returning to England. Her intention was to live the rest of her life in the Netherlands and to acquire Dutch nationality. Therefore, on the day when the application for divorce was filed, the wife was either domiciled in China or the Netherlands, and it was more likely that she had acquired a domicile of choice in the Netherlands.

Sylvester v Sylvester [2014] WTLR 127 was a claim under the I(PFD)A 1975. Mrs Sylvester was born in Carriacou but moved to London in 1957 with her husband. They had four children. She acquired British nationality but continued to have close links with her family and bought a house in Carriacou, where they spent a considerable amount of time when they retired. On her husband's death in 2004 in London, she inherited the entirety of his estate. On her death in 2007, she left her estate to only one of her children. Her last visit to Carriacou was in 2006. One of the siblings made a claim for financial provision under the Act. Mrs Sylvester's domicile was raised as a preliminary issue in the proceedings. In those proceedings, the evidence revealed that although she had acquired British citizenship, she had renewed her Grenadian passport, and therefore her nationality, for the rest of her life. She had seriously considered retiring in Carriacou, where she owned property and spent time. On the other hand, she had also owned property in London, and after her husband's death she spent more time in London. She only made short visits to Grenada twice. She had completed a medical questionnaire in 2003 in which she had indicated that she intended to live in England permanently. It was held that her continued stay in London had not been dictated by her need for medical care, but by her genuine wish to remain there, and her actions after her husband's death were clear indications that she had made a free choice to remain there for the rest of her life. Her domicile of choice was England at the date of her death.

In *U v J* [2017] EWHC 449 (Fam), in divorce proceedings, the court had to consider: (a) whether the applicant, whose domicile of origin was Ireland, acquired a domicile of choice in England, and, if so, whether that domicile of choice subsisted; (b) whether the respondent, whose domicile of origin was India, acquired a domicile of choice in England, and, if so, whether that domicile of choice subsisted. Both parties had led peripatetic lives for over two decades. In determining the issue, the court reviewed 'the scene as a whole' with each fact adding 'to the landscape'. In relation to the applicant, the court took into account the strong practical, financial and fiscal links with the United Kingdom; the fact that she had always returned to the United Kingdom for medical treatment; that she had viewed London as her 'base' and her 'adopted home' and that she had developed a singular and distinctive relationship with London which had replaced that which she had with Ireland. These factors were balanced against the absence of emotional warmth or attachment to England as a country. But after some hesitation it concluded that London had become the 'centre of gravity' and a place of her permanent home (see [63]). With regard to the respondent, having reviewed all the evidence, Cobb J concluded that although the respondent had initially acquired a domicile of choice in England and retained it over decades, he had lost it about 10 years previously and had not acquired another domicile of choice elsewhere, resulting in the revival of his Indian domicile of origin more particularly because, said Cobb J (at [68]):

> This revival coincides with, though is not driven by, the fact that his daughter, son-in-law and grandson now live there. I note that the Respondent indicates that he wishes to spend his final years in either India or Italy, and has, by his most recent will, indicated his wish to be buried in India 'in my father's village of birth … where I believe my reincarnation was rooted at the time of my father's birth'.

In *Kelly v Pyres* [2018] EWCA Civ 1368 (a divorce case), the wife was born in England to Irish parents but moved to Ireland at a very young age. Her domicile of origin was therefore Ireland. The longest period that she lived in England as an adult was 18 months. She eventually took up employment overseas. Her husband was born in India but spent most of his adult life in England. The couple married in Italy in 2005 and their children were born there. In 2015 the marriage broke down. She filed her divorce application in England relying on habitual residence and her domicile of choice in England. On appeal, the Court of Appeal ruled that when she lived in England it was specifically to obtain her Master's degree and she had not formed the necessary intention to remain in England permanently or indefinitely. The second period of her stay in England was under a fixed term contract of employment but within 4 months she was looking for employment abroad. Thereafter, she had not demonstrated any personal nexus to England. Her future intention to retire in England in 2037 was not enough to establish a domicile of choice in England.

In *Proles v Kohli* [2018] EWHC 767 (Ch), the claim was made under the Act by the deceased's child born out of wedlock for financial provision from the deceased's estate where the deceased's widow inherited the whole estate under his will. The deceased was born and bred in India and had married an Indian woman in India. His children were born in India and the family lived there until he was in his 40s, when he began to travel and acquired properties and business assets in England. He had formed a relationship with the claimant's mother and, when the claimant was born, he had acknowledged her as his daughter and committed to her. When he was diagnosed with cancer and during the period when he was attempting to settle his affairs, he had indicated what his intentions were and where he considered himself to be domiciled. In 2015 he returned to India for a break from his cancer treatment and died there. The court held that the deceased had acquired a domicile of choice in England and his return to India did not result in the abandonment of that domicile because all the indications were that his return to India was temporary and his intention was to return to England.

Henkes v HMRC [2020] UKFTT 159 (TC) was a tax case in which the grandchildren appealed a decision that they had acquired a domicile of choice in the United Kingdom for tax purposes, relying on their argument that their grandfather had acquired a domicile of choice in Brazil and consequently their father's and their domicile of origin was Brazil. Factors that were considered by the court, to rule that the father had acquired a domicile of choice in the United Kingdom, were his length of stay for 40 years in the United Kingdom; his ties to England; his recruitment into the British Army; his ties and close family members; and social and centre of interest and location of property and assets.

In *Re Z (Parental Order: Child's Home)* [2021] EWHC 29 (Fam), the issue of domicile arose in an application for a parental order under the HFEA 2008 made by AB and CD who were in a same sex relationship. Both had been born in the United Kingdom and were UK citizens. They had lived overseas in connection with AB's employment. They returned to the United Kingdom in May 2020 and subsequently applied for a parental order for Z, who had been born following a surrogacy arrangement entered into in Columbia. One of the conditions on which the court has to be satisfied under s 54 of the Act is that at the time of the application and the making of the order, either or both of the applicants must be domiciled in the United Kingdom or in the Channel Islands or the Isle of Man. The court held that since the couple's residence abroad related to the country where AB was employed and they could only remain there for as long as AB remained in active employment, their residence there was therefore in no way permanent, particularly because neither had taken any steps to revoke their UK citizenship or obtain the right to remain permanently in another country. Therefore, since neither had taken any steps to abandon their UK citizenship or obtain the right to remain permanently in another country, neither had taken any steps to abandon their domicile of origin nor had they acquired a domicile of choice.

2.6.6 Summary

Hence, unless satisfactory evidence is produced to show that a domicile of choice was acquired by the deceased and had been retained by them until their death, the presumption that the domicile of origin subsisted will prevail.

Residence by itself, even if it is for a long period, without evidence of the necessary intent to abandon the domicile of origin and to remain in the country of choice, does not lead to the acquisition of a domicile of choice. Reference should be made to works on the conflict of laws for the law relating to domicile and on the distinction between habitual residence and domicile. Case law under the Child Abduction and Custody Act 1985, where the issue of habitual residence is frequently raised, may also assist in distinguishing between habitual residence and domicile.

In order to establish a domicile of choice, the evidence must establish that the deceased's intention to change their domicile was not influenced by external pressures; that they intended to live permanently and indefinitely in England and Wales; and that the circumstances in their life and up to their death do not disclose any suggestion of any indecision on their part or anything which would suggest that they had not made up their mind.

Before challenging the issue of domicile, consideration should be given to the effect this might have on the estate, both in terms of the possible reduction in the value of the estate if inheritance tax becomes payable and the costs of litigation.

Chapter 3

Time Limits

3.1 INTRODUCTION

Time limits have always applied to claims for financial provision from a deceased's estate, ever since the right to make such claims was introduced by the I(FP)A 1938. The Act limited the time within which an application could be made to 6 months from the issue of a grant of representation, with a provision for time to be extended with leave of the court. The Intestates' Estates Act 1952 introduced a provision for the court to extend the time limit of 6 months in specified circumstances.

The Family Provision Act 1966 repealed the earlier provisions and gave the court a general discretion to extend the limitation period. This provision is now incorporated in I(PFD)A 1975, s 4, which provides that:

> an application for an order under section 2 of the Act shall not, except with the permission of the court, be made after the end of the period of six months from the date on which representation with respect to the estate of the deceased is first taken out.

It is thus essential that a claim for an order under I(PFD)A 1975, s 2 is issued within the prescribed time limit.

However, pursuant to the Inheritance and Trustees' Powers Act 2014, as from 1 October 2014, s 4 has been amended to enable an application under the Act to be made before the grant of representation is taken out. Civil Procedure Rules 1998 (SI 1998/3132) (CPR), r 57.16 has also been amended to provide that where no grant has been obtained, the claimant may make an application without naming a defendant and apply for directions. In any case, where the deceased died before 1 October 2014, the previous provisions of s 4 continue to apply. The provisions of the amended s 4 and the new procedural rules are considered at para 3.3.1.

3.2 COMMENCEMENT OF THE PERIOD OF 6 MONTHS

I(PFD)A 1975, s 23 provides that, in considering when representation with respect to the estate of a deceased person was taken out, a grant limited to settled land or trust property is to be left out of account; and a grant limited to real estate or to personal estate is to be left out of account unless a grant limited to the remainder of the estate has previously been made or is made at the same time. The Act makes no other provision for determining the date for the commencement of the 6-month limitation period, nor does it make any reference to grants which are limited for a particular purpose. Thus, the effects of these grants for the purposes of the time limit under the Act are unclear. They are dealt with briefly below.

3.2.1 Grant *ad colligenda bona*

A grant of letters of administration *ad colligenda bona* is applied for when it is necessary to prevent loss to the estate because there is no one authorised to administer it. The grant is limited to the purposes of collecting and getting in and receiving the deceased's estate and doing such acts as may be necessary to preserve the estate, until further representation is granted. The grant ceases when the object for which it was granted has been achieved or a full grant has been issued.

It is submitted that, by reason of its limited nature, a grant *ad colligenda bona* does not operate to start time running in respect of claims under the I(PFD)A 1975.

3.2.2 Grant pending determination of claim

Under Senior Courts Act 1981, s 117, a limited grant of letters of administration pending determination of a probate claim commenced in the Chancery Division may be issued as a matter of urgency when there is a dispute which gives rise to a probate claim, for example, to determine the validity of a testator's will. In such cases, the administrator has all the rights and duties of a general administrator except that they are subject to the immediate control of the court and must act under its direction. The object of this grant is to enable the administrator to collect and safeguard assets pending the outcome of the claim. Once the claim has been determined, the grant terminates and the person entitled as a result of the probate claim may take out a grant of probate or administration.

In this case, too, it is unlikely that time will begin to run in respect of any claim under the I(PFD)A 1975, but it would be prudent, if it is intended to make a claim under the Act, to notify the executors and the beneficiaries of that intention. In some cases, it may be desirable to have all issues relating to the deceased's will and estate to be determined by the same tribunal. If a probate claim is pending, the court's direction should be sought (see, also, para 3.3 on claims made before a grant is issued).

3.2.3 Grant ad litem

A grant *ad litem* enables proceedings to be begun or continued on behalf of the deceased's estate or against it. It is limited to bringing or defending a claim, or otherwise being a party to a claim. Once the proceedings are over, application may be made for a general grant, and on the issue of a general grant the limited grant terminates.

In *Re Johnson (Paul Anthony) (Deceased)* [1987] CLY 3882, a grant limited to solicitors for the purposes of issuing a claim for negligence in respect of the deceased's estate was held not to be the first taking out of representation in respect of the estate of the deceased. On the basis of the decision in *Re Johnson*, a general proposition is often made that a grant *ad litem* does not start time running in respect of claims under the I(PFD)A 1975. It is, however, submitted that the decision is not unequivocal, because such a grant may be issued to commence or defend proceedings brought under the Act itself, and in such circumstances the limitation period should start running as soon as the grant is issued.

On the other hand, such a grant does not allow the administrator to distribute the estate. The administrator may not have full knowledge of the extent and nature of the estate or the identity of the beneficiaries entitled, and therefore time ought not to run. In such cases the practitioner will need to consider the nature of the proceedings in respect of which the grant was issued, and make a decision whether time may begin to run.

If the circumstances are unclear, it may be wise to err on the side of caution and, to avoid any risk, proceedings under the I(PFD)A 1975 should be commenced to protect the client; if necessary, an application should be made to adjourn the proceedings generally or for the proceedings to be stayed until the outcome of any pending proceedings.

3.2.4 Grant in common form

Where a grant in common form is followed by a grant in solemn form in respect of the same will, time begins to run from the date on which the grant in common form was granted (see *Re Miller, Miller v De Courcey* [1969] 1 WLR 583).

3.2.5 Successive grants

Where letters of administration are replaced by a grant of probate, for example, because a will is subsequently found, time begins to run from the grant of probate (see *Re Bidie, Bidie v General Accident Fire and Life Assurance Corporation* [1949] Ch 121). In *Re Bidie*, the deceased made a will on 10 February 1937. He died on 16 January 1945. The will was not found. On 13 April 1945, letters of administration were issued to his widow and one of their children. The will was later found and probate was granted on 7 September 1946. On 8 January 1947, the widow applied for financial provision under the I(FP)A 1938. Her claim was allowed to proceed as it had been made within 6 months of the grant of probate.

Similarly, where the grant of probate is revoked and replaced by letters of administration, time begins to run from the grant of letters of administration, because, for the purposes of I(PFD)A 1975, s 4, time begins to run from the date on which 'effective' or 'valid' representation was 'first taken out'. (See *Re Freeman, Weston v Freeman* [1984] 1 WLR 1419, for the absurd situation which would have prevailed if the court had taken a different view.)

3.2.6 *De bonis non* grant

A grant of letters of administration *de bonis non* is made following the death of the sole or last personal representative who obtained a grant in relation to the estate of the deceased but died before completing its administration. The grant relates only to the estate remaining unadministered. It is a second effective and valid grant, but it does not relate to the whole estate. Time therefore runs from the date of the original grant (see, also, *cessate* grant, at para 3.2.7).

3.2.7 *Cessate* grant

A *cessate* grant issues when the first grant was conditional or limited and the condition or limitation has been fulfilled or the grantee dies without fulfilling the purpose for which the grant was made. Unlike a *de bonis non* grant, a *cessate* grant operates in respect of the whole estate. In this case, time begins to run from the original grant, because the second grant is a re-grant.

3.2.8 Authority to the Official Solicitor to obtain a grant: Senior Courts Act 1981, section 116

Where there is no one able or willing to obtain a grant, the applicant wishing to make a claim under the I(PFD)A 1975 may apply to the court under Senior Courts Act 1981, s 116 for an order authorising the Official Solicitor to obtain a grant.

Where it is proposed to make such an application, the Official Solicitor should be notified and given details of the circumstances that necessitates his intervention, and he should be requested to act. The contact details of the Official Solicitor are:

Official Solicitor and Public Trustee
Post Point 0.53
102 Petty France
London SW1H 9AJ
Tel: 020 3681 2759/020 3681 2600 (Trusts and Deputy Services)
Fax: 020 3681 2762
DX Post Point 0.53 DX 152384 Westminster 8 UK
Email: enquiries@ospt.gov.uk

Costs incurred by the Official Solicitor will be met out of the estate. Note, however, that the Official Solicitor cannot be used to give advice on the claimant's case or how the claim should be made.

3.2.9 Standing search for grant

To ensure that a claimant is notified of the issue of a grant of representation, facilities are available for a standing search to be made for an office copy of every grant of representation which tallies with the particulars given on the application, and which either was issued in the 12 months before receipt of the application or is issued within 6 months thereafter.

The procedure is governed by Non-Contentious Probate Rules 1987 (SI 1987/2024) (as amended by the Non-Contentious Probate (Amendment) Rules 2018 (SI 2018/1137)), r 43, which requires the applicant to send a notice in Form 2 of the Rules with the prescribed fee of £3, together with additional fee for the search and copies if required, either by post or by electronic means to any Registry or sub-registry. However, the current guidance suggests that if death has occurred within the last 6 months, the application should be made by completing Form PA1S (available at www.gov.uk/government/publications/find-a-will-or-probate-document-form-pa1s and set out at Appendix A1) and sending it with the prescribed fee (currently £3) to The Postal Copies and Search Department, District Probate Registry, York House, 31 York Place, Leeds LS1 2BA, DX 26451 Leeds Park Square. The fee includes a copy of the will and the grant. Further copies may be obtained on payment of an additional fee of 50 pence per copy. A confirmation letter will be sent to the applicant confirming the receipt of the application and the date when the standing search was entered. An extension beyond the 6 months may be applied for if made within 1 month of the expiry date and on payment of a further fee of £3 (see Non-Contentious Probate Rules 1987 (as amended), r 43). If the death has occurred later than within 6 months of the initial application, the applicant should apply for a general search and if no result is found then that notification should be sent with the application for a standing search. Further information including applying for the search online is available at www.gov.uk/search-will-probate.

It should also be noted that *Practice Direction (Names of Deceased: Death Certificates)*, 12 January 1999 [1999] 1 WLR 259 directs that in all instances where the deceased died in the United Kingdom and the death has been recorded in the Register of Deaths:

(1) the names and dates of birth and death of the deceased as recorded in the register must be included in the oath lodged in support of an application made through a solicitor or probate practitioner for a grant of representation;
(2) the names and date of death of the deceased as recorded in the register must be included in the notice for a standing search or caveat;
(3) in any case where the name of the deceased or by which the deceased was known differs from that recorded in the register, the name must also be included in the oath or the notice, as the case may be.

Pursuant to the *President's Direction: Probate Records: Grants of Representation*, 3 November 1998 [1999] 1 FLR 102, as from November 1998, records of all grants of representation made in the Principal Registry of the Family Division and in district probate registries after that date, kept pursuant to Senior Courts Act 1981, s 111, are maintained in the form of computer records. Records from 1980 to 1988 are maintained on microfilm. The annual calendar books continue to be maintained for the years prior to 1980. The information comprises:

(1) the full names of the deceased and any alias names;
(2) the last address of the deceased;
(3) the date of death and domicile of the deceased;
(4) the name(s) and address(es) of the executor(s) or administrator(s);
(5) the type of grant;
(6) the gross and net values of the estate or, in the case of an exempted estate, the limits within which the estate falls;
(7) the name and address of the extracting solicitor (if any) or the fact that the grant was obtained by way of personal application;
(8) the date of the grant and the issuing registry.

3.3 CAN A CLAIM BE MADE BEFORE GRANT?

Before the Inheritance and Trustees' Powers 2014 came into force on 1 October 2014, there were two conflicting authorities on whether a claim for an order under

I(PFD)A 1975, s 2 could be issued before the grant of representation has been taken out.

In cases under the I(FP)A 1938, it had been held that a claim which is made before the time on which representation was taken out is not invalid (see *Re Searle, Searle v Siems* [1949] Ch 73). In *Re Searle, Searle v Siems*, the originating summons was issued before probate was granted. A grant of representation was obtained before the final hearing. It was argued that an application made before the grant had been taken out was a nullity. Roxburgh J rejected this submission because it would have been contrary to natural justice to prevent the applicant from making the claim. He also considered that the objection raised was one of procedure and could be dispensed with, particularly as it had not been made at any stage prior to the final hearing.

It had also been argued that the decision in *Re Searle, Searle v Siems* does not apply to applications under the I(PFD)A 1975 by reason of the provisions of s 4 (before its amendment; see below) and the CPR which applied to such applications.

I(PFD)A 1975, s 4 in its original form provided:

> An application for an order under section 2 of the Act shall not, except with the permission of the court, be made after the end of the period of six months from the date on which representation with respect to the estate of the deceased is first taken out.

The practice and procedure for claims under the I(PFD)A 1975 were governed by CPR r 57.15 (before its amendment) and the General Pre-Action Conduct and Protocols Practice Direction.

CPR r 57.16(3) provides that:

> The written evidence filed and served by the claimant with the claim form must have exhibited to it an official copy of—
>
> (a) the grant of probate or letters of administration in respect of the deceased's estate; and
> (b) every testamentary document in respect of which probate or letters of administration were granted.

Both the provision of I(PFD)A 1975, s 4 and the rules are mandatory and therefore appear to suggest that no application should be issued unless some grant or representation in the estate has been granted.

In addition, in *Re McBroom Deceased* [1992] 2 FLR 49, it was held that it was essential for a grant of probate or letters of representation to have been obtained before an application under I(PFD)A 1975, s 2 could be issued. In *Re McBroom*, the applicant issued proceedings before a grant of representation had been issued, seeking orders under s 9 against the deceased's severable share in property jointly owned. No attempt had been made to obtain a grant before the final hearing, nor was there any indication whether or not a grant of representation would be obtained before the final hearing. Eastham J struck out the claim on the basis that it was premature.

It is arguable that had the grant been obtained in the preliminary stages of the proceedings or before the final hearing, the result is likely to have been different. The right to make a claim arises as a result of the provisions of I(PFD)A 1975, s 1. Section 1(1) provides that where a person dies domiciled in England and Wales and is survived by any of the persons referred to in the section, such a person may apply to the court for an order under s 2 on the grounds set out in the section. The right to make a claim therefore accrues against the estate on the death of the testator, not on the grant of representation.

In setting the time limit within which such a claim may be made, I(PFD)A 1975, s 4 (before its amendment) provided that the claim cannot, except with the permission of the court, be made after the end of 6 months from the date on which representation with respect to the estate of the deceased is first taken out. It therefore fixed the moment from which time begins to run, not the point at which the right to make a claim accrues. There is no provision in the Act which prohibits the making of a claim until a grant of representation has been issued. Furthermore, if a claim for financial provision under the Act could not be made until a grant of representation has been taken out, the court would be deprived of its power to preserve property pending trial.

If it were the case that the claim does not accrue until the first effective grant of representation is issued, the consequence would be that, if the will is contested, the claim for financial provision could not be commenced until the probate claim has been concluded. The resultant delay in pursuing the claim for financial provision would lead to injustice and possibly more expense. There may be situations where the person contesting the will could also have a claim under the I(PFD)A 1975. The two matters could be conveniently and expeditiously dealt with by the same court simultaneously if the claim under the Act does not have to await the result of the probate claim. If the decision in *Re McBroom* is to be followed, then, where there is a contested probate claim which fails, it is inevitable that the claim for financial provision under the Act will be out of time because it is not until the probate claim has been determined that it will become clear whether the grant of representation issued, if any, is effective. It is inevitable that this claim will take longer than 6 months. If the challenge fails and the grant is found to be effective, then the claimant will be out of time. It is therefore submitted that, in the absence of any specific provision in the Act preventing the issue of proceedings until after the grant of representation has been issued, a claimant under the Act should be able to proceed as soon as practicable after the deceased's death.

Where there is no person willing or able to take out a grant of representation, application should be made to the court to appoint an appropriate person to act, or for the Official Solicitor to represent the estate of the deceased.

In cases where there is, or is likely to be, a dispute over who is to take a grant, it is possible for a claimant to apply for a grant to a nominated person under the Senior Courts Act 1981, on the grounds that there are special circumstances that make it necessary and expedient for the court to appoint a person other than the person entitled to the grant. This procedure, if adopted, is particularly useful where the claim includes an application for interim relief and has the benefit of avoiding delay.

As a result of the amendment made to s 4, by the Inheritance and Trustees' Powers Act 2014, it is unlikely that there are now any cases outstanding where death has occurred before 1 October 2014.

3.3.1 The position post-1 October 2014

Inheritance and Trustees' Powers Act 2014, Sch 2, para 6 amends I(PFD)A 1975, s 4 to provide that:

> An application for an order under section 2 of this Act shall not, except with the permission of the court, be made after the end of the period of six months from the date on which representation with respect to the estate of the deceased is first taken out (*but nothing prevents the making of an application before such representation is first taken out*) (emphasis added)

Thus the time limit for bringing the claim within 6 months from the date on which representation is first taken out remains, but the section as amended now clearly enables the claimant to issue an application before such a grant is taken out.

CPR r 57.16 has been amended to include two new provisions, as follows:

> (3A) Where no grant has been obtained, the claimant may make a claim without naming the defendant and may apply for directions as to the representation of the estate. The written evidence must—
>
> (a) explain the reason why it has not been possible for a grant to be obtained;

(b) be accompanied by the original or a copy (if either is available) of the will or testamentary document in respect of which probate or letters of administration are to be granted; and

(c) contain the following information, so far as is known to the claimant—

(i) brief details of the property comprised in the estate, with an approximate estimate of its capital value and any income that is received from it;

(ii) brief details of the liabilities of the estate;

(iii) the name and addresses of the persons who are in possession of the documents relating to the estate; and

(iv) the names of the beneficiaries and their respective interests in the estate.

(3B) Where a claim is made in accordance with paragraph (3A), the court may give directions as to the parties to the claim and as to the representation of the estate either on the claimant's application or on its own initiative.

Although the court will not be able to progress the application to a final hearing before there is a grant, an application issued before grant of representation will at least ensure that the claimant will not have to overcome the hurdle of seeking permission for an extension of time. The court's power to give direction as to the representation of the estate also means that those responsible for obtaining the grant do not drag their feet in doing so.

However, as soon as it becomes apparent that a claim under the I(PFD)A 1975 may be made, whether this is before or after the grant of representation has been obtained, it is incumbent on the applicant to comply with the General Pre-Action Conduct and Protocols Practice Direction and the *Chancery Guide 2022* (Courts and Tribunals Judiciary, 2022), and to ensure that proceedings are issued at the first opportunity thereafter and in any event before the expiry of 6 months from the date of the grant. Failure to comply with the Protocol may lead to costs implications. Where it becomes apparent during negotiations which are being undertaken and the Protocol's procedure is being followed that there is a risk of time running out, immediate steps should be taken to issue proceedings and to apply for directions. This will avoid having to cross the hurdle of seeking permission for an extension of time, as delay in issuing the application within the time limit without good and, most likely, exceptional reasons could also result in any application for leave to issue out of time being refused (see, further, below).

It is thus essential for practitioners to ensure that the pre-action letter is sent as soon as it appears that their client may have a claim under the I(PFD)A 1975, and to identify the following:

(1) whether the grant of representation has been taken out, and, if not, when it is likely to be taken out;

(2) if a clear answer is not given, to issue proceedings and apply for directions including direction as to representation and, if necessary, either to seek a long adjournment or to apply for a stay to enable negotiations to be undertaken and completed;
(3) in any event, the date from which the commencement of the 6 months is calculated, and to ensure that proceedings are commenced within the time limit.

In the alternative, an application may be made for a grant *ad litem* (see para 3.2.3) and to issue the claim promptly.

3.4 APPLICATIONS IN RESPECT OF JOINT PROPERTY – I(PFD)A 1975, SECTION 9

Before the Inheritance and Trustees' Powers Act 2014 came into force on 1 October 2014, an application under I(PFD)A 1975, s 9, to treat the deceased's severable share of a joint tenancy as part of the net estate of the deceased (see para 9.8), had to be made within the period of 6 months from the date on which representation with respect to the deceased's estate was first taken out. The court did not have the power to extend the time limit imposed by statute in cases under s 9. This time limit no longer applies in relation to applications issued after 1 October 2014. Where it is proposed to make an application for an order under s 9, the relief should be sought within the substantive claim so that if there has been a delay in making the substantive application within the time limit under s 4, the issue is considered together at the same time (see, further, para 9.8).

3.5 EXTENSION OF TIME

3.5.1 Powers of the court

In addition to setting the time limit for bringing a claim under the I(PFD)A 1975, s 4 confers on the court a general discretion to extend the time limit. The Act does not, however, set out any criteria or principle which the court should apply when considering an application for an extension of time, nor does it in any way restrict the court's power. The court thus has unfettered discretion, and the circumstances in which the court may be asked to exercise its discretion are limitless. However, now that it is possible to issue proceedings before grant is taken out, it will be in very exceptional circumstances that the court is likely to exercise its discretion in favour of the applicant. Practitioners should also pay heed to the overriding objectives set out in the CPR and the General Pre-Action Conduct and Protocols Practice Direction and the costs provisions set out in r 44.2(4) and (5) which entitle the court to take account of conduct of the parties when exercising its discretion as to costs.

In dealing with an application for an extension of time, guidance is often sought from case law following the I(FP)A 1938 under which the time limit of 6 months was first imposed. Regard should, however, be had to the fact that, as respects the estates of persons dying after 1952 and before 1967, when the Family Provision Act 1966 came into force, the court's discretion to extend the 6-month period was limited by the Intestates' Estates Act 1952. That Act provided that the period could be extended only in limited specified circumstances, and then only if it could be shown to the satisfaction of the court that the time limit would operate 'unfairly'. The pre-1966 case law may be said to be of limited value to an application under I(PFD)A 1975, s 4, particularly as social conditions and attitudes have changed significantly and continue to do so.

However, the cases may be of relevance in so far as CPR r 1.1 requires the court when dealing with any case to apply the 'overriding objective' with a view to dealing with the case justly and fairly and ensuring that the parties are on an equal footing.

Additionally, the court is now obliged in determining any issue to have regard to the provisions of the Human Rights Convention. In an application under I(PFD)A 1975, s 4 for an extension of time, the provisions of Art 6 of the Convention, which entitles every person to a fair and public hearing, will be a significant factor in the determination of the application. It should also be borne in mind that social conditions and attitudes have changed significantly and continue to do so.

In exercising its discretion, the court will take account of all the circumstances of the case, carry out a balancing exercise between the merits of each party's case, exercise its discretion on the basis of what is just and fair, and give reasons for its decision (see *Fielden and Graham v Cunliffe* [2005] EWCA Civ 1508, [2006] 1 FLR 745). Case law provides some guidance on the principles which have been considered as relevant to such applications.

3.5.2 The relevant criteria to be applied in an application for extension of time

Case law provides guidance on the factors which will be relevant in an application to bring a claim out of time. The leading case which gives such guidance and which has been consistently followed is *Re Salmon (Deceased), Coard v National Westminster Bank* [1981] Ch 167.

The principles formulated by Megarry VC in his judgment in *Re Salmon (Deceased), Coard v National Westminster Bank* (applied in *Berger v Berger* [2013] EWCA Civ 1305) are generally relied on by courts when exercising the discretion under I(PFD)A 1975, s 4. These principles are:

(1) The discretion is unfettered and one that is exercised judicially in accordance with what is just and proper.
(2) The onus lies on the applicant to establish sufficient grounds for taking the case out of the general rule and depriving those who are protected by it of its benefits. Furthermore, the time limit prescribed is a substantive provision laid down in the I(PFD)A 1975 itself, and is not merely a procedural time limit imposed by rules of court which may be treated with indulgence appropriate to procedural rules. The burden on the applicant is thus not a triviality. The applicant must make out a substantial case for it being just and proper for the court to exercise its statutory discretion to extend the time.
(3) The court must consider how promptly and in what circumstances the applicant is seeking an extension of time. The whole of the circumstances must be looked at, including the reasons for the delay and how promptly the applicant gave a warning to the defendant of the proposed application.
(4) It is material whether or not negotiations have been commenced within the time limit; if they have, and time has run out while they are proceeding, this is likely to encourage the court to extend the time. Negotiations commenced after the time limit has expired might also aid the applicant, at any rate, if the defendants have not taken the point that time has expired.
(5) It is relevant to consider whether the estate had been distributed before the claim was notified.
(6) The court should also consider whether refusal to extend time would leave the applicant without redress against anybody.

In *Re Dennis (Deceased), Dennis v Lloyds Bank* [1981] 2 All ER 140, Browne-Wilkinson J, while applying the principles stated by Megarry VC, formulated two further factors which should be adopted when exercising the court's discretion. These are:

(7) The applicant must show that 'he has an arguable case, a case fit to go to trial and that in approaching that matter the court's approach is rather the same as it adopts when considering proceedings for summary judgment' (see CPR Part 24).
(8) Where, after a full understanding of the nature of the claim and the prospect of success, the applicant makes a conscious decision not to

make a claim and then later changes his/her mind, the court ought not to permit the claim to be made irrespective of the length of time which has elapsed, save only that no distribution has taken place (see *Escritt v Escritt* (1982) 3 FLR 280).

In *Re Dennis (Deceased)*, the applicant was the son of the deceased. He had received £90,000 by way of a gift, with other sums, during the deceased's lifetime. The deceased had left him a legacy, free of duty, of £10,000, and £30,000 in trust. Probate was granted on 17 January 1978. On 19 February 1980, the son applied for financial provision and for an extension of time. His claim was limited to such sums as would enable him to discharge the capital transfer tax on the £90,000 received during the deceased's lifetime. The court found the application totally unmeritorious.

In *Cowan v Foreman* [2019] EWCA Civ 1336, the Court of Appeal further expanded on these principles applying the earlier decisions in *Nesheim v Kosa* [2006] EWHC 2710 (Ch) and *Berger v Berger* [2013] EWCA Civ 1305. Asplin LJ held at [44]–[48] that:

(1) 'First, it seems to me that the concept of a "stale claim" is of little relevance in the 1975 Act context. It is borrowed from and is more apposite to the consideration of matters under the Limitation Act 1980. Section 4 contains no long stop provision. Furthermore, the assessment, for the purposes of the substantive claim, is made at the date of the hearing and, therefore, concerns about the loss of evidence and witnesses over time are of much less importance than they might be. As Briggs J (as he then was) pointed out in *Nesheim v Kosa*, section 4 exists for the purpose of avoiding unnecessary delay in the administration of estates which would be caused by the tardy bringing of proceedings and to avoid the complications which might arise if distributions from the estate are made before the proceedings are brought. This dovetails with section 20 of the 1975 Act. It provides express protection for the executors/personal representatives of an estate from any liability which might otherwise arise as a result of having made a distribution from the estate more than six months after the grant of probate/letters of administration, on the ground that they ought to have taken into account that the Court might permit a claim to be made after the end of that period. Section 4 is not designed, therefore, to protect the court from stale claims as the Judge explains. On the contrary, if the circumstances warrant it, the power in section 4 can be exercised in order to further the overriding objective of bringing such claims before the court where it is just to do so, and, in such circumstances, the personal representatives have the protection

afforded by section 20. The power must be considered in the context in which it arises.'

(2) There is nothing in s 4 or in the principles distilled in *Berger v Berger* which requires 'a robust application of the extension power'. The factors set out in the overriding objective to the CPR are not relevant to the exercise of discretion under s 4. These factors are all concerned with 'managing a claim proportionately and fairly once it has been commenced, whereas section 4 is concerned with whether, given all the circumstances of the case and the delay, it is appropriate to allow a claim to be issued more than six months after a grant of probate/letters of administration.'

(3) 'There is no disciplinary element to section 4. Unlike the provisions of the CPR, the six-month time limit in section 4 is not to be enforced for its own sake. The time limit is expressly made subject to permission of the court to bring an application after the six months has elapsed. It is designed to bring a measure of certainty for personal representatives and beneficiaries alike. When determining whether a claim should be brought outside the six-month period, nevertheless, the court must consider all of the relevant circumstances of the case in question and the factors which were highlighted in *Berger v Berger* [[2013] EWCA Civ 1305]. The rationale of CPR 3.9(1) with which the "*Denton* jurisprudence" is concerned, on the other hand, just like the overriding objective in CPR 1.1, is that court rules should be obeyed so that once commenced, litigation should proceed expeditiously and at proportionate cost and that court resources should not be wasted. As Chief Master Marsh neatly described it recently in *Bhusate v Patel* [2019] EWHC 470 (Ch) at [64], to have regard to the overriding objective or the approach to relief against sanctions in the *Denton* case when exercising the discretion under section 4 "involves conflating issues that, if they are related, are at best distant cousins."'

(4) Although it is necessary to put forward a substantial case 'it is also necessary to consider the statutory power in the context in which it arises. It is for those reasons that the factors distilled in *Berger v Berger* are relevant to the exercise of the power'.

The principles set out in the above two cases are 'guidelines' and should assist the practitioner in advising whether the case merits an application being made under the I(PFD)A 1975 and for permission to apply for the application out of time and the nature of the evidence which will be required for the application for permission to apply out of time to succeed.

The application of each of the above eight factors to the facts of individual cases, and the consideration of them by the courts, are reviewed below.

3.5.3 Merits of the claim

In *Re Salmon (Deceased), Coard v National Westminster Bank*, it was held that the applicant must show a substantial case for it being just and proper for the court to exercise its statutory discretion to extend the time. It would seem from the authorities, however, that, to take the case out of the general rule, the applicant must not only establish sufficient reason for the delay in making the application but must also show a good prospect of succeeding in the claim. The following cases further illustrate the court's approach to an application for leave to extend time.

In *Re Stone* (1969) 114 SJ 36, the Court of Appeal stated that the applicant must establish that there is a triable issue and satisfy the court that in all the circumstances of the case the court ought to exercise its discretion.

In *Re Dennis (Deceased), Dennis v Lloyds Bank*, it was held that, in exercising its discretion, a factor to which the court was required to have regard, in addition to other matters, was whether the applicant was able to satisfy the court that he had an arguable case that he was entitled to reasonable financial provision out of the estate. The criterion to be applied in deciding whether the applicant had an arguable case was the same as that applied by the court in deciding whether a defendant should have leave to defend (see CPR Part 24), but note also that under this rule the test appears to be whether there is a 'real prospect' of success, or 'compelling' reasons. In *Re Dymott, Spooner v Carroll*, CAT, 15 December 1980, the principle applied was whether there was any merit in the application, rather than whether the applicant had an arguable case.

In *Smith v Loosley*, CAT, 18 June 1986, the issue was decided on the basis of whether the applicant had an arguable case. The applicant was 7 weeks out of time. She did not understand what a life interest meant and she had been involved in a dispute with one of the members of the extended family. The delay was not regarded as excessive. In addition, a warning letter had been sent by her solicitors to the executors 1 day before the time expired.

In *Polackova v Sobiewski*, CAT, 28 October 1985, there had been inactivity for 6 months after the solicitors and the applicant discovered that probate had been granted, and the application was made 3 months out of time. No satisfactory explanation for the delay was given, but leave was granted on the basis that, at the date of the hearing, the applicant had an arguable case. It is difficult to reconcile this decision with the principles set out by Megarry VC in *Re Dennis (Deceased)* and the other authorities. It can be explained only on the basis that the court took the view that as the applicant was the former spouse of the deceased, the case must have some merit.

These authorities seem to suggest that the onus on the applicant has gradually shifted from having to 'make a substantial case' to: (1) having to show an 'arguable case' or a 'triable issue' (*Re Dennis (Deceased)*); (2) showing that the applicant's case has merit (*Re Dymott*); and (3) if *Polackova v Sobiewski* is to be regarded as good law, to a 'triviality' and an inquiry which is superficial. *Polackova v Sobiewski* should not, however, be regarded as setting a new standard, but as a case which turned on its own facts. The correct approach is to show that the applicant has a good arguable case on the merits which ought to be tried, or that the applicant has a 'real prospect of success'.

In *Re C (Deceased)* [1995] 2 FLR 24, leave was granted although there had been a delay of 2 years before the mother of the deceased's child sought to make a claim. The delay was not properly explained. There had not been any distribution of the estate. If leave was refused, the child would have suffered as a result of her mother's default. The court considered the merits of the application and the prospects of success if the child's claim was allowed to be made. It was inevitable that there would be a substantial provision out of the estate in favour of the child for the child's ordinary maintenance requirements. Wilson J (as he then was) stated that in none of the reported cases to which he had been referred had the prospects of substantial success been so clear as in this case, and 'in the end the task is to determine whether the net weight of the relevant factors is such as to justify permission outside the normal period'.

In *Budd v Fowler* [1999] CLY 4635, the widower of the deceased, having accepted a lump sum of £700 in full and final settlement of all claims against the estate of the deceased, including all claims under the I(PFD)A 1975, applied to make a claim out of time. In determining the application, the court, *inter alia*, applied the test of whether the claimant had reasonable grounds for making a claim and whether there was a real and substantial question to be tried. On the facts, the application for permission to bring a claim under the Act was refused because the applicant had agreed to settle all claims including those under the Act and the applicant's case lacked merit.

In *McNulty v McNulty* [2002] EWHC 123 (Ch), [2002] WTLR 737, the applicant succeeded in her application for permission to issue her claim against the estate of the deceased although she was in excess of 3 years out of time. The court found on the facts that her case had merit, the estate had not been distributed and there would be no prejudice to any of the beneficiaries if permission was granted (see, further, under claims by those with disability).

In *Stock v Brown* [1994] 1 FLR 840, the court granted permission notwithstanding the fact that there had been a delay in excess of 6 years. The court struck a balance between the length of the delay and the merit of the case, the fact that there would be no prejudice to or objections from any beneficiaries, the applicant's age which disabled her from seeking independent legal advice, and other extraneous circumstances.

In *Berger v Berger* [2013] EWCA Civ 1305, proceedings were issued 6 years after the grant of probate. Although the widow's application had merit, the delay could not be explained, especially taking into consideration the fact that she had not been receiving sufficient income.

In *Zarrinkhat v Kamal* [2013] WTLR 1477, the application for an extension of time was refused as the applicant had delayed in seeking advice, and also because the delay was partly due to his legal advisers, against whom she had a possible claim.

3.5.4 Delay in bringing the claim

In considering an application for an extension of time, the court looks not only at the length of time that has elapsed, but at the whole of the circumstances. In *Re Salmon (Deceased), Coard v National Westminster Bank* (at paras 3.5.2 and 3.5.3), the reasons for the delay, as well as the promptness with which the applicant gave warning to the defendants of the proposed claim, were regarded as important considerations. In *Re Ruttie (Deceased) Ruttie v Saul* [1970] 1 WLR 89, the court considered the hardship to the applicant if an extension was not granted, the fact that the estate had not yet been distributed and the fact that the application was just 6 weeks out of time against the fact that there would be no prejudice whatsoever to the defendants except what was inevitably involved in any extension of time, that is, the loss of the advantage of a rigid time limit. The delay in making the application earlier was explained on three grounds, namely:

(1) there had been lengthy negotiations with a view to reaching a compromise, during which arose the question whether the doctrine of community of property under Polish law would be applicable;
(2) the applicant had been ill;
(3) in concentrating on the issue of community of property, the solicitors had overlooked the time limit.

In *Re Gonin (Deceased), Gonin v Garmeson* [1979] Ch 16, where the delay was of 2 years, the court refused the application because the applicant had been in control throughout and the delay had occurred as a result of the negligence of the applicant's solicitors and the advice they gave her. The applicant had a good case against her solicitors, and the injustice to her could therefore be remedied by an action against them.

In *Re Bone (Deceased), Bone v Midland Bank* [1955] 1 WLR 703, an issue had arisen as to the construction of the deceased's will. The widow's solicitors were informed that an application would be issued for the question to be determined by the court. The application was not made, so the widow issued an application under the I(FP)A 1938. The application was 2 days out of time and leave was sought to extend time. Leave was granted because the executor's solicitors had led the widow to suppose that proceedings would be commenced; the delay was short; and refusal would have caused hardship.

In *Re Trott, Trott v Miles* [1958] 1 WLR 604, the deceased had died on 8 October 1954. Probate was granted on 17 November 1954. The widow applied for financial provision for herself. On 13 April 1955, the widow gave birth to the deceased's daughter. The application on behalf of the daughter was not issued until 11 July 1955, almost 2 months out of time. Leave was granted, as it was plain that on the birth of the child, another circumstance affecting the administration or distribution of the estate arose. No time had been wasted between the date of the child's birth and the date of the application; an application for the child to be represented by means of public funds had also been in progress.

In *Re McNare, McNare v McNare* [1964] 1 WLR 1255, the deceased died in 1961. Probate was granted to his son on 8 May 1962. The deceased had left nothing to his widow, who was blind, crippled and 71 years of age, and who had not discovered the deceased's death until the end of October 1962. She had no information regarding the deceased's assets. Her sister, on her behalf, sought legal advice and as a result the son was contacted, but he refused to give any information. Solicitors were instructed on the widow's behalf and there then followed preliminary negotiations between them and the son's solicitors. There was deadlock. The widow then issued the application for financial provision and sought an extension of time. Leave was granted because:

(1) the applicant had not had any information about the deceased's estate;
(2) there were negotiations between solicitors;
(3) refusal to extend the time would have caused hardship and would have operated unfairly against the applicant.

In *Re Longley (Deceased), Longley and Longley v Longley* [1981] CLY 2885, the application for an extension of time was refused because there had been a delay of about 14 months before making the application; distribution of the estate had taken place; there had been no negotiations for a settlement; and the applicant had a good case for negligence against her solicitors.

In *Re Adams, Adams and Adams v Schofield and Adams* (1981) [2004] WTLR 1049, an appeal succeeded because the judge had placed too great an emphasis on the fact that the delay was wholly due to the negligence of the solicitors and that the applicant would have had a good claim against them; and had failed to give due weight to the other factors in favour of the applicant (see, also, *Zarrinkhat v Kamal* (at para 3.5.3)).

In *Escritt v Escritt* (1982) 3 FLR 280, despite the fact that the applicant had been properly advised, she had delayed for 3 years in bringing her claim, to avoid differences within the family. Leave to apply out of time was refused.

In *Sargeant v Sargeant* [2018] EWHC 8 (Ch), [2019] WTLR 1451, the claimant had delayed 10 years before applying for an extension of time although she had been advised to take legal advice on what if any options were available to her, but in *Bhusate v Patel* [2019] EWHC 470 (Ch) permission was granted although the widow's application was 26 years out of time because the court found that her substantive claim had merit and that the delay was the consequence of the conduct of her step-children who stood to benefit if she did not proceed and the fact that she would be left homeless. This decision was upheld on appeal (*Thakare v Bhusate* [2020] EWHC 52 (Ch)).

In *Kaur v Bolina* [2021] EWHC 2894 (Fam), where the delay was for 5 months, in exercising its discretion and granting leave the court took account of the factors set out in s 3 of the Act, the conduct of the executors and beneficiaries, the circumstances that had led to the delay and the fact that when the applicant had applied for a caveat she had not been advised that probate had already been granted. (See, also, *Begum v Ahmed* [2019] EWCA Civ 1794, where there was a delay of 16 months and *Antonio v Williams* [2022] EWHC 2383 (Ch), where the claimant was a minor, and where the delay was said to be a period of 6 months.)

In *Antonio v Williams* [2022] EWHC 2383 (Ch), the claim made was on behalf of a minor and was 6 months out of time. The delay was caused in consequence of a history of disputes amongst the family in relation to whether the deceased had made a will and the challenge to the validity of the will. This had resulted in the grant not being obtained or granted, notwithstanding that 3 years had elapsed from the deceased's death. Permission was granted for the claim to be brought out of time.

Where there are related proceedings with regard to the construction or validity of the deceased's will, the issue of a possible claim under the I(PFD)A 1975 can be easily overlooked, as occurred in *Anthony v Donges* [1998] 2 FLR 775. In such cases, it is advisable to issue a claim under the Act to protect the claim from being out of time and then either to apply for a stay of the proceedings or for the matter to be consolidated with the probate action.

3.5.5 Negotiations

Where delay has occurred because the parties have been attempting to negotiate a settlement, the court is likely to consider an application for permission to bring a claim out of time favourably. The basis of the application will obviously include the fact that the executors and any beneficiaries were made aware of the claim, and therefore there would be no prejudice to them. If assurances were given whilst negotiations were being undertaken that the issue of the time limit under I(PFD)A 1975, s 4 would not be relied on against the claimant if negotiations failed, the application for permission will be granted. Now that under the CPR the emphasis is on mediation and attempting a settlement before issuing any claim and following the General Pre-Action Conduct and Protocols Practice Direction, if delay has occurred in pursuit of effecting a settlement, the court is likely to treat an application under s 4 sympathetically. However, so as to protect the claimant in such cases, it is desirable that the pre-action letter includes a request for confirmation that the 'time' factor will not be raised against the claimant, to enable negotiations to be undertaken and to avoid the costs of issuing a claim and then having to apply for a stay.

Cases where this principle is demonstrated include *Re McNare, McNare v McNare* (at para 3.5.4). See, also, *Re Ruttie* (at para 3.5.4), where the negotiations with a view to compromising the claim had commenced before the grant of probate and had continued for the whole of the period of 6 months.

In *Re John, John v John* (1966) 111 SJ 115, the application was made by the widow of the deceased 3 years after probate was taken out because she had relied on promises made to her by the legatees which never materialised. Her application was granted.

In some instances where the claimant has given notice of a possible claim being made, agreement is reached between the parties to attempt to reach a settlement and pending the process of negotiations to enter into a 'standstill agreement'. However, as Asplin LJ stated in *Cowan v Freeman* [2019] EWCA Civ 1336, an agreement not to take any point on the issue of delay is not binding and there is always a risk that the court may not grant permission to issue proceedings out of time although an attempt to negotiate a settlement is to be encouraged (at [73]). King LJ in her judgment also pointed out (at [90]) that:

> whilst the final decision always rests with the court, where there is a properly evidenced agreement to which no objection has been taken by the Executors and beneficiaries, it is unlikely that in the ordinary way, a judge would dismiss an application for an extension of time.

She stressed (at [91]) however that:

if parties choose the 'stand-still' route, there should be clear written agreement setting out the terms/duration of such an agreement and each of the potential parties should be included in the agreement. In the event that proceedings have, in due course to be issued, the court should be presented with a consent application for permission to be granted notwithstanding that six months has elapsed.

3.5.6 Distribution of the estate

I(PFD)A 1975, s 20(1) stipulates that the provisions of the Act do not render the personal representative of the deceased person liable for having distributed any part of the estate of the deceased, after the end of the period of 6 months from the date on which representation with respect to the estate of the deceased is first taken out, on the ground that he ought to have taken into account the possibility that the court might permit the making of an application after the end of 6 months, or might exercise its powers under s 6 (see, further, para 8.11). The section goes on to provide that this does not prejudice any power to recover, by reason of the making of an order under the Act, any part of the estate distributed. If, therefore, distribution has taken place, the prejudice to the beneficiaries will be that much greater by reason of the conversion of hope and expectation to reality when they received their shares:

> For most people, there is a real difference between the bird in the hand and the bird in the bush. In addition, of course, the beneficiaries are more likely to have changed their position in reliance on the benefaction if they have actually received it than if it lies merely in prospect. If it is always prejudicial to claimants not to receive money that they are entitled to receive at the earliest moment, it is likely to be even more prejudicial to have taken away from them money that they have actually received and have begun to enjoy. The point is strengthened if they have changed their position in reliance on what they have received, as by making a purchase or gifts they would otherwise not have made. (per Megarry VC in *Re Salmon (Deceased)* [1981] Ch 167 (at paras 3.5.2 and 3.5.3))

Although Megarry VC referred to the fact that the court could go behind the fact of distribution, it is unlikely for a claim made out of time where distribution has taken place to succeed unless the applicant for an extension of time is able to establish compelling reasons and exceptional circumstances. Of relevance will also be the extent of the distribution, the nature of the property/assets distributed, whether any part of the assets distributed were nominated or were included in a *donatio mortis causa*, the identity and status of those who have benefited from the distribution. There have been no reported cases of leave being granted after distribution has taken place. In *Re Longley (Deceased), Longley and Longley v Longley* [1981] CLY 2885, distribution had taken place when the application was made. It was a factor which the court took into account when refusing leave. In *Berger v Berger* [2013] EWCA Civ 1305 distribution of the deceased's assets had only partially been undertaken and there was sufficient capital within the estate to meet the claimant's claim. The court having considered all the relevant factors such as reasons for the delay, whether negotiations had taken place within the time limit, the merit of the applicant's case and what if any steps that been taken to notify the defendants of the claim within the time limits and whether the applicant had a possible claim against a third party, nevertheless refused the application. In *Hendry v Hendry* [2019] EWHC 1976 (Ch), on the facts permission to bring a claim was refused although the delay was for no more than about 57 days. The applicant had issued divorce proceedings in November 2016 in which she made a claim for financial provision, and her solicitors had indicated to the deceased's solicitors that she intended to do so although she had entered into a pre-nuptial agreement. Mr Hendry died in February 2017. The applicant and her solicitors were aware of the time limit to bring a claim under the Act but took no steps to do so nor could they explain sufficiently the reason for the delay. Apart from notifying the deceased's solicitors in the divorce proceedings of the applicant's intentions to make a claim, no further steps had been taken towards negotiating a settlement. The court also took into account the fact that the applicant had a possible claim against her solicitors for negligence because they had admitted their error in not issuing her claim within the time limit. Although the estate had not been distributed, it was in itself insufficient to outweigh all the other factors and in particular the failure to provide sufficient and convincing reasons or explanation for the delay.

See, also, *Antonio v Williams* [2022] EWHC 2383 (Ch), where the claim related to a minor. There were a number of factors taken into account, including the fact that distribution of the estate had not taken place.

Compelling and exceptional circumstances may, for instance, include a situation where the distribution has occurred very recently, or where the assets distributed are still in the hands of the beneficiary, or can be traced with little or no prejudice to the beneficiary who has received the asset. It could also arise where negotiations have led to an agreement which has not yet been put into effect or where the defendant reneged on the agreement and distributed the estate without any prior warning to the claimant.

3.5.7 Claimant's possible claim against third parties or solicitors

In *Re Salmon (Deceased), Coard v National Westminster Bank* [1981] Ch 167, Megarry VC stated that a relevant factor in exercising the court's discretion when dealing with an application for permission to bring a claim under the I(PFD)A 1975 was the fact that the applicant had a possible claim against a third party. Subsequent cases, however, have not considered this factor as tipping the balance against the applicant, but only as one of the factors which the court will take into account when assessing all the circumstances of the individual case. The decision in *Re Adams, Adams and Adams v Schofield and Adams* (1981) [2004] WTLR 1049, supports this view because, on appeal, it was held that the trial judge had placed too great an emphasis on the fact that the claimant had a possible claim against his legal advisers and had failed to give sufficient weight to the other factors which supported the claimant's case. In *Re Longley (Deceased), Longley and Longley v Longley* [1981] CLY 2885, the claimant's remedy against her lawyers was one amongst other relevant factors considered by the court in exercising its discretion and refusing permission. In that case, the deceased had made a will appointing his mistress executor, and bequeathed to her his house, in which she was then living with her daughter. The remainder of his estate devolved on his widow on a partial intestacy. The mistress wished to make a claim against the estate under the Act. She renounced probate in the widow's favour. Thereafter, although her solicitors were involved, the matter did not result in any settlement. The solicitors took no further action to pursue the claim on behalf of the mistress or her child. The mistress took further advice, but when she issued proceedings the claim was 14 months out of time and the estate had been distributed. Her application for an extension of time was refused because of the delay, the fact that distribution had taken place and that she had a claim against her former solicitors. In exercising its discretion and carrying out the balancing exercise, the court had regard to all the important issues involved. See, also, *Hendry v Hendry* (at para 3.5.6), where the claimant's solicitors had accepted their error in not issuing proceedings within the time limit, and the permission was refused although the estate had not been distributed. It seems, therefore, that where the application for an extension of time is opposed on the basis that the applicant has a possible claim against a third party, the success or otherwise of the application will depend on the circumstances of the individual case. It is unlikely that the court will deny the claimant the right to pursue a rightful and meritorious claim simply on the basis that they may have a possible claim against a third party, particularly where the claimant is a vulnerable individual or a child (for an example, see *Re C (Deceased)* [1995] 2 FLR 24 (at para 3.5.3); see, also, *Zarrinkhat v Kamal* [2013] WTLR 1477 (at para 3.5.3)).

3.5.8 Conscious decision not to make a claim

Where the applicant has been properly advised but seeks not to pursue a claim promptly or makes a conscious and informed decision not to pursue the claim and then changes their mind, it is unlikely that an application for permission will succeed (see *Escritt v Escritt* (1982) 3 FLR 280 and para 3.5.4). In contrast, in *Re C (Deceased)* (at para 3.5.3), the court took a different view on the facts and more particularly as the applicant was a child and dependent on the decision of her mother.

3.5.9 Claimant under disability

In the case of civil litigation, Limitation Act 1980, s 28(1) extends the limitation period where the claimant is a person under disability. The I(PFD)A 1975 does not make any special provision for a claimant who is physically or mentally disabled. The disabled claimant should not, however, be disadvantaged or prejudiced by the absence of any specific provisions since the court has an unfettered discretion under I(PFD)A 1975, s 4. In exercising its discretion, the court is obliged to have regard to all the circumstances, including human rights issues under the Human Rights Convention, and to consider whether it is reasonably clear that the extension of time is required in the interests of justice.

The constraints of time are often more pressing when the practitioner has to deal with a client under disability, particularly if the client has learning difficulties or otherwise lacks capacity or has a speech impediment or is hard of hearing. In the case of a claimant who has severe learning difficulties or lacks capacity, consideration should be given to the appointment of a litigation friend or a receiver or, in appropriate cases which fall within the Mental Capacity Act 2005, the intervention of the Court of Protection. In such a case, delay is likely, and steps must be taken to safeguard the interest of the claimant under disability. The duty and burden on the solicitor are necessarily heavy ones. Time may have begun to run or may have expired before advice is sought. It is essential that a meticulous note is kept of every step taken in the proceedings to show that the matter was dealt with expeditiously and efficiently. If there is any likelihood of delay before a claim can be issued, contact with the personal representatives or their solicitors must be maintained to ensure that they are kept informed and, if possible, to obtain an extension of time by agreement, but in this event it is essential to follow the guidance given by King LJ in *Cowan v Freeman* [2019] EWCA Civ 1336 referred to at para 3.5.5. In some cases, it may be appropriate to apply for leave to issue the claim without the necessary supporting evidence, to protect the claim and then seek directions from the court or apply for a stay to enable the necessary inquiries and investigations to be made to pursue the claim.

Where delay has occurred and it is necessary to apply for an extension of time, the principles set out above should be taken into account when preparing the supporting evidence. In addition, the extent and nature of the claimant's disability and the reason for the delay in making the claim are relevant factors, particularly if the delay is solely attributable to the claimant's disability. The claimant, through their solicitor, must set out any other factor which establishes that it would be just and fair for the court to exercise its discretion in favour of the person under disability. Evidence which indicates that the matter was dealt with diligently, efficiently and expeditiously will be relevant.

The following are some of the cases where the court has waived the time limits, where the applicant has been a person under disability:

- *Re McNare, McNare v McNare* (at para 3.5.4), where the applicant was blind, crippled and 71 years of age and did not discover the death of the deceased until 5 months after the grant of probate had been issued to her son.
- *Re Wood (Deceased), Wood v Wood* [1982] LS Gaz R 774, where the deceased had died intestate in April 1980. She was survived by a severely mentally handicapped child and the deceased's husband who was not the child's natural father. The estate was valued at £26,737. The husband inherited £25,000, the child the balance. The husband died in January 1981, leaving his entire estate to his natural son. The child's application, brought out of time, was allowed.
- *Re C (Deceased)* (at para 3.5.3), where a claim on behalf of a child was allowed despite the fact that it was 2 years out of time and notwithstanding the fact that the mother of the child, who could have made the claim on behalf of the child on time, could not give any reason for the delay.
- *Stock v Brown* [1994] 1 FLR 840, where the applicant was 85 years of age when probate was granted and had not had the opportunity to obtain independent legal advice. Permission to bring a claim despite a delay of 6 years was granted due to the exceptional circumstances, the merits of the case and the fact that there was no prejudice to the beneficiaries.
- *Antonio v Williams* [2022] EWHC 2383 (Ch) where the delay in making a claim on behalf of a minor was caused by family disputes and challenges on whether the deceased who was the aunt of the claimant had made a valid will.

3.5.10 Delay caused by application for public funding

Solicitors should be mindful of the fact that there is no guarantee that any delay in issuing a claim, resulting from the time taken by the Legal Aid Agency to deal with an application for public funding, will be treated by the court sympathetically. It is the duty of the solicitor to ensure that the Legal Aid Agency is made fully aware of the urgency when making the application and subsequently by sending regular reminders to the Agency that time is running out. If it appears that the application will take some time to process, then it would be advisable to seek an emergency certificate, or one limited to issuing the proceedings.

It is also well worth notifying the personal representatives or their solicitors of the application for public funding, keeping them informed at all times of the progress of the application, and seeking an extension by agreement. If all else fails, the solicitor should advise the client of the implications, with a view to ascertaining whether the client is able to meet the costs of issuing the claim out of their own resources. It is also possible to apply to the court for leave to issue the proceedings without the supporting evidence on the undertaking that the evidence will be filed upon the determination of the application for a public funding certificate.

3.6 PROCEDURE

An application under I(PFD)A 1975, s 4 for permission to bring a claim after the 6-month period has lapsed must be made in the claim form and supported by evidence (see Chapter 12).

3.7 BURDEN OF PROOF

The overall burden of proof rests on the applicant to establish that there are good grounds for the delay and that the interests of justice justify leave to be granted.

Chapter 4

Claimants

4.1 INTRODUCTION

I(PFD)A 1975, s 1(1), as amended by Law Reform (Succession) Act 1995, s 2, CPA 2004, s 71, Sch 4, the Marriage (Same Sex Couples) Act 2013 and the Inheritance and Trustees' Powers Act 2014, sets out the classes of person entitled to make an application for an order under s 2 for financial provision on the ground that the disposition of the deceased's estate effected by their will, or the law of intestacy, or the combination of their will and that law, is not such as to make reasonable financial provision for the applicant. These classes are:

(a) the spouse or civil partner of the deceased;

(b) a former spouse or civil partner of the deceased but not one who has formed a subsequent marriage or civil partnership;

(ba) a cohabitant of the deceased;

(c) a child of the deceased;

(d) any person (not being a child of the deceased) who in relation to any marriage or civil partnership to which the deceased was at any time a party, or otherwise in relation to any family in which the deceased at any time stood in the role of a parent was treated by the deceased as a child of the family;

(e) any person (not being a person included in the foregoing classes) who, immediately before the death of the deceased, was being maintained, either wholly or partly, by the deceased.

4.2 SPOUSE OF THE DECEASED

Before 17 July 2013, only a marriage between a man and woman was recognised as a valid marriage, Since 17 July 2013, when the Marriage (Same Sex Couples) Act 2013 came into force, marriage between same sex couples is recognised as valid. Section 11(1) of the Act provides that a marriage has the same effect in relation to same sex couples as it has in relation to opposite sex couples. All legislation passed in England and Wales whenever passed or made has effect in accordance with this provision (Sch 3, para 1(1)(a) and (b)).

Marriage (Same Sex Couples) Act 2013, Sch 3, para 5(2) defines the meaning which applies to the expressions 'husband', 'wife', 'widow' and 'widower' as follows:

> (a) 'husband' includes a man who is married to another man;
> (b) 'wife' includes a woman who is married to another woman;
> (c) 'widower' includes a man whose marriage to another man has ended with the other man's death;
> (d) 'widow' includes a woman whose marriage to another woman has ended with the other woman's death;
>
> and related expressions are to be construed accordingly.

Until 4 April 2005 a male–female transsexual and a man could not claim a right to marry (see *Sheffield and Horsham v United Kingdom* (1998) 27 EHRR 163). The Gender Recognition Act 2004 now enables a person who has undergone a gender realignment to be recognised in the acquired gender (see, further, below).

4.2.1 Proof of marriage

A claimant spouse of the deceased will have to establish that they were the deceased's spouse and that the marriage was a valid marriage recognised under English law and was subsisting at the time of death.

There is usually no dispute about the identity of the person who was the wife or husband of the deceased immediately before death, and in most cases the production of a valid marriage certificate suffices. The parties remain married until the marriage has been dissolved by a final divorce order (formerly a decree absolute). The remarriage of the widow or widower of the deceased after the claim under the I(PFD)A 1975 is issued but before the claim is finally determined does not affect the validity of the claim. It is, however, a factor which the court is entitled to consider when determining whether reasonable financial provision was made by the deceased and, if not, what orders the court should make having regard to all relevant circumstances of the case and the criteria set out in s 3.

In the case where the marriage was not celebrated in the United Kingdom, the provisions of Family Procedure Rules 2010 (SI 2010/2955) (FPR 2010), PD 7A provide that the validity of a foreign marriage may be established by the production of a certified copy of the foreign marriage where the existence and validity of the marriage is not in dispute. Where the marriage certificate is in a foreign language, a translation of the document certified by a notary public or authenticated by a statement of truth will be required (FPR 2010, PD 7A, para 3.1).

Where there is any doubt about the validity of a foreign marriage, the claimant's evidence of the formalities of that marriage, the production of a certified copy of the marriage certificate, if available, and the evidence where appropriate of an expert in the local law to establish that the marriage certificate would be accepted in the country of origin of a valid marriage will be required.

Where a marriage certificate is not available, the claimant's evidence, corroborated by any witness who was present at the ceremony of the marriage, describing the formalities of the ceremony, and the evidence of an expert in the local or customary law to confirm that the formalities described would be accepted in the country of origin as evidence of a valid marriage, will be necessary. Where the foreign marriage certificate issued overseas has been lost and a certified copy cannot be obtained, for example due to civil war, the problem may be overcome by following the procedure in family proceedings for dissolution of marriage set out in FPR 2010, PD 7A, paras 3.3 and 3.5 and explaining, in a written statement made by the applicant or the lawyer representing the surviving spouse, circumstances of the loss/unavailability of the certificate, and the efforts, if any, that have been made to obtain a certified copy or other reason why a copy cannot be obtained.

Where the parties have gone through a ceremony of marriage in accordance with customary law, it is for the claimant to establish that the ceremony of marriage complied with customary law and would be recognised as a valid marriage in the country where the marriage occurred. It is possible to challenge the validity of a customary marriage on the ground that the ceremony did not comply with the customary law or on the basis that one of the parties to the marriage lacked capacity or the necessary intention to marry and that the actions of that party during the ceremony were equivocal (see *A-M v A-M (Divorce Jurisdiction: Validity of Marriage)* [2001] 2 FLR 6). In some cases, resolving the issue of whether or not a subsisting marriage exists can result in long-running litigation. An example is the Nigerian case of *Moses-Taiga v Taiga* [2005] EWCA Civ 1013, [2006] 1 FLR 1074; *MT v T* [2006] EWHC 2494 (Fam), [2007] 2 FLR 925; *M-T v T (Marriage: Strike Out)* [2013] EWHC 2061 (Fam), which took a decade to resolve. *MO v RO* [2013] EWHC 392 (Fam) is another Nigerian case where the court, having heard the evidence of an expert in Nigerian law and numerous family members, concluded on the balance of probabilities that the parties did not participate in customary or civil marriage, that the applicant had assumed the respondent's first wife's identity and had become well practised in deception. In some instances, the court may need to determine not only whether a customary marriage took place, but also whether it had been validly dissolved under customary law. In *GE v KE* [2013] EWHC 1938 (Fam), two women claimed to be the deceased's surviving spouse. The first wife, GE, claimed that she had married the deceased by customary marriage in Nigeria and that the marriage was subsisting when the deceased died. The second wife, KE, claimed that she and the deceased were married in a register office in England in 1957 and they continued to live together until his death. On the evidence adduced before the court, it was held that the first marriage had been dissolved under customary law and that at the date of the deceased's death, the only subsisting marriage was that with KE. In *N v D (Customary Marriage)* [2015] EWFC 28, N and D, both Nigerians, had lived together for 9 years. They had four children. N contended that they had been married under customary law and she sought a declaration under the Family Law Act 1986. Expert evidence confirmed that Nigerian law recognised presumption of marriage where there had been a long period of cohabitation. Having heard extensive factual and expert evidence, the court was satisfied that the parties were married under customary law (see, also, *GE v KE and AE (Nigerian Customary Marriage and Divorce*) [2013] EWHC 1938 (Fam)).

Where the validity of the marriage is challenged on the grounds that it was bigamous and not recognised under the law in England and Wales, it will be necessary to obtain expert evidence, and in transnational cases the impact of Family Law Act 1986, ss 45–46 will need to be considered. For examples, see *Padero-Mernagh v Mernagh* [2020] EWFC 27 and *Parveen v Hussain* [2022] EWCA Civ 1434 (for details, see para 4.2.2) and *MM v NA (Declaration as to Marital Status)* [2020] EWHC 93 (Fam). Where the validity of a foreign marriage has been proved in proceedings in a court in England and Wales, there will not be any need for further evidence to be adduced.

4.2.2 Polygamous and potentially polygamous marriages

Where the deceased and the claimant have entered into a polygamous marriage overseas in the country of the parties' domicile – under whose laws polygamy is permitted – the marriage is recognised in England and Wales, and the claimant may pursue a claim under the I(PFD)A 1975 as a spouse of the deceased. In *Re Sehota (Deceased), Kaur v Kaur* [1978] 1 WLR 1506, the claimant and the deceased were married in India in 1937. The marriage was potentially polygamous under Indian law. In 1948, the deceased married again. The deceased and his two wives subsequently acquired English domicile. In 1976, the husband died, leaving his entire estate to his second wife. The first wife applied for an order for financial provision as a wife of the deceased. She was adjudged to be the wife of the deceased notwithstanding that the marriage was polygamous. It was held that s 1(1)(a) should be construed in the light of the then Matrimonial Proceedings (Polygamous Marriages) Act 1972, s 1, under which matrimonial relief may be granted in cases where the marriage is polygamous. This Act was repealed but Matrimonial Causes Act 1973, s 47 confirms that the court is not precluded from granting matrimonial relief or making a declaration concerning the validity of a polygamous marriage.

Under Matrimonial Causes Act 1973, s 11(d) (before it was amended – see below), a marriage celebrated after 31 July 1971 was considered void if it was a polygamous marriage entered into outside England and Wales and either party was, at the time of the marriage, domiciled in England and Wales. Thus, in *Hussain v Hussain* [1982] 3 All ER 369, a man domiciled in England and Wales married a woman domiciled in Pakistan, where the law permits a man to take more than one wife, but does not extend the like right to women. It was held that since, under the law of domicile of both parties, neither could enter into a second marriage, the marriage was monogamous. Had the woman been domiciled in England and Wales and the man in Pakistan, the marriage would have been potentially polygamous as the man would have been permitted under the law of Pakistan to take a second wife.

Private International Law (Miscellaneous Provisions) Act 1995, s 5, has, however, amended Matrimonial Causes Act 1973, s 11(d), to provide that a marriage celebrated after 31 July 1971 shall be void in the case of a polygamous marriage entered into outside England and Wales in a country which permits polygamy, where either party was, at the time of the marriage, domiciled in England and Wales. The effect is to render void only a marriage entered into in a foreign country by a person domiciled in England and Wales which is actually polygamous, not one which is potentially polygamous.

If a party to a marriage is already legally married and is domiciled in England and Wales at the time they enter into a second marriage outside England and Wales, that marriage will be void.

A court in England and Wales is not precluded from granting matrimonial relief or making a declaration concerning the validity of a marriage by reason only that either party to the marriage is, or has, during the subsistence of the marriage been married to more than one person (Matrimonial Causes Act 1973, s 47).

The status of a polygamous marriage has been recognised for the purposes of administering a deceased's estate and for the purposes of determining succession right on intestacy (see *Coleman v Shang (alias Qartney)* [1961] AC 481, [1961] 2 All ER 406). For a case where the deceased was married to several wives, in accordance with the law of his domicile which permitted polygamy, died intestate and was domiciled outside England and Wales with real and personal property in England and Wales, see *Official Solicitor to the Senior Courts v Yemoh* [2010] EWHC 3727 (Ch), [2011] 1 WLR 1450. In deciding how the intestacy rules should apply, Mr Elleray QC sitting as a deputy High Court Judge held that:

(a) 'a spouse lawfully married in accordance with the law of his domicile to someone dying intestate, is entitled to be recognised in this country in relation to property, including real property, of the intestate being administered here, as a surviving spouse for the purpose of section 46 of the 1925 Act' (at [20]);
(b) 'the surviving polygamous spouses of the intestate in this case together constitute the "spouse" for the purposes of section 46 ... and that there is a single statutory legacy rather than seven or eight, depending on the number of polygamous widows, statutory legacies. This case happens to be informative on its facts, because if there were, as it were, any number of statutory legacies, the estate would be wholly exhausted by statutory legacies, which would seem to defeat the construct of section 46 and its provisions, as they divide matters, according to Parliament, on an intestacy between the surviving spouse and issue' (at [21]);
(c) on the issue of 'whether the spouses should share the statutory legacy as beneficial joint tenants in common ... it does follow ... that there is a single statutory legacy flowing from the death of the intestate and charged on his residue, that that fell to be paid with statutory interest between those who were widows, recognised in accordance with the law of Ghana, in equal shares' (at [23]);
(d) '... Since the widows are treated as a surviving spouse, on the death of one of them the remaining spouses hold the life interest until the death of the last of them to die, when that half of residue will fall in for the benefit of children' (at [24]);
(e) on the issue of 'whether benefits received, whether by widows or children under the deceased's Ghanaian intestacy, have to be brought into account' the deputy High Court Judge applied the reasoning of the then Vice Chancellor Sir Nicolas Browne-Wilkinson in *Re Collens (Deceased)* [1986] Ch 505 at 512D:

> ... in my judgment section 46 can only impose a charge for the statutory legacy on the proceeds of the English immovables. There is no way in which it can be made to impose a charge on assets not devolving under English law since such charge is part of the English law of succession. Mr. Simmonds has accepted that there is no implied statutory hotchpot. In the absence of such statutory hotchpot I can see no way in which the charge on the English immovable estate can be said to have been satisfied out of the overseas assets of the deceased.

(f) on the issue of whether all of the deceased's children living at the date of the deceased's death are entitled on his intestacy regardless of their legitimacy, the deputy High Court Judge concluded that since the deceased died after the passing of the Family Law Reform Act 1969, under ss 14 and 15, illegitimate children of a deceased are expressly entitled to share in the estate of an intestate parent. Where the illegitimate child dies, his issue shall be entitled to take any interest therein to which he or such issue would have been entitled if he had been born legitimate (at [26]).

Where a divorce has been obtained overseas it may be necessary to ensure that the divorce was validly granted and that its validity would be recognised by the courts in England and Wales. Family Law Act 1986, ss 45 and 46 set out the grounds for recognition of an overseas divorce annulment or legal separation. In *Hussain v Parveen* [2021] EWFC 73 at first instance, it was held that where the divorce process (in this case the pronouncement of the talaq) takes place in England but the proceedings are concluded in a foreign country (Pakistan in this case where the wife was then living) with the registration of the divorce in accordance with its laws, the proceedings were transnational and therefore could not be recognised in England under the provisions of the Family Law Act 1986. Consequently, the wife remained married to her first husband when she remarried and therefore that marriage was void. On appeal (*Parveen v Hussain* [2022] EWCA Civ 1434), the Court of Appeal agreed that, because the proceedings in relation to wife's divorce from her first husband had partly taken place in England and partly in Pakistan, it was a transnational divorce and not entitled to recognition under the Family Law Act 1986. This, however, is not determinative of the issue whether she had capacity to marry her second husband on 19 December 2008. The Family Law Act 1986 does not expressly state what the effect of non-recognition is on capacity to marry. Having analysed extensively the Law Commission Reports and other authorities and the provisions of Matrimonial Causes Act 1973, ss 11 and 14, which the court considered to be more relevant than the provisions of the Family Law Act 1986, the court ruled that the rules governing marriage should be given priority over rules relating to the recognition of divorce. Of relevance was also what justice requires. The court held at [89]–[90]:

> The public policy objectives would be sufficiently achieved by denying recognition of the divorce to the wife's previous husband because of his connections with the UK.
>
> In conclusion, therefore, the wife's marriage to the husband is valid as she had the capacity to marry because her previous divorce was effective under the law of Pakistan. The fact that that divorce is not entitled to recognition under the FLA 1986 does not mean that she did not have the capacity to marry.

4.2.3 Void marriages

A void marriage is one that is regarded, in any case in which the existence of the marriage is in issue, as never having taken place. It may be put in issue at any time, even after one or both parties to it has died.

Matrimonial Causes Act 1973, s 11 provides that a marriage is void on the following grounds only:

> (a) that it is not a valid marriage [in that]—
>
> > (i) the parties are within the prohibited degrees of relationship;
> > (ii) either party is under the age of eighteen (formerly before 27 February 2023 sixteen) [see further under para 4.2.3]; or
> > (iii) the parties have intermarried in disregard of certain requirements as to the formation of marriage;
>
> (b) that at the time of the marriage either party was already lawfully married;
> (c) that the parties are not respectively male and female;
> (d) in the case of a polygamous marriage entered into outside England and Wales, that either party was at the time of the marriage domiciled in England and Wales.

For the purposes of para (d), a marriage is not polygamous if, at its inception, neither party had any spouse additional to the other.

4.2.4 Rights of spouse to void marriage under the I(PFD)A 1975

The rights of a party to a void marriage, if that marriage is subsisting at the time of the deceased's death, are preserved by the provision of I(PFD)A 1975, s 25(4) provided certain conditions are satisfied. Section 25(4) provides:

> (4) For the purposes of this Act any reference to a wife or husband shall be treated as including a reference to a person who in good faith entered into a void marriage with the deceased unless either—
>
> > (a) the marriage of the deceased and that person was dissolved or annulled during the lifetime of the deceased and the dissolution or annulment is recognised by the law of England and Wales; or
> > (b) that person has during the lifetime of the deceased formed a subsequent marriage or civil partnership

4.2.5 Marriage entered into in good faith

As will be observed, the provisions of I(PFD)A 1975, s 25(4) apply only if the claimant entered into a void marriage with the deceased in good faith and that marriage has not been dissolved or annulled during the lifetime of the deceased or the claimant has not during the lifetime of the deceased entered into another later marriage. Thus the claimant must have believed that the ceremony entered into was one of marriage and did not know or have reason to believe that the marriage was not a valid one. If the claimant was aware or had reason to suspect that the marriage for whatever reason was not valid, the claimant will fail to establish that it was entered into in good faith. The issue of whether the marriage between the deceased and the claimant is void but was entered into in good faith will be determined on the facts. An example of a case which illustrates the effect of the provisions of s 25(4) is *Ghandi v Patel* [2002] 1 FLR 603. In that case the claimant had undergone, at an Indian restaurant in London, a Hindu ceremony of marriage with the deceased who was separated from his first wife, but whose marriage to his first wife was still subsisting at the date of his marriage to the claimant. The marriage between the claimant and the deceased was conducted to comply with the rituals and requirements of the Hindu faith, but no effort was made to comply with the English legal requirements to constitute a lawful marriage. Thereafter, the claimant and the deceased had a stormy and troubled relationship and, following the birth of their second child, they lived separate lives. The claimant had, during the lifetime of the deceased, issued proceedings against the deceased seeking the transfer to her of one of the deceased's properties. In those proceedings, she maintained that she was not married to the deceased. On his death, she applied for financial provision under the Act on the basis that, while she accepted that her marriage to the deceased was void by reason of the bigamy, she had nevertheless entered into the marriage with the deceased in good faith and was therefore entitled to claim as his spouse. On the facts, the court held that the claimant had not established 'good faith' within the meaning of s 25(4) because marriage requires the participation of two people – a man and a woman – and the ceremony must purport to be a marriage of the kind contemplated by the Marriage Acts and must comply with the requirements of English law or purport to do so. On the evidence adduced, it was held that the Hindu ceremony did not comply with the requirements of English law and did not purport to do so. The Hindu marriage did not give rise to a void marriage. It was a 'non-marriage'. It was further held that even if the ceremony had created a void marriage, by reason of its bigamous nature, known to the claimant, she had not entered into the marriage in good faith. Her claim therefore failed.

4.2.6 Distinction between void marriage and non-marriage

A distinction needs to be made between a void marriage and a non-marriage. A void marriage is one which falls within the provisions of Matrimonial Causes Act 1973, s 11. A non-marriage is one which is conducted in England or Wales, but the ceremony of marriage is not of a kind contemplated by the Marriage Acts. The cases of *Ghandi v Patel* (at para 4.2.5) and *El Gamal v Al Maktoum* [2011] EWHC B27 (Fam) are good illustrations of a non-marriage. In *El Gamal v Al Maktoum*, the parties believed they had taken part in an Islamic ceremony of marriage in a flat in Knightsbridge. The wife petitioned for nullity on the grounds that since the marriage had not complied with the formalities of English law it was void. The husband denied that any marriage ceremony had taken place and that it was so far removed from marriage in English law as to be considered even a void marriage. On the facts, it was held that an Islamic ceremony of marriage had taken place, but since there was no written contract as would generally be required in Islamic courts, a valid marriage had not taken place and therefore it was a non-marriage (see, also, *Dukali v Lamrani* [2012] EWHC 1748 (Fam), [2012] 2 FLR 1099). In contrast, in *MA v JA and the Attorney General* [2012] EWHC 2219 (Fam), [2013] 2 FLR 68, a religious ceremony conducted by an authorised person and celebrated in an authorised venue, and where both parties believed that they had taken part in a valid marriage recognised under English law, was held to be valid.

4.2.7 Effect of annulment of void marriage to claim under the I(PFD)A 1975

Where a void marriage has been annulled, a party to it who has not remarried may claim as a former spouse. If the decree of nullity was granted within 12 months of the death of the deceased, under the provisions of I(PFD)A 1975, s 14, the claimant may be able to claim for financial provision as a surviving spouse (see para 4.4.2).

4.2.8 Voidable marriage

Matrimonial Causes Act 1973, s 12 provides that a marriage is voidable on the following grounds:

(a) that the marriage has not been consummated owing to the incapacity of either party to consummate it;
(b) that the marriage has not been consummated owing to the wilful refusal of the respondent to consummate it;
(c) that either party to the marriage did not validly consent to it, whether in consequence of duress, mistake, unsoundness of mind or otherwise;
(d) that at the time of the marriage either party, though capable of giving a valid consent, was suffering (whether continuously or intermittently) from mental disorder within the meaning of the Mental Health Act 1983 of such a kind or to such an extent as to be unfitted for marriage;
(e) that at the time of the marriage the respondent was suffering from venereal disease in a communicable form;
(f) that at the time of the marriage the respondent was pregnant by some person other than the petitioner.

4.2.9 Marriage with a transsexual – Gender Recognition Act 2004

Before 4 April 2005, where a person's biological and sexual characteristics at birth were congruent, those characteristics determined the person's sex for the purposes of marriage. It was for the court to determine, by assessing the facts of the individual case, whether a person was male or female. In his dissenting judgment in *Bellinger v Bellinger* [2001] EWCA Civ 1140, [2002] 2 WLR 394, Thorpe LJ considered that other factors, including psychological considerations, should be considered by the court; that the family justice system should be sufficiently flexible to accommodate social change; and that one of the objectives of statute law reform and of the family justice system in this field must be to ensure that the law reacts to and reflects social change in the construction of existing statutory provisions. On appeal ([2003] UKHL 21, [2003] 2 WLR 1174), the House of Lords (now the Supreme Court) confirmed that, in determining whether a person was male or female for the purposes of Matrimonial Causes Act 1973, s 11(c), the test set out in *Corbett v Corbett (Otherwise Ashley)* [1971] P 83, still applied; and that any change in the law was a matter for Parliament, particularly as the government had already announced its intention to introduce primary legislation on the subject. The House of Lords also held, however, that the non-recognition of gender change for the purpose of marriage was incompatible with Arts 8 and 12 of the Human Rights Convention, and made a declaration to that effect in respect of Matrimonial Causes Act 1973, s 11(c). See, also, *Goodwin v United Kingdom* [2002] ECHR 588, (2002) 35 EHRR 18 and *I v United Kingdom* [2002] ECHR 592, [2002] 2 FLR 518, where the European Court of Human Rights held that to deny legal recognition to transsexuals was no longer sustainable and was a violation of their rights under Arts 8 and 12. As a result, the Gender Recognition Bill was introduced into Parliament in November 2003 and led to the Gender Recognition Act 2004 receiving Royal Assent on 1 July 2004 and coming into force on 4 April 2005. The Act made provision for the establishment of a gender recognition panel with authority to issue gender recognition certificates to transsexuals who no longer wish to be associated with their birth gender. For a person to qualify for a gender recognition certificate, they must provide a declaration stating that they have lived in the new gender for a period of at least 2 years; to confirm whether they are married; and any other information required by the panel or the Secretary of State. The application must be supported by medical evidence from a general practitioner practising in gender dysphoria, and one other medical practitioner or a chartered psychologist practising in gender dysphoria.

4.2.10 Separation of married couples by judicial separation order (formerly decree of judicial separation)

The marriage of a claimant, who was separated from the deceased at the time of death, by a judicial separation order (formerly a decree of judicial separation) and remained separated at the date of the deceased's death, is considered to be subsisting and the survivor is regarded as the spouse of the deceased (see

Re Sehota, Surjit Kaur v Gian Kaur [1978] 1 WLR 1506). If the order/decree was made within 12 months of the deceased's death, the provisions of I(PFD)A 1975, s 14 apply, subject to the conditions set out in that section (see paras 4.4.2 and 4.5.2). Where the order/decree was made over 12 months before the deceased's death, the claimant will not be entitled to receive the same financial provisions which a widow/widower of the deceased would be entitled to receive. Where the separation was by agreement but a judicial separation order/decree of judicial separation has not been obtained, the claimant will be entitled to make a claim as a spouse of the deceased.

4.3 CIVIL PARTNER OF THE DECEASED

The CPA 2004 as amended enables same sex couples and opposite sex couples to register a civil partnership. Once the partnership is registered, it gives the couple the same legal rights as those enjoyed by couples who enter into a marriage. A civil partnership may be terminated on the ground of nullity or the partnership may be dissolved by one partner issuing a petition for dissolution of the partnership or a legal separation or, where appropriate, applying for a presumption of death order. The same rules apply to the dissolution of a civil partnership as they do to the dissolution of a marriage. Civil partnership was initially not available to opposite sex couples. Following the Supreme Court's decision in *R (Steinfeld and Keidan) v Secretary of State for International Development (in substitution for the Home Secretary and the Education Secretary)* [2018] UKSC 32, the Civil Partnerships, Marriage and Death Registration etc) Act 2019 and the Civil Partnership (Opposite-sex Couples) Regulations 2019 (SI 2019/1458) extended civil partnership to opposite sex couples with effect from 2 December 2019.

4.3.1 Proof of civil partnership

The production of a civil partnership registration certificate will suffice to establish proof of the civil partnership.

A civil partnership formed at the British Consulate outside England and Wales, Scotland and Northern Ireland, or in the case of the armed forces personnel at their barracks, will be recognised as valid, provided the conditions set out in CPA 2004, s 210 in the case of the former and s 211 in the case of the latter are met. Where the civil partnership has been registered in a foreign country under the laws of that country, it will be recognised as valid (s 215) on the production of a certified copy of the registration document. In any other case the principles which apply in relation to proving a foreign marriage also apply to the recognition of a civil partnership registered overseas.

4.3.2 Void civil partnership

A nullity of the partnership may be obtained if the parties to the civil partnership were not eligible to register as civil partners or there was some irregularity in the registration of the partnership and both parties were aware of it at the time of registration.

A civil partnership will be considered void if the couple or either of them was not eligible to register as civil partners. CPA 2004, s 3(1), as amended, provides that two people are not eligible to register as civil partners of each other (see below) if:

- (b) either of them is already a civil partner or lawfully married,
- (c) either of them is under 18 [formerly 16], or
- (d) they are within prohibited degrees of relationship.

Section 3(1) has now been further amended by the Marriage and Civil Partnership (Minimum Age) Act 2022, which came into force on 27 February 2023 pursuant to the Marriage and Civil Partnership (Minimum Age) Act 2022 (Commencement and Transitional Provisions) Regulations 2023 (SI 2023/88), to substitute in s 3(1)(c) the minimum age for entering into a civil partnership from 16 to 18 years. Since the 2022 Act has, as from 27 February 2023, increased the eligibility from 16 to 18 years, s 4 which deals with parental consent or court's authorisation for under 18-year-olds will also be omitted. Similarly, CPA 2004, s 54, which deals with the validity of civil partnerships registered outside England and Wales, will be amended to insert an additional sub-section (aa) to provide that where the partnership is registered in Scotland the partnership will be void if the civil partnership was registered when: (1) one of the two people was domiciled in England and Wales; and (2) one of the two people was under 18. Additionally, s 54(2) and s 54(2A) will also be amended in relation to civil partnerships registered in Northern Ireland. These changes will not affect civil partnerships or marriages entered into before 27 February 2023.

For those who are within the 'prohibited degree of relationship', see CPA 2004, Sch 12.

A civil partnership will also be void if at the time the parties entered into the civil partnership they both knew: (1) that the notice of proposed civil partnership has not been given; (2) that the civil partnership document has not been duly issued; (3) that the civil partnership document is void under CPA 2004, s 17(3) or s 27(2) (registration after the end of time allowed for registering); (4) that the place of registration is a place other than that specified in the notices of proposed civil partnership and the civil partnership document; and (5) that the civil partnership registrar is not present. It will also be void if the civil partnership document is void under Sch 2, para 6(5).

4.3.3 Voidable civil partnership

A civil partnership will be considered voidable if:

(1) either of the parties did not validly consent to its formation (whether as a result of duress, mistake, unsoundness of mind or otherwise);
(2) at the time of its formation either of them, though capable of giving a valid consent, was suffering (whether continuously or intermittently) from a mental disorder of such a kind or to such an extent as to be unfit for civil partnership;
(3) at the time of its formation, the respondent was pregnant by some person other than the applicant;
(4) an interim gender recognition under the Gender Recognition Act 2004 has after the time of its formation been issued to either civil partner;
(5) the respondent is a person whose gender at the time of its formation had become the acquired gender under the Gender Recognition Act 2004.

A nullity order will not, however, be granted where the applicant to such an order conducted themselves in relation to the respondent to the application in such a way as to lead the respondent reasonably to believe that they would not seek to do so and that it would be unjust to the respondent to make the order (CPA 2004, s 51).

4.3.4 Civil partnership entered into in good faith

I(PFD)A 1975, s 25(4A) preserves the position of a person who entered into a void civil partnership in good faith. Section 25(4A) provides:

> For the purposes of this Act any reference to a civil partner shall be treated as including a reference to a person who in good faith entered into a void civil partnership with the deceased unless either—
>
> (a) the civil partnership between the deceased and that person was dissolved or annulled during the lifetime of the deceased and the dissolution or annulment is recognised by the law of England and Wales; or
> (b) that person has during the lifetime of the deceased formed a subsequent civil partnership or marriage.

See, further, para 4.2.5.

4.3.5 Effect of dissolution or annulment of civil partnership

On the dissolution or annulment of the civil partnership, civil partners are entitled to apply for financial ancillary relief. The financial provisions to which they are entitled mirror those which are available to couples on the dissolution or nullity of their marriage. Civil partners have the same rights to make a claim under the I(PFD)A 1975 on the death of one of the civil partners as couples who are married. The Act has been amended by the CPA 2004 to give same sex and opposite sex civil partners the same status and rights as a spouse.

4.3.6 Effect of marriage overseas between same sex couples

Before the Marriage (Same Sex Couples) Act 2013 came into force on 29 March 2014, the effect of a marriage entered into by two people of the same sex, who were both domiciled in England and Wales, in a foreign country where such a marriage was recognised as valid, was treated as a civil partnership under CPA 2004, ss 212–218 (see *Wilkinson v Kitzinger and Another (No 2)* [2006] EWHC 2022 (Fam), [2007] 1 FLR 295). Marriage between same sex couples is now recognised in England and Wales, and same sex married couples have the same rights as opposite sex couples. If the marriage ceremony took place in England and Wales, it must be a civil ceremony in a register office or approved premises or, provided the religious organisation concerned is in agreement, on religious premises and the marriage is solemnised through a religious ceremony. Same sex marriage celebrated overseas must be proved in the same way as marriage between opposite sex couples (see para 4.2.1).

4.3.7 Separation order in the case of civil partnership

A separation order may be obtained by a civil partner on similar grounds as those under the Matrimonial Causes Act 1973 (CPA 2004, s 179) with like effect as a judicial separation order obtained by a married couple. If the separation order was made within 12 months of the deceased's death, the provisions of I(PFD)A 1975, s 14A apply, subject to the conditions set out in that section (see para 4.5.1). Where the separation order was made over 12 months before the deceased's death, the claimant will not be entitled to receive the same financial provisions which a widow/widower of the deceased would be entitled to receive. Where the separation was by agreement, but a separation order has not been obtained, the claimant will be entitled to make a claim as a spouse of the deceased.

4.3.8 Effect on claim made by surviving spouse/civil partner by the subsequent marriage/civil partnership before the claim is determined

To qualify as a spouse, or a former spouse, or surviving civil partner or former partner of the deceased, the claimant must not have remarried or entered into a subsequent civil partnership at the date when proceedings are issued. It matters not whether any such remarriage or subsequent civil partnership is void or voidable. I(PFD)A 1975, s 25(5) provides that:

> Any reference in this Act to the formation of, or a person who has formed, a subsequent marriage or civil partnership includes (as the case may be) a reference to the formation of, or to a person who has formed, a marriage or civil partnership which is by law void or voidable.

If, therefore, the surviving spouse/civil partner of the deceased remarries or enters into a subsequent civil partnership whilst an application under the I(PFD)A 1975 for financial provision is pending, that will not affect their status as the surviving spouse/civil partner as long as the application was issued before the remarriage or subsequent civil partnership. It is, however, likely to affect the decision of the court when it considers the factors which the court has to consider under s 3 (see Chapter 7) in determining whether the deceased made reasonable financial provisions for the applicant and, if not, the extent of the provision which the court should provide in the circumstances.

4.4 FORMER SPOUSE OF THE DECEASED WHO HAS NOT REMARRIED

A 'former spouse' means a person whose marriage with the deceased was, during the lifetime of the deceased:

(1) dissolved or annulled by a final divorce order/decree of divorce or of nullity of marriage order/decree of nullity of marriage, made/granted under the law of any part of the British Islands; or
(2) dissolved or annulled in any country or territory outside the British Islands by a divorce or annulment which is entitled to be recognised as valid by the law of England and Wales (I(PFD)A 1975, s 25, as amended); and
(3) that person has not remarried before the death of the deceased.

Where a conditional order/decree nisi has been granted, but the deceased dies before the order/decree has been made final/absolute, the marriage is regarded as subsisting and the claimant is eligible to make a claim as the spouse of the deceased. The court is, however, entitled to have regard to any financial settlement reached between the parties or ordered by the court when considering what, if any, financial provision should be ordered (see, further, paras 4.4.2 and 4.5.2 and Chapter 7).

Family Law Act 1986, s 44(1) provides that:

> subject to section 52(4) and (5)(a) of this Act, no divorce or annulment obtained in any part of the British Islands shall be regarded as effective in any part of the United Kingdom unless granted by a court of civil jurisdiction.

4.4.1 Overseas divorce and talaq

The validity of an overseas divorce, annulment or legal separation obtained by means of proceedings must be recognised if the divorce, annulment or legal separation is effective under the law of the country in which it is obtained, and at the relevant date either party to the marriage (Family Law Act 1986, s 46(1)):

(a) was habitually resident in the country in which the divorce, annulment or legal separation was obtained; or
(b) was domiciled in that country; or
(c) was a national of that country.

The validity of an overseas divorce, annulment or legal separation obtained otherwise than by means of proceedings must be recognised if the divorce, annulment or legal separation is effective under the law of the country in which it was obtained, and at the relevant date (Family Law Act 1986, s 46(2)):

(a) each party to the marriage was domiciled in that country; or
(b) either party to the marriage was domiciled in that country and the other party was domiciled in a country under whose law the divorce, annulment or legal separation is recognised as valid; and
(c) neither party to the marriage was habitually resident in the United Kingdom throughout the period of one year immediately preceding that date.

Most Islamic countries now require registration of talaq. Sanctions are imposed if the registration requirements are not complied with. The following are some examples of cases where the validity of a talaq has been considered by the English courts.

In *Al Sulaiman v Al Juffali* [2001] EWHC 556 (Fam), [2002] 1 FLR 479, both parties were Saudi nationals of, and domiciled in, Saudi Arabia. They were married in Saudi Arabia. In 2001, the husband pronounced a bare talaq in England

and then registered it with a Sharia court in Saudi Arabia, thus dissolving the marriage under Sharia law as applied in Saudi Arabia. The wife issued divorce proceedings in England. The husband contested the proceedings on a number of grounds, including the fact that the marriage had already been dissolved. It was held, applying the provisions of Family Law Act 1986, s 44(1), that, irrespective of the parties' domicile and religion, informal divorces obtained in England and Wales otherwise than by proceedings in a court of civil jurisdiction will not be recognised. A bare talaq pronounced in England does not, therefore, operate to dissolve the marriage because it is not obtained in any proceedings in a court of civil jurisdiction.

In *El Fadl v El Fadl* [2000] 1 FLR 175, however, it was held that the pronouncement of the talaq before witnesses, which was registered by a Lebanese Sharia court that was properly convened and took formal declarations, was a divorce obtained by means of proceedings, although the Sharia court did not have judicial jurisdiction to make it. See, also, *Wicken v Wicken* [1999] 1 FLR 293, where a letter of divorce was recognised.

In *H v S (Recognition of Overseas Divorce)* [2011] EWHC B23 (Fam), the court was provided with a substantial review of the law and authorities to determine whether the pronouncement of talaq by the husband in Saudi Arabia and the lodging of a deed of confirmation before the Sharia court should be recognised as a valid divorce. Having considered the evidence and the English and Islamic concept of marriage and law of several Islamic countries, the judge was satisfied that the husband had engaged in proceedings under Saudi law and was entitled to recognition.

For other cases where talaq has been considered, see *Quazi v Quazi* [1980] AC 744 (HL), *R v Secretary of State for the Home Department ex parte Ghulam Fatima* [1986] AC 527 and *Chaudhary v Chaudhary* [1985] Fam 19.

Family Law Act 1986, Part II does not apply where Arts 14–20 of Council Regulation (EC) No 1347/2000 of 29 May 2000 on jurisdiction and the recognition and enforcement of judgments in matrimonial matters and in matters of parental responsibility for children of both spouses [2000] OJ L160/19 (Council Regulation 1347/2000) apply. These Articles require that a judgment given in a Member State relating to divorce, annulment of marriage or legal separation is to be recognised in any other Member State without any special procedure being required; and that recognition may not be refused because the law of the Member State in which recognition is sought would not have allowed the dissolution or annulment of the marriage or a legal separation on the same facts (Art 18). (Note, however, that post-Brexit the provisions under Council

Regulation 1347/2000 no longer apply with effect from midnight on 31 December 2020. It is possible that agreement may be reached on this issue of cross border recognition at some time in the future.)

In relation to the interpretation of the Family Law Act 1986 on transnational proceedings where the talaq proceedings are commenced in country A and the rest of the proceedings are completed in country B, see *Parveen v Hussain* [2022] EWCA Civ 1434 and para 4.2.2 where the issue is dealt with.

Article 15(1) of Council Regulation 1347/2000 provides:

> A judgment relating to a divorce, legal separation or marriage annulment shall not be recognised:
>
> (a) if such a recognition is manifestly contrary to the public policy of the Member State in which recognition is sought;
> (b) where it was given in default of appearance, if the respondent was not served with the document which instituted the proceedings or with an equivalent document in sufficient time and in such a way as to enable the respondent to arrange for his or her defence unless it is determined that the respondent has accepted the judgment unequivocally;
> (c) if it is irreconcilable with a judgment given in proceedings between the same parties in the Member State in which recognition is sought;
> (d) if it is irreconcilable with an earlier judgment given in another Member State or in a non-Member State between the same parties, provided that the earlier judgment fulfils the conditions necessary for its recognition in the Member State in which recognition is sought.

Applying these provisions in *Ivleva v Yates* [2014] EWHC 554 (Fam), a Ukrainian decree was refused recognition because sufficient steps had not been taken to give the husband notice of the proceedings.

Article 16 of Council Regulation 1347/2000 provides that a court of a Member State may, on the basis of an agreement on the recognition and enforcement of judgments, not recognise a judgment given in another Member State. Under Art 19, 'under no circumstances may a judgment be reviewed as to its substance'. (Note, however, that post-Brexit the provisions under Council Regulation 1347/2000 no longer apply with effect from midnight on 31 December 2020. It is possible that agreement may be reached on this issue of cross border recognition at some time in the future.)

Prior to the enactment of the MFPA 1984, a person whose marriage was dissolved in a foreign country was not eligible to apply for financial provision under the I(PFD)A 1975 as a former spouse of the deceased. MFPA 1984, s 25 now enables a person whose marriage was dissolved outside England and Wales to apply for an order under I(PFD)A 1975, s 2.

4.4.2 Application of I(PFD)A 1975, section 14

In cases where, within 12 months from the date on which a divorce order/decree of divorce or nullity of marriage order has been made final, or a judicial separation order has been granted, a party to the marriage dies and an application for financial relief or property adjustment order under Matrimonial Causes Act 1973, ss 23 and 24 has not been made by the other party to the marriage, or such an application has been made but is pending at the time of the death of the deceased, and the former spouse applies for an order under I(PFD)A 1975, s 2, the court has power, if it thinks it just to do so, to treat the former surviving spouse as if the divorce order/decree of divorce, or nullity of marriage order had not been made final or the judicial separation order had not been made. However, in the case where a judicial separation order has been granted, the provisions of s 14 will only apply if at the date of death of the deceased the order/decree was in force and the separation was continuing (s 14(2)).

4.4.3 Restrictions imposed in matrimonial proceedings under I(PFD)A 1975, sections 15 and 15A

Before making a claim on behalf of a former spouse of the deceased, the order for financial remedy should be checked to ascertain whether or not an order under I(PFD)A 1975, s 15 or s 15A was included in the order. Pursuant to s 15, on the making of a divorce order/decree of divorce, nullity of marriage/decree of nullity of marriage or a judicial separation order/decree of judicial separation, or at any time thereafter, the court if it considers it just to do so, may on the application of either party to the marriage order that the other party to the marriage shall not on the death of either party apply for an order under I(PFD)A 1975, s 2 (s 15(1), as amended).

In the case of a divorce or nullity of marriage order/decree of divorce or nullity of marriage, an order under I(PFD)A 1975, s 15(1) may be made before or after the decree is made final/absolute, but if it is made before the order/decree is made final/absolute, it will not take effect unless the order/decree is made final/absolute (s 15(2) as amended). Where the order does take effect then on the death of the other party to the marriage, the court cannot entertain an application for an order under I(PFD)A 1975, s 2 by the surviving former spouse (s 15(3)).

Where an order under I(PFD)A 1975, s 15 is made on the making/granting of a judicial separation order/decree of judicial separation, if the other party to that marriage dies while the order/decree is in force and the separation is continuing, the court cannot entertain any application for an order under I(PFD)A 1975, s 2 (s 15(4)).

Similar provisions have been inserted into the I(PFD)A 1975 under s 15A by the MFPA 1984 in respect of marriages which have been dissolved or annulled overseas or where the parties have been legally/judicially separated and the other party dies while the legal separation is continuing.

In either case, if an order under I(PFD)A 1975, s 15 or s 15A is made and one of the parties dies before the order/decree is made final/absolute, the financial remedy is of no effect (*McMinn v McMinn* [2002] EWHC 1194 (Fam), [2003] 2 FLR 823) (see, further, paras 7.11–7.11.1).

4.5 FORMER CIVIL PARTNER OF THE DECEASED

A 'former civil partner' means a person whose civil partnership with the deceased was during the lifetime of the deceased either (I(PFD)A 1975, s 25(1)):

- (a) dissolved or annulled by an order made under the law of any part of the British Islands, or
- (b) dissolved or annulled in any country or territory outside the British Islands by a dissolution or annulment which is entitled to be recognised as valid by the law of England and Wales.

See, further, para 6.3.

4.5.1 Application of I(PFD)A 1975, section 14A

Similar provision as applies to married couples is included in the I(PFD)A 1975 to provide equality to civil partners. Section 14A provides that where in relation to a civil partnership one of the civil partners dies within 12 months from the date on which a dissolution order, nullity order, separation order or presumption of death order has been made, and an application for financial relief or a property adjustment order under CPA 2004, Sch 5, Part 1 or Part 2 has not been made by the other civil partner or such an application has been made, but the proceedings on the application have not been determined at the time of the death of the deceased, then if an application is made by the surviving partner for an order under I(PFD)A 1975, s 2, the court has the power, if it thinks it just to do so, to treat the surviving civil partner as if the civil partnership was subsisting, save that in the case of a separation order this principle would apply only if the separation order was still in force at the date of the death of the deceased and the separation was continuing.

4.5.2 Restrictions imposed in proceedings for the dissolution, etc of a civil partnership on an application under I(PFD)A 1975, section 15ZA

The court has similar powers as those which apply to married couples under I(PFD)A 1975, ss 15 and 15A (see para 4.4.3) to restrict an application to be brought for a claim under the Act by a former civil partner when making a dissolution order, nullity order, separation order or presumption of death order under CPA 2004, Part 2, Chapter 2 or at any time thereafter (I(PFD)A 1975, s 15ZA(1)–(5)).

The court's powers to impose restrictions in relation to financial orders made in proceedings following an overseas dissolution, etc of partnership are set out in I(PFD)A 1975, s 15B(1)–(4) (see, further, paras 7.11–7.11.1).

4.6 COHABITANT OF THE DECEASED

I(PFD)A 1975, s 1(1)(ba) and (1A), introduced by the Law Reform (Succession) Act 1995, extended the categories of person who may apply for financial provision to include a cohabitant of the deceased. A cohabitant is, however, eligible to apply as a cohabitant only if the deceased died on or after 1 January 1996, and, during the whole of the period of 2 years ending immediately before the date when the deceased died, the person was living:

(1) in the same household as the deceased; and
(2) as the husband or wife of the deceased.

This provision was introduced in response to cases such as *Bishop v Plumley* [1991] 1 WLR 582 (CA), where the claimant had to prove 'dependency' in order to succeed. Although, pursuant to the Marriage (Same Sex Couples) Act 2013, the reference to husband and wife is equally applicable to those in a same sex relationship, under this provision the effect is academic because same sex couples living together would inevitably fall under the provision relating to civil partners under s 1(1B) (see para 4.6.4). The revised provisions are, however, subject to certain limitations. There are three conditions which must be satisfied to establish eligibility, namely:

(1) Cohabitation must have continued for the 'whole of the two years immediately before the death of the deceased'. There are thus two separate issues to consider, namely what is meant by:

   (a) the whole of the period of 2 years; and
   (b) immediately before the death of the deceased.

(2) The claimant must prove that the claimant was living in the same household as the deceased (see *Re Watson* [1999] 1 FLR 878 at para 4.6.1). This means living together as one unit, and does not include living in the same property but as two separate independent entities.
(3) The claimant must prove that the claimant was living 'as the husband or wife or as the civil partner of the deceased'.

4.6.1 Whole of the 2 years immediately before the date when the deceased died

The words 'whole of the two years' implies that there must have been continuous cohabitation without a break for the full 2 years and if this cannot be proved the claim will fail. It could, however, be argued that where the evidence establishes that, although the parties may have been physically apart, and their separation was not voluntary, the relationship was continuing and the household was being maintained as a single unit for both the deceased and the claimant, the claim should be allowed. To rule otherwise would mean a total disregard of social and economic changes which compel couples to be apart for short periods, for example, where one partner has to work away from home or is posted overseas for a short time, or one partner has to care for a sick relative or has, by agreement, taken a holiday without the other, or the separation is the result of one party's illness (see, further, below).

Likewise, the second ingredient, 'ending immediately before the date when the deceased died', should not, it is suggested, be applied too strictly. If the test relating to claimants under I(PFD)A 1975, s 1(1)(e) is applied (see para 4.9), where the language of the statute is 'immediately before the death of the deceased', then, if cohabitation has ceased, no matter for how short a period, s 1(1A) may not apply. It is submitted that a common-sense approach should be taken and the provision interpreted to allow for circumstances beyond the parties' control which cause cohabitation to cease or to be interrupted immediately before the death of the deceased. The test applied under the Matrimonial Causes Act 1973 (before its amendments by the Divorce Dissolution and Separation Act

2020) to cases of separation for 2 or 5 years, where the relationship was not regarded as at an end if separation had been brought about by illness, should be applied.

In *Jelley v Iliffe* [1981] Fam 128, Griffiths LJ held that:

> The words 'immediately before the death of the deceased' in section 1(1)(e) cannot be construed literally as applying to the de facto situation at death but refer to the general arrangements for maintenance subsisting at the time of death. So that if, for example, the deceased had been making regular payments to the support of an old friend, the claim would not be defeated if those payments ceased during a terminal illness because the deceased was too ill to make them.

An admission to hospital followed by death in hospital, for example, is a circumstance where the parties would be physically separated immediately before death but neither would have regarded their relationship as at an end. The break in the cohabitation could not be regarded as one of choice and should be disregarded as constituting an act of separation. The issue is not simply whether the deceased and the claimant were physically living together, but whether they remained bound together emotionally and socially and did not consider their relationship at an end (see *Gully v Dix* [2004] EWCA Civ 139, discussed at para 4.6.2).

Although the above two issues were not argued in the case of *Re Watson* [1999] 1 FLR 878, the judgment of Neuberger J supports the view set out above. In *Re Watson*, the claimant and the deceased had had a relationship for over 30 years. From 1995 until April 1996, when the deceased died, the arrangement between them had been that the deceased provided the running living costs for both of them and the claimant looked after the home and contributed towards the service bills. They did not share the same bedroom and did not have a sexual relationship. The deceased was taken into hospital about 3 weeks before his death. Neuberger J (as he then was) held that:

> So far as s 1(1A) is concerned, it is not in dispute that during the whole of the period of two years ending immediately before the date when [Mr Watson] died Miss Griffiths was living … in the same household as [Mr Watson]. The Treasury Solicitor has not argued that Miss Griffiths' application should fail because this condition was not satisfied during the last three weeks of Mr. Watson's life when he was in hospital, and it is right to record that, in my view, that is not an argument which could respectably have been advanced. In the first place as a matter of ordinary language, the fact that someone is in hospital for a period, possibly for a long period, at the end of which he dies, does not mean that, before his death, he ceased to be part of the household of which he was part, until he was forced by illness to go to hospital, and to which he would have returned had he not died. Secondly, even if it had involved straining the language of section 1(1A) of the Act to arrive at that result, it would appear to me to

> be appropriate so to do; it would be contrary to the whole purpose and thrust of the section, if someone, who otherwise fell within it, was wholly deprived of its benefit because the deceased had been forced to spend time in hospital immediately prior to his death. Even if the deceased had returned from hospital for his last few days of life, as not infrequently occurs, a person who otherwise fell within section 1(1A) of the Act might still be deprived of its benefit if the Treasury Solicitor's concession is wrong, because it could then be argued that the deceased and the applicant were not 'living … in the same household' for 'the whole of the period of two years ending with the death'.

This view was applied in *Baynes v Hedger and Others* [2008] EWHC 1587 (Ch), [2008] 2 FLR 1805, also at [2009] EWCA Civ 374, [2009] 2 FLR 767, CA (see para 7.4), where the court confirmed that where two people are living in the same household they will not necessarily stop doing so merely because they are temporarily separated.

In *Lindop v Agus, Bass and Hedley* [2009] EWHC 1795 (Ch), the deceased and the claimant had begun a relationship in 2001, and in 2002 she moved in to live with the deceased in his house. However, she maintained a postal address at her father's house. In determining her claim as a cohabitant of the deceased, the court held that there was nothing inconsistent in her relationship as a cohabitant of the deceased whilst at the same time maintaining a postal address elsewhere.

Guidance may also be found in the test applied in matrimonial cases where the court has had to determine whether the parties have lived separately and apart for the relevant period. Enforced periods of separation are brought about by external factors, such as where the couple have spent time away from each other whilst on holiday or to get medical treatment, or where their circumstances compel one or both to live apart due to work commitments, or for example where the separation is due to the absence of the husband at sea (see *Lilley v Lilley* [1960] P 158). It implies the fact of physical separation as well as the intention to bring cohabitation between the parties to an end. (See *Santos v Santos* [1972] Fam 247 where the court considered the issue of whether the parties had been living separate and apart and when it could be inferred that they had made that decision.)

Much will depend on the factual circumstances, the evidence to support the case and the evidence adduced by those who wish to challenge the claim.

4.6.2 Living in the same household

The claimant must prove that they were living in the same household as the deceased (see *Re Watson* [1999] 1 FLR 878). This means living together as one unit and does not include living in the same property but as two separate independent entities.

The issue is not simply whether the deceased and the claimant were physically living together, but whether they remained bound together emotionally and socially and did not consider their relationship at an end:

> The relevant word is 'household' not 'house' ... Thus they will be in the same household if they are tied by their relationship. The tie of that relationship may be made manifest by various elements, not simply their living together under the same roof, but the public and private acknowledgement of the mutual protection and support that binds them together. In former days one would possibly say one should look at the whole consortium vitae. For present purposes it is sufficient to ask whether either has demonstrated a settled acceptance or recognition that the relationship is in truth at an end. If the circumstances show an irrevocable breakdown of the relationship, then they no longer live in the same household and the Act is not satisfied. If, however, the interruption is transitory, serving as a pause for reflection about the future of a relationship going through difficult times but still recognised to be subsisting, then they will be living together in the same household and the claim will lie. (Ward LJ in *Gully v Dix* [2004] EWCA Civ 139)

In *Gully v Dix* [2004] EWCA Civ 139, the claimant, who had lived with the deceased for about 27 years, had left him following an incident when he had threatened her with a knife. She had then remained apart from him for about 3 months during which time the deceased had telephoned the claimant's daughter on several occasions to ask the claimant to come back. The daughter did not pass on the messages to her mother for fear that she would return to live with the deceased. It was held that, on the facts, the relationship had not ended. The deceased had genuinely wanted the claimant to return home and the claimant would have returned had she known of the deceased's telephone calls.

In *Re Watson* [1999] 1 FLR 878, where the couple had lived together and had sexual relations in the early years of that relationship, but in the latter years they had abstained from sexual relationship, Neuberger J (as he then was) held that when considering whether a person falls within I(PFD)A 1975, s 1(1A) one must 'beware of indulging in too much over-analysis'. The court should take account of the multifarious nature of marital relationships and should 'ask itself whether, in the opinion of a reasonable person with normal perceptions, it could be said that the two people in question were living together as husband and wife'. The deceased's assumption of responsibility for the applicant and the nature and length of the relationship were relevant factors. The test applied in *Re Watson* [1999] 1 FLR 878 by Neuberger J (as he then was) was applied in *Patel v Vigh* [2013] EWHC 3403 (Ch).

In *Kaur v Dhaliwal* [2014] EWHC 1991 (Ch), the deceased and the claimant had lived together between July and September 2006 and between July 2007 and June 2009. The issue for determination was whether the earlier period of cohabitation in 2006 could be considered as cohabitation within the meaning of I(PFD)A 1975, s 1(1A). Applying *Gully v Dix*, Barling J stated (at [41]):

> 41. In my view the Judge correctly directed himself as to the principles to be applied. Nor do I accept that the conclusion he reached in the application of that approach was not open to him on the facts, as submitted by Mr Blackett-Ord. I agree that the particular facts of *In re Dix (deceased)* were very different from those of the present case. In that case the hurdle for the claimant was a different one, in that the parties were clearly not living under the same roof 'immediately before the date when the deceased died' within subsection 1(A). But the different factual circumstances do not affect the nature of the test, which is encapsulated in the questions posed by Lord Justice Ward:
>
> (1) Whether there is a settled relationship creating a tie between the parties, evidenced not simply by 'their living under the same roof but by the public and private acknowledgment of their mutual society and the mutual protection and support that binds them together', and, if so,
> (2) Whether that relationship has irretrievably broken down or, rather, is merely suspended, with any interruption being transitory.
>
> (See paragraph 24 of the judgment in that case.)

The judge had clearly taken into account the fact that (at [42]):

> … day in, day out, throughout the disputed period, the parties were together working in the Deceased's cafe (save for the period when he visited India); that their settled establishment at 33 Sandown Close was interrupted in September 2006 for family reasons unrelated to the ongoing state of their own relationship; that they were undoubtedly under the same roof (Gagan's) for some 2 weeks in May/June 2007 before resuming a permanent establishment at 42 Solway Close in July 2007; and that their engagement to marry subsisted throughout with the knowledge of their respective families.

The claimant's continued links with their country of origin, the fact that they continued to retain a property there and had a child by a previous relationship are also relevant factors in considering whether the relationship between the deceased and the applicant was one as a cohabitant or simply as a dependant. In *Witkowska v Kaminski* [2006] EWHC 1940 (Ch), [2007] 1 FLR 1547, on balance on the facts, the court found that the claimant had been cohabiting with the deceased before his death, notwithstanding the fact that she had retained a property in Poland in which her son lived. Although she repeatedly returned to Poland, the deceased had transferred funds to her and she and the deceased had conducted a close relationship for about 5 years before his death.

In an earlier case of *Kotke v Saffarini* [2005] EWCA Civ 221, [2005] 2 FLR 517, the court had held that the retention of a property which was used occasionally by the claimant was not in itself a barrier to establishing that the deceased and the claimant were cohabiting together as husband and wife unless it was clear that they had not committed themselves to such an arrangement. The fact that a couple have cohabited together but ceased to have sexual intercourse for 2 years and all communication between them has been conducted by written notes does not necessarily lead to the conclusion that their relationship has come to an end, but is comparable to a marriage in the last stages of breaking up (see *Adeoso v Adeoso* [1980] 1 WLR 1535, CA).

These cases demonstrate that the nature of the relationship between the claimant and the deceased will be the deciding factor.

Cases decided under the Fatal Accidents Act 1976, the Rent Act 1977, the Housing Act 1988 and the Matrimonial Causes Act 1973 have been considered by the court when determining the issue of whether the deceased and the claimant were cohabiting in the same household immediately before the deceased's death. For a review of some of the authorities on this issue, see the observations made by Ward LJ in the judgment in *Amicus Horizon Ltd v The Estate of Mabbot (Deceased)* [2012] EWCA Civ 895. This was a housing case. The tenancy was in the name of the deceased female partner and her partner wished to succeed to the tenancy. On the evidence, Ward LJ held that there is both an objective and a subjective element in the test of whether the parties were living together as husband and wife. In the case before him, he concluded that, although the parties had presented their relationship to the outside world as 'important and lasting', the deceased had cherished her financial independence and therefore had not made the necessary level of commitment for them to qualify. Among the important factors taken into consideration were the facts that the parties had continued to claim benefits individually rather than as a couple, and that the applicant had retained his mother's address for all correspondence.

In *Nutting v Southern Housing Group* [2004] EWHC 2982 (Ch), [2005] 1 FLR 1066, Evan-Lombe J's approach was to consider whether the relationship was a loving and committed one in which the parties offered each other emotional and practical support to an extent far beyond what could be expected between even the closest of friends, until death parted them. The other factor taken into account was the fact that the claimant's children had accepted the deceased as her partner, and that they appeared from the outside to be husband and wife. At [9] and [17], Evans-Lombe J approved the test applied by the recorder at first instance, i.e.:

> Is the relationship an emotional one of mutual lifetime commitment rather than simply one of convenience, friendship, companionship or the living together of lovers? ...

> subject to the qualification ... that the relationship must be openly and unequivocally displayed to the outside world ...

This approach was adopted in *Swetenham v Walkley* [2014] WTLR 845.

It will be observed from the examples given above that success or otherwise of a claim under this head will depend very much on the circumstances of the individual case, the evidence adduced by both the claimant and those who are seeking to challenge the claim and the assessment of that evidence by the court.

4.6.3 As the husband or wife of the deceased

Third, the claimant must prove that they were living 'as the husband or wife or civil partner of the deceased'. The case of civil partnership is considered below.

This rules out cases where the parties were living in the same household but in a relationship other than that of a husband and wife. It is not necessary to prove that the claimant and the deceased were in a sexual relationship as long as they were in a relationship which was for all intents and purposes that of a couple cohabiting together. In *Re Watson* [1999] 1 FLR 878, Neuberger J (as he then was) held that when considering whether two people are living together as husband and wife, it would be wrong to conclude that they do so simply because their relationship is one which a husband and wife would have. If the test were as wide as that, then, bearing in mind the enormous variety of relationships that can exist between husband and wife, virtually every relationship between a man and a woman living in the same household would fall within I(PFD)A 1975, s 1(1A). When considering whether the claimant was living as the wife or husband of the deceased the court should determine the matter by asking whether, in the opinion of a reasonable person with normal perceptions, it could be said that the two people were living together as husband and wife, although the multifarious nature of marital relationships should not be ignored.

In an earlier decision, *Adeoso v Adeoso* [1980] 1 WLR 1535 (CA), where the court was concerned with the provisions of Domestic Violence and Matrimonial Proceedings Act 1976, s 1(2), the parties were living together but had not had a sexual relationship with each other for 2 years. They slept in separate bedrooms. They had not spoken to each other and had communicated with each other only by way of notes. The applicant had stopped cooking and washing for the respondent. The Court of Appeal held that the parties' relationship was comparable to a marriage in the last stages of breakdown, and the fact that the parties had severed their living arrangements did not mean that they were living in different households (see, further, para 4.6.2).

4.6.4 Same sex cohabitants post-5 December 2005

By reason of the amendments made to the I(PFD)A 1975 by the CPA 2004, I(PFD)A 1975, s 1(1B) now provides that same sex couples who are in a relationship but have not entered into a civil partnership have the same rights as opposite sex couples if, for the whole of the period of 2 years ending immediately before the date when the deceased died, the person was living:

(a) in the same household as the deceased, and
(b) as the civil partner of the deceased.

The principles set out above under paras 4.6.1–4.6.3 apply to same sex couples who have not entered into a civil partnership. If these conditions are not met, it may still be possible to make a claim under I(PFD)A 1975, s 1(1)(e) (see para 4.9).

4.6.5 Same sex cohabitants pre-5 December 2005

Before the CPA 2004 came into force, arguments raised in cases decided by the courts in statutory provisions other than the I(PFD)A 1975 were relied upon and enforced with those brought about by the CPA 2004 to support a claim by same sex cohabitants who were in a relationship.

I(PFD)A 1975, s 1(1A) before its amendment, referred to the claimant living 'as the husband or wife of the deceased'. 'Cohabitant' is not defined in the Act as amended. There was no specific reference to gender in s 1(1A), and therefore the provision was capable of being construed as applying to both opposite sex and same sex relationships. There are no decided cases on this issue under the Act, but Family Law Act 1996, s 62 before its amendment defined 'cohabitants' as 'a man and a woman who, although not married to each other, are living together as husband and wife'. Section 62 now defines cohabitants as 'two persons who are neither married to each other nor civil partners of each other but are living together as husband and wife or as if they were civil partners', and 'cohabit' and 'former cohabitants' are 'to be read accordingly, but the latter expression does not include cohabitants who have subsequently married each other or become civil partners of each other'. Decisions under the Rent Act 1977, in matrimonial proceedings, and of the European Court of Human Rights under the Human Rights Convention, were relied on to suggest that the I(PFD)A 1975 should apply to same sex relationships.

In the cases under the Rent Act 1977, the courts have overcome the problem by two separate routes. In *Fitzpatrick v Sterling Housing Association Ltd* [1998] Ch 304, the appellant and the tenant lived together for 17 years in a loving, faithful, monogamous same sex relationship. When the tenant suffered a stroke the appellant gave up work and nursed him for 8 years. The issue for consideration was whether, as the same sex partner of the lawful tenant, he was entitled to succeed to a statutory tenancy under Rent Act 1977, Sch 1, paras 2(2) and 3(1) as a 'person living with the original tenant as his or her wife or husband' or as 'a member of the original tenant's family'. The Court of Appeal, by a majority, held that the provisions applied only to opposite sex relationships and that only persons who were bound together by the ties of kinship could be regarded as 'member[s] of the original tenant's family'. Ward LJ, in his dissenting judgment, stated that if a same sex couple was asked in what manner they lived together, the couple's answer would not be different from that given by an opposite sex couple save only in the one respect – that in their case their sexual relations were between two people of the same sex, Ward LJ stated:

> no distinction can sensibly be drawn between the two couples in terms of love, nurturing, fidelity, durability, emotional and economic inter-dependence – to name but some and by no means all of the hallmarks of a relationship between a husband and his wife with regard to the only distinguishing feature, sexual activity, that is a function of the relationship of a husband and wife, a man and his mistress and it is a function of homosexual [same sex] lovers. That the activity takes place between members of different sexes or of the same sex is a matter of form not function ... I would say that there is no essential difference between a homosexual [same sex] and a heterosexual couple [opposite sex] and accordingly, I would find that the appellant had lived with the deceased tenant as his husband and wife ... The common man may be vaguely disapproving of the homosexual [same sex] relationship which is not for him but having shrugged his shoulders, he would recognise that the relationship was to all intents and purposes a marriage between those partners. They lived a life akin to that of any husband and wife. They were so bound together that they constituted a family.

On appeal, the House of Lords (now the Supreme Court) concluded that the appellant could not be treated as the spouse of the deceased tenant because the language of the statutory provisions could be interpreted as referring only to opposite sex relationships, but stressed that this interpretation was confined to the particular provision of the Rent Act 1977. However, in *Mendoza v Ghaidan* [2002] EWCA Civ 1533, [2003] 1 FLR 468, the application of Rent Act 1977, Sch 1, para 2(1) as amended was considered again by the Court of Appeal in a case involving a same sex relationship. It was held that Sch 1, para 2(1) as construed by *Fitzpatrick v Sterling Housing Association Ltd* infringed Art 14 of the Human Rights Convention. Having regard to its duty under the Human Rights Act 1998, the court concluded that the words of the section 'as his or her wife or husband' should be read to mean 'as if they were his or her wife or husband'. On appeal ([2004] UKHL 30), the House of Lords affirmed the decision of the Court of Appeal. In his leading judgment, Lord Nicholls of Birkenhead said (at [17]):

> A homosexual [same sex] couple, as much as a heterosexual [opposite sex] couple, share each other's life and make their home together. They have an equivalent relationship. There is no rational or fair ground for distinguishing the one couple from the other in this context.

The protection afforded to a cohabiting opposite sex couple is therefore equally applicable to the survivor of a same sex couple. (See, also, *Saunders v Garrett* [2005] WTLR 749 (case under the I(PFD)A 1975) where the court, applying the principles set out in *Fitzpatrick v Sterling Housing Association Ltd*, concluded that the applicant who had been in a same sex relationship with the deceased was entitled to make the application for financial provision under I(PFD)A 1975, s 1(1)(ba).) As the law stood then, the court was obliged to take account of the Human Rights Convention and Human Rights Act 1998, s 3, which requires the court to read in words which change the meaning of enacted legislation, so as to make it Convention-compliant. The court can therefore modify the meaning of provisions to make it Convention-compliant. Hence it is possible in order to make the provisions of the I(PFD)A 1975 Convention-compliant to give it an interpretation which is expansive and which provides equality of treatment to same sex couples when there is no legitimate reason justifying discrimination. (See, also, *M v Secretary of State for Works and Pensions; Langley v Bradford Metropolitan District Council* [2004] EWCA Civ 1343, [2005] 1 FLR 498, where the court construed the words to read 'as if he had been the husband or wife of the deceased'.)

These cases serve as a reminder that where a same sex person is for any reason now unable to bring a claim under I(PFD)A 1975, s 1(1A) or (1B), such a claimant may have a good case under s 1(1)(e) as a person who immediately before the death of the deceased was being maintained whether wholly or partly by the deceased.

4.7 CHILD OF THE DECEASED

A 'child' includes:

(1) an illegitimate child;
(2) a child *en ventre sa mere* (i.e. a child who has been conceived but not born at the death of the deceased (I(PFD)A 1975, s 25(1));
(3) an adult child (see *Re Coventry, Coventry v Coventry* [1980] Ch 461 and *Re Callaghan (Deceased)* [1985] Fam 1);
(4) an adopted child, that is, a child adopted in England and Wales or in any foreign country if the adoption is recognised in England and Wales.

4.7.1 Presumption of legitimacy

Where the parents of a child were married to each other at the time of their birth, the presumption of legitimacy arises and the husband of the mother is presumed to be the father of the child unless the contrary is proved. The presumption can be relied on to prove parenthood until the presumption is rebutted. A certified copy of the claimant's birth certificate is regarded as sufficient evidence of legitimacy, provided it contains the relevant information on parenthood. If an appropriate birth certificate is not available and there is no other evidence to prove the claimant's parenthood, an order for DNA profiling to be carried out could be applied for.

Where a child is born not later than the period of gestation after the marriage has been dissolved, the presumption of legitimacy may arise. In *Re Overbury (Deceased)* [1955] Ch 122, a child was born less than 9 months from the date when the mother's first marriage was dissolved, but during the subsistence of her second marriage. On the basis of the common law presumption of legitimacy, the child was presumed to be the child of both the former husband and the mother's current husband. The court ruled, on the evidence, that the child was the legitimate child of the first husband. Today, however, the matter would be established by DNA profiling, not by legal presumption or inference.

4.7.2 Legitimation

Where the parents of an illegitimate child marry then, provided that the father is domiciled in England and Wales at the time of the marriage, the child is legitimated at the date of the marriage (Legitimacy Act 1976, s 2). Where the father is not domiciled in England and Wales at the date of the marriage, the child is legitimated if the law of the domicile of the father legitimates the child by marriage (Legitimacy Act 1976, s 3).

4.7.3 Legitimation and same sex female partners

The Legitimacy Act 1976 as amended by the HFEA 2008 now provides for a child born to same sex female couples who subsequently enter into a civil partnership to be legitimated. Legitimacy Act 1976, s 2A provides that where:

(a) a person ('the child') has a parent ('the female parent') by virtue of section 43 of the Human Fertilisation and Embryology Act 2008 (treatment provided to woman who agrees that second woman to be parent);

> (b) at the time of the child's birth, the female parent and the child's mother are neither married nor civil partners of each other;
> (c) the female parent and the child's mother subsequently enter into a civil partnership; and
> (d) the female parent is at the date of the marriage or the formation of the civil partnership domiciled in England and Wales,
>
> the marriage or the civil partnership shall render the child, if living, legitimate from the date of the formation of the civil partnership.

Where the female parent is domiciled outside England and Wales at the time of the marriage or the formation of the civil partnership, Legitimacy Act 1976, s 3 as amended to include sub-section (2), now provides that where:

> (a) a person ('the child') has a parent ('the female parent') by virtue of section 43 of the Human Fertilisation and Embryology Act 2008 (treatment provided to woman who agrees that second woman to be parent);
> (b) at the time of the child's birth, the female parent and the child's mother are neither married nor civil partners of each other;
> (c) the female parent and the child's mother subsequently marry or enter into a civil partnership; and
> (d) the female parent is not at the time of the marriage or the formation of the civil partnership domiciled in England and Wales but is domiciled in a country by the law of which the child became legitimated by virtue of the civil partnership,
>
> the child, if living shall in England and Wales be recognised as having been so legitimated from the date of the marriage or the formation of the civil partnership notwithstanding that, at the time of the child's birth, the female parent was domiciled in a country the law of which did not permit legitimation by subsequent marriage or civil partnership.

4.7.4 Child of void marriage

Legitimacy Act 1976, s 1 as amended provides that a child of a void marriage or a void civil partnership, whenever born, shall, subject to I(PFD)A 1975, s 1(2) and Sch 1, be treated as the legitimate child of his parents if at the time of the insemination resulting in the birth, or where there was no such insemination, the child's conception (or at the time of the celebration of the marriage or of the formation of the civil partnership if later), both or either of the parties reasonably believed that the marriage or civil partnership was valid. For this provision to apply, the father of the child must be domiciled in England and Wales at the time of the birth or, if he died before the birth, he must have been so domiciled immediately before his death (s 1(2)). Similarly, if a woman is treated as the female parent of a child by virtue of the HFEA 2008, that female parent was domiciled in England and Wales at the time of the birth or if she died before the birth, was so domiciled immediately before her death, the child will be treated as a legitimate child of the couple.

The phrase 'child of a void marriage' does not extend to an illegitimate child born before the void marriage or the formation of the civil partnership took place. Such a child is not the child of a void marriage or civil partnership, but a child of their parents; the child is not legitimated by the subsequent void marriage or the formation of a civil partnership of the parents. I(PFD)A 1975, s 1(1) applies only to a child born after a void marriage or a void civil partnership has been celebrated (see *Re Spence (Deceased)* [1990] Ch 652).

A child born or conceived during the subsistence of the marriage or the formation of the civil partnership is legitimated notwithstanding the subsequent annulment of the marriage or the civil partnership (Matrimonial Causes Act 1973, s 16).

4.7.5 Adopted child

Under the law relating to adoption as set out in the Adoption Act 1926, an adopted child remained the child of their birth parents. Section 5(2) provided that:

> An adoption order shall not deprive the adopted child of any right to or an interest in property to which, but for the order, the child would have been entitled under any intestacy or disposition, whether occurring or made before or after the making of the adoption order, or confer on the adopted child any right to or interest in property as a child of the adopter, and the expression 'child,' 'children' and 'issue' where used in any disposition whether made before or after the making of an adoption order, shall not, unless the contrary intention appears, include an adopted child or children or the issue of an adopted child.

This provision was amended by the Adoption and Children Act 1949, which provided that adopted children are to be treated as the children of their adopters and not their birth parents. Similar provisions were made in Adoption Act 1976, s 39. Neither this provision nor those set out in Sch 2, para 6 to the Act, which set out transitional provisions were repealed or amended when the Adoption and Children Act 2002 was passed. The status conferred by adoption on an adopted child is now set out in Adoption and Children Act 2002, s 67. These provisions are not retrospective.

A child of the deceased who is adopted after the death of their biological parent, but before making a claim under the I(PFD)A 1975 is not a child of the deceased within the meaning of s 1(1)(c). This applies whether the adoption order was made under the Adoption Act 1976 or the Adoption and Children Act 2002. An adopted child is not eligible to make a claim under the I(PFD)A 1975 because, by virtue of Adoption Act 1976, s 39(2) and Adoption and Children Act 2002, s 67, an adopted child is treated in law as the child of the adopters and as such loses the right to make a claim against the estate of their biological parent, but is eligible to make a claim under the I(PFD)A 1975 as the child of the adopters because the child is treated in law as the child of the adopters in all respects. A testamentary disposition made before the child was adopted by the adopters will be interpreted so as to give the adopted child inheritance rights under the disposition.

The provisions of the Adoption Acts are not retrospective so that an illegitimate child who is adopted by their father cannot inherit under a will made prior to the statutory provisions coming into effect. In *Timothy Everard Upton v National Westminster Bank plc and Others* [2004] EWHC 1962 (Ch), an illegitimate grandson who had been adopted by his father could not inherit under his grandfather's will made in 1930 and codicil in 1935. The Human Rights Act 1998 had come into force shortly before the grandfather died, but it appears that neither the effect of its provisions nor EU case law were taken into account when the case was heard and judgment handed down. The court therefore concluded that under the domestic law then in force, illegitimate children were not included in the disposition. The status of an illegitimate and an adopted child should now be considered in the light of Arts 8 and 14 of the Human Rights Convention and Art 1 of the First Protocol to the Convention. In *Marckx v Belgium* (Application No 6833/74) [1979] ECHR 2, similar issues as those which arose in the *Upton* case were considered by the European Court of Human Rights. It ruled that Belgian law contravened the Convention because it resulted in a lack of respect for the illegitimate child's family rights, as Art 8 does not make any distinction between legitimate and illegitimate children. In *Pla and Puncernau v Andorra* (Application No 69498/01) [2004] 2 FCR 630, the European Court of Human Rights held that any interpretation of a disposition which discriminates against an adopted child would be contrary to Art 14 of the Human Rights Convention, and that the disposition should be interpreted in the light of the social, economic and legal changes and the application of the Convention, and not to the conditions which existed at the time when the will was made (see, also, *Brauer v Germany* (Application No 3545/04) [2010] ECHR 74 and *Fabris v France* (Application No 16574/08) [2013] ECHR 427). The issue of the status of an adopted child was considered in *Hand and Another v George and Another* [2017] EWHC 533 (Ch), where the question in a claim made under the I(PFD)A 1975 was whether adopted children count as 'children' for the purposes of a will made in 1946. It was conceded that under the domestic law in force at the time, the claimants, who were adopted grandchildren of the deceased, were not included in the trust. Reliance was therefore placed on the infringement of the claimant's Convention rights. Rose J considered the decision in *Re Erskine 1948 Trust* [2012] EWHC 732 (Ch). She disapproved of the approach adopted by the judge in *Erskine* on the basis that it was inconsistent with the decision of *Wilson v First County Trust Ltd (No 2)* [2003] UKHL 40 on the issue of retrospectivity (see [62]–[67]). Rose J, having considered both the domestic and European case law, concluded that the domestic law infringed the claimants' rights under Arts 8 and 14 by failing to legislate to ensure that the interpretative provision in Adoption Act 1926, s 5(2) has no continuing effect where a will falls to be construed after the Convention came into force. She said at [76]:

> The ECtHR has consistently held that Article 14 in conjunction with Article 8 precludes legislation which confers more limited rights on adopted children to their adoptive parents' estate, than are conferred on natural children. The ECtHR has also consistently rejected arguments put forward by respondent governments that the discriminatory law should remain applicable to instruments that pre-date the change in social attitudes which now requires equal treatment for adopted children. The ECtHR addressed the problem of retrospectivity of the Convention in this regard in *Marckx*. It held that arguments based on legal certainty or the need to protect the expectations of the deceased and their families must be subordinate to the imperative of equal treatment. Discrimination cannot be regarded as a proportionate response to such concerns ... .

In any event, the adopted child would be eligible to make a successful claim under the I(PFD)A 1975 against the estate of the deceased if the will is not interpreted in a way which is Convention-compliant.

The status of an adopted child as set out above does not prejudice:

(1) any qualifying interest, i.e. an interest vested in possession in the adopted person before the adoption;
(2) an interest expectant (whether immediately or not) upon a qualifying interest (Adoption and Children Act 2002, s 69(4));
(3) as from 1 October 2014, any contingent interest (other than a contingent interest in remainder) which the adopted person has immediately before the adoption in the estate of a deceased person whether testate or intestate (inserted into Adoption and Children Act 2002, s 69(4)(c) by Inheritance and Trustees' Powers Act 2014, s 4).

Furthermore, neither Adoption Act 1976, s 42(4) nor Adoption and Children Act 2002, s 69(4) before its amendment conferred on an adopted child an 'interest expectant', as they did not have an enforceable right against the estate of the deceased. The I(PFD)A 1975 merely conferred a right to apply to the court for relief and thus they only had a cause of action (see *Re Collins (Deceased)* [1990] 2 All ER 47). The court in *Re Collins* was reinforced in this view by the decision in *Whyte v Ticehurst* [1986] Fam 64, where a wife who had applied for financial provision under the I(PFD)A 1975 died before the hearing of her claim. Her personal representatives applied to carry on with the proceedings on behalf of her estate. In dismissing the application, Booth J stated that the claim under the Act arose from the relationship of the two parties and was a personal one. On the death of the claimant, it ceased to exist. In *Re Bramwell (Deceased), Campbell v Tobin* [1988] 2 FLR 263, it was held that the right to apply for financial provision under the Act was a mere hope or contingency and not a cause of action. However, as from 1 October 2014, s 69(4) has been amended by inserting a paragraph (c) as set out above. This enables a child who has a contingent interest in the estate of his deceased biological parent immediately before he was adopted to keep that interest. This provision applies to interests under a will or on intestacy. It does not affect the rule that an adopted child cannot bring a claim against the estate of his biological parent.

4.7.6 Child born as a result of infertility treatment

In view of the advancement in science in the development of human assisted reproduction, the law of parentage has evolved over the last two decades and is likely to continue to evolve. An outline of the various changes in the law is set out below simply as a quick guide to assist the practitioner. The issues of parentage of a child born as a result of reproductive treatment are set out in the following statutory provisions:

(1) the Family Law Reform Act 1987;
(2) the Human Fertilisation and Embryology Act 1990 (HFEA 1990);
(3) the Human Fertilisation and Embryology (Deceased Fathers) Act 2003;
(4) the HFEA 2008.

These statutes deal with the case where reproductive treatment is provided:

(1) to those in an opposite sex married relationship;
(2) to opposite sex unmarried couples;
(3) to same sex female couples in a civil partnership or married at the time of treatment;
(4) to same sex female couples who are not registered as civil partners or married; and
(5) for the posthumous use of sperm/embryo by all the above four categories.

The issue of surrogacy and parental orders and the parentage of a child when a parental order is made in favour of same sex male couples is considered at para 4.7.8.

There is a need to consider these provisions where a child has been conceived as a result of infertility treatment, such as artificial insemination, gamete intra-fallopian transfer (GIFT), or in vitro fertilisation (IVF), to identify the legal status of the child and to ascertain who, in law, are the child's parents. The statutory provisions require clinics and those who provide treatment to be licensed and to follow a prescribed procedure, especially in relation to the obtaining of consents.

Unfortunately, following an audit undertaken of all UK fertility clinics, it was discovered that in a large number of cases the correct procedure had not been followed. Consequently, the parents who were affected were notified, and this resulted in those parents applying to the High Court for a declaration of parentage to confirm that they are the legal parents of the child born to them. In order to do justice and to promote the welfare of the children concerned, Sir James Munby P dealt with these cases by finding evidential solutions and employing the equitable relief of rectification to found a basis for making a declaration of parentage under Family Law Act 1986, s 55A (see para 4.7.9).

Married opposite sex couples – Family Law Reform Act 1987

Where a child was born as a result of IVF or GIFT, or where sperm taken from the husband or partner of the mother was used to inseminate her (AIH), the legal relationship between the child and the parent can be established on the basis of blood ties. The child is the child of the mother and her husband or partner, and if the parents were married or entered into a civil partnership, the child would be legitimate.

Family Law Reform Act 1987, s 27 applied where a child was born to a married woman after 4 April 1988 in England and Wales as a result of artificial insemination of the woman (whose marriage had not at the time been annulled or dissolved), and she was artificially inseminated with the semen of some person other than her husband. In such a case, unless it was proved to the satisfaction of any court by which the matter had to be determined that the husband did not consent to the insemination, the child was treated in law as the child of the parties to the marriage. If the husband had not consented to the insemination of his wife, then he was not regarded as the child's father and the child was fatherless.

Married opposite sex couples – HFEA 1990

Family Law Reform Act 1987, s 27 was replaced, as from 1 August 1991, by the provisions of the HFEA 1990. HFEA 1990, s 28, headed 'Meaning of "father"', provided:

> (1) This section applies in the case of a child who is being or has been carried by a woman as the result of the placing in her of an embryo or of sperm and eggs or her artificial insemination.
>
> (2) If—
>
> (a) at the time of the placing in her of the embryo or the sperm and eggs or of her insemination, the woman was a party to a marriage, and
>
> (b) the creation of the embryo carried by her was not brought about with the sperm of the other party to the marriage,

then, subject to subsection (5) below, the other party to the marriage shall be treated as the father of the child unless it is shown that he did not consent to the placing in her of the embryo or the sperm and eggs or to her insemination (as the case may be).

(3) If no man is treated, by virtue of subsection (2) above, as the father of the child but—

(a) the embryo or the sperm and eggs were placed in the woman, or she was artificially inseminated, in the course of treatment services provided for her and a man together by a person to whom a licence applies, and
(b) the creation of the embryo carried by her was not brought about with the sperm of that man, (*donor sperm*)

then, subject to subsection (5) below, that man shall be treated as the father of the child.

(4) Where a person is treated as the father of the child by virtue of subsection (2) or (3) above, no other person is to be treated as the father of the child.

(5) Subsections (2) and (3) above do not apply—

(a) in relation to England and Wales and Northern Ireland, to any child who, by virtue of the rules of common law, is treated as the legitimate child of the parties to a marriage, ...
(b) to any child to the extent that the child is treated by virtue of adoption as not being the child of any person other than the adopter or adopters.

(6) Where—

(a) the sperm of a man who had given such consent as is required by paragraph 5 of Schedule 3 to this Act was used for a purpose for which such consent was required, or
(b) the sperm of a man, or any embryo the creation of which was brought about with his sperm, was used after his death,

he is not to be treated as the father of the child.

(7) The references in subsection (2) above to the parties to a marriage at the time there referred to—

(a) are to the parties to a marriage subsisting at that time, unless a judicial separation was then in force, but
(b) include the parties to a void marriage if either or both of them reasonably believed at that time that the marriage was valid; and for the purposes of this subsection it shall be presumed, unless the contrary is shown, that one of them reasonably believed at that time that the marriage was valid.

(8) This section applies whether the woman was in the United Kingdom or elsewhere at the time of the placing in her of the embryo or the sperm and eggs or her artificial insemination.

(9) In subsection (7)(a) above, 'judicial separation' includes a legal separation obtained in a country outside the British Islands and recognised in the United Kingdom.

Thus, a child born to a married woman after 1 August 1991 as a result of artificial insemination with the semen of someone other than her husband is treated as the child of the woman and her husband unless it is shown that the husband did not consent to the artificial insemination (HFEA 1990, s 28(2)).

HFEA 1990, s 29(3) provides *inter alia* that references to any relationship in any deed or other instrument (whenever passed or made) are to be construed accordingly. It follows, therefore, that the child will be treated as legitimate. These provisions apply only in relation to children born as a result of artificial insemination or *in vitro* fertilisation carried out on or after 1 August 1991. However, they are retrospective in the sense that the rules of construction they introduce apply to all instruments 'whenever made' and, accordingly, apply to instruments made before as well as after that date. Where, however, the parents remain married, the common law presumption of legitimacy arises, because s 28(5) provides that s 28(2) does not apply to any child who, by virtue of the rules of common law, is treated as the legitimate child of the parties to a marriage. If paternity is disputed, the dispute will have to be resolved by the court. If the presumption of legitimacy applies, it can be rebutted by evidence which establishes that the person could not be the father, for example, that he was impotent, and if necessary by DNA profiling. In a case in France on 6 November 1997, a court in Paris ordered the exhumation of the body of Yves Montand, the French film actor who had died 6 years previously, to enable the applicant, who alleged that she was his daughter, to establish paternity.

Opposite sex married couples – HFEA 2008

The HFEA 2008 provides a definition for both the terms 'mother' and 'father'. It confirms the position under the HFEA 1990 that the woman who carries the child as a result of assisted reproduction anywhere in the world is the mother of the child unless that child is subsequently adopted or made the subject of a parental order (HFEA 2008, s 33).

Where the woman is married to a man at the time of treatment when there was placed in her an embryo or the gametes involving donor sperm, her husband will be treated as the father of the child conceived as a result of the assisted reproduction unless it is shown that he did not consent to his wife's treatment. It matters not whether the woman was in the United Kingdom or elsewhere when she received the treatment (HFEA 2008, s 35). In this case no other person will be treated as the father of the child (s 38(1)) thus preserving the previous position of the donor that he cannot have the status of a father. Section 38(2) also confirms the presumption at common law that a child born to a married couple is the legitimate child of the parties to the marriage.

Unmarried woman and her male partner – HFEA 1990

Where an unmarried woman is artificially inseminated in the course of licensed treatment services provided for her and her male partner together, the partner will be treated in law as the father of the child (HFEA 1990, s 28(3)). Where the treatment was provided abroad, and therefore by a non-licence holder, the provisions of s 28(3) do not apply to confer paternity on the man. In such cases the issues which may arise include whether the treatment was provided 'together'; whether there was appropriate counselling; and whether the man was warned of the consequences and given a full opportunity to make an informed choice. Similarly, where treatment was provided to a couple together but is administered by a person who was not licensed under the Act, section 28(3) will not apply to confer paternity on the man (see *U v W (AG Intervening)* [1998] 1 FCR 526).

The question whether the treatment services were provided for the couple 'together' was considered in *Re B (Parentage)* [1996] 2 FLR 15, where the father had given sperm with which the mother was inseminated. At the time of insemination, the relationship between the mother and the father had ended. The father accepted that he was the biological father of the twins born to the mother. The issues were whether the parties had been receiving treatment together, and whether the father had consented. On the facts, it was found that the father had not given his express consent, but it was held that he was deemed to have given his consent as he and the mother had been receiving treatment together and he had not at any stage before insemination withdrawn his consent.

For paternity to be established where the man has no biological connection with the embryo, the embryo must have been placed in the mother at a time when treatment services were being provided for the couple together. Thus, where the relationship between the couple had ended before the embryo was placed in the mother and the mother had misled the medical authority by falsely representing that the relationship with the man was subsisting, the man was held not to be the legal father of the child by reason of HFEA 1990, s 28(3) (see *Re R (IVF: Paternity of Child)* [2003] EWCA Civ 182, [2003] 1 FLR 1183).

In *Re Q (Parental Order)* [1996] 1 FLR 369, an unmarried mother acted as a surrogate mother for a married couple. She gave birth to a child created from the egg of the wife and fertilised by sperm from a donor under a licensed arrangement. Under HFEA 1990, s 28(6), the donor could not be treated as the father of the child. Section 28(3) did not apply as the husband had not received treatment services together with the woman. It followed that no man could be treated in law as the father of the child.

Unmarried woman and her male partner – HFEA 2008

The HFEA 2008 now makes provision for the male partner of an unmarried woman, who has no female partner, to be the father of a child conceived by the woman using donor sperm provided the 'fatherhood conditions' set out in s 37 are met and provided that:

(1) the woman is treated in the United Kingdom by a person who is licensed to provide the treatment;
(2) the 'fatherhood conditions' set out in s 37 are met;
(3) the man remained alive at the time; and
(4) the creation of the embryo carried by the woman was not that of her male partner.

The 'fatherhood conditions' set out in HFEA 2008, s 37 which must be satisfied to enable the man to be treated as the father of the child are:

(1) both the man and the woman must have given written notice that they both consent to the man being treated as the father of any child resulting from the treatment provided to the woman under the licence;
(2) neither the woman nor the man has, since giving notice of their consent, given subsequent notice of the withdrawal of that consent;
(3) the woman has not since giving her consent given a further notice that she consents to another man being treated as the father of any resulting child or that she consents to a woman being treated as a parent of the resulting child; and
(4) the woman and the man must not be within the prohibited degrees of relationship in relation to each other.

In cases where the form on which the consent of the man has been given cannot be found or there has been a clerical error in completing the form or the wrong form has been used, the court may rectify the error to give effect to the parties' intention and the requirements of the Act and grant a declaration of parentage under Family Law Act 1986, s 55A (see *X & Y v St Bartholomew's Hospital Centre for Reproductive Medicine* [2015] EWFC 13, *Human Fertilisation and Embryology Act 2008 (Cases A–H)* [2015] EWHC 2602 (Fam) and *Human Fertilisation and Embryology Act 2008 (Cases AD, AE, AF, AG, AG (No 2))* [2017] EWHC 1782 (Fam)).

Same sex female couples – HFEA 2008

HFEA 2008, ss 42–44 make new provisions to give same sex female couples similar rights as those which apply to opposite sex couples. Where two females are in a relationship and one of them gives birth to a child conceived as a result of donor insemination, she alone will be considered the mother of the child (HFEA 2008, s 33(1)). In order to qualify as a parent of the child, the other partner will need to satisfy certain conditions which vary according to whether or not the couple have entered into a civil partnership. These conditions mirror those which apply to opposite sex couples.

Same sex female couples in a civil partnership

If at the time the woman who received treatment was a party to a civil partnership, she will be the mother of the child born to her as a result of donor insemination. Her partner will be a parent of the child unless she did not consent to the mother receiving the treatment (HFEA 2008, s 42(1)).

Same sex female couples not in a civil partnership

Where two women who are in a relationship have not entered into a civil partnership, the woman who carries the child will be the child's mother. Her partner will be treated as the legal parent, provided certain conditions set out in HFEA 2008, s 43 and the 'female parenthood' conditions set out in s 44 are satisfied.

The conditions in HFEA 2008, s 43, are:

(1) the embryo or the sperm and eggs were placed in the woman or the woman was inseminated in the course of treatment services provided in a licensed clinic in the United Kingdom;
(2) at the time when the treatment was provided, the agreed female parenthood conditions set out in s 44 were met in relation to the other woman in relation to the treatment provided to the woman who will carry the child; and
(3) the other woman remained alive at that time.

'Female parenthood' conditions

The 'female parenthood' conditions which much be satisfied by the woman who is not carrying the child are similar to those which apply to a male partner where the parties are in an opposite sex relationship. The conditions are as follows:

(1) Both parties must have given to the person responsible for providing the treatment a written notice stating that they both consent to the other woman being treated as the parent of the resulting child.
(2) Neither women has given a subsequent notice of withdrawal of consent to the person responsible for providing the treatment.
(3) The woman must not have given a subsequent notice of consent to another woman being treated as the parent of the child.
(4) The woman must not subsequently have given notice of consent to another man being treated as the child's father under HFEA 2008, s 37(1)(b).
(5) The female couple must not be within the prohibited degree of relationship in relation to each other.
(6) Where the above conditions are satisfied, the other woman will be treated as the parent of the child, and no man will be treated as the father of the child (s 45(1)).

Posthumous use of sperm (opposite sex couples) – HFEA 1990 as amended by the Human Fertilisation and Embryology (Deceased Fathers) Act 2003

Following the decision in *R v Human Fertilisation and Embryology Authority ex parte Blood* [1997] 2 FLR 742, the HFEA 1990 was amended to deal with the use of a deceased father's sperm. In *R v Human Fertilisation and Embryology Authority ex parte Blood*, the claimant wished to be artificially inseminated with sperm taken from her husband at her request by doctors treating him when he was unconscious and receiving treatment in hospital. The sperm was stored in a licensed institution. The husband died. The Human Fertilisation and Embryology Authority refused to release the sperm to the applicant on the ground that no written consent had been obtained from the husband and he had not received counselling as required by the provisions of the Act. On appeal, it was held that the provisions of the Act had been breached and therefore the sperm should not have been preserved and stored. The court directed that in future those responsible for treating a man and a woman together should take the precaution of having the necessary consent not only to storage, but also to the continuation of treatment if the man should die before the sperm is used. Leave was, however, given for the sperm to be released so that the woman could receive treatment in Belgium. A child born as a result of such treatment is not considered the child of the husband (s 28(2) and (3)).

The Human Fertilisation and Embryology (Deceased Fathers) Act 2003 amended the HFEA 1990 to permit a man to be registered as the child's father if the child was conceived by using the man's sperm after his death or embryo created by using his sperm before his death.

Posthumous use of sperm – HFEA 2008

HFEA 2008, s 39 replaces the provision inserted in the HFEA 1990 by the Human Fertilisation and Embryology (Deceased Fathers) Act 2003 (see above) by setting out the conditions that must be satisfied before a man may be treated as the father of a child born to a woman by using the man's sperm after his death or using an embryo created with the man's sperm before his death but placed in the woman after his death, but only for the purposes of registering the birth of the child.

The conditions are:

(1) the man must have consented in writing to the use of his sperm or embryo after his death and to being treated as the father of any resulting child for the purposes of registering the birth of the child;
(2) the man must not have withdrawn his consent;
(3) the woman must elect in writing not later than the end of the period of 42 days from the day on which the child was born for the man to be treated for the purposes of birth registration as the father of the child; and
(4) no one else is to be treated:

  (a) as the father of the child by virtue of s 35 or s 36 or by virtue of s 38(2) or (3) (see paras 4.7.1 and 4.7.2: opposite sex married and unmarried couples and the provision of common law presumption of legitimacy);
  (b) no one else is to be treated as a parent of the child by virtue of s 42 or s 43 (see below); or
  (c) no one else is treated as a parent of the child by virtue of adoption.

Posthumous use of donated sperm where the couple are married

Where the child has been carried by a married woman as a result of the placing in her of an embryo created by donated sperm and her husband died before the embryo was placed in the woman then the husband will be treated as the father of the resulting child, provided the conditions set out in HFEA 2008, s 40 are satisfied.

The conditions are:

(1) the woman must have been married when the embryo was created;
(2) the husband died before the embryo was placed in the woman;
(3) the husband must have consented in writing and not withdrawn his consent to the placing of the embryo in the woman after his death and to being treated as the father of any resulting child for the purposes of birth registration;
(4) the woman has elected in writing no later than the end of the period of 42 days from the day on which the child was born for the man to be treated for the purposes of birth registration as the father of the child;

(5) no one else is to be treated as the father of the child by virtue of s 35 or s 36 (see above) or s 38(2) or (3); or as a parent of the child by virtue of s 42 or s 43 (see below);
(6) no one else is to be treated as a parent of the child by virtue of adoption.

Posthumous use of donated sperm where the couple are unmarried

Similar conditions as apply to married couples must be satisfied to ensure that the man is to be treated as the father of the resulting child. In addition, the woman must not have been a party to a marriage or a civil partnership at the time when the embryo was created, which must have been in the course of licensed treatment provided to the woman in the United Kingdom and immediately before the man's death, and the agreed 'fatherhood conditions' set out in HFEA 2008, s 37 must have been met in relation to treatment proposed to be provided to the woman in the United Kingdom by a licensed person (s 40(2)).

Same sex female couples in a civil partnership or marriage at the time of treatment – HFEA 2008

The HFEA 2008 for the first time introduces provisions providing for same sex female couples to have the same rights as those which apply to opposite sex couples.

HFEA 2008, s 42 provides that where, at the time of placing in her of the embryo or sperm and eggs or her artificial insemination, a woman was a party to a civil partnership or a marriage, then the other party to the civil partnership is to be treated as a parent of the child unless it is shown that she did not consent to the mother's treatment. The woman who carried the child will be the child's mother (s 33(1)).

Same sex female couples not in a civil partnership or marriage

Where two women are in a relationship but they have not entered into a civil partnership or marriage, the woman who carries the child will be the mother and her partner will be treated as a parent of the child, provided that the 'female parenthood' conditions set out in HFEA 2008, s 44 are met.

The 'female parenthood' conditions are:

(1) both parties must have given written notice of their respective consent to the other woman to be treated as the parent of any child resulting from treatment provided to the woman who is to carry the child;
(2) neither of them must have withdrawn their consent;

(3) the woman must not have subsequently given notice that she consents to another woman being treated as a parent of any resulting child or a notice that she consents to a man being treated as the father of any resulting child;
(4) the female couple must not be within the prohibited degrees of relationship in relation to each other.

Posthumous transfer of embryo after death of female spouse, civil partner or intended parent

In line with the provisions set out in HFEA 2008, s 40 relating to transfer of embryo after the death of the male spouse, civil partner or intended parent who did not provide sperm, s 46 provides for the registration of the deceased same sex female partner to be treated as a parent of the resulting child provided certain conditions are met.

HFEA 2008, s 46 provides that where a child has been carried by a woman as the result of the placing in her of an embryo which was created at a time when she was a party to a civil partnership or marriage with another woman and the other party to the civil partnership or marriage dies before the placing of the embryo in the woman, then provided the conditions set out in s 46(1)(d)–(f) are met, the other party to the civil partnership or marriage is to be treated as a parent of the child for the purposes of birth registration. The conditions are:

(1) that the other party to the civil partnership or marriage consented in writing (and did not withdraw that consent) to the placing of the embryo in the woman after the death of the other party and to being treated as the parent of any resulting child for the purposes of birth registration;
(2) the woman has elected in writing not later than 42 days from the day on which the child was born for the other party to the civil partnership or marriage to be treated for the purposes of birth registration as the parent of the child;
(3) no one else is to be treated as the father of the child by virtue of s 35 or s 36 or by virtue of s 45(2) or (3) (conditions which apply to opposite sex married and unmarried couples) or as a parent of the child by virtue of s 42 or s 43;
(4) no one else is to be treated as a parent of the child by virtue of adoption.

Posthumous transfer of embryo after death of same sex partner where the couple are not in a civil partnership or marriage

Where a child has been carried by a woman as a result of the placing in her of an embryo and the embryo was not created at a time when the woman was a party to a marriage or civil partnership but was created in the course of licensed treatment provided to the woman in the United Kingdom, the woman's female partner may be treated as the parent of the resulting child provided the following conditions are satisfied:

(1) the other female partner consented in writing (and did not withdraw that consent) to the placing of the embryo in the woman after her own death and to being treated as the parent of any resulting child for the purposes of registration of birth;
(2) the other female partner died before the placing of the embryo in the woman;
(3) immediately before the death of the other female partner, the agreed 'female parenthood' conditions set out in HFEA 2008, s 44 (see above) were met in relation to the licensed treatment provided in the United Kingdom to the woman bearing the child;
(4) the woman carrying the child had elected in writing not later than the end of the period of 42 days from the day on which the child was born for the other woman to be treated as the parent of the resulting child for the purposes of registration;
(5) no one else is treated as the father or parent of the child (see above);
(6) if no one else is treated as the parent of the child by virtue of adoption then the other woman is to be treated as the parent of the child for the purposes of birth registration.

4.7.7 Mistaken transfer of sperm

Where, by mistake of the hospital authorities, the sperm used for IVF treatment was not, as intended, that of the woman's husband but of another man, the husband cannot be treated as the father of the child born to the mother as he had not consented to the use of the donor sperm. The presumption of legitimacy can be displaced by DNA tests to establish that the husband is not the father of the child born to the mother (see *Leeds Teaching Hospital NHS Trust v A & B* [2003] EWHC 259 (QB), [2003] 1 FLR 1091).

The law in this area is evolving and new scenarios will emerge. The statutory provisions and cases cited above are provided as an illustration of the difficulties that may arise and the hurdles to be crossed. It is not intended to be a full exposition of the law in this area. It is essential to be vigilant and aware of new developments. In case of doubt, advice from an expert in this field of law is advised.

4.7.8 A child who is the subject of a parental order

HFEA 1990, s 30 allowed a court to make a 'parental order' providing for a child, who is genetically the child of the husband or wife or both, but has been carried by a surrogate mother, to be treated in law as the child of the husband and wife. Before such an order could be made the court had to be satisfied that:

(1) the husband and wife were married and had attained the age of 18 at the date of the making of the order;
(2) they were domiciled in the United Kingdom or in the Channel Islands or the Isle of Man;
(3) the child had had his home with the husband and wife;
(4) the application for an order was made within 6 months of the birth of the child.

A child who is the subject of a parental order is treated as the child of the marriage or civil partnership (see below) of the couple in whose favour the order is made. The child is not regarded as illegitimate.

The HFEA 2008 repealed HFEA 1990, s 30 and replaced it with the provisions set out in HFEA 2008, s 54.

The first change that has been made by the new provision is to extend the categories of applicants who can apply for a parental order to civil partners, unmarried opposite sex couples and same sex couples who are not in a civil partnership. Initially, a single person could not apply for a parental order. In *Z (A Child: HFEA: Parental Order)* [2015] EWFC 73, Sir James Munby stated the provision could not be 'read down to include an application for a parental order by one person alone because Parliament had made a clear distinction and the provision could not be stretched to go against that grain. However, this situation has now been corrected by inserting an additional section – s 54A (Human Fertilisation and Embryology Act 2008 (Remedial) Order 2018 (SI 2018/1413)) – which now enables one applicant alone to make an application for a parental order if:

(a) the child has been carried by a woman who is not the applicant, as a result of the placing in her of an embryo or sperm and eggs or her artificial insemination;
(b) the gametes of the applicant were used to bring about the creation of the embryo;
(c) the child's home has been with the applicant who is domiciled in the United Kingdom or in the Channel Islands or the Isle of Man; and
(d) the application is made within 6 months of the child's birth.

In addition, the court must be satisfied that the applicant has attained the age of 18 and that the surrogate and any other person who is a parent of the child but is not the applicant (including any person under the fatherhood or female parenthoods conditions set out above) has freely and with full understanding of what is involved agreed unconditionally to the making of the order.

The conditions that must be satisfied before a parental order can be made can be summarised as follows:

(1) the application must be made by two people who must both be 18 years of age or over;
(2) the applicants must be: (a) husband and wife; (b) civil partners of each other; (c) two persons who are living together in an enduring family relationship and are not within prohibited degrees of relationship in relation to each other;
(3) the child must have been carried by a surrogate mother who is not one of the applicants;
(4) the gametes of at least one of the applicants must have been used to bring about the creation of the embryo;
(5) at the time of issuing the application and the making of the order either or both the applicants must be domiciled in the United Kingdom or in the Channel Islands or the Isle of Man;
(6) the child must have his home with the applicants;
(7) the application must be made within 6 months of the child's birth; and
(8) the court must be satisfied that:

    (a) the woman who carried the child and any other person who is a parent of the child but is not one of the applicants have, with full understanding of what is involved, freely and unconditionally agreed to the making of a parental order;
    (b) no money or other benefit (other than for expenses reasonably incurred) has been given or received by either of the applicants for or in consideration of the making of the order or any agreement required for the making of the application or the handing over of the child to the applicants, or the making of arrangements with a view to the making of the order unless authorised by the court;
    (c) the agreement of the woman was given within 6 weeks of the birth of the child.

The agreement of a person who cannot be found or is incapable of giving consent is not required. (See, further, under the commentary in *The Family Court Practice 2022* (LexisNexis, 2022), paras 2.752–2.753 on the issues raised with regard to these considerations and case law on the subject.)

4.7.9 Declaration of parentage, legitimacy and legitimation

The Family Law Act 1986, as amended by the Family Law Reform Act 1987, states that any person may apply to the court for a declaration that:

(a) a person named in the application is or was his parent;
(b) he is the legitimate child of his parents;
(c) he has become a legitimated person;
(d) he has not become a legitimated person.

In order to make the application, the applicant must establish that they are domiciled in England and Wales on the date of the application, or have been habitually resident in England and Wales throughout the period of 1 year preceding the application.

This relief has been repeatedly relied upon by parents in numerous cases resulting from errors made in following the correct procedures or the use of incorrect forms by the registered clinics (see, for example, *Re I (HFEA 2008)* [2016] EWHC 791 (Fam) and *In the Matter of HFEA 2008 (Case M)* [2016] EWHC 1572 (Fam)).

The procedure to be followed is set out in FPR 2010, Part 8, Chapter 5. The application is made on Form C63 issued in the High Court or the Family Court for a declaration. The application must contain the information required on the form and the information set out in FPR 2010, Part 19. A copy of the birth certificate of the person whose parentage is in issue, and a supporting statement which must be verified by a statement of truth, must accompany Form C63. The court may, at any stage of the proceedings, of its own initiative or on the application of any party to the proceedings, direct that the Attorney General be served with the proceedings.

The respondents to the application will generally be the parents, if alive, and the person whose parentage is in issue (if the application is not made by that person, see FPR 2010, r 8.20). In the case where a parent has died, the executors, the beneficiaries and any other person who may be affected by the declaration sought should be made a party to the application for the declaration. Service should be effected in accordance with FPR 2010, Part 6 and PDs 6A–6C. The respondents to the application should file an acknowledgement of service and any statement in answer within 14 days of service (FPR 2010, rr 19.5 and 19.7). The applicant may file a reply within 14 days of the respondents' statement.

The procedure set out in FPR 2010, Part 19 and PD 19A applies to an application for a declaration. The applicant must be heard by a judge. The court may give directions for scientific tests to be undertaken to determine paternity. If paternity is established, the court must make a declaration that the person named in the application is or was the parent of the person whose parentage is in issue.

A similar procedure is followed where a declaration of legitimacy or legitimation is sought under Family Law Act 1986, s 56. The FPR 2010 again apply to such an application. Any declaration made is on Form M31.

4.8 ANY PERSON TREATED AS A CHILD OF THE FAMILY

I(PFD)A 1975, s 1(1)(d), as amended by the CPA 2004 (with effect from 5 December 2005), provided that any application for an order under I(PFD)A 1975, s 2 may be made by 'a person who (not being a child of the deceased) in the case of any marriage or civil partnership to which the deceased was a party was treated by the deceased as a child of the family in relation to that marriage or civil partnership'.

I(PFD)A 1975, s 1(1)(d), as now amended by Inheritance and Trustees' Powers Act 2014, Sch 2, para 2(2), extends this category of potential claimants in relation to deaths occurring after 1 October 2014 to include any person (not being a child of the deceased) who in relation to any marriage/civil partnership to which the deceased was at any time a party or otherwise in relation to any family in which the deceased at any time stood in the role of a parent, was treated by the deceased as a child of the family.

The term 'child of the family' does not, here, have the meaning given to it in the Matrimonial Causes Act 1973. The Family Law Act 1996 does not provide any new definition of 'child of the family'.

Unlike the case under the Matrimonial Causes Act 1973, there is no age limit. An adult child of the deceased has been regarded as a child of the family and entitled to claim under the I(PFD)A 1975. For a claim to proceed in relation to deaths occurring after 1 October 2014, however, the deceased must have been married or in a civil partnership, or otherwise stand in the role of a parent in any family, and the claimant must have been treated by the deceased as a child of the family within that marriage/civil partnership, or otherwise must have been treated as a child of the family in which the deceased stood in the role of a parent. In relation to deaths occurring before 1 October 2014, it will be necessary to show that there was a marriage or civil partnership in relation to which the claimant was treated as a child of the family. In relation to a claim made before October 2014, whether a claimant falls within this category depends on the facts of the individual case. In relation to a case where there was no marriage or civil partnership, the claimant will have to establish that the claimant was a member of a family and that within that family the deceased by his conduct towards the claimant stood as a parent figure and the claimant was treated as a child within that family. The important factor will be the nature of the relationship which the deceased and the claimant had. Since the relationship is now no longer linked to a marriage or civil partnership, it can extend to include a single person or an unmarried couple who lived together with the claimant as part of a family in which the claimant stood as a child; or the relationship could be a relative or relatives who assumed the role of a parent towards the claimant.

The following examples of decided cases may assist.

In *Re Callaghan (Deceased)* [1985] Fam 1, the claimant was a step-son of the deceased. He was 6 years old when his natural father died. Three years later, the deceased came to live in his mother's home as a lodger. Subsequently, the deceased and the mother lived together as man and wife. The deceased treated the claimant as his son. In 1960, the claimant married, but continued to maintain a close relationship with his mother and the deceased. In 1972, the claimant's mother and the deceased married. The mother died in 1980. The claimant continued to care for the deceased until his death. In considering the claim, Booth J said:

> In this case the acknowledgement by the deceased of his own role of grandfather to the plaintiff's children, the confidences as to his property and financial affairs which he placed in the plaintiff, and his dependence on the plaintiff to care for him in his last illness are examples of the deceased's treatment of the plaintiff as a child, albeit an adult child of the family. All these things are part of the privileges and duties of two persons who, in regard to each other, stand in the relationship of parent and child; it is the existence of that relationship that enables the plaintiff to apply under section 1(1)(d) of the Act. My view is not altered by the fact that, in considering an application by a person coming within section 1(1)(d), the court is required to have regard to the education or training of the applicant and must also consider the extent to which the deceased has assumed responsibility for his maintenance.

In *Re Leach (Deceased), Leach v Linderman* [1986] Ch 226, when the claimant's father remarried, the claimant was 32 years of age and was living away from home. The claimant never lived with her father and her step-mother in one household. The claimant's father died in 1974, and the step-mother died in 1981. The claimant applied for an order under I(PFD)A 1975, s 2 for a half share in the net estate. The claim was allowed because the step-mother had, after her marriage and on the death of her husband, expressly and impliedly assumed the position of a parent towards the claimant. Her treatment of the claimant after the death of the claimant's father was a consideration which the court could take into account as it stemmed from the marriage. In his judgment, Slade J said:

> I do not think it is necessary or appropriate to imply any similar temporal limitation in the construction of section 1(1)(d) of the 1975 Act, which is directing attention solely to the treatment of the child by one party to the marriage. The phrase used is not 'during the subsistence of the marriage', it is the wider phrase 'in relation to the marriage'. It seems to me that the treatment of an applicant by a surviving spouse after the death of the other spouse may be a relevant factor in deciding whether the applicant qualifies under section 1(1)(d), provided that such treatment is referable to or 'stems from' the marriage.

Where grandparents or other relatives take on the responsibility of caring for a grandchild or a child related to them, that child may become a child of the family both within Matrimonial Causes Act 1973, s 52, and within the I(PFD)A 1975 (see *Re A (A Child of the Family)* [1998] 1 FLR 347, CA and *Re Debenham (Deceased)* [1986] 1 FLR 404, discussed at paras 6.3 and 7.5). In such cases, the court considers the matter objectively in order to determine the relationship between the grandparents/relative and the child, and whether the services were provided by them by way of support in an emergency, or whether they had assumed primary responsibility for the foreseeable future and cared for and treated the child as their own.

In Antonio v Williams [2022] EWHC 2383 (Ch), the evidence clearly showed that the claimant had been provided with a home and been cared for as part of his aunt's family and maintained by his aunt since his birth and that her will clearly demonstrated her intention to ensure that his needs were provided for. It was eventually accepted that in the circumstances the claimant was treated by the deceased as the child of her family, and that in any event he was eligible to make a claim under I(PFD)A 1975, s 1(1)(e). In a claim made under this head, therefore, the applicant will need to establish that the deceased expressly or impliedly assumed the position of a parent towards the applicant with the attendant responsibilities, obligations and privileges of that relationship.

To summarise, therefore:

(1) 'child', for the purposes of this section, includes an adult child;
(2) the relevant 'treatment' is the behaviour of the deceased towards the claimant;
(3) the treatment need not stem from marriage or civil partnership. It is the nature of the relationship between the claimant and the deceased and the conduct of the deceased towards the claimant that is relevant;
(4) the mere display of affection, kindness and hospitality by a surviving step-parent towards a step-child is not sufficient. Proof that the deceased expressly or impliedly assumed the position of a parent or took on the

role of a parent towards the claimant, with the attendant responsibilities and privileges of that relationship, are the relevant factors.

4.9 ANY PERSON (NOT BEING A PERSON INCLUDED IN THE FOREGOING PARAGRAPHS) WHO IMMEDIATELY BEFORE THE DEATH OF THE DECEASED WAS BEING MAINTAINED EITHER WHOLLY OR PARTLY BY THE DECEASED

This provision applies as a net to enable any other person who does not fall within the specific categories referred to above to make a claim. The words in parentheses suggest that the claim cannot be made by a person who falls within I(PFD)A 1975, s 1(1)(a)–(d). However, this does not prevent a person who falls within the other categories to apply for financial provision under this class in the alternative, for instance, where the claimant is not sure that they will be able to establish the required relationship between them and the deceased, for example, a cohabitant where the period of cohabitation is in dispute or a claimant who makes a claim as a child of the family where there is a dispute as to the nature of the relationship between the claimant and the deceased. Note, however, that to fall within this class, the claimant must establish that, immediately before the death of the deceased, they were being maintained wholly or partly by the deceased. This is further qualified by the provision set out under s 1(3), which identifies the nature of the financial dependence which the claimant must be able to establish. How this is assessed is dependent on whether the deceased died before or after 1 October 2014 because s 1(3) has been amended by the Inheritance and Trustees' Powers Act 2014 which came into force on 1 October 2014. Therefore, the factors in relation to the nature of the dependency which will need consideration will depend on whether the deceased died before or after 1 October 2014. The issues that need to be considered in relation to this class are discussed below.

4.9.1 Being maintained

In relation to deaths occurring before 1 October 2014, I(PFD)A 1975, s 1(3) (before its amendment) provides that:

> (3) For the purposes of subsection (1)(e) above, a person shall be treated as being maintained by the deceased, either wholly or partly, as the case may be, if the deceased, *otherwise than for full valuable consideration*, was making a substantial contribution in money or money's worth towards the reasonable needs of that person. (emphasis added)

In relation to deaths occurring after 1 October 2014, the amended I(PFD)A 1975, s 1(3) provides:

> (3) For the purposes of subsection (1)(e) above, a person is to be treated as being maintained by the deceased (either wholly or partly, as the case may be) only if the deceased was making a substantial contribution in money or money's worth towards the reasonable needs of that person, other than a contribution made for full *valuable consideration pursuant to an arrangement of a commercial nature*. (emphasis added)

The I(PFD)A 1975 does not make any other reference to the meaning of 'being maintained'. Thus it will be observed that in relation to a claim made under s 1(1)(e), where the deceased died before 1 October 2014 a claimant had to show that the contribution made if any was not for full valuable consideration irrespective of whether or not it was pursuant to an arrangement of a commercial nature.

In addition, although not a bar to a claim, in assessing the merit of the claim factors which the court is required to take into account under I(PFD)A 1975, s 3(4) are relevant. Before s 3(4) was amended, amongst the factors which the court was required to consider when determining a claim under s 1(1)(e) was 'to have regard to the extent to which and the basis on which the deceased assumed responsibility for the maintenance of the applicant and the length of time for which the deceased discharged that responsibility'.

I(PFD)A 1975, s 3(4) as amended by the Inheritance and Trustees' Powers Act 2014 now provides that:

> (4) ... where an application for an order under section 2 of this Act is made by virtue of section 1(1)(e) of this Act the court shall, in addition to the matters specifically mentioned in paragraphs (a) to (f) of that subsection, have regard—
>
> (a) to the length of time for which and basis on which the deceased maintained the applicant, and to the extent of the contribution made by way of maintenance;
> (b) to whether and, if so, to what extent the deceased assumed responsibility for the maintenance of the applicant.

Therefore, under the amended I(PFD)A 1975, s 3(4), the emphasis is on ascertaining to what extent the deceased maintained the applicant.

These provisions read together identify what must now be established. This includes:

(1) the contribution made by the deceased must be a substantial contribution in money or money's worth;
(2) the contribution must have been for the maintenance of the claimant and to provide for their reasonable needs;
(3) the contribution must not have been made for full and valuable consideration pursuant to an arrangement of a commercial nature;
(4) the payments must have been made immediately before the death of the deceased;
(5) the length of time for which, and the basis on which, the deceased maintained the applicant and the extent of the contribution made by way of maintenance and whether and, if so, to what extent the deceased assumed responsibility for the maintenance of the applicant.

What needs to be established is the fact that the claimant was being *maintained* by the deceased; that their contribution towards the claimant's maintenance was *substantial*; and that it was to meet the *reasonable needs* of the claimant.

4.9.2 Substantial contribution

I(PFD)A 1975, s 1(3), both in its original and amended forms, requires that the contribution made by the deceased towards the maintenance of the claimant must be 'substantial'. Before October 2014, the issue of whether there was valuable consideration for such contribution resulted in the court assessing what the deceased was contributing against what the claimant's contributions were. Where the claimant was contributing more than the deceased or where the contributions were equal, there would be no dependency. Where there was doubt about the balance tipping in favour of the deceased's contribution being the greater, then the claimant was given the benefit of any doubt and entitled to succeed. See *Jelley v Iliffe* [1981] Fam 128, where Griffiths LJ stated that:

> the court must use common sense and remember that the object of Parliament in creating this extra class of persons who may claim benefit from an estate was to provide relief for persons of whom it could truly be said that they were wholly or partially dependent on the deceased.

In *Jelley v Iliffe*, the claimant was a widower, and had lived with his daughter before he went to live with the deceased. The deceased lived in a house which had been conveyed to her by her children on the understanding that she would leave it to them on her death. The claimant and the deceased shared the accommodation and pooled their resources. The claimant also did the household jobs and the gardening. He lived in the house rent-free. On her death, the deceased left all her property to her children and nothing to the claimant. The claimant's claim was allowed.

In determining whether the deceased had made a 'substantial contribution' to the claimant's needs, the court must approach the problem in the round, apply a common-sense approach, and avoid fine balancing computations involving the value of normal exchanges of support in the domestic sense (see *Bishop v Plumley* [1991] 1 WLR 582).

In *Malone v Harrison* [1979] 1 WLR 1353, the deceased had failed to make any provision for his second mistress, who had been wholly supported by the deceased; she was awarded a lump sum.

In *Lindop v Agus, Bass and Hedley* [2009] EWHC 1795 (Ch), the claimant, in addition to claiming that she and the deceased had lived together as husband and wife, also claimed in the alternative that she had been maintained by him as he had provided her with a home for which he had paid all the outgoings until his death and that he had also provided her with transport to travel to and from work and had also paid for her holidays and her wardrobe.

In *Bouette v Rose* [2001] 1 FLR 363, the deceased's financial affairs were managed by the Court of Protection and the deceased's mother who cared for her disabled daughter and to whom regular payments were made by the Court of Protection. On the daughter's death, the mother made a claim under the I(PFD)A 1975. On appeal, the Court of Appeal held that it must have been obvious to the Court of Protection that the payments made to the mother would necessarily be used to meet the mother's financial and material needs, particularly as, on the facts, the mother had made no contribution toward the household expenses. There was nothing absurd in the notion of the Court of Protection acting as the conscience of the patient and making provision for those to whom the patient would have felt a moral obligation if the patient had been of full capacity. On the facts, it would have been obvious to the Court of Protection that the payments made to the mother were also providing the financial and material needs of the mother throughout the deceased's life.

Antonio v Williams [2022] EWHC 2383 (Ch) provides a recent example of a case where had the child not been considered to be a child of the deceased's family, the claim would have succeeded under I(PFD)A 1975, s 1(1)(e) because of the deceased's assumption of responsibility for the maintenance and other needs of the minor claimant during her lifetime and her intention to ensure that he would continue to have his needs provided for from her estate.

Thus whether the deceased made a substantial contribution to another's reasonable needs depends, therefore, on the circumstances of the parties and their relationship. All the contributions made, whether in kind or otherwise, are taken into account. The deceased's 'motives or intentions are irrelevant except insofar as s 3(4) makes them relevant to the court's task of deciding whether or not to make provision for the claimant and if so in what form and what scale' (per Walker LJ in *Bouette v Rose* [2001] 1 FLR 363). The court has to consider whether the deceased, otherwise than for valuable consideration, was in fact making a substantial contribution in money or money's worth towards the reasonable needs of the applicant on a settled basis which either was still in force immediately before the deceased's death, or would have lasted until death, but for the approach of death and the consequent inability of either party to continue to carry out the arrangement, unless the circumstantial evidence suggests that the deceased had made it clear that they did not assume such responsibility or that their actions should not be taken to mean that the support afforded to the claimant would continue. It is not necessary, however, to prove that the deceased had intended to maintain the claimant after the deceased's death. Such an intention may be inferred from the conduct of the deceased, particularly where the conduct was such that the claimant had been made wholly or partly dependent on the deceased, as was the case in *Graham v Murphy* [1997] 1 FLR 860. There, the deceased and the claimant had lived together from 1976 until 1993 when the deceased died. The deceased had a substantial income, whereas the claimant was a lorry driver with an average wage of £160 per week. By reason of the deceased's income, the couple were able to live a comfortable life including eating out and going for holidays abroad which were paid for by the deceased. In 1990, the deceased became ill. Throughout her illness until her death the claimant cared for and provided support for the deceased. The claim was allowed, although the court referred to it as 'quite close to borderline'. The provisions of Law Reform (Succession) Act 1995, s 2 were not then in force. Had they been, the claimant would have succeeded in any event as a cohabitant of the deceased.

A situation similar to that in *Graham v Murphy* arose in *Bishop v Plumley* (see para 4.6). In *Re Haig, Powers v Haig* [1979] LS Gaz R 476, the claimant had lived with the deceased as his wife for 3 years preceding his death. She was given the right to occupy his house rent-free.

4.9.3 Reasonable needs

In determining the issue of whether the deceased had maintained the claimant to provide for their reasonable needs it will be necessary for the court to consider the interaction between the provisions of I(PFD)A 1975, ss 1(3) and 3. The claimant will need to satisfy the court not only that the claimant was being maintained either wholly or partly by the deceased immediately before their death, but also the duration and extent of, and the basis on which, the contributions were made and whether and, if so, to what extent the deceased had assumed responsibility for the claimant (see *Antonio v Williams* [2022] EWHC 2383 (Ch) for a recent example where the deceased had assumed responsibility for her nephew). An outright gift of a house many years before the death of the deceased may not constitute maintenance even if the claimant continued to live in the house, as it would be an asset over which the deceased had no control (see *Baynes v Hedger and Others* [2009] EWCA Civ 374, [2009] 2 FLR 767).

In considering the claim, the court is required to look not at the *de facto* state of the maintenance existing at the moment of death, but at the state and extent of the maintenance arrangement generally between the deceased and the claimant, using the date of death on which the arrangement would be considered.

Case law provides some guidance on what would have to be proved to establish 'reasonable needs'. In *Re Coventry, Coventry v Coventry* [1980] Ch 461, Goff J referred to cases in which the meaning of maintenance was considered. He said:

> In particular, in this country there is *Re E, E v E* ([1966] 1 WLR 709, [1966] All ER 44), in which Stamp J said that the purpose was not to keep a person above the breadline but to provide reasonable maintenance in all the circumstances. If I may say so with respect, 'breadline' there would be more accurately described as 'subsistence level'. Then there was *Millward v Shenton* ([1972] 1 WLR 711, [1972] 2 All ER 1025) in this court. I think I need only refer to one of the overseas reports … *Duranceau* ([1952] 3 DLR 714) where, in somewhat poetic language, the court said that the question is 'Is the provision sufficient to enable the dependant to live neither luxuriously or miserably, but decently and comfortably according to his or her station in life?'. What is proper maintenance must in all cases depend upon all the facts and circumstances of the particular case being considered at the time, but I think it is clear on the one hand that one must not put too limited a meaning on it; it does not mean just enough to enable a person to get by, on the other hand, it does not mean anything which may be regarded as reasonably desirable for his general benefit or welfare.

Reasonable needs may also mean reasonable requirements, and in considering this the court must necessarily consider the factors which it is required to take into account under I(PFD)A 1975, s 3. In *Harrington v Gill* (1983) 4 FLR 265 (CA), the deceased and the claimant had cohabited together for 8 years before the deceased's death in the deceased's house. The claimant had retained the tenancy of her council flat. She carried out all the household duties and the deceased had paid all the outgoings. The claimant, who worked, also spent all her earnings on household extras, clothes and other necessaries. She made no contribution towards her board and lodgings. The deceased died intestate and his estate, worth about £65,000, went to his daughter, who was financially comfortable. At the date of the hearing the claimant was 74. Her income consisted of the state pension. She was living in the deceased's house, but had surrendered the council tenancy. On appeal, it was held that, in considering the needs of the claimant, the court will, among other things, consider the extent to which the deceased had undertaken responsibility for the claimant, the standard of living enjoyed by the claimant during the deceased's lifetime, and the extent to which the deceased contributed to that standard of living. Dunn LJ said:

> The scheme of the Act, as set out in the sections, is a little complicated, but at the end of the day the court must ask itself the question: What testamentary provision would a reasonable man in the position of this deceased have made for the plaintiff in all the circumstances, including the matters set out in section 3?
>
> In *Re Watson (Deceased)* [1999] 1 FLR 878 the deceased and the applicant had had a relationship over 30 years but they had not lived together until 1985 when they ceased to have the responsibility of caring for their elderly parents. Thereafter, the claimant moved in to live with the deceased until he went into hospital where he died. In considering her 'reasonable needs' and whether it requires the court to take into account the resources and assets of the applicant at the relevant time Neuberger J (as he then was) said, "I am not sure that that is a question which is capable of being answered unequivocally in the abstract. Bearing in mind the purpose of the Act it appears to be wrong, at least in general, to seek to fetter the meaning of any particular expression in it further than the legislature has done. However, it is fair to say that one would, on the face of it, expect the word 'needs' in section 1(3) to have the same meaning, for instance, as the word 'needs' in s 3(1)(a), (b) and (c) of the same Act."

However, he pointed out that a contrast needs to be made between the provision of I(PFD)A 1975, ss 1(3) and 3 as the 'needs' referred to in s 1(3) related to the needs of the applicant at and a little time before the deceased's death, whereas the 'needs' referred to in s 3 referred to the needs at the date of the hearing and for the foreseeable future (s 3(5)).

In *Re Viner (Deceased), Kreeger v Cooper* [1978] CLY 3091, the claim was by a woman aged 74. She had been widowed for a year before her brother's death, and was left in difficult circumstances. The brother had been persuaded by another sister, to whom he was voluntarily paying £10 per week, partly to maintain the claimant. He agreed to divide the weekly payments of £10 between his two sisters, and grudgingly paid £5 per week to the claimant for 6 months prior to his death. By his will, the deceased left an annuity to his unmarried sister, but nothing to the claimant. The residue of his estate was left to a person with whom he had worked. On the facts, the claimant succeeded.

In *Rees v Newbery and the Institute for Cancer Research* [1988] 1 FLR 1041, for almost 10 years before the death of the deceased, the claimant had lived in a flat owned by the deceased. He had paid to the deceased rent below the market rent. The deceased had given instructions for a new will which was to provide that the claimant should continue living at the property under the existing arrangements for life. Before the will could be executed, the deceased died. The claim was allowed because the deceased had not only expressly indicated his intention, but the arrangement between the deceased and the claimant before death led to the inference that the claimant had been maintained by the deceased, that he had assumed responsibility for the claimant's maintenance, and that he was making a substantial contribution towards the reasonable needs of the claimant. For a recent example, see *Antonio v Williams* [2022] EWHC 2383 (Ch), where although the claim succeeded on the basis that the claimant was a child of the deceased's family, it was also observed that in view of the deceased's substantial maintenance of the claimant since his birth, the claim would have succeeded under I(PFD)A 1975, s 1(1)(e). The case illustrates the extent to which the evidence will be scrutinised to assess the claimant's assumption of responsibility.

4.9.4 Otherwise than for full valuable consideration pursuant to an arrangement of a commercial nature

I(PFD)A 1975, s 25(1) defines 'full valuable consideration' to exclude 'marriage or a promise of marriage'. This will also exclude a civil partnership or a promise to enter into a civil partnership with the claimant. In relation to cases where the deceased has died after 1 October 2014, the fact that there has been full valuable contribution will not affect the claim unless it was made as a result of a commercial arrangement between the deceased and the claimant. In cases falling before the amendments made to the Act, the court will need to evaluate the contribution that was made by the claimant to assess whether the contributions of the deceased and those made by the claimant, if any, would amount to '*full* valuable consideration'. Where some valuable consideration was accepted by the deceased from the claimant for meeting the claimant's needs, the nature and extent of the consideration they received will be relevant. For example, *Rees v Newbery and the Institute for Cancer Research* (see para 4.9.3), where the claimant had paid to the deceased rent below the market rent and the deceased had clearly expressed his intention that this arrangement should continue after his death for life, is a good example of a case where it was held that the deceased had maintained the claimant and that the rent received could not be said to be in 'full' consideration of that privilege.

In *Re Wilkinson (Deceased), Neale v Newell* [1978] Fam 22, Arnold J, when assessing the value of the contributions made by the claimant, said:

> It is not very easy, when one is dealing with the question of what is full valuable consideration, to measure in purely financial terms the sort of things which the applicant was doing for the deceased and the sort of thing which the applicant represented to the deceased ... Somehow it seems to me I have to measure those matters in order to see whether, fairly looked at, they were a full valuable requital or return for that which the applicant received from the deceased.

In *Re Wilkinson*, the sister of the deceased had left her employment at the age of 61 to look after the deceased. The deceased had paid for all the food and met the household expenses. The claimant had done the light housework and the cooking. The heavier tasks were carried out by a home help and a sister-in-law. Having carried out a balancing exercise, the court held that the deceased had made a substantial contribution to the claimant's needs, and that the duties that the claimant performed for the deceased could not be regarded as full valuable consideration in return for the contribution made by the deceased. See, also, para 4.9.2.

King v Dubrey [2014] EWHC 2083 (Ch) is another helpful example on how the court deals with the issue of contributions made by the deceased. The deputy judge set this out as follows (at [63] and [64]):

> 63. In relation to the 1975 Act claim I find as follows (1) Mr King moved into June's house in 2007. The purpose of moving in was to care for her, and he did so until she died (2) in return for the care, he was receiving board and lodging, expenses and small sums of money (3) that followed a settled pattern and involved assumptions of responsibility on both sides – on June's side for maintaining Mr King and on Mr King's side for looking after June (4) Mr King did not work during the period when he was caring for June, with very modest exceptions, nor realistically could he do so (5) since June died, Mr King has not worked and has not been able to maintain himself (6) whilst one might say that there was a balance to be struck between Mr King's services as a carer and the board, lodging and money he received from June, so that there was no dependency, adopting the approach in *Jelley v Iliffe*, I do not think such an approach would be correct. The realistic analysis is that there was maintenance in money and money's worth for a lengthy period and an assumption of responsibility for such maintenance by the deceased to a considerable extent and on a settled basis. (7) [T]he evidence of the failed wills seems to me that June accepted that she had assumed a responsibility for Mr King.
>
> 64. I find that Mr King falls within s1(1)(e) of the 1975 Act and that June otherwise than for full valuable consideration was making a substantial contribution in money or money's worth towards the reasonable needs of that person.

Although the examples all relate to cases before 1 October 2014, they give an indication of the nature and extent of the contributions made by the deceased which the court has taken into account. For cases that fall within the amended I(PFD)A 1975, s 1(3), the issue of full valuable contribution will apply only if the arrangement between the parties was of a commercial nature, for example, where paid services were provided.

4.9.5 Immediately before the death of the deceased

In claims under I(PFD)A 1975, s 1(1)(e), the relationship between the deceased and the claimant must have been continuing at the date of the death, and the claimant must show that the deceased was maintaining the claimant immediately before the death of the deceased. If the arrangement had ceased before the date of death, the claim will fail no matter how short the period. Thus, where cohabitation between the deceased and the claimant had ended 2 years before the death of the deceased, the claim failed (see *Layton v Martin* [1986] 2 FLR 227).

Where the deceased had left his mistress 9 days before he died, it was held that she was not being maintained by him immediately before his death and the claim failed (see *Kourkgy v Lusher* (1983) 4 FLR 65).

In *Sen v Headley* [1991] Ch 425, the claimant was obliged to make a claim under the doctrine of *donatio mortis causa* as she was not being maintained by the deceased immediately before his death.

On the other hand, the court does have regard to the circumstances which led to the break. Dependence is not measured in days or weeks, particularly where the separation has been forced or is involuntary, for example where the deceased becomes terminally ill and has to be admitted to hospital. In *Re Beaumont (Deceased), Martin v Midland Bank Trust Co Ltd* [1980] Ch 444, Megarry VC said:

> If one is to reject a mere examination of the de facto state of affairs existing at the instant of death, and seek to discover something more substantial and enduring than that, then an assumption by the deceased of responsibility for the maintenance of the applicant seems to me to be the relationship which has to be considered. If immediately before the death of the deceased such an assumption of responsibility by the deceased for the applicant was in existence, and under it the applicant was being maintained, wholly or partly, by the deceased, then the applicant may claim under the Act. In such a case the degree of maintenance would not be whatever degree existed at the instant before death but whatever degree normally and habitually existed under the assumption of responsibility which was then in existence.

In *Re Kirby (Deceased), Hirons v Rolfe* (1982) 3 FLR 249, the court applied the test of 'the settled pattern of arrangements between the parties ignoring any transitory interruption owing to changes of circumstances occurring immediately before the death and possibly in anticipation of it'. In *Re Watson (Deceased)* [1999] 1 FLR 878, although the point was not raised by the Treasury Solicitor, Neuberger J (as he then was) said that if it had, it was not an argument which in his view could respectably have been advanced, and that as a matter of ordinary language, the fact that someone is in hospital for even a long period at the end of which he dies does not mean that 'he ceased to be part of the household of which he was a part until he was forced by illness to go to hospital and to which he would have returned had he not died'.

It would seem, therefore, that the court will not apply the words of the section strictly, but consider the facts and the circumstances which led to the separation, and the parties' relationship, and take a broad and practical decision (see, further, para 4.6.1).

Chapter 5

Forfeiture

5.1 INTRODUCTION

The forfeiture rule is a common law rule of public policy which, in certain circumstances, precludes a person who has unlawfully killed another from acquiring a benefit in consequence of the killing. It applies to succession under wills and intestacy.

Such an offender may not take any benefit which would otherwise accrue to them under a disposition made in the victim's will, or on the victim's intestacy. The whole of any disposition in favour of the offender fails. The offender and their successors in title are prevented from acquiring any benefit under any disposition made by the deceased in their will or under the laws of intestacy. The forfeiture rule does not apply to the interest of a discretionary beneficiary under a lifetime trust settled by the beneficiary's victim, who was the ultimate beneficiary of the trust (see *Henderson v Wilcox* [2015] EWHC 3269 (Ch); and see, further, para 5.6). Thus where the offender is the only child of the victim, their inheritance goes to other relatives. All descendants of the offender are excluded, for example the offender's child and the grandchild of the victim, as occurred in *Re DWS (Deceased)* [2001] Ch 568, CA, where a person killed both his parents, neither of whom left a will. The offender was not allowed to inherit from them by reason of the forfeiture rule. The Court of Appeal decided that not only he, but also his son, was excluded from inheriting and the deceased's estate passed to other relatives. This consequence was rectified by the Estates of Deceased Persons (Forfeiture Rule and Law of Succession) Act 2011, which came into force on 1 February 2012. This Act now provides that, irrespective of whether the deceased died testate or intestate, the unlawful killer is deemed to have died immediately before the deceased. This means that as from 1 February 2012: (1) where an intestacy arises, the issue (including the children of the unlawful killer), will be able to inherit under the intestacy rules; and (2) where the deceased made a will, the person next entitled to the property in place of the unlawful killer will be able to inherit, unless a contrary intention is expressed.

However, under Forfeiture Act 1982, s 2, the court is empowered to modify and mitigate to some extent these effects. It has limited the operation of the rule in respect of claims made under the I(PFD)A 1975 in cases where the claimant is convicted of unlawful killing after 13 October 1982, the date the Forfeiture Act 1982 came into force. The Forfeiture Act 1982 enables a person who has unlawfully killed another to make a claim under any of the provisions of the I(PFD)A 1975 for financial provision from the estate of the deceased. Note, however, that this provision is limited to 'unlawful killing'. It does not apply where the person is convicted of murder.

5.2 ORDER MODIFYING THE EFFECT OF THE RULE

Forfeiture Act 1982, s 2(1), empowers the court, when determining a claim under I(PFD)A 1975, s 2, to make an order modifying the effect of the forfeiture rule. Forfeiture Act 1982, s 2 provides as follows:

> (1) Where a court determines that the forfeiture rule has precluded a person (in this section referred to as 'the offender') who has unlawfully killed another from acquiring any interest in property mentioned in subsection (4) below, the court may make an order under this section modifying the effect of that rule.
>
> (2) The court shall not make an order under this section modifying the effect of the forfeiture rule in any case unless it is satisfied that, having regard to the conduct of the offender and of the deceased and to such other circumstances as appear to the court to be material, the justice of the case requires the effect of the rule to be so modified in that case.
>
> (3) In any case where a person stands convicted of an offence of which unlawful killing is an element, the court shall not make an order under this section modifying the effect of the forfeiture rule in that case unless proceedings for the purpose are brought before the expiry of the period of three months beginning with his conviction.
>
> (4) The interests in property referred to in subsection (1) above are—
>
> (a) any beneficial interest in property which (apart from the forfeiture rule) the offender would have acquired—
>
> (i) under the deceased's will … or the law relating to intestacy or by way of *ius relicti*, *ius relictae* or *legitim*;
> (ii) on the nomination of the deceased in accordance with the provisions of any enactment;
> (iii) as a *donatio mortis causa* made by the deceased; or
> (iv) under a special destination (whether relating to heritable or moveable property); or
>
> (b) any beneficial interest in property which (apart from the forfeiture rule) the offender would have acquired in consequence of the death of the

deceased, being property which, before the death, was held on trust for any person.

(5) An order under this section may modify the effect of the forfeiture rule in respect of any interest in property to which the determination referred to in subsection (1) above relates and may do so in either or both of the following ways, that is—

(a) where there is more than one such interest, by excluding the application of the rule in respect of any (but not all) of those interests; and
(b) in the case of any such interest in property, by excluding the application of the rule in respect of part of the property.

(6) On the making of an order under this section, the forfeiture rule shall have effect for all purposes (including purposes relating to anything done before the order is made) subject to the modifications made by the order.
(7) The court shall not make an order under this section modifying the effect of the forfeiture rule in respect of any interest in property which, in consequence of the rule, has been acquired before the coming into force of this section by a person other than an offender or a person claiming through him.
(8) In this section—

'property' includes any chose in action or incorporeal moveable property; and 'will' includes codicil.

It will be observed that the court's powers are limited in the following respects:

- The court's power is discretionary (s 2(2)).
- The court cannot make an order modifying the effect of the rule unless it is 'satisfied, having regard to the conduct of the offender and of the deceased and to such other circumstances as appear to the court to be material, that the justice of the case requires the effect to be modified' in that case. The moral culpability of the offender and the justice of the case are matters which are relevant (s 2(2)).
- The court cannot make an order modifying the effect of the rule unless proceedings for the modification of the rule are commenced before the expiry of 3 months from the date of the offender's conviction. There is no power to extend the time limit (s 2(3)).
- The court cannot modify the rule in respect of any interest in property which, in consequence of the rule, has been acquired before the coming into force of s 2 by a person other than the offender or a person claiming through them (s 2(7)).
- The court has no power to modify the effect of the rule if the offender has been convicted of murder.
- The court may modify the rule by totally or partially excluding the forfeiture rule's application to relevant property or interest.
- Property includes all benefits by way of succession.

If the court decides that relief should be granted, it may:

(1) order that the forfeiture rule should not apply to any of the property, thus allowing the property to devolve as if no cause for forfeiture existed; or
(2) reject the application of the rule to the whole of the property (see *Dalton v Latham* [2003] EWHC 796 (Ch));
(3) apply the rule to some parts of the property and to others by identifying the particular assets, interests or property or percentage of the estate; or
(4) make other provisions for the property, for example order that the proceeds of an insurance policy be put into a trust for a child (see *Re S (Deceased) (Forfeiture Rule)* [1996] 1 WLR 235).

Forfeiture Act 1982, s 3 provides that the forfeiture rule shall not be taken to preclude any person from making an application under the I(PFD)A 1975. This appears to include an unlawful killing, including murder.

Although Forfeiture Act 1982, s 3 clearly entitles a claimant convicted of unlawfully killing to make an application under the I(PFD)A 1975, in view of the decision in *Re Royse (Deceased), Royse v Royse* [1985] Fam 22 (see below), it was thought that the forfeiture rule prevented such an application to be made or, if made, from succeeding.

In *Re Royse (Deceased), Royse v Royse*, the claimant was convicted of the manslaughter of her husband and committed to hospital under Mental Health Act 1959, s 60. On 31 March 1981, she was discharged from hospital and returned to live in the former matrimonial home, which was valued at £30,000, and which comprised the major part of the net estate of £32,000. The claimant was the sole beneficiary of the deceased's estate under his will. The claimant applied for financial provision to be made for her, because she was precluded from acquiring any benefit by reason of the forfeiture rule. The application failed because the absence of reasonable financial provision was a consequence of a rule of public policy which precluded her from receiving any benefit under the will. It was not and could not be attributed to her husband's will, which had made reasonable provision for her. The court also ruled that the forfeiture rule, apart from Forfeiture Act 1982, s 3(1) applied to the I(PFD)A 1975 and, therefore, the court did not have any discretion to consider making an order. The claimant's application under the Forfeiture Act 1982 also failed since that Act was not in force when she made the claim. This would not apply today by virtue of the fact that in any case issued after 13 October 1982, the provisions of the Forfeiture Act 1982 apply. It would also be considered as Convention non-compliant and, by reason of Human Rights Act 1998, s 3, the court is under an obligation to construe statutory provisions, in this case the Forfeiture Act 1982, in a way which make them Convention-compliant.

The case of *Land v Land* [2006] EWHC 2069 (Ch) confirms that it is unlikely that the court will adopt this position in future. In *Land*, the applicant was the sole executor and beneficiary under his mother's will. He was convicted on his plea of guilty of manslaughter of his mother. He applied for relief under Forfeiture Act 1982, s 2(1), but the application was made out of time, so his claim failed; whereupon he made an application under the I(PFD)A1975. Having regard to the decision in *Re Royse (Deceased), Royse v Royse*, the issue for determination was whether the court could make an order for financial provision in his favour even though his mother had, in fact, made proper provisions for him in her will, which could not take effect because of the forfeiture rule. The court on this occasion took the view that Forfeiture Act 1982, s 3 permitted the court to make an order even though it was the forfeiture rule and not the deceased's will which gave rise to the situation where no reasonable financial provision had been made for the claimant. The judge also took into account the impact of the Human Rights Convention on UK legislation.

Hence, it would seem that a claimant who is convicted of unlawful killing may either seek relief under the Forfeiture Act 1982 or pursue a claim under the I(PFD)A 1975. The decision on which route to follow may depend on which process entitles the claimant to a greater benefit. It will be more advantageous to apply for relief under the Forfeiture Act 1982 if the claimant's entitlement under the deceased's will or intestacy is greater than that which they would receive by way of 'reasonable financial provision' under the I(PFD)A 1975. Note, however, that any application under the Forfeiture Act 1982 must be made within 3 months of the date of the conviction. The court does not have the power to extend this time limit.

5.3 THREE-MONTH TIME LIMIT – WHEN TIME BEGINS TO RUN

As noted above, the 3-month time limit beginning with the conviction for bringing a claim under the Forfeiture Act 1982 is a fixed period with no power given to the court to exercise its discretion to extend the period. The question therefore arises – what is the date from which time begins to be calculated, particularly where there is a delay between the end of the trial and the jury's verdict and sentence or where there is an appeal pending on the conviction and or the sentence imposed? Where a person is convicted after a trial of murder but that conviction is quashed on appeal and a retrial is directed, time does not begin from the date of the conviction or the end of the appeal because the conviction is quashed. Where there is delay in the retrial and the eventual date when the person is sentenced or between conviction and sentence, the relevant date for the purposes of Forfeiture Act 1982, s 2(1) when time begins to run is the date when the accused person is finally sentenced (see *Challen v Challen* [2020] EWHC 1330 (Ch)).

5.4 RELEVANT FACTORS FOR MODIFYING THE EFFECT OF THE ACT

Forfeiture Act 1982, s 2(2) restricts the court's power to modify the effect of the forfeiture rule unless it is satisfied that having regard to the conduct of the offender and the deceased and to such other material circumstances, the justice of the case requires the effect of the rule to be modified. Case law provides some guidance on how the courts have interpreted the factors set out in s 2(2) to meet the justice of the case. The result, however, is that there are no strict principles that apply, and much depends on the facts and circumstances of each case.

In *Dunbar v Plant* [1998] Ch 412 (see para 5.5), Mummery LJ said (at p 427):

> [Section 2(2)] requires that the judge should look at the case in the round, pay regard to all the material circumstances, including the conduct of the offender and the deceased, and then ask whether 'the justice of the case requires' a modification of the effect of the forfeiture rule ... The court is entitled to take into account a whole range of circumstances relevant to the discretion, quite apart from the conduct of the offender and the deceased: the relationship between them; the degree of moral culpability for what has happened; the nature and gravity of the offence; the intentions of the deceased; the size of the estate and the value of the property in dispute; the financial position of the offender; and the moral claims and wishes of those who would be entitled to take the property on the application of the forfeiture rule.

And Phillip LJ stated (at p 438) that:

> The discretion is a broad one, and it is legitimate to have regard to all the consequences of the order, but it is not right to approach the exercise of the discretion as if dealing simply with an *inter partes* dispute … The first, and paramount consideration, must be whether the culpability attending the beneficiary's criminal conduct was such as to justify the application of the forfeiture rule at all …

The end result will be governed by what appears to the court to meet with the justice of the case.

Conduct of the offender and the deceased is a specific factor that the court is required to take into account along with any other relevant circumstances. So the canvas on which the decision is made is fairly wide, with the importance given to what 'the justice of the case requires'. Abuse suffered by the offender at the hands of the deceased is a material factor, as is the fact that the actions of the offender were not intentional or where the act is done out of mercy, such as by those involved in assisted dying. The cases of *Challen v Challen* [2020] EWHC 1330 (Ch) (see below), *Amos v Mancini* [2020] EWHC 1063 (Ch) and *Ninian v Findlay* [2019] EWHC 297 (Ch) are examples where these issues were found to be relevant and material.

In *Challen v Challen* [2020] EWHC 1330 (Ch), the deceased and the applicant had been in a relationship for many years. Throughout their relationship and cohabitation the applicant suffered serious frequent and intolerable domestic abuse and controlling and coercive behaviour at the hands of the deceased. Her will eventually broke and one day she used a hammer on him which caused his death. At the second trial, she pleaded guilty to manslaughter but due to the time she had spent in custody she was discharged from custody. Thereupon she applied for the disapplication of the forfeiture rule to enable her to inherit the former matrimonial home. Apart from the court having to determine when time begins to run for the purposes of the statutory 3-month time limit, the court also considered the test to be applied in such cases and whether the exceptional circumstances of the applicant's case were such as to justify, in the interests of justice, for the court to exercise its discretion for relief to be granted to her. Although the case clearly came within the forfeiture rule the court took into account the level of abuse the applicant had suffered during the whole of the 40-year relationship between her and the deceased, the views of the applicant's children who supported her application, the fact that the deceased died intestate and the sentencing judge's remarks when sentencing her. When allowing her application the court emphasised that 'the fact of this terrible case are so extraordinary with such a fatal combination of conditions and events that I would not expect them to be replicated in any other'.

In *Amos v Mancini* [2020] EWHC 1063 (Ch), the deceased died from the injuries he suffered when the car driven by his wife was involved in a road traffic accident caused due to a lapse of concentration and therefore not a deliberate act with intent to cause harm. The beneficiaries who stood to inherit were not opposed to the wife's application for the court to disapply the forfeiture rule. All these factors were considered sufficient to justify the court exercising its discretion.

In *Ninian v Findlay* [2019] EWHC 297 (Ch), the deceased's wife was the applicant. She had accompanied him to the Dignitas clinic at his insistence, although she had made it absolutely clear that she was opposed to this. The evidence adduced at the hearing established that she had done all she could to dissuade him. The fact that she was not prosecuted for any offence was also a factor taken into account by the court. Her application was granted.

5.5 FURTHER ILLUSTRATION OF THE APPLICATION OF SECTION 2(2)

The following older cases also provide further illustration of how the court has considered the application of Forfeiture Act 1982, s 2(2).

In *Re K (Deceased)* [1985] Ch 85, there had been a history of ill-treatment of the wife by the deceased during their marriage. On 30 September 1982, during an altercation, the deceased was killed at short range by a shotgun held by the wife. The wife was charged with murder but pleaded guilty to manslaughter. She was placed on probation. The deceased had bequeathed his residuary estate on trust to his widow for life and thereafter to four named beneficiaries. The estate was worth £412,000. The matrimonial home was held on a joint tenancy, so the widow was entitled to the deceased's half share. The residuary beneficiaries contended that, notwithstanding the provisions of Forfeiture Act 1982, s 7(4), which enabled the court to modify the operation of the forfeiture rule, and whether the killing occurred before or after the I(PFD)A 1975 came into force, the court could not make an order under the Act in respect of an interest in property which had been acquired before the Act came into force. Vinelott J held that, on the true construction of Forfeiture Act 1982, s 2(7), an interest in property acquired before the coming into force of the I(PFD)A 1975 denoted property which had actually been transferred to the person entitled to it by virtue of the operation of the forfeiture rule, or who had acquired an indefeasible right to have it transferred to them. It did not include property which, at the time the section came into force, was held by the personal representatives who had not completed the administration; such property could therefore be the subject of an order under the Forfeiture Act 1982.

Although by reason of the wife's conduct the forfeiture rule applied, the purpose of the I(PFD)A 1975 was to require the court to form a view of the culpability attending the killing, in order to see whether, in the particular case, the effect of the rule should be modified. On the facts, since the widow had been a loyal wife, who had been subjected to violence by the deceased, and since there were no other persons to whom the deceased owed a moral obligation, it was held that it would be unjust for the widow to be deprived of the benefits which the deceased had conferred on her by his will and those which had accrued to her by survivorship. The rule was modified and she was allowed to take under the will. The conduct of the deceased towards his wife would also be a relevant consideration under Forfeiture Act 1982, s 2(3).

In *Re S (Deceased)* [1996] 1 WLR 235, a husband, who had entered into a joint insurance endowment policy with his wife, was convicted of her manslaughter. They had one son. The wife died intestate and her estate therefore passed to the son. The husband sought an order under the Forfeiture Act 1982 in respect of the policy on the ground that it came within s 2(4)(b) and was held on trust before the death of the wife pursuant to Married Women's Property Act 1882, s 11. The court held that the insurance policy could be treated as two separate policies for the husband and wife individually, for the benefit of each other. But for the application of the forfeiture rule, the beneficial interest under the policy would have passed to the husband. However, the policy constituted property held on contingent trust for him which had existed before the wife's death and thus came within Forfeiture Act 1982, s 2(4)(b). In the circumstances, the court held that it would be appropriate to apply the proceeds of the policy to a trust set up for the benefit of the son.

In *Re Jones, Jones v Midland Bank Trust Co Ltd* [1998] 1 FLR 246 (CA), the testatrix's will provided that her entire estate should pass to her son; if he predeceased her, then her two nephews were to take in equal shares. The son killed his mother and was convicted of her manslaughter. He was sentenced to a community rehabilitation order. The son applied for relief under the Forfeiture Act 1982. A preliminary issue was raised whether the residuary estate was to be held for those entitled on the deceased's intestacy, or for her two nephews. On appeal, applying the decision in *Re Sinclair, Lloyds Bank plc v Imperial Cancer Research Fund* [1985] FLR 965 (CA), it was held that the estate should devolve as on the deceased's intestacy as the gift over could take effect only if the son had predeceased the testatrix. It was not possible to speculate what provisions she would have made had she known that her son would kill her and forfeit his claim unless the court exercised its discretion.

In *Jones v Roberts* [1995] 2 FLR 422, the applicant was suffering from mental illness and killed both his parents. He pleaded guilty to manslaughter on the grounds of diminished responsibility. He was ordered to be detained under Mental Health Act 1983, s 37. The parents had died intestate. The claimant applied to the court for a determination whether, in view of his mental illness, he was precluded from taking on his father's intestacy. *Gray v Barr (Prudential Assurance Co Ltd, third party)* [1971] 2 QB 554 was relied on in support of a submission that the forfeiture rule did not apply automatically in every unlawful killing case, but only where the claimant had been guilty of deliberate and intentional manslaughter, violence or threats of violence. In rejecting the submission, the court distinguished the other cases cited. It found that the claimant's case was not one of insanity, nor of accident or recklessness. The defence of diminished responsibility reduced the charge of murder to manslaughter but the defendant was still criminally liable for his action. His application was refused.

In *Dalton v Latham* [2003] EWHC 796 (Ch), the claimant was convicted of manslaughter and sentenced to a term of imprisonment. He had a history of mental illness. His application was refused on the grounds that his conviction for manslaughter on the grounds of diminished responsibility had resulted simply in the claimant's responsibility for his actions being 'reduced not extinguished', but he still remained criminally liable for his actions and that the interests of justice did not require that the forfeiture rule should be modified. His plea that he had taken care of the deceased was rejected, the court finding that he had taken advantage of the deceased.

In *Dunbar v Plant* [1998] Ch 412, which was a case of suicide, the claimant's son (the deceased) and the defendant were lovers. They had purchased a property in joint names with a collateral insurance policy. The son had a like policy for the benefit of the defendant. They had planned to marry. The defendant was then accused of fraud and decided to commit suicide. She told her fiancé (the deceased) of her decision. They agreed to commit suicide together. On the third attempt, the claimant's son (the deceased) died and the defendant survived. It was held that the forfeiture rule applied to offences under the Suicide Act 1961, but the court had a discretion under the Forfeiture Act 1982 to modify the rule and had to consider s 2(2) when doing so. On the facts, the court directed that the forfeiture rule should not apply and granted the defendant full relief.

In *Mack v Lockwood and Others* [2009] EWHC 1524 (Ch), the applicant was convicted of manslaughter on the basis of provocation, but his application was nevertheless refused.

In *Chadwick v Collinson and Others* [2014] EWHC 2055 (Ch), the applicant was convicted of manslaughter on the basis of diminished responsibility. He lived with his partner and their son in a house which they jointly owned. He was also a residuary beneficiary under his partner's will. He killed his partner and their son. His application under the Forfeiture Act 1982 for the rule not to apply was refused, the court taking into account the level of culpability, the nature and gravity of the offences and the fact that the source of the deceased's estate had, in the most part, been funded through the efforts of the deceased.

In *Henderson v Wilcox* [2015] EWHC 3469 (Ch) (see para 5.6), the court on the evidence held that the serious nature of the offence and the degree of culpability of the claimant outweighed all other factors (for which, see [57]–[59] of the judgment).

5.6 DOES THE FORFEITURE RULE AFFECT TRUSTS?

Where the deceased and the claimant are joint owners of property, the survivor will, in any event, be entitled to their half share irrespective. The issue to be determined will be whether the forfeiture rule should be modified (see *Re K (Deceased)* and *Dunbar v Plant* (above)). Where there is a trust settled by the deceased (the victim of the claimant's unlawful killing), the court will need to consider two questions, namely: (1) what crime or acts are sufficient to engage the forfeiture rule; and (2) what are the interests affected by the rule? In *Henderson v Wilcox* [2015] EWHC 3469 (Ch), after referring to a number of cases including *Dunbar v Plant* and *Re K (Deceased)* (see above), His Honour Judge David Cook held that, in relation to a claimant who is a discretionary beneficiary under a trust (at [17] and [18]):

> 17. … that status on the execution of the trust and his interest is neither created nor enlarged by her death. If the trustees exercise their powers to pay any income or capital to him, he will receive it as a result of the decision of the trustees (albeit one they may make in light of the death) and not by virtue of the death itself. The position is *a fortiori* in the case of his own trust; the property settled (a joint interest in the house) was his before death and even if he had retained it in his own name he would not have had it removed from him by the forfeiture rule (cf Ms Plant's existing share in *Dunbar v Plant*). The effect of each joint owner separately dealing with their own beneficial interest (by declaring the Family Protection Trusts) would be to sever the beneficial joint tenancy. Ian's separate share is now held by the trustees (there is no suggestion that the trust is invalid) and his present interest in it derives from the terms of the trust and not in any respect from the death of Mrs Henderson.
> 18. In my judgment then the forfeiture rule has no application to any interest now existing or in future created under either of the trusts. The trustees are not prevented from exercising their discretion under those trusts in favour of Ian by the forfeiture rule if they think fit, and if they do so he will not be prevented by that rule from taking any benefit conferred by the trustees. Accordingly no question of relief under the Forfeiture Act arises in relation to any such interest or benefit.

5.7 SUMMARY

In summary, therefore, the language of Forfeiture Act 1982, s 2(2) is wide in its terms and the court is required to consider the justice of each case. In so doing, it will consider:

- the intention of the offender, particularly of the survivor of a suicide pact, as a relevant factor;
- the wishes of the beneficiaries, which are also material and must be given weight (see *Re K (Deceased)* (see para 5.5));
- the conduct of the offender and the deceased;
- any moral obligation the deceased owed to the applicant and any other beneficiaries, which will be given due weight;
- in the case of property held on constructive trust, giving effect to the trust so as to provide a benefit to a third party, for example, a son of the deceased;

- the applicant's culpability, as a relevant factor;
- the fact that the forfeiture rule will not be modified in cases where a charge of murder has been reduced to manslaughter by reason of diminished responsibility;
- as per the court's duty, what would be just in all the circumstances.

Chapter 6

Basis of the Claim

6.1 GROUNDS ON WHICH A CLAIM MAY BE MADE

There is only one ground upon which a claim under the I(PFD)A 1975 may be made, namely that (s 1(1)):

> the disposition of the deceased's estate effected by his will or the law relating to intestacy, or the combination of his will and that law, is not such as to make reasonable financial provision for the applicant.

The concept of reasonable financial provision is made central to the court's jurisdiction to depart from the will or intestacy rules. Therefore, a claimant, who falls into one of the categories of persons who are eligible to claim, will need to get over several hurdles. This is so because the Act in section 2 distinguishes what is 'reasonable financial provision' in relation to a spouse or civil partner of the deceased and that which is for other claimants (see, further, below). Section 3 of the Act also provides some guidance on the test to be applied by setting out a range of factors that must be taken into account when determining the reasonableness of the financial provision or lack of it made by the deceased in their will or under the intestacy rules. Some of these factors are common to all those who are eligible to make a claim and others only relate to a surviving spouse and civil partner of the deceased. The Supreme Court in *Ilott v The Blue Cross and Others* [2017] UKSC 17 has pointed out the danger of slipping into the error of applying the wrong test and for courts to be alert to the danger 'because the two tests will by no means invariably arrive at the same answer' (at [17]) (see the examples of such situations by reference to the cases of *Re Hancock deceased* [1998] 2 FLR 346 and *Re Jennings deceased* [1994] Ch 286 referred to in the judgment). The test of reasonable provision is objective. It is not simply whether the deceased behaved reasonably or otherwise in leaving the will they did or choosing not to leave one.

The s 3 factors are discussed in detail in Chapter 7, so the material in this chapter should be read in conjunction with Chapter 7.

6.2 MEANING OF 'REASONABLE FINANCIAL PROVISION'

The statutory definition of 'reasonable financial provision' is provided in I(PFD)A 1975, s 1(2) as amended by the CPA 2004. A distinction is drawn between what financial provision means in respect of:

(1) a claimant who is a surviving spouse/civil partner of the deceased, with special provisions in relation to those spouses who were judicially separated but where the separation was not continuing and those who fall within I(PFD)A 1975, s 14; and
(2) all other categories of claimants.

The amendments made to the I(PFD)A 1975 by the CPA 2004 set out how the court should deal with an application made by the surviving civil partner or former partner of the deceased. These are set out in s 1(2)(aa). They are similar to those which apply to married couples.

6.2.1 Surviving spouse/civil partner and judicially separated spouse/civil partner

I(PFD)A 1975, s 1(2)(a) and (b), as amended by the Divorce, Dissolution and Separation Act 2020 which came into force on 6 April 2022, provides that in respect of a surviving spouse/civil partner (except where the marriage/civil partnership with the deceased was the subject of a judicial separation order/ decree of judicial separation and at the date of death the order/the decree was in force and the separation was continuing), 'reasonable financial provision' means:

> such financial provision as it would be reasonable in all the circumstances of the case for a husband or wife/civil partner of the deceased to receive, *whether or not that provision is required for his or her maintenance.* (emphasis added)

This provision must be read with the provisions of I(PFD)A 1975, s 3(2), under which in relation to this category of claimants the court must have regard to the provision that the spouse or civil partner might have been expected to receive in the event of a divorce or dissolution of the civil partnership (see, further, Chapter 7).

It will be observed that the section makes an exception in relation to a surviving spouse who was separated from the deceased under a judicial separation order/decree of judicial separation, which was in force at the date of death. A judicially separated spouse/civil partner is excluded from receiving the wider financial provision which applies to a surviving spouse/civil partner of the deceased, and they fall within the provision which applies to all other claimants (see below).

If, however, despite the judicial separation order/decree of judicial separation or separation order (in the case of a civil partnership), the parties were living together and therefore the order was not in force and the separation was not continuing, then the claimant would be entitled to receive financial provision as set out under I(PFD)A 1975, s 1(2)(a) above, which applies to a surviving spouse/civil partner, i.e. wider provision not limited to maintenance.

The I(PFD)A 1975 makes one further exceptional provision in respect of a claimant who is a former spouse/civil partner of the deceased. This exception is set out in ss 14 and 14A, as amended by the CPA 2004.

I(PFD)A 1975, s 14 deals with the exception provided in respect of a surviving former spouse. Where the deceased dies within 12 months of the divorce order/decree absolute of divorce or nullity of marriage order has been made final/absolute or a judicial separation order/decree of judicial separation has been made/granted, but where:

(1) an application for a financial provision order under Matrimonial Causes Act 1973, s 23 or a property adjustment order under s 24 has not been made by the other party to that marriage, or
(2) such an application has been made but the proceedings thereon have not been determined at the time of the death of the deceased,

then if an application for an order under I(PFD)A 1975, s 2 is made, the court is empowered, notwithstanding anything in s 1 or s 3, if it thinks it just to do so, to treat that party for the purposes of the application as if the divorce order/decree of divorce or nullity of marriage order had not been made final/absolute or the judicial separation order had not been made, as the case may be, and therefore as if the marriage was still subsisting.

The provisions in relation to civil partners are contained in I(PFD)A 1975, s 14A. Section 14A, inserted by CPA 2004, Sch 4, para 20, provides that where:

(1) a dissolution order, nullity order or presumption of death order has been made under the CPA 2004, Pt 2, chapter 2 in relation to a civil partnership,
(2) one of the civil partners dies within 12 months from the date on which the order is made, and

(3) either an application for a financial provision order under CPA 2004, Sch 5, Part 1 or a property adjustment order under Sch 5, Part 2 has not been made by the other civil partner, or such an application has been made but the proceedings on the application have not been determined at the time of death of the deceased,

then if an application is made for an order under I(PFD)A 1975, s 2 by a surviving civil partner, notwithstanding anything in ss 1 and 3, the court shall have power, if it thinks just to do so, to treat the surviving former civil partner as a surviving partner.

There are four matters of note within these two sections. The first is that, provided the conditions are satisfied, a former spouse/civil partner's claim for financial provision will be considered on the basis of what the outcome would have been in the matrimonial proceedings. Second, that although the provision is drafted in mandatory terms by the use of the words 'the court shall', on closer scrutiny it will be observed that the court is given a discretion by the words, 'if it thinks just' whether or not to treat such a claimant as a surviving spouse/civil partner. Third, in the case where there has been a judicial separation or, in the case of a civil partner, a separation order which was in force, and the separation was continuing at the date of the death of the deceased, any claim made by the surviving spouse/civil partner of the deceased will be limited to financial provision which would be reasonable in all the circumstances of the case for the claimant to receive for their maintenance and not the generous provisions which apply to a surviving spouse/civil partner. Thus in the case of a surviving spouse/civil partner, the claim for financial provision is not limited to maintenance. The governing criterion is what the court considers to be reasonable provision unqualified by consideration of maintenance, although there may be cases where the order made will be restricted to maintenance in such cases. Lastly, in the case of a civil partnership, I(PFD)A 1975, s 14A refers to an additional order, namely that of a 'presumption of death order' which is not referred to in s 14 and does not apply to a surviving spouse. A married person was able to obtain a decree of presumption of death and dissolution of marriage where their spouse had been missing for a period of 7 years or more, pursuant to Matrimonial Causes Act 1973, s 19. This provision was repealed by Presumption of Death Act 2013, Sch 2, para 1. In relation to civil partnerships, CPA 2004, s 55 provides that the court may make a presumption of death order if for a period of 7 years or more the other civil partner has been continually absent from the applicant and the applicant has no reason to believe that the other civil partner has been living within that time. This merely creates a rebuttable presumption of death. Although CPA 2004, s 55 mirrors the provisions which were set out in the repealed Matrimonial Causes Act 1973, s 19, CPA 2004, s 55 has not been repealed. However, the court's jurisdiction to make a presumption of death order has been limited in that the original provisions set out in CPA 2004, s 222(a) and (b) have been repealed. Under s 222 as amended, the court has jurisdiction to entertain an application for a presumption of death order only if:

> (ba) at the time the application is made, the High Court does not have jurisdiction to entertain an application by that civil partner under section 1 of the Presumption of Death Act 2013 for a declaration that the other civil partner is presumed dead, and
>
> (c) the two people concerned registered as civil partners of each other in England and Wales and it appears to the court to be in the interests of justice to assume jurisdiction in the case.

The court's jurisdiction to make a declaration of presumed death is now set out in the Presumption of Death Act 2013 and future application for a declaration of presumed death should be made under the 2013 Act. It would seem that the provision now contained in CPA 2004, s 222 is a saving provision where, for any reason, the jurisdiction under Presumption of Death Act 2013, s 1 does not apply.

6.2.2 Surviving spouses/civil partners and those who come within I(PFD)A 1975, sections 14 and 14A

In the case of a surviving spouse and a spouse who comes within I(PFD)A 1975, s 14, the statutory definition makes clear that the court's considerations are not restricted to what would be reasonable for the spouse to receive by way of 'maintenance'. However, in determining what would be reasonable, the court is required to consider what the surviving spouse would have received had the marriage/civil partnership ended in a divorce/dissolution order rather than death, and then make a judgment, having regard to all the factors set out in s 3, as to what it considers to be just in the circumstances. In the words of Oliver LJ in *Re Besterman (Deceased), Besterman v Grusin* [1984] Ch 458:

> The Inheritance (Family Provision) Act 1938, which first introduced the concept of reasonable testamentary provision into English Law, was an Act to provide for the maintenance of dependants. The present Act remains such an Act in relation to dependants other than surviving spouses, but this section expressly provides that in the case of a surviving spouse the governing criterion is to be what the court considers to be 'reasonable' provision unqualified by any such consideration. There may, of course, be cases where that reasonable provision in all the circumstances might be restricted to maintenance, but the sub-section makes it clear that the court, in making such reasonable provision, is not to be inhibited by what I may call 'the 1938 concept' that maintenance is the only criterion or, indeed, even that that is the dominant consideration.

In *Re Besterman (Deceased), Besterman v Grusin*, the deceased and the claimant were married for 18 years. The deceased had been extremely wealthy, and his wife had enjoyed a very high standard of living. Under the deceased's will, the widow received personal chattels and a life interest in war stocks, which produced an income of £3,500 per annum. The principal beneficiary was Oxford University. The widow had no financial resources, other than a state pension. She applied for financial provision to be made for her. An interim order was made, granting her a lump sum of £75,000 to purchase a property, and interim periodical payments of £15,000 per annum. At the substantive hearing, a lump sum of £259,000 was awarded to her. The widow appealed on the ground that the provision made for her was considerably less than she might reasonably have expected to receive under the Matrimonial Causes Act 1973, which was a factor the court was required, by I(PFD)A 1975, s 3(2), to have regard to when calculating reasonable financial provision. On appeal, the lump sum was increased to £378,000 (see, also, Chapter 7).

The following cases further illustrate how the court has dealt with this special provision in respect of a surviving spouse:

- In *Re Bunning (Deceased), Bunning v Salmon* [1984] Ch 480, the claimant had married the deceased when she was 35 and he was 56. Soon after the marriage, the claimant had given up her job; she had found it impossible to continue working and to run a home and give assistance to the deceased in his business. In 1971, the deceased retired. In 1978, the claimant left him. Between 1968 and 1973, the deceased had given the claimant various capital funds. On his death in 1982, he left various legacies, including legacies to the Royal Society for the Protection of Birds and the Department of Veterinary Medicine at Cambridge University. At the time of his death, the widow's assets were estimated at £98,000 and her income consisted of an investment income, the state pension and other pensions. She had an earning capacity. There were no dependants. In considering her claim, the court had regard, as required by I(PFD)A 1975, s 3(2), to the lump sum she would have been awarded on an application under the Matrimonial Causes Act 1973. The court also had regard to her age and the likely length of widowhood, and took into account the fact that the assets had been built up largely by the deceased's own efforts before the marriage. In determining what the wife would have received under the Matrimonial Causes Act 1973, the court took into account the husband's likely future needs, and on that basis, the maximum the widow would have received would have been £36,000. The court would not interfere with the deceased's right to dispose of his assets as he willed, save to make reasonable provision for the wife. She was awarded £60,000 which, added to her existing assets, gave her about one half of the total assets of the parties.
- In *Re Rowlands (Deceased)* [1984] FLR 813, the claimant widow was aged 90. She had lived apart from the deceased for about 43 years when

the deceased died in 1981. She lived with her daughter and son-in-law. The deceased left his entire estate, worth about £100,000, to his two sons. On her application, the widow was awarded £3,000. She appealed. The court, in dismissing her appeal, took into account her special position as a surviving spouse and the matters set out in I(PFD)A 1975, s 3(2), but found that she was not able to formulate what her needs were and what she would do if a substantial award was made in her favour. There was no indication how her life would be enhanced if periodical payments or a lump sum were awarded to her.

- In *Stead v Stead* [1985] FLR 16, the claimant and the deceased had married when they were 55 and 63, respectively. The deceased had two children by his first marriage. The parties worked in their farming business and the claimant also worked as a nursery nurse. On their retirement, they sold the farm and purchased a new home, and thereafter the claimant took in paying guests. The deceased was 88 when he died. By his will, he gave his widow a life interest in the home on condition that she discharged all the outgoings, and bequeathed a sum of £60,000 on trust to be invested to give her an income for life. On her claim under the I(PFD)A 1975, she was awarded a lump sum and periodical payments of £1,500 per year.
- In *Re Krubert* [1997] Ch 97 (CA), at first instance the widow received what was in effect 85 per cent of the net estate and the deceased's brother and sister, in whose favour a trust in the residuary estate had been set up, received legacies of £7,000 each. On appeal, it was held that, in considering an appropriate award for a surviving spouse, the figure resulting from what would have been a s 25 exercise in ancillary relief proceedings under the Matrimonial Causes Act 1973 was merely one of the factors to which the court must have regard, subject to the overriding consideration of what was reasonable in all the circumstances. The Court of Appeal preferred the approach in *Re Besterman*, stating that it was more in accordance with the intention of the I(PFD)A 1975 read as a whole.

It will be noted from the above decisions that the court has used the matrimonial concept as a yardstick when determining a claim by a surviving spouse. However, as was pointed out in *Re Krubert*, this approach is merely one of the factors to which the court must have regard, subject to the overriding consideration of what was reasonable in all the circumstances. It is submitted that there is nothing in the statutory provisions which suggests that this factor should be given importance or more weight than other factors referred to in I(PFD)A 1975, s 3. Section 3(2), as amended by the Inheritance and Trustees' Powers Act 2014, now provides that 'nothing requires the court to treat such provisions as setting an upper or lower limit on the provision which may be made by an order under section 2' (see, further, Chapter 7). Many of the decisions on this issue have adopted the approach in *Re Krubert*.

In *Moody v Stevenson* [1992] Ch 486, a notional divorce provision was treated as the starting point. In *P v G, P and P (Family Provision: Relevance of Divorce Provision)* [2004] EWHC 2944 (Fam), [2006] 1 FLR 431, Black J (as she then was) pointed out that the provisions of the I(PFD)A 1975 which relate to a surviving spouse/civil partner do not contemplate the playing out of the entire fictional ancillary relief case. To do so would involve the court in a spurious exercise. The court should, however, 'reach sufficient of a conclusion about how it would have been resolved to take that factor into account in considering what would be reasonable financial provision' under the Act.

In *Fielden and Graham v Cunliffe* [2005] EWCA Civ 1508, [2006] 1 FLR 745, the Court of Appeal took the view that the approach adopted in ancillary relief cases should be used and that result then checked against the yardstick of equality of division in cases under the I(PFD)A 1975, but pointed out that there was no presumption that the division of the assets should be in favour of an equal division. The court in cases under the Act had to carry out a balancing exercise between the various factors which had be to be taken into consideration when determining a claim under the Act. Referring to *Re Besterman*, Wall LJ said that the case should be 'viewed with a substantial element of caution not least because Oliver LJ giving the leading judgment, warned against using it as basis for drawing general decisions of principle to be applied in other and probably quite different cases'. Reference was also made to the fact that the case predates the amended provision of Matrimonial Causes Act 1973, s 25, the decision in *White v White* [2000] UKHL 54, [2000] 2 FLR 981 and the *Duxbury* Tables (see *Duxbury v Duxbury* [1992] Fam 62).

In *Baker v Baker (Financial Provision: Divorce Comparison)* [2008] EWHC 977 (Ch), [2008] 2 FLR 1956, the court applied *Fielden and Graham v Cunliffe* (see above). The court confirmed that the concept of equality had to be approached with caution in the context of family provision. Whilst acknowledging that in the case of a spouse the financial provision was not confined to reasonable maintenance, the court nevertheless had to take into account other factors. On the facts of the case, the court took into account the impact of any order on other beneficiaries, on the continuation of the family business run by the deceased's sons, and the difficult 'circumstances which prevailed in extricating the estate's interest in the business', together with the fact that the parties had agreed that there was a need for a clean break, when deciding what financial provision would be appropriate for the widow. Similar views were expressed in *Barron v Woodhead* [2008] EWHC 810 (Ch), [2009] 1 FLR 747, where on the facts the court's principal concern was to ensure that the claimant had a roof over his head and sufficient means for his everyday needs.

In *Moore v Holdsworth and Others* [2010] EWHC 683 (Ch), [2010] 2 FLR 1501, in evaluating the widow's claim against the estate, the court took account of

I(PFD)A 1975, s 3 factors together with the divorce comparator. The court concluded that it was unlikely that she would have received the whole estate as she claimed. The court struck a balance and awarded her a life interest.

In *Iqbal v Ahmed* [2011] EWCA Civ 900, [2012] 1 FLR 31, the deceased's will gave the widow the right to occupy the matrimonial home and a legacy of £8,000. The remainder of the estate was left to his son. On her claim under the I(PFD)A 1975, the court applied the statutory cross check of what the widow might have reasonably expected to receive on divorce, and the decisions in *Miller v Miller; McFarlane v McFarlane* [2006] UKHL 24, [2006] 1 FLR 1186. She was awarded a life interest in the home, the net proceeds to be held on trust for sale in equal shares with her son and the residuary estate was transferred to the widow. On appeal, the Court of Appeal approved the award (see, also, *Lilleyman v Lilleyman* [2012] EWHC 821 (Ch); see, in respect of civil partnerships, *Lawrence v Gallagher* [2012] EWCA Civ 394; and see para 6.2 and Chapter 7).

Following the Law Commission report, *Matrimonial Property, Needs and Agreements*, Law Com No 343 (TSO, February 2014) and its recommendations, which included that the Family Justice Council should issue guidance and a formula to be used in financial disputes, the Family Justice Council has issued guidance for litigants in person, *Sorting out Finance on Divorce* (Family Justice Council, April 2016) and *Guidance on 'Financial Needs' on Divorce* (Family Justice Council, June 2016), which is directed at judges and professionals. The aim of the guidance is to clarify the meaning of needs and the objective that financial orders made must be to achieve and encourage consistency of approach by courts across England and Wales. Although the guidance is aimed at divorcing couples and dissolution of partnerships, its approach will also be useful in determining reasonable financial provisions in claims made under the I(PFD)A 1975 (see, further, Chapter 7).

To summarise, therefore, in claims made by a surviving spouse the court will have regard to the following:

- that what is reasonable financial provision for a surviving spouse should not be restricted to maintenance;
- that there may be circumstances where what is reasonable financial provision may be restricted to maintenance;
- that the divorce/dissolution comparator is only one of the relevant factors, not the paramount factor in determining the competing claims;
- that the I(PFD)A 1975 does not contemplate the playing out of the whole matrimonial ancillary relief exercise, but its use is merely as a yardstick against which to measure what would be the appropriate reasonable financial provision for the surviving spouse/civil partner;

- that the other factors set out in s 3 must be considered alongside the divorce/dissolution comparator in achieving a just result;
- that unlike an application for ancillary relief under the Matrimonial Causes Act 1973, where the court is only concerned with striking a balance between two living spouses where one or both may have earning capacity, in a claim under the I(PFD)A 1975 the court is concerned with striking a balance between the surviving spouse/civil partner and the competing claims of other beneficiaries from the estate;
- that the test applied in *Re Besterman* should be applied with a 'substantial element of caution', and to note that that case was one of a blameless widow of a wealthy man who was, on the facts, entitled to financial security commensurate to the lifestyle she had enjoyed;
- that the overriding consideration is what would be reasonable in all the circumstances of the case;
- that where the surviving spouse/civil partner is unable to formulate what their needs are and what they would do if a substantial award were to be made in their favour, it would be difficult for the court to allow a claim for a substantial award (see *Re Rowlands* [1984] 1 FLR 813 and *Gregory, Gregory v Goodenough* [1970] 1 WLR 1455).

6.2.3 Claim by surviving husband

The I(FP)A 1938 makes no distinction between a claim by a surviving husband and a claim by a surviving wife. In the early cases, however, the courts appeared to be disinclined, save in exceptional circumstances, to grant relief where the claim was made by a surviving husband. This is illustrated by two cases in particular. In *Re Sylvester, Sylvester v Public Trustee* [1941] Ch 87, the parties were married in 1931. The husband subsequently gave up his employment and thereafter did all the housework and nursed his wife during her illness. The wife had her own income. The husband had none. She died in 1940. She bequeathed to him an annuity of £525 per annum and gave her residuary estate to a number of charities. The husband made a claim against the estate for his maintenance under the I(FP)A 1938. Farwell J, in allowing the husband's claim and awarding him 3 shillings a week, stated:

> I do not consider that, in the ordinary way, applications by husbands for this sort of assistance should be readily entertained. *Prima facie* a husband should be able to maintain himself, and ought not to ask the court to give him, out of his wife's estate, more than she thought fit to provide for him. There are, of course, exceptional cases in which such an application may be justified, but personally I should not be very willing to assist husbands in cases of this sort, unless the circumstances were indeed exceptional.

In *Re Styler, Styler v Griffiths* [1942] Ch 387, the deceased had made an agreement with her second husband that, on his making a will in her favour, she would make a will leaving the income of her estate to him for life. They both made wills in accordance with the agreement. Subsequently, the wife made another will leaving all her estate to her daughter by her first marriage. On the wife's death, the husband applied for reasonable provision. In refusing his application, Morton J approved the judgment of Farwell J in *Re Sylvester* (above) and criticised his own decision in *Re Pointer* [1941] Ch 60. He stated:

> Having now had more experience of administering the Act since I decided that case, I do not think that I should now make any provision, as I did there for a husband with a pension of £180 a year, an annual income of £124 from investments and £25 a year net from property, unless the circumstances were exceptional.

The court's approach today would be different, having regard to decisions concerning applications for financial relief under the Matrimonial Causes Act 1973, and more particularly to the decisions in *White v White* [2000] UKHL 54, [2000] 2 FLR 981 and *Cowan v Cowan* [2001] EWCA Civ 679, [2002] Fam 97. In *White v White*, Lord Nicholls of Birkenhead stated, 'There is one principle of universal application which can be stated with confidence. In seeking to achieve a fair outcome, there is no place for discrimination between husband and wife and their respective roles' (see, further, Chapter 7). (See, also, *Barron v Woodhead* [2008] EWHC 810 (Ch), [2009] 1 FLR 747, where in a claim made by a surviving husband, the court was concerned with providing the claimant with the security of a roof over his head.)

6.2.4 Judicially separated spouse/civil partner and former spouse/civil partner

A surviving spouse/civil partner who is judicially separated from the deceased, and a former spouse/civil partner, are placed in the same category as other claimants. This distinction may well have been made because a judicially separated spouse/civil partner or spouse/civil partner whose marriage/civil partnership has been dissolved would have been entitled to apply for ancillary relief under the Matrimonial Causes Act 1973 and the CPA 2004, respectively, and such an application would have been considered and dealt with under the very wide jurisdiction provided by both Acts. It will thus be difficult for such a claimant to satisfy the court that the deceased's will or the law of intestacy or the combination of the will and that law has failed to make reasonable financial provision for the claimant. Any claim for financial provision made under the I(PFD)A 1975 by a former spouse/civil partner would, therefore, be additional to the relief already obtained in the matrimonial proceedings. However, I(PFD)A

1975, ss 15 and 15ZA entitle the court when considering an application for financial relief, on making a divorce, nullity of marriage or judicial separation order, or in the case of a civil partnership on making a dissolution order, nullity order separation order or presumption of death order, to exclude the parties to the matrimonial proceedings from seeking an order under the Act. Similar restrictions may also be imposed under ss 15A and 15B of the Act in proceedings for financial provisions under the MFPA 1984 and CPA 2004, Sch 7 (overseas divorces and dissolution of civil partnership) (see para 7.11.1). The court in those circumstances will be reluctant to interfere with the deceased's disposition of their estate. It will only do so if it is satisfied that the deceased has not been reasonable, and will decide the issue 'by ordinary canons of human behaviour and decency balancing generosity against parsimony, and the duty to a family against the claim of an ex-wife' (see *Re Talbot* [1962] 1 WLR 1113).

Some confirmation for the basis of this distinction can also be found in the special and exceptional provision made by I(PFD)A 1975, ss 14 and 14A in respect of a claimant whose marriage/civil partnership was dissolved or annulled, or who was granted a judicial separation order/decree of judicial separation, within 12 months of the date of the deceased's death, and the application under the Matrimonial Causes Act 1973 or the CPA 2004 has not yet been made or is still pending (see, further, under paras 6.2.1 and 6.2.2).

In view of the court's powers, under the Matrimonial Causes Act 1973 and the CPA 2004, to make capital adjustments between spouses and civil partners on a divorce, dissolution, annulment of marriage/civil partnership or judicial separation/separation order, there will be few cases in which it will be possible for a former spouse/civil partner to satisfy the condition that the deceased's will or the law of intestacy, or the combination of their will and that law, failed to make reasonable financial provision for the former spouse/civil partner. The former spouse/civil partner will have to show exceptional circumstances. These exceptional circumstances were referred to by Ormrod and Purchas LJJ in *Re Fullard (Deceased)* [1981] 3 WLR 743. Purchas LJ said:

> There must be some exceptional developments or conditions present which would make the analysis of what is reasonable as at the date of the death, which is the time when considerations under the Act must be made, different from the circumstances which existed at the dissolution of the marriage when these matters were carefully canvassed and resolved. There may well, of course, be developments which would enable an ex spouse to seek relief with some chances of success under this Act. Where there has been a long period of time since the dissolution of the marriage in circumstances in which a continuing obligation to support the ex spouse has been established by an order of the court, by consent, or otherwise, under which periodical payments have been, and continue to be made up to the date of death there may be circumstances such as envisaged by counsel for the applicant, where the death itself unlocks a substantial capital sum of which the testator should have been aware and

> from which had he made a will, at the time immediately before his death, he ought, within the criteria of the 1975 Act have made provision. There may be other incidents of further accretion of wealth but I doubt that the mere fact of accretion of wealth after the dissolution of the marriage would justify an application. An application would only be justified if all the circumstances of the case and all the considerations set out in the Act, made it reasonable that the testator should have made some provision as at the time of his death for the applicant.

The test in such cases is whether the former spouse/civil partner is reasonably provided for, and it is only if such a claimant is not so provided for that the court will interfere. See, also, *Whiting v Whiting* [1988] 2 FLR 189.

Where the surviving former spouse/civil partner has been in receipt of secured periodical payments, they may succeed in making a claim under the I(PFD)A 1975 (see *In Re Eyre* [1968] 1 WLR 530).

In recent proceedings for financial relief following a divorce/dissolution of civil partnership, the court has set aside orders made where the respondent has not made full and frank disclosure or misrepresented their financial situation to such an extent that if the true position had been known, the order obtained or consented to would have been different (see *Gohill v Gohill* [2015] UKSC 61 and *Sharland v Sharland* [2015] UKSC 60). In *Roocroft v Ball* [2016] EWCA Civ 1009, two women had been in a same sex relationship for 18 years and in a civil partnership for about a year when they separated. Within proceedings for financial relief an agreed order was made on the basis of the assets known to the claimant and disclosed by the respondent. Following the death of the respondent in 2013, the surviving former partner discovered that the deceased had far more assets than she had disclosed. She applied to have the order set aside on the grounds of non-disclosure. Her appeal against the dismissal of her claim was allowed. The Court of Appeal held that the court should make findings on the issue of non-disclosure and address its impact on the agreement that had been reached.

In *Goddard-Watts v Goddard-Watts* [2023] EWCA Civ 115 on appeal where there had been fraudulent non-disclosure which had resulted in a third application being made and in which the initial order had been set aside, the Court of Appeal held that the wife's application should have been completely reconsidered.

In such cases, it will be necessary to consider whether an application should be made to set aside the order in the matrimonial proceedings under FPR 2010, r 41(6) or to seek relief within proceedings under the I(PFD)A 1975.

Another instance where a claim may be justified is where the evidence discloses that when the consent order in favour of the surviving spouse was made, they had lacked capacity (see *MAP v RAP (Consent Order: Appeal: Incapacity)* [2013] EWHC 4784 (Fam)).

The following are some of the cases which illustrate the distinctly different principles which apply to such claims:

- In *Re Talbot* [1962] 1 WLR 1113, the claimant was 52. Her marriage to the deceased had been annulled and on her application for ancillary relief an order by consent was made in her favour for her maintenance at the rate of £432 per annum. A year later, she gave birth to a child of whom the deceased was not the father. The deceased nevertheless continued to maintain the claimant. The deceased remarried and had three children by his second wife, all of whom were minors at the date of his death. His estate, worth £19,397, was left to his second wife. When dismissing the claimant's claim Baker J said:

  > Before I sit in the testator's chair to amend his last will, I must be satisfied that he has not been reasonable in his solution to the dilemma which faced him. Would any testator have done other than did the deceased in the circumstances which existed immediately before his death? I think not. Such a man would regard interference with his disposition as an unwarranted statutory and judicial defeat of his intentions. It may be said that all testators who fail to make provision for a former wife are unreasonable if a substantial maintenance order is suddenly to be cut off at death. But that problem should be decided by the ordinary canons of human behaviour and decency, balancing generosity against parsimony and the duty to a family against the claim of an ex-wife.

- In *Lusternik v Lusternik* [1972] Fam 125, the claim succeeded because the deceased had not made a full, frank and honest disclosure of his means.
- In *Re Crawford (Deceased)* (1983) 4 FLR 273, the deceased's marriage was dissolved in 1968. A consent order was made, providing periodical payments to the wife and her continuing occupation of the former matrimonial home, the outgoings of which were to be paid for by the respondent husband. In 1975, the former matrimonial home was sold and another property purchased for the former wife. The respondent thereafter failed to make the payments under the order. He remarried and had two children. On his retirement, he received a lump sum of £69,767, which was paid into a joint account with his second wife. He also received an index-linked pension. In 1979, he suggested to his former wife that she should apply for a lump sum order on a 'clean break' basis but before the application was heard, he died. The claimant (former wife of the deceased) did not receive anything from his estate. The widow, on the other hand, received substantial lump sum payments from a pension fund which did not form part of the net estate and an index-linked pension for herself and for the benefit of the two children. In addition, the widow had an interest in one-half of the former wife's house and a life interest in another property

> under the will. She also had capital of £69,767.21. The former wife had capital of £1,500 and state benefits of £34.28 per week.
>
> It was conceded that the deceased had failed to make reasonable financial provision for the claimant and that a lump sum should be awarded. The issue related to the amount which should be awarded. In deciding the amount, the court took into account the fact that in assessing the amount to be awarded to a former wife, the court had to look at all the matters set out in I(PFD)A 1975, s 3(1) and (2). On the facts, the court concluded that the former wife needed an annuity of £4,000, and made an order which would fund such a payment by severing the deceased's severable interest from the jointly owned property.

See, also, *Re Farrow (Deceased)* [1988] 1 FLR 205.

Where, however, a former wife's claims for income and capital have been finally settled, she is unlikely to succeed in obtaining an order under I(PFD)A 1975, s 2. In *Brill v Proud* [1984] Fam Law 59 (CA), on the dissolution of their marriage the parties had obtained a consent order in full and final settlement of their claims for financial relief. The former wife had, under the terms of the settlement, received the former matrimonial home in return for a small lump sum. Her income was higher than her husband's. On his death, she made a claim which failed.

In *Cameron v Treasury Solicitor* [1996] 2 FLR 716, the claimant's marriage to the deceased had been dissolved in 1971. They had no children. The claimant had received a lump sum payment on the dissolution of the marriage by way of a clean break provision. The deceased died intestate and the estate devolved on the Crown as *bona vacantia*. The former wife's claim under the I(PFD)A 1975 failed on appeal, despite the fact that she was in difficult financial circumstances and in poor health, on the grounds that the clean break order had been obtained over 19 years before the death of the deceased and there was no evidence that he had had any continuing obligation towards her and she had not made out a case that it was not reasonable for the deceased to have not made any financial provision for her (cf *Wyatt v Vince* [2015] UKSC 14, an exceptional case where a former wife applied for financial relief after 30 years when she discovered that the husband had acquired a fortune).

In *Barrass v Harding* [2001] 1 FLR 138 (CA), following a divorce between the claimant and the deceased there had been a clean break settlement in 1964. The deceased remarried, but his second wife predeceased him. He made a will leaving his estate to his sister-in-law. The former wife was living with her son in poor circumstances. Her claim failed.

Although not a case under the I(PFD)A 1975, in *Benson v Benson* [1996] 1 FLR 692, within 6 months of financial settlement in divorce proceedings the wife died. The husband by way of an appeal sought to have the order set aside on the grounds that the order was still executory. The appeal was dismissed on the grounds that where the parties had been legally represented and the agreement reached between them which had led to the order was clear, unambiguous and made for good consideration, the court would not interfere with the consent order. The death of the wife was not an event which was contemplated by the parties. Additionally, the appeal was lodged over a year after the wife's death.

6.2.5 All other claimants

In the case of all other claimants, 'reasonable financial provision' means (I(PFD)A 1975, s 1(2)(b)):

> such financial provision as it would be reasonable in all the circumstances of the case for the claimant to receive for his maintenance.

It will be noted that the test for those for a surviving spouse/civil partner is wider than that for other classes of claimants. In respect of claimants other than a surviving spouse/civil partner, the test of what is 'reasonable financial provision' is limited to what would be reasonable for the claimant to receive for their maintenance. The I(PFD)A 1975 does not define 'maintenance'. It is considered to be a deliberately vague legislative choice but, nevertheless, an important one (see *Ilott v The Blue Cross and Others* [2017] UKSC 17, [13]). In determining the issue, the court is required to take into account the range of factors set out in I(PFD)A 1975, s 3. The assessment on what is reasonable financial provision for this category will turn largely on need, but as the Supreme Court stated by reference to the observation of Oliver J in *Re Coventry, Coventry v Coventry* [1980] Ch 461 (see, also, para 7.5), need is not by itself a sufficient condition for an order.

Disapproving of the approach adopted by the Court of Appeal, Lord Hughes stressed (at [34]) that the I(PFD)A 1975:

> does not require the judge to fix some hypothetical standard of reasonable provision and then either add to it, or discount from it, by percentage points or otherwise, for variable factors. To the contrary the section 3 factors, which are themselves variables and which are likely often to be in tension one with another, are all to be considered so far as they are relevant, and in the light of them a single assessment of reasonable provision is made.

Baroness Hale, while approving the observations made by Black LJ in her judgment ([2011] EWCA Civ 346, [88]) that '[a] dispassionate study of each of the matters set out in section 3(1) will not provide the answer to the question whether the will makes reasonable financial provision for the applicant no matter how careful and thorough it is', posed the question of how is the court to distinguish between the deserving and the undeserving and stated that even in the case of a large estate it might be thought that the children ought to inherit even if they are not in need, adding that 'this would run counter to the restriction of their claims to reasonable maintenance. It would also run counter to the approach long taken in the law of *inter vivos* financial provision for adult children' (*Ilott v The Blue Cross and Others* [2017] UKSC 17, [62]).

(See, further, below and Chapter 7.)

6.3 MEANING OF 'MAINTENANCE'

There is no definition of the term 'maintenance' in the I(PFD)A 1975, but case law provides guidance on the approach of the courts on what can be regarded as reasonable maintenance. In *Ilott v The Blue Cross and Others* [2017] UKSC 17, the Supreme Court, in determining what this means for the claimants in this class, stated (at [16]) that:

> these are words of objective standard of financial provision, to be determined by the court. The Act does not say that the court may make an order when it judges that the deceased acted unreasonably. That too would be an objective judgment, but it would not be the one required by the Act.

The Supreme Court approved the test set out by Oliver J *Re Coventry, Coventry v Coventry* [1980] Ch 461 on determining what is *reasonable maintenance*:

> It is not the purpose of the Act to provide legacies or rewards for meritorious conduct. Subject to the court's powers under the Act and to fiscal demands, an Englishman still remains at liberty at his death to dispose of his own property in whatever way he pleases or, if he chooses to do so, to leave that disposition to be regulated by the laws of intestate succession. In order to enable the court to interfere with and reform those dispositions it must, in my judgment, be shown, not that the deceased acted unreasonably, but that, looked at objectively, his disposition or lack of disposition produces an unreasonable result in that it does not make any or any greater provision for the applicant – and that means, in the case of an applicant other than a spouse, for that applicant's maintenance. It clearly cannot be enough to say that the circumstances are such that if the deceased had made a particular provision for the applicant, that would not have been an unreasonable thing for him to do and therefore it now ought to be done. The court has no carte blanche to reform the deceased's dispositions or those which statute makes of his estate to accord with what the court itself might have thought would be sensible if it had been in the deceased's position.

The Supreme Court referred to some of the earlier decisions which had determined what the term 'maintenance' does not mean. It is thus necessary to consider these cases in order to ascertain what, if any, further guidance is given in *Ilott v The Blue Cross and Others* in relation to the concept of 'maintenance':

- 'Maintenance' includes payments which directly or indirectly enable the claimant in the future to discharge the cost of living. It does not include a capital sum to enable the claimant to discharge their tax liability (see *Re Dennis (Deceased), Dennis v Lloyds Bank* [1981] 2 All ER 140 at 145–6) or for a mortgage to be discharged where the claimant has a comfortable standard of living (*Re Jennings, deceased* [1994] (Ch) 286).
- The fact that the claimant is in necessitous circumstances is not enough (see *Re Coventry, Coventry v Coventry* [1980] Ch 461 (CA)). In *Re Coventry*, the claimant was the only child of the deceased. He returned home when he was aged 26. Shortly afterwards, the mother left home and she lived separately from the deceased. The son looked after the home, did all the tasks and contributed towards the general outgoings. When he married, his wife took over the task, but the marriage broke down. A year later, the deceased died intestate. His entire estate passed to his widow. The son, who was on a low income and had no savings, made a claim. His claim failed.
- 'Maintenance' does not mean whatever may be desirable for the claimant's general benefit or welfare (see *Re Coventry*, discussed above).
- 'Maintenance' means what is sufficient to enable the claimant to live decently and comfortably according to the station in life to which the claimant has been accustomed. It does not merely mean enough to bring the claimant to subsistence level, but it does not mean sufficient to give the claimant a life of luxury (see Ewbank J in *Re Debenham (Deceased)* [1986] 1 FLR 404, adopting the decision in *Re Duranceau* [1952] 3 DLR 714). In *Re Debenham*, the claimant was an unwanted child of the deceased, who had always been aloof, distant and cruel to the claimant. The claimant was brought up by her grandparents in South Africa. When she was aged 21, she came to England to see her mother, but she was totally rejected by her. Subsequently, the mother had led her to believe that she would be 'all right' if anything happened to the mother. The deceased left the claimant a legacy of £200, and most of the residue of her estate was left to six charities. The claimant was 58, an epileptic and a sick woman. She and her husband lived on a pension of £500 per annum and state benefits. In allowing her application, the court had regard to the matters set out in I(PFD)A 1975, s 3; the fact that there were no other claimants; and the fact that the deceased had no obligations or responsibilities to the charities. The court considered that the deceased owed the claimant a moral obligation and responsibility, and awarded her a lump sum of £3,000 and periodical payments of £4,500 per annum. The case was distinguished from that of *Re Coventry* (above).

- 'Maintenance' means no more or less than the claimant's and their family's way of life and well-being, their health and financial security. In *Graham v Murphy* [1997] 1 FLR 860, on the facts, it was decided that maintenance did not mean that the claimant should be provided with a lavish lifestyle or such as would relieve the claimant from working, or such as would provide the claimant with a high standard of life for the rest of the claimant's life. See, also, *Re Scott-Kilvert (Deceased), Robinson v Bird* [2003] WTLR 529, on luxury items not coming within the meaning of 'maintenance'.
- An award of a lump sum to pay off past debts does not fall within the concept of 'maintenance' unless the payment of such debts enables the claimant to derive a future income, or the debts represent living expenses since the death of the deceased (see *Baynes v Hedger and Others* [2009] EWCA Civ 374, [2009] 2 FLR 767).
- Some moral obligation of maintenance over and above blood ties must be established. In *Re Goodchild, Goodchild v Goodchild* [1997] 1 WLR 1216, the deceased and his wife had executed simultaneous wills in favour of the survivor of them and then in favour of their adult son. After his wife's death, the deceased remarried and made a new will leaving his entire estate to his second wife. On the son's claim, it was held that the wills were not mutually binding, but that when the first wife made her will, it had been on the clear understanding that her husband would give effect to their mutual intention. That gave rise to a moral obligation to provide for the son. The deceased was in breach of that obligation which left the son in financial difficulties; in those circumstances, the court had to ensure that adequate financial provision was made for the son to provide for his reasonable needs for maintenance and support.
- It is not enough to establish relationship and necessity. A child must also establish special circumstances, which must be relevant to the issues before the court. Moral obligation is the most obvious special circumstance although not the only one (see *Re Abrams* [1996] 2 FLR 379). In *Re Pearce (Deceased)* [1998] 2 FLR 705 (CA), the deceased's son had worked hard on the deceased's farm without pay and was told repeatedly by the deceased that he would leave the farm to him. The deceased and his wife divorced and the deceased started cohabiting with the defendant. The deceased made a will leaving all his property to her. She subsequently moved out, but the deceased did not alter his will. The son was on a low income. He had five children and lived in a property which required considerable improvement. The court found that the deceased owed a moral obligation to his son and had not made reasonable financial provision for him.
- In *Re Hancock (Deceased)* [1998] 2 FLR 346, the deceased did not make any provision for one of his daughters because sufficient funds were not

available, but stipulated that, in the event of his wife's predeceasing him, his money was to be divided between his beneficiaries, which included his daughter. The deceased's assets included a plot of land, which was valued at £100,000, and which he left to his other children. The land was sold at a price higher than had been expected and the children received a windfall. The daughter's claim succeeded on the basis that the deceased's will clearly indicated that he would have made provision for her if he had believed he had sufficient assets available. A periodical payments order of £3,000 per annum was awarded.

For other examples where an award was made, see *Rees v Newbery and the Institute for Cancer Research* [1988] 1 FLR 1041 and *Re Watson* [1999] 1 FLR 878 (see Chapter 4).

- Failure by the deceased to provide for the claimant during the claimant's minority does not entitle the claimant to apply for financial provision from the deceased's estate when they become an adult (see *Re Jennings (Deceased)* [1994] Ch 286 (CA)).
- In *Re Christie (Deceased), Christie v Keeble* [1979] Ch 168, an order was made to redress the balance between the two children of the deceased. The court interpreted I(PFD)A 1975, s 1(2)(b) thus:

> In my judgment, the financial provision that is thus contemplated is not necessarily financial provision that would be 'required' for the applicant's maintenance. The contrast between paragraphs (a) and (b) of section 1(2), in my judgment, makes it clear. Nor in my judgment does the use of the word 'maintenance' carry with it any implication that the applicant, in order to qualify, must be in any way in a state of destitution or financial difficulty. Nor in my judgment, is it useful to refer to the test as being an objective test, whatever that word may mean, in the context of this Act which directs the court to consider the particular and personal matters set out in section 3. In my judgment the word 'maintenance' refers to no more and no less than the applicant's way of life and well-being, his health, financial security and allied matters such as the well-being, health and financial security of his immediate family for whom he is responsible.

The Supreme Court's decision has confirmed the earlier decisions in that it has emphasised the principle that, although the concept of maintenance is broad, 'the distinction made by the differing paragraphs in I(PFD)A 1975, s 1(2) shows that it cannot extend to any or every thing which it would be desirable for the claimant to have. It must import provision to meet the everyday expenses of living' (at [14]) (*Re Jennings deceased* and *Re Dennis deceased* applied). Lord Hughes (at [15]) said:

> The level at which maintenance may be provided for is clearly flexible and falls to be assessed on the facts of each case. It is not limited to subsistence level. Nor, although maintenance is by definition the provision of income rather than capital, need it

> necessarily be provided for by way of periodical payments, for example under a trust. It will very often be more appropriate, as well as cheaper and more convenient for other beneficiaries and for executors, if income is provided by way of a lump sum from which both income and capital can be drawn over the years, for example on the *Duxbury* model familiar to family lawyers (see *Duxbury v Duxbury (Note)* [1992] Fam 62). Lump sum orders are expressly provided for by section 2(1)(b). There may be other cases appropriate for lump sums; the provision of a vehicle to enable the claimant to get to work might be one example and, as will be seen, the present case affords another. As Browne-Wilkinson J envisaged (*obiter*) in *In re Dennis* (above) there is no reason why the provision of housing should not be maintenance in some cases; families have for generations provided for the maintenance of relatives, and indeed for others such as former employees, by housing them. But it is necessary to remember that the statutory power is to provide for maintenance, not to confer capital on the claimant. Munby J (as he then was) rightly made this point clear in *In re Myers* [2004] EWHC 1944 (Fam); [2005] WTLR 851 at paras 89–90 and 99–101. He ordered, from a very large estate, provision which included housing, but he did so by way not of an outright capital sum but of a life interest in a trust fund together with power of advancement designed to cater for the possibility of care expenses in advanced old age. If housing is provided by way of maintenance, it is likely more often to be provided by such a life interest rather than by a capital sum.

The court also accepted that sums (including substantial sums) needed to be spent on 'items which could properly be described as necessities for daily living' including 'such things as essential white goods, basic carpeting, floor covering and curtains, and the replacement of worn out and broken beds' could fall within the concept of maintenance, and also (at [41]) stated that the I(PFD)A 1975 is not designed to provide a claimant to be gifted a 'spending spree', but that this kind of 'necessary replacement of essential household items is not such an indulgence; rather it is the maintenance of daily living'.

Lady Hale, when analysing the options that were open to the district judge who first heard the case, acknowledged that 'housing is undoubtedly one of the first things that anyone needs for her maintenance, along with food and fuel', but went on to elaborate that 'it is difficult to reconcile the grant of an absolute interest in real property with the concept of reasonable provision for maintenance: buying a house and settling it upon her for life with reversion to the estate would be more compatible with that' (at [65] (2)). A few days earlier, Marcus Smith J giving judgment in an appeal in *Martin v Williams* [2017] EWHC 491 (Ch) had also concluded that account needs to be taken of Mrs Williams' (a cohabitant of the deceased) housing needs because 'it is obvious that reasonable financial provision for Mrs Williams involves ensuring a roof over head', but having regard to all the circumstances he considered that vesting a life interest would meet those needs. In *Thompson v Raggett* [2018] EWHC 688 (Ch), the claimant was 79 years of age. She had lived with the deceased for 42 years and had been financially dependent on him. She had worked on his farm and his business without pay.

When he died they were living in a cottage purchased by him. In his will the deceased left the entire estate valued at £1.5 million to friends and tenants, and he left a note setting out his reason for not making any financial provisions for the claimant or her children from a previous relationship – that the claimant had her own assets. Her assets however were savings of £2,500 and her only income was from state benefits. She was in poor health. She applied for the cottage to be transferred to her absolutely and a lump sum to cover the costs of the move and the running costs of living in the cottage. The court ordered an outright transfer of the cottage to her and a lump sum payment of £28,844 to cover the costs of renovating the cottage and moving costs, and a further lump sum of £160,000 for her living costs.

As regards the situation of cohabitants, in view of the government's response to the recommendations made in the report, *The rights of cohabiting partners*, published on 4 August 2022 by the Women and Equalities Committee (a cross-party group of MPs), no change is anticipated. It is therefore essential that when advising a client, practitioners ensure that the client is advised to make provisions for the cohabitant (see under Chapter 1 and for the full report, see https://publications.parliament.uk/pa/cm5803/cmselect/cmwomeq/92/report.html). Due to the publicity that the case of *Ilott v The Blue Cross and Others* received, it was hoped that the Supreme Court would give a comprehensive guidance on how the competing claims should be assessed and balanced. The difficulty the court faced is demonstrated by the three options which Lady Hale stated were open to the district judge when he determined the case (see para 6.3.1). Unfortunately, the court was not able to give guidance because, as Lady Hale stated (at [49]):

> This case raises some profound questions about the nature of family obligations, the relationship between family obligations and the state, and the relationship between the freedom of property owners to dispose of their property as they see fit and their duty to fulfil their family obligations. All are raised by the facts of this case but none is answered by the legislation which we have to apply or by the work of the Law Commission which led to it.

She added that the case demonstrates 'the unsatisfactory state of the present law, giving as it does no guidance as to the factors to be taken into account in deciding whether an adult child is deserving or undeserving of reasonable maintenance', and regretted that the Law Commission did not reconsider the fundamental principles underlying such claims when it last dealt with this topic in 2011 (at [66]).

Additionally, the court also approved Black LJ's observations in the Court of Appeal ([2011] EWCA Civ 346, [88]):

> A dispassionate study of each of the matters set out in section 3(1) will not provide the answer to the question whether the will makes reasonable financial provision for the applicant, no matter how thorough and careful it is. ... [S]ection 3 provides no guidance about the relative importance to be attached to each of the relevant criteria. So between the dispassionate study and the answer to the first question lies the value judgment to which the authorities have referred. It seems to me that the jurisprudence reveals a struggle to articulate, for the benefit of the parties in the particular case and of practitioners, how that value judgment has been, or should be, made on a given set of facts.

However, this does not mean that claims made under the I(PFD)A 1975, especially by adult children, are doomed to fail. It will require the potential claimant and their advisers to ensure that the claimant's case is carefully prepared in order to establish it, especially where a claimant is reliant on state benefits of any kind (see below).

6.3.1 Maintenance in relation to claimants on state benefits

Issues have sometimes arisen regarding the relevance of state benefits when the court is considering a claim under the I(PFD)A 1975 and the level of award which should be made in such cases. State benefits have been disregarded in considering whether reasonable financial provision has been made for the claimant by the deceased. In *Re Collins* [1990] Fam 56, the deceased died intestate. The claimant was her daughter who was mentally disabled, unemployed and on state benefits. She was awarded £5,000 and her entitlement to state benefits was disregarded.

The fact that the claimant is on state benefits should not preclude the person from seeking or being granted an award unless, as occurred in *Re E, E v E* [1966] 1 WLR 709, the estate is so small that it would not benefit anyone to make any awards. Since those under disability, particularly those with mental disability, are often treated in the community, an award can provide them with some basic needs and comfort which would otherwise not be available. See *Hanbury v Hanbury* [1999] 2 FLR 255, where an award of £39,000 was settled on a discretionary trust. Where a person is on benefits, and particularly where the recipient of such benefits is under some disability, it is essential to ascertain the maximum capital which a person is entitled to have and still remain eligible for benefits.

In *Gold v Curtis* [2005] WTLR 673, the deceased had left her entire estate to her daughter, indicating that she had not made any provision for her son as he had had enough from her during her lifetime and that they had been estranged. The son had, in fact, received only two modest payments from his mother of £1,200 and £600. Before her death, they had become reconciled and the deceased saw her grandchildren during their childhood. One of the grandchildren was mentally disabled and would remain dependent on her father. On the facts, it was held that the deceased had not made reasonable financial provision for her son having regard to his inadequate circumstances and the fact that his disabled child would remain wholly dependent on him (see, also, *Myers v Myers* [2004] EWHC 1944 (Fam), [2005] WTLR 851). However, in *Wellesley v Wellesley* [2019] EWHC 11 (Ch), the deceased's daughter's claim failed although she was receiving state benefits because the evidence adduced established that she could support herself adequately. It was stressed by the court that where it is suggested that an adult child of the deceased is impecunious their needs must be well supported by evidence, and arguments put forward on human rights and public policy issues were by themselves insufficient to outweigh the s 3 factors that the court is required to consider when determining what if any orders should be made.

The Supreme Court in *Ilott v The Blue Cross and Others* [2017] UKSC 17 has now confirmed that state benefits are part of the resources of the claimant, and that it is relevant to consider whether they will continue to be received and what impact any order made will have on the claimant's entitlement to such benefits. However, the decision taken at all levels of the court in the *Ilott case* is a clear indication of the difficulties that arise when the court seeks to resolve issues when a claimant is on state benefits and attempts to ensure that the claimant's financial needs can be met by an award under the I(PFD)A 1975 without impacting on the state benefits received by the applicant. In *Ilott v The Blue Cross*, the Supreme Court referred to at least three different solutions. The first was that adopted by the first instance judge who had evaluated Mrs Ilott's claim and awarded her £50,000, thereby depriving her of her means-tested benefits. The district judge did not expressly consider, and was not presented with, the information to enable him to consider what effect that this would have on the family's entitlements, and in particular the fact they would lose their entitlement to housing benefit until their capital was reduced to below £16,000. The second alternative was that adopted by Eleanor King J, which was to decline to make any order because the claimant was regarded as self-sufficient, albeit largely dependent on public funds. The third option available was what the Court of Appeal did, i.e. increasing the lump sum awarded to the claimant to enable her to buy the home where she lived with her family and to have an additional award of a sum, which would not affect the state benefits she received, to meet future needs, and as Lady Hale commented, it 'preserved the family's claims to means-tested income benefits. It was benefits-efficient from the public point of view because it saved sums payable in housing benefits.' It was, in the end, a value judgment, as Black LJ observed in her judgment ([2011] EWCA Civ 346) and referred to with approval by Lady Hale.

Since the first option was rightly open for the district judge to take on the evidence, he could not be said to have fallen into an error of law or fact. The Supreme Court allowed the appeal, and the order made by the district judge, awarding Mrs Ilott £50,000, was reinstated. The court, whilst acknowledging that it was up to Mrs Ilott how she used the award, stated that if a substantial part of it were spent on necessary household items, the impact on the family's state benefits would be minimised 'because she could put the household into a much sounder footing without for long retaining capital beyond the £16000 ceiling at which entitlement to Housing and Council Tax benefits is lost'.

Practitioners' attention is drawn to the Law Commission report, *Cohabitation: The Financial Consequences of Relationship Breakdown*, Law Com No 307 (TSO, 2007), p 207, which recommends the need for the removal of the 'maintenance' ceiling in relation to cohabitants and extending it to cover what would be reasonable in all the circumstances of the case irrespective of whether the provision is required for the applicant's maintenance, i.e. to bring it in line with the test applied in claims made by spouses and civil partners. It also recommends that a person should be entitled to apply for provision under the I(PFD)A 1975 where the applicant was living in the same household as the deceased immediately before the deceased's death, and: (1) either: (a) the applicant and the deceased had lived for a period of 2 years immediately before the deceased's death, or (b) the applicant and the deceased had a child together; and (2) that the court should not have discretion to dispense with these requirements. The Law Commission has also suggested that a person who had cohabited with the deceased, but whose relationship ended shortly before the deceased's death, should be entitled to make a claim.

The government has so far shown a disinclination to implement these recommendations or the observations made by Lady Hale in *Ilott v The Blue Cross and Others* or the recommendations made in the recent report, *The rights of cohabiting partners*, published on 4 August 2022 by the Women and Equalities Committee (available at https://publications.parliament.uk/pa/cm5803/cmselect/cmwomeq/92/report.html) (see, also, Chapter 1).

Chapter 7

Matters to which the Court is to Have Regard

7.1 INTRODUCTION

Once the court is satisfied on the preliminary issues, namely that: (1) the application has been made within the time limit, or if out of time, leave to apply has been considered; (2) the deceased died domiciled in England and Wales; and (3) the claimant comes within the categories of persons who are eligible to make a claim against the estate, it can go on to consider:

(1) whether the disposition of the deceased's estate effected by the deceased's will or the law of intestacy, or the combination of the will and that law, has failed to make reasonable financial provision for the claimant;
(2) if the court determines that reasonable financial provision has not been made, whether and in what manner and to what extent the court should exercise its powers under I(PFD)A 1975, s 2 to make reasonable financial provision for the claimant.

In determining whether the deceased failed to make reasonable financial provision for the claimant and in what manner and to what extent the court should make a financial provision order, it must have regard to the factors set out in s 3. The issue for determination is not whether the deceased acted unreasonably, but whether, looked at objectively and having taken into account all the factors under s 3, the provisions made or the lack of disposition produce an unreasonable result in not making any or inadequate provision for the claimant. If it decides this issue in the affirmative, it must then consider whether to exercise its discretion regarding the appropriate order it should make under s 2 (see Chapter 8) by applying the factors set out in s 3.

There is therefore a two-stage process and in considering both stages the s 3 factors will be relevant. This approach was specifically referred to by Lord Hughes in his judgment *Illott v The Blue Cross and Others* [2017] UKSC 17, [23].

Lord Hughes also went on to elaborate on how the court should approach these issues and to emphasise that an appellate court will be slow to interfere with the decision of the court of first instance unless it is established that the judge erred in principle or in law. He said at [24]:

> The Act plainly requires a broad brush approach from the judge to very variable personal and family circumstances. There can be nothing wrong, in such cases, with the judge simply setting out the facts as he finds them and then addressing both questions arising under the Act without repeating them. Nor should there normally be any occasion for a split hearing. Moreover, Goff LJ's observations ought not to be thought to mean that the approach of an appeal court should differ as between the two parts of the process. Whether best described as a value judgment or as a discretion (and the former is preferable), both stages of the process are highly individual in every case. The order made by the judge ought to be upset only if he has erred in principle or in law. An appellate court will be very slow to interfere and should never do so simply on the grounds that its judge(s) would have been inclined, if sitting at first instance, to have reached a different conclusion. The well-known observations of Lord Hoffmann in *Piglowska v Piglowski* [1999] 1 WLR 1360 esp at 1373–1374 are directly in point. It is to 'kill the parties with kindness' to permit marginal appeals in cases which are essentially individual value judgments such as those under the 1975 Act should be. The present case, as it happens, is an example of much to be regretted prolongation, and presumably expensive prolongation, of the forensic process.

7.2 RELEVANT DATE FOR CONSIDERATON OF SECTION 3 FACTORS

The requirements of I(PFD)A 1975, s 3 are mandatory. It requires the court when determining the issues and the matters to which the court is required to have regard, to take into account all the matters set out in s 3(2) and to the facts as known *at the date of the hearing* (s 3(5)) (see *Ilott v Mitson* [2011] EWCA Civ 346, [2012] 2 FLR 170, *Re Coventry, Coventry v Coventry* [1980] Ch 461, *Re Rowlands (Deceased)* [1984] FLR 813 and *Re Hancock* [1998] 2 FLR 346). The issue as to the date at which the facts fall to be assessed was raised in the appeal to the Supreme Court in *Ilott v The Blue Cross and Others* [2017] UKSC 17. The court confirmed that 'where a court has to assess whether reasonable financial provision has been made, and/or what it should be the relevant date is the date of hearing' and that if on appeal 'the question is whether the trial judge made an error of principle the facts and evidence must be taken as they stood before him. And if it should fall to the appellate court to remake the decision on the merits, as ordinarily it should not, any request to adduce further evidence will have to be judged by ordinary *Ladd v Marshall* principles (see [1954] 1 WLR 1489)' (at [25]). The court will therefore require up-to-date information about the parties' circumstances and the values of all assets, including those of the parties. It is thus important to ensure that the evidence is updated to reflect the changes in the circumstances of the parties between the commencement of the proceedings and the date of the hearing. Where the claimant lives overseas, evidence of the cost of living in the foreign country should be adduced (see *Witkowska v Kaminski* [2006] EWHC 1940 (Ch), [2007] 1 FLR 1547). The value of the estate should also be updated as the court is unlikely to allow any orders to be set aside and the matter to be reheard where there has been a fluctuation of the valuation of the assets (see *Myerson v Myerson (No 2)* [2009] EWCA Civ 282, [2009] 2 FLR 147). Having regard to the decision of the Supreme Court in *Ilott v The Blue Cross and Others* (above), in the case of a claimant other than a surviving spouse/civil partner, it is essential to ensure that the case is carefully prepared and that all the evidence to establish what is necessary maintenance for the claimant to meet their needs is adduced before the court. In a case where the claimant is on state benefits, this includes up-to-date information on the benefits and credits received by the claimant, the benefits that the claimant may be entitled to but not claimed due to ignorance or otherwise; what impact any capital payments would have on these benefits and credits and the housing needs of the claimant, and how best to formulate the client's case to achieve the best outcome. The ill thought-out submissions made on behalf of Mrs Ilott, referred to by Lord Hughes at [37], serve as a good example. Where it is necessary to instruct an expert to assess any entitlement or asset, application should be made for permission to do so and for any other directions pursuant to CPR Part 35.

As stated by Morton J in *Re Styler, Styler v Griffiths* [1942] Ch 387, when dealing with the claim, the court should not:

> interfere with a testatrix's or testator's disposition merely because the judge may think that he would have been inclined, if he were in the position of the testator or testatrix, to make some provision for a particular person. I think that the court has to find that it was unreasonable on the part of the testatrix or the testator to make no provision for the person in question, or that it was unreasonable not to make a larger provision.

See, also, *Re Talbot* [1962] 1 WLR 1113, 'Nothing in the 1975 Act undermines the basic proposition that a citizen of England and Wales is at liberty at his death to dispose of his own property in whatever way he pleases'. There is no concept of 'forced heirship', see for example, *Ilott v The Blue Cross and Others* (above), where both Lord Hughes and Lady Hale referred to the significance attached in English law to testamentary freedom and of the fact that the I(PFD)A 1975 did not introduce a general power to rewrite the testator's will. In *Myers v Myers* [2004] EWHC 1944 (Fam), [2005] WTLR 851, Munby J (as he then was) expressed similar views when he stated that the adult child is not entitled to succeed because the reasons for excluding that adult child from the will may not commend themselves to the modern judge. The question the court has to consider is whether the *provision* was unreasonable. The background history may be relevant, but the court must, when determining whether the provision is unreasonable, apply the criteria in I(PFD)A 1975, s 3 objectively.

7.3 CRITERIA IN I(PFD)A 1975, SECTION 3

The matters which the court is required to take into account in deciding whether reasonable financial provision has been made and, if not, whether and in what manner to exercise its powers, vary according to the status of the claimant. There are general matters which apply to all claimants. There are additional factors to which the court must have regard in relation to a claim by:

(1) a surviving spouse;
(2) a former spouse;
(3) a cohabitant of the deceased;
(4) a child of the deceased or a child of the family; and
(5) any other person who was being maintained by the deceased.

The court is required to take into consideration all the matters set out in I(PFD)A 1975, s 3. The section does not indicate that any one of these factors is of greater importance than another factor. The weight of each of the matters specified in the section will depend upon the facts of the particular case. That is not to say that in an individual case one or two factors may not have a magnetic or even a decisive influence on the outcome.

7.3.1 Surviving spouse/civil partner

In the case of a claim by a surviving spouse/civil partner of the deceased, the court must have regard to the following matters (I(PFD)A 1975, s 3(1) and (2)):

(1) the financial resources and financial needs which the claimant has or is likely to have in the foreseeable future;
(2) the financial resources and financial needs which any other claimant for an order under s 2 has or is likely to have in the foreseeable future (see *Re Debenham (Deceased)* [1986] 1 FLR 404);
(3) the financial resources and financial needs which any beneficiary of the estate of the deceased has or is likely to have in the foreseeable future (see *Re Besterman (Deceased), Besterman v Grusin* [1984] Ch 458 and *Re Debenham* (above));
(4) any obligations and responsibilities which the deceased has towards any claimant for an order under s 2 or towards any beneficiary of the estate of the deceased (see *Rajabally v Rajabally* [1987] 2 FLR 390, 396);
(5) the size and nature of the estate of the deceased (for the definition of 'net estate', see Chapter 9 and see *Re Besterman* (above));
(6) any physical or mental disability of any claimant for an order under s 2 or any beneficiary of the deceased;
(7) any other matter, including the conduct of the claimant or any other person, which in the circumstances of the case the court may consider relevant;

(8) the age of the claimant and the duration of the marriage/civil partnership;
(9) the contribution made by the claimant to the welfare of the family of the deceased, including any contribution made by looking after the home or caring for the family;
(10) the provision which the claimant might reasonably have expected to receive if, on the day on which the deceased died, the marriage/civil partnership, instead of being terminated by death, had been terminated by a decree of divorce/dissolution of partnership (see, also, *Re Besterman* (above) and *Re Bunning* (above)), but nothing requires the court to treat such provision as setting an upper or lower limit on the provision which may be made by an order under s 2. In the case of a civil partner of the deceased, the court must, unless at the date of death a separation order under CPA 2004, Part 2, Chapter 2 was in force and the separation was continuing, have regard to similar considerations as those which apply to a surviving spouse (see *Kaur v Singh* [2023] EWHC 304 (Fam) where applying all these factors the court awarded the widow for whom no provision was made in the deceased will one half of the net estate valued at about £2 million).

7.3.2 Former spouse/civil partner of the deceased who has not remarried or formed a subsequent civil partnership, and cohabitants

Where the claimant is a former spouse/civil partner of the deceased, and who has not remarried or formed a subsequent civil partnership, the court must have regard to (I(PFD)A 1975, s 3(1) and (2)):

(1) the financial resources and financial needs which the claimant has or is likely to have in the foreseeable future (see *Ilott v The Blue Cross and Others* (above);
(2) the financial resources and financial needs which any other claimant for an order under s 2 has or is likely to have in the foreseeable future (see *Re Debenham* (above));
(3) the financial resources and financial needs which any beneficiary of the estate of the deceased has or is likely to have in the foreseeable future (see *Re Besterman* (above) and *Re Debenham* (above) and Chapter 5), but see, also, *Ilott v The Blue Cross and Others* (above), where the Supreme Court confirmed the position of charities as beneficiaries and that they should not have to justify a claim under the Act;
(4) any obligations and responsibilities which the deceased has towards any claimant for an order under s 2 or towards any beneficiary of the estate of the deceased (see *Rajabally v Rajabally* [1987] 2 FLR 390);

(5) the size and nature of the estate of the deceased (for the definition of 'net estate', see Chapter 9 and see *Re Besterman* (above));
(6) any physical or mental disability of any claimant for an order under s 2 or any beneficiary of the deceased;
(7) any other matter, including the conduct of the claimant or any other person, which in the circumstances of the case the court may consider relevant;
(8) the age of the claimant and the duration of the marriage/civil partnership, or, in the case of a cohabitant, the length of the period during which the claimant lived as the husband or wife or civil partner of the deceased and in the same household;
(9) the contribution made by the claimant to the welfare of the family of the deceased, including any contribution made by looking after the home or caring for the family.

7.3.3 Child of the deceased

In the case of a claim by a child of the deceased, the criteria in I(PFD)A 1975, s 3(1) and (3) are as follows:

(1) the financial resources and financial needs which the claimant has or is likely to have in the foreseeable future;
(2) the financial resources and financial needs which any other claimant for an order under s 2 has or is likely to have in the foreseeable future (see *Re Debenham* (above));
(3) the financial resources and financial needs which any beneficiary of the estate of the deceased has or is likely to have in the foreseeable future (see *Re Besterman* (above) and *Re Debenham* (above) and Chapter 5);
(4) any obligations and responsibilities which the deceased has towards any claimant for an order under s 2 or towards any beneficiary of the estate of the deceased (see *Rajabally v Rajabally* (above));
(5) the size and nature of the estate of the deceased (for the definition of 'net estate', see Chapter 9, and see *Re Besterman* (above));
(6) any physical or mental disability of any claimant for an order under s 2 or any beneficiary of the deceased;
(7) any other matter, including the conduct of the claimant or any other person, which in the circumstances of the case the court may consider relevant;
(8) the manner in which the claimant was being, or in which they might have expected to be, educated or trained.

7.3.4 Person treated as a child of the family

Where the claim is made by a person (not being a child of the deceased) who, in relation to any marriage/civil partnership to which the deceased was at any time a party, or otherwise in relation to any family in which the deceased at any time stood in the role of a parent, was treated by the deceased as a child of the family, the court must take into account (I(PFD)A 1975, s 3(1) and (3)):

(1) the financial resources and financial needs which the claimant has or is likely to have in the foreseeable future;
(2) the financial resources and financial needs which any other claimant for an order under s 2 has or is likely to have in the foreseeable future (see *Re Debenham* (above));
(3) the financial resources and financial needs which any beneficiary of the estate of the deceased has or is likely to have in the foreseeable future (see *Re Besterman* (above) and *Re Debenham* (above) and Chapter 5);
(4) any obligations and responsibilities which the deceased has towards any claimant for an order under s 2 or towards any beneficiary of the estate of the deceased (see *Rajabally v Rajabally* (above));
(5) the size and nature of the estate of the deceased (for the definition of 'net estate', see Chapter 9, and see *Re Besterman* (above));
(6) any physical or mental disability of any claimant for an order under s 2 or any beneficiary of the deceased;
(7) any other matter, including the conduct of the claimant or any other person, which in the circumstances of the case the court may consider relevant;
(8) the manner in which the claimant was being, or in which they might have expected to be, educated or trained;
(9) whether the deceased maintained the applicant and, if so, to the length of time for which and the basis on which the deceased did so, and to the extent of the contribution made by way of maintenance;
(10) whether and, if so, to what extent the deceased assumed responsibility for the claimant's maintenance;
(11) whether, in maintaining or assuming responsibility for maintaining the applicant, the deceased did so knowing that the claimant was not their own child; and
(12) the liability of any other person to maintain the claimant.

7.3.5 Any other person who was being maintained by the deceased

In the case of a claim by any other person who, immediately before the death of the deceased, was being maintained, either wholly or partly, by the deceased, the court must have regard to (I(PFD)A 1975, s 3(1) and (4)):

(1) the financial resources and financial needs which the claimant has or is likely to have in the foreseeable future;
(2) the financial resources and financial needs which any other claimant for an order under s 2 has or is likely to have in the foreseeable future (see *Re Debenham* (above));

(3) the financial resources and financial needs which any beneficiary of the estate of the deceased has or is likely to have in the foreseeable future (see *Re Besterman* (above) and *Re Debenham* (above));
(4) any obligations and responsibilities which the deceased has towards any claimant for an order under s 2 or towards any beneficiary of the estate of the deceased (see *Rajabally v Rajabally* (above));
(5) the size and nature of the estate of the deceased (for the definition of 'net estate', see Chapter 9, and see *Re Besterman* (above));
(6) any physical or mental disability of any claimant for an order under s 2 or any beneficiary of the deceased;
(7) any other matter, including the conduct of the claimant or any other person, which in the circumstances of the case the court may consider relevant;
(8) the length of time for which and the basis on which the deceased maintained the claimant, and to the extent of the contribution made by way of maintenance;
(9) whether and, if so, to what extent the deceased assumed responsibility for the maintenance of the claimant.

7.4 FINANCIAL RESOURCES AND FINANCIAL NEEDS – I(PFD)A 1975, SECTION 3(1)(A)–(C)

In all cases, the court must take account of the financial resources and financial needs of the claimant(s) and beneficiaries. There is no formal definition provided in the I(PFD)A 1975 for the terms 'financial resources' and 'financial needs', but s 3(6) provides that in considering the 'financial resources' of any person, the court must take into consideration the person's earning capacity, and in considering the 'financial needs' of any person, account must be taken of that person's 'obligations and responsibilities'.

7.4.1 Financial resources

The I(PFD)A 1975 requires the court to take account of not only the present financial resources of the claimant(s) and beneficiaries, but also their foreseeable future resources. This therefore includes information not only about current earnings, but about future prospects. Earnings from investments, such as dividends from shareholdings, interest on savings and income from other sources such as from a trust, must be provided. In respect of a person receiving state benefits, it is necessary to consider the different types of benefit and the amounts of each type to which the person is entitled (for an example of the various benefits and tax credits that need to be considered, see *Ilott v The Blue Cross and Others* (above)). Any pension rights, whether under a state pension or an occupational or private pension, are relevant. Information about, and valuations of, capital and other assets, including real property, savings, shareholdings and any other item of value, must be disclosed. Any entitlement under an insurance policy should be disclosed, including the surrender value and its value on maturity. Where there is a real prospect of the claimant(s) receiving an inheritance from family or friends this should be disclosed. In the age of cryptocurrency and digital assets, these are likely to be treated as property and therefore to be accounted for by the personal representatives and all the parties.

The *Legal Statement on Cryptoassets and Smart Contracts*, published on 18 November 2019 by the UK Jurisdiction Taskforce, chaired by Sir Geoffrey Vos, stated that in principle English Law recognises cryptocurrencies as property and smart contracts as enforceable. The statement can be found at www.judiciary.uk/the-chancellor-of-the-high-court-sir-geoffrey-vos-launches-legal-statement-on-the-status-of-cryptoassets-and-smart-contracts/.

Since then, there have been a number of cases in which the High Court has treated this form of assets as property (see, for example, *Tulip Trading Ltd (Seychelles company) v Van Der Laan and Others* [2022] EWHC 667 (Ch) where this issue is reviewed).

In relation to earning capacity and future earnings, much will depend on the individual circumstances of the claimant(s) and/or beneficiary/beneficiaries, but merely because the claimant is in necessitous circumstances will not be sufficient to entitle the claimant to seek a variation in the dispositions made by the deceased, particularly when the circumstances are brought about by the action of the claimant, for example in choosing not to work when they have an earning capacity, see *H v J's Personal Representatives, Blue Cross, RSPB and RSPCA* [2009] EWHC 3114 (Fam), [2010] 1 FLR 1613, and the reversal of the decision by the Court of Appeal reported as *Ilott v Mitson* [2011] EWCA Civ 346, [2012] 2 FLR 170. Note also that the Supreme Court in *Ilott v The Blue Cross and Others* [2017] UKSC 17 has now ruled that 'benefits are part of the resources of the claimant and it is relevant to consider whether they will continue to be received'.

The court is likely to consider these issues in the same way as it does when assessing claims for damages in personal injury cases and in proceedings for ancillary relief under the Matrimonial Causes Act 1973 or the CPA 2004. The age, health and skills of the individual will be relevant (see below). In the case of claimants with young children, personal circumstances, the cost of care for the children, the availability or otherwise of a support network and the prospect of the person obtaining employment when the children are older are all relevant issues. Depression in the labour market in any specific area of employment in which the claimant's skill lies or evidence of the effect of recession on the labour market generally may also be relevant.

Form E, which is used in applications for ancillary relief, provides a good guide to the information required and can be referred to in claims cases under I(PFD)A 1975, s 2 as a way of ensuring all the relevant evidence is collected. Form E is available on the website of HM Courts & Tribunals Service at www.gov.uk/government/organisations/hm-courts-and-tribunals-service.

Preparation of a schedule of assets, income and expenditure in the form usually prepared in matrimonial cases will be a good guide and starting point, and beneficial to the court. Similarly, it would also be useful, both in terms of considering the nature of the evidence which may be relevant and to get a 'bird's eye view' of the merits of the case and the possible orders which may be appropriate, to prepare a schedule similar to that which is prepared in civil actions such as personal injury claims.

7.4.2 Financial needs

'Financial needs' means reasonable requirements, and in assessing this factor the court may take into account the standard of living enjoyed by the claimant during the lifetime of the deceased, and the extent to which the deceased contributed to that standard (see *Harrington v Gill* (1983) 4 FLR 265 (CA), discussed at para 4.9.3, *Malone v Harrison* [1979] 1 WLR 1353, discussed at para 4.9.2, *Stead v Stead* [1985] FLR 16, discussed at para 6.2.2, *Re Besterman (Deceased), Besterman v Grusin* [1984] Ch 458, discussed at para 6.2.2, and *Re Bunning (Deceased), Bunning v Salmon* [1984] Ch 480, discussed at para 6.2.2).

The needs of a claimant or beneficiary depend on their standard of life and the extent to which the deceased provided for that standard. In a claim by a surviving spouse or cohabitant, the lifestyle enjoyed by the claimant and the deceased, to which the deceased contributed, is highly relevant, but not a claim where the needs are assessed on speculation rather than based on facts and disregards the claimant's earning capacity and ability to obtain lucrative employment (see *Wooldridge v Wooldridge* [2016] Fam Law 451). The success fee under a conditional fee agreement was taken into account as a factor in determining the claimant's future needs, financial obligations and responsibilities in *Bullock v Denton* (HHJ Gosnell, Leeds County Court, 15 April 2020, unreported) and *Re H (Deceased), SH v NH* [2020] EWHC 1134 (Fam), [55]–[60]. In *Higgins v Morgan* [2021] EWHC 2846 (Ch), the court included the sum of £14,200 in respect of the success fee as reasonable need in awarding the claimant a lump sum of £55,000. In *Hirachand v Hirachand* [2021] EWCA Civ 1498, it was held that it was within the discretion of the trial judge to include such provisions to ameliorate the impact on the needs of the claimant. However, in *Clarke v Allen* [2019] EWHC 1193 (Ch), the court held that the widow's needs did not include her lawyer's success fee under a conditional fee agreement and that the responsibility for the success fee must remain with the party who entered into the conditional fee agreement (at [196]).

Whether the claimant's reasonable needs can be met will depend on the size of the estate and the competing claims of other claimants and beneficiaries. The competing claims of a beneficiary which is a charitable organisation are no less important. It is not the function of the court to re-write the deceased's will, but to carry out a balancing exercise between the competing interests, while giving effect to the deceased's intention. The Court of Appeal in *Ilott v Mitson* (above) had taken the view that charities did not rely on any competing need and would not suffer prejudice if a higher award than the court would otherwise make was made to Mrs Ilott. The Supreme Court has, however, disagreed with this view and ruled (at [46]) that the claim of the charities was not on a par with that of Mrs Ilott, and that although it was not based on personal need, they nevertheless relied heavily on testamentary bequests for their work which was for public benefit and humanitarian purposes. Additionally, since the bequest made to the charities was freely made by the testatrix, the charities should not be required to justify their claim. Lord Hughes emphasised (at [47]) that:

> it is not the case that once there is a qualified claimant and a demonstrated need for maintenance, the testator's wishes ceased to be of any weight. They may of course be overridden, but they are part of the circumstances of the case and fall to be assessed in the round together with all other relevant factors.

Lady Hale in her judgment referred (at [66]) to the charities' position as follows:

> This is not to down-play the public interest in charitable giving and the importance of legacies in the funding of charitable activities. But just as the applicant has no expectation of a legacy, neither did the charities. However, the greater the weight attached to testamentary freedom, the smaller the provision which might be thought reasonable in an unusual case such as this …

What is reasonable is relative and much will depend on the individual facts of each case. However, in *White v White* [2000] UKHL 54, [2000] 2 FLR 981, the House of Lords (now the Supreme Court) disapproved any evaluation of a wife's needs solely or even largely by reference to 'reasonable requirements' on the basis that the Matrimonial Causes Act 1973 does not refer to an entitlement being assessed in that manner. The only yardstick that the court can now use is that of fairness between the parties with the objective of achieving a fair outcome. In *Miller v Miller; McFarlane v McFarlane* [2006] UKHL 24, [2006] 1 FLR 1186, Lord Nicholls stated that the hopes, aspiration and expectations of the parties were not an appropriate basis on which to assess financial needs. Baroness Hale made the observation that, 'the court has to take some account of the standard of living enjoyed during the marriage: section 25(2)(c). The provision should enable a gentle transition from that standard to the standard that she could expect as a self-sufficient woman.'

Both the above cases relate to financial provision following a dissolution of marriage but the decisions are relevant in claims under the I(PFD)A 1975 where the claimant is a surviving spouse/civil partner, although only as a starting point. In a claim under the Act the court has to balance the needs of the claimant against the needs of any beneficiary, not simply those of the spouses/civil partners. This issue has now been resolved to some extent by the amendment made to I(PFD)A 1975, s 3(2) by the Inheritance and Trustees' Powers Act 2014, which provides that nothing requires the court to treat such provision as setting an upper or lower limit on the provision which may be made by an order in the case of a surviving or former spouse/civil partner of the deceased.

The I(PFD)A 1975 requires the court to consider both present and foreseeable future needs. It is under this head that information relating to the parties' future prospects, in terms of both income and capital, is relevant. In addition, the needs of those for whom the claimant or beneficiary is and will continue to be responsible, for example, children, an adult disabled child and other members of the family, are relevant. Any other liability which the claimant or a beneficiary has is also a relevant factor. Where a claimant or beneficiary or their dependant is suffering ill-health, medical evidence should be provided about the person's present condition and the prognosis; in appropriate cases it may be useful to adopt the approach taken in personal injury cases (see *Hanbury v Hanbury* [1999] 2 FLR 255 (see para 8.5)).

In this regard, entitlement to future pension benefits and any contingent or postponed interests may be relevant if it is possible to provide a realistic estimation of their value.

When considering whether the deceased has made reasonable financial provision for the claimant, the court is concerned with whether the provisions made or not made were reasonable in the circumstances as they exist, and not as the deceased may have thought they existed. For example, in *Millward v Shenton* [1972] 1 WLR 711, the claimant was suffering from *dystrophia myotonica* and was an invalid living on benefits. His mother made no provisions for any of her six children as she believed they were self-supporting. See, also, the approach adopted by the Supreme Court in *Ilott v The Blue Cross and Others* (above) and in the evaluation of needs in relation to reasonable financial provisions and maintenance discussed in Chapter 6. In *Iqbal v Ahmed* [2011] EWCA Civ 900, [2012] 1 FLR 31, the Court of Appeal considered the options that were open to the widow (at [31]), i.e.:

> first to remain in a house in a bad state of repair and probably too large for her needs, and spend such capital as is available to her on necessary repairs. The second option would be to sell and buy a smaller, cheaper property. There was no evidence before the judge of property values in the area. The third option would be to sell and move into rented accommodation. If the respondent has a half beneficial share outright, a part of the proceeds of sale will go to her and she will have a 'capital cushion' ... to assist her in future years.

7.5 DECEASED'S OBLIGATIONS AND RESPONSIBILITIES – I(PFD)A 1975, SECTION 3(1)(D)

The obligations and responsibilities which the deceased had towards the claimant or beneficiary, to be taken into account when considering a claim, must have existed immediately before the death of the deceased. A claim by an adult child of the deceased, without any evidence to show special circumstances, will generally fail. Failure by the deceased to provide for their child during the child's minority does not entitle the child, when the child reaches adulthood, to found a claim unless there are exceptional circumstances which establishes that having regard to the claimant's circumstances the deceased had a responsibility and obligation to have made financial provisions. The fact that an adult child of the deceased is in necessitous circumstances does not in itself justify a conclusion that the deceased failed to make reasonable provision for the child (see *Re Coventry, Coventry v Coventry* [1980] Ch 461). Where the claimant is of working age with a job or capable of obtaining a job which would be available to them but chooses not to work, they are unlikely to succeed unless there are some special circumstances to justify the conclusion that the failure to make any or insufficient provision for the claimant was unreasonable. This point was raised in the *Ilott* case, both at first instance and on appeal (see *Ilott v Mitson* [2011] EWCA Civ 346, [2012] 2 FLR 170, where the Court of Appeal reversed the decision in *H v J's Personal Representatives, Blue Cross, RSPB and RSPCA* [2009] EWHC 3114 (Fam), [2010] 1 FLR 1613, but this issue did not feature in the Supreme Court's decision). However, where the claimant has given up employment to care for the deceased and has long been out of employment, that factor has been considered to be relevant in considering whether in the circumstances the deceased had failed to discharge his obligation. But see the observations made by Lady Hale (at [62]) of the difficulties faced by the court in distinguishing 'between deserving and the undeserving'. In *Espinosa v Bourke* [1999] 1 FLR 747, when the deceased was aged 79, he and his grandson moved in with his adult daughter who gave up her part-time employment to care for him and his grandson. When the deceased was aged 87, the daughter left to marry, leaving the deceased to be cared for by his grandson and a cleaner. The deceased left his estate including the portfolio of shares he had inherited from his wife to the grandson and excluded his daughter, despite the fact that he had promised his wife that he would leave the shares to the daughter. In allowing the appeal against the decision of the trial judge who had dismissed the daughter's claim, it was held that the trial judge had focused too much on the requirement that an adult child must show moral obligation and her conduct in leaving the deceased and had failed to take account of the criteria in I(PFD)A 1975, s 3 in the balancing exercise. The judge had failed to take account of the claimant's age and the fact that she had been out of employment for a long time. He had also failed to take account of the promise he had made to leave his wife's portfolio of shares to the daughter. She was awarded £60,000 (see, also, below).

In *Re Jennings (Deceased)* [1994] Ch 286, the claimant's father had not made any financial contribution for the claimant's maintenance during his minority and had had no contact with him. The father died without leaving any other children or other dependants. He left his estate to remote relatives and three charities. The claimant lived comfortably. At first instance, the judge had held that he was entitled to take into account the deceased's total failure to fulfil his financial and moral obligations towards the claimant during his minority and awarded the claimant £40,000 to enable him to reduce his mortgage. On appeal, it was held that Parliament had not intended that the I(PFD)A 1975 should revive defunct obligations and responsibilities as a basis for a claim under the Act. As a general rule, the obligations and responsibilities of the deceased referred to in s 3(1)(d) are those which the deceased had immediately before his death, and if the claim did not come within para (d) it could not be brought under the general provision of s 3(1)(g). Blood relationship between a parent and child did not impose a continuing moral obligation which could found a claim under the Act. Furthermore, on the facts, the claimant had failed to satisfy the test in s 1(1)(b) that the provision was necessary for his maintenance to enable him to discharge the cost of his daily living at the standard appropriate to him. See, also, *Williams v Johns* [1988] 2 FLR 475.

In *Adams v Lewis* [2001] WTLR 493, although the deceased's daughters were on state benefits, had little if any savings and lived modestly, their claim against the estate failed. The court found that there was no moral or other obligation on the deceased to provide for the daughters.

In *H v J's Personal Representatives, Blue Cross, RSPB and RSPCA* [2009] EWHC 3114 (Fam), [2010] 1 FLR 1613, where the claimant was estranged from her mother since she was 17 and three attempts at reconciliation had failed, the daughter's claim against the estate failed although she was in necessitous circumstances relying mainly on state benefits for income. The claimant did not work and her husband worked only part time. The mother had set out her reason for not making any provision for her daughter in a letter. On appeal, the court held that necessitous circumstances could not, in itself, be a reason to alter the disposition made by the deceased, particularly as the claimant had the ability to work but had chosen not to do so. 'The ordinary family obligations of a mother towards her only child who was an independent adult' was not a weighty factor and on the facts there was no obligation on the part of the deceased to make provision for her daughter. However, on further appeal to the Court of Appeal, the court reversed the decision. The court held that the issue of whether the mother's failure to make financial provision for her estranged daughter was a value judgment, and the district judge's decision should not be disturbed when the reasons for the exercise of his discretion had been fully and clearly explained, unless it was plainly wrong (reported as *Ilott v Mitson* [2011] EWCA Civ 346, [2012] 2 FLR 170). This issue of the relationship between Mrs Ilott and her mother was further considered by the Supreme Court. The court observed that the circumstances of the relationship between the deceased and the claimant may affect what is the just order to make, and that sometimes the relationship will have been such that reasonable provision is the maximum which the estate can afford. In other situations, because of the distance of the relationship or because of the conduct of one or other or both parties, the provision which it is reasonable to make will be limited to the needs of the claimant. In some cases, this will be of importance where, for example, there was a close relationship between the deceased and the claimant (see [22] and [35]). Lady Hale referred to the issue of family relationships and family obligations and that of the state and the freedom of testamentary disposition, and the fact that these issues have not been dealt with in the I(PFD)A 1975. In particular, she emphasised the difficulty faced by the court in distinguishing between the deserving and non-deserving child (see [49] and [62]). She specifically mentioned that 'one factor which is not on the list (of s 3 factors) but which does feature in family law, is the public interest in family members discharging their responsibilities towards one another so that these do not fall upon the state', and went on (at [63]–[65]) to pose the question:

> So what, if anything, is the relevance of the fact that an applicant's household is very largely dependent on state benefits (in this case 75% of their income) to the threshold question, let alone to the quantification of any order to be made.

Lady Hale emphasised (at [66]) that the state of the present law was unsatisfactory, given that it does not give any guidance as to the factors to be taken into account in deciding whether an adult child is deserving or undeserving of reasonable maintenance.

Similarly, in *Garland v Morris* [2007] EWHC 2 (Ch), [2007] 2 FLR 528, a claim made by an adult daughter, who had not spoken to her father for 15 years, against her father's estate failed. In *Baynes v Hedger and Others* [2009] EWCA Civ 374, [2009] 2 FLR 767, it was held that the deceased, who was the claimant's godmother, did not have obligations or responsibility to make provisions for her goddaughter. She had fulfilled her obligations to her goddaughter during her lifetime by providing financial assistance to her in her lifetime.

As shown by the above cases, the morality of a claim, or the deceased's moral obligation, though not always enough to substantiate a claim, may be relevant when weighing up all the other factors under I(PFD)A 1975, s 3 and carrying out the balancing exercise. The Supreme Court in *Ilott v The Blue Cross and Others* (above) (at [20]) stated that there is no requirement for a moral claim as a '*sine qua non*' for all applications under the I(PFD)A 1975 and case law does not impose one, but in the case of an adult child capable of living independently, something more than a qualifying relationship is needed to found a claim and that additional something could only be a moral claim.

In the case of an adult child, it is not necessary to show exceptional circumstances. While a claim by an adult child who is able to support themselves, without any other relevant circumstances, is unlikely to succeed, it does not follow that a claim by an adult child will always fail. The test is whether, after applying the s 3 criteria to the particular facts of the case, which include the deceased's obligations towards the claimant, it is established that the deceased did not make such provision as would be reasonable in all the circumstances of the particular case for the claimant to receive for their maintenance. The Act does not in any way restrict the interpretation to be given to the word 'obligations'.

Re Coventry, Coventry v Coventry [1980] Ch 461 is often cited as authority that an adult child of the deceased is not entitled to make a claim unless it can be shown that there are exceptional circumstances; reliance for this proposition is placed on the judgment of Oliver J where he said, 'applications for maintenance by able-bodied and comparatively young men in employment and able to maintain themselves must be relatively rare and need to be approached, I would have thought, with a degree of circumspection'. But the learned judge also said:

> It cannot be enough to say, 'Here is a son of the deceased; he is in necessitous circumstances; there is property of the deceased which could be made available to assist him, but which is not available if the deceased's dispositions stand: therefore those dispositions do not make reasonable provision for the applicant'. There must it seems to me, be established some sort of moral claim by the applicant to be maintained by the deceased, or at the expense of his estate, beyond the mere fact of a blood relationship, some reason why it can be said that, in the circumstances, it is unreasonable that no or no greater provision was in fact made.

In *Re Debenham (Deceased)* [1986] 1 FLR 404, the deceased had never recognised her obligations towards the claimant, her daughter, whom she had rejected since her birth, and consistently repulsed efforts by the daughter to form a relationship with her, although she had indicated to the claimant that she would be well provided for in her will. The deceased left the claimant £200, even though she was aware that her daughter suffered from epilepsy and was unable to work; her life expectancy was lower than average and she and her husband lived on a small income. The deceased left the rest of her estate to six animal charities to whom she had no obligations. It was held that although the deceased did not owe any legal obligation to the claimant who was an adult, she owed her a moral obligation and responsibility.

Case law supports the view that the deceased's moral obligation to the claimant justifying an award may be established where promises were made; or where the deceased took advantage of the services of the claimant; or by evidence of the deceased's conduct towards the claimant, as occurred in *Re Debenham* [1986] 1 FLR 404; or where the deceased had said that they owed the claimant such an obligation. In *Re Abrams (Deceased)* [1996] 2 FLR 379, a claim was made by an adult son of the deceased. The son had worked for the deceased in the family business for many years at a low wage in expectation that one day it would be his. He had been forced by the mother's ill-treatment of him to leave the business. The court found that moral obligation was the most obvious circumstance to be taken into account and that, on the facts of the case, the deceased's moral obligation or special circumstances and failure to make provision had been overwhelmingly established to justify an award.

In *Re Pearce* [1998] 2 FLR 705, the claimant, the deceased's son, had worked hard on the deceased's farm without pay and was told by the deceased that he would leave the farm to his son on his death. The deceased, on his divorce, formed a relationship with the defendant. He made a will leaving all his property to the defendant. She then left him and did not live with him again. The deceased did not change his will. The claimant was on a low income and lived with his wife and five children in a home which was in need of substantial improvements. It was held that the deceased had a moral obligation to his son to make financial provision for him.

See, also, *Re Callaghan (Deceased)* [1985] Fam 1, where the deceased, who had been cared for by his adult step-son, was held to have owed the step-son considerable obligations.

In *Re Rowlands (Deceased)* [1984] FLR 813, in his will the testator after making some bequests left the residue to two of his sons who had worked on the family farm. The testator's intention was the continuation of the farm within the family. The widow, who was 90 years of age, and the testator's two daughters made a claim under the Act. The couple had separated after 9 years of marriage but had remained married so that at his death they had been married for 62 years. The widow lived in one of the dilapidated cottages on the farm with one of the couple's daughters her husband and her son. The daughter had cared for her mother, who was bed-ridden, in very difficult circumstances. The court held that having regard to all the relevant factors, the long period of separation should reduce the claim but that the widow's housing needs required improvements which could be provided with an award of £5,000 and which the estate could raise without affecting the ability of the sons to retain the farm within the family. In relation to the daughter's claim, the court held that, although the deceased owed an obligation towards his wife, the same was not applicable to the daughter's claim, which failed. The sons appealed against this decision. Their appeal failed.

In *Re Hancock* [1998] 2 FLR 346, the deceased, when not making any provision for the claimant, who was one of his daughters, had expressed that he would have done so if there had been sufficient money available, and had made provision that if his wife predeceased him, his money was to be divided between his children, including the claimant. The estate received a windfall as a result of the sale of a plot of land. It was held that, in determining the claim, the windfall should be taken into account, along with the expressed intention and obligation of the deceased.

It may be possible to establish a claim grounded in moral obligation on the basis of estoppel, where the deceased's actions led and encouraged a person to act in the belief thereby arising, as occurred in *Re Goodchild, Goodchild v Goodchild* (at para 6.3; and see para 7.8.4).

Moral obligation is also owed by the deceased where the claimant is mentally disabled or suffers from disability, or where the claimant cared for a disabled child. See *Hanbury v Hanbury* [1999] 2 FLR 255 (see para 8.5), where the claimant, an adult child of the deceased, was physically and mentally disabled and the deceased had deliberately taken steps to avoid a claim by his daughter. See, also, *Re Wood (Deceased), Wood v Wood* [1982] LS Gaz R 774 and *Bouette v Rose* [2001] 1 FLR 363 (see para 4.9.2). Arden LJ in the *Ilott* case in the Court of Appeal had expressed the view that the same consideration applies to the case where a party has extra financial needs because she relies on state benefits, but this was disapproved of by the Supreme Court.

In the case of a claim by a former spouse, the deceased does not owe any obligation or responsibility where there has been a 'clean break' settlement by agreement or court order; indeed, the court may specifically have directed, pursuant to I(PFD)A 1975, s 15, that neither party is entitled, on the death of the other, to apply for financial provision under s 2. Where, however, a continuing obligation has been imposed by an order made on marriage breakdown, or it becomes evident that the deceased had not given a full and frank disclosure of their assets, it could be argued that the deceased owed the former spouse obligations and responsibilities (see, further, Chapter 4).

To summarise some of the points raised above, there are unlikely to be any obligations in the following circumstances:

- necessitous circumstances in itself will not be sufficient to justify an award;
- failure by a parent to provide for an adult child during their minority will not suffice to raise a special obligation owed by the deceased to an adult child;
- the fact that a claimant is on state benefits will not raise a moral or legal obligation on the deceased to make provision;
- where an adult child has made a choice not to pursue employment it does not raise any legal or moral obligations on the part of the deceased;
- blood ties alone are insufficient to found a claim;
- where the adult child is self-sufficient, independent and has a comfortable standard of living;
- where the claimant's conduct towards the deceased has been reprehensible;
- where the adult child and deceased parent have been estranged it may reduce the weight of the obligation owed by the deceased;
- where a marriage/civil partnership has ended with a clean break settlement, the court is unlikely to find a continuing obligation unless there was a continuing financial order.

Legal and moral obligation on the part of the deceased may arise:

- where the claimant or any beneficiary is physically and/or mentally disabled;
- where an adult child has cared for a deceased parent or step-parent;
- where the deceased had wholly or partially supported and maintained the claimant and undertaken responsibility for the claimant;
- where promises have been made by the deceased to the claimant;
- where the conduct of the deceased gives rise to an equitable obligation or constructive trust (see para 7.8.3);
- where the deceased has taken advantage of the services of the claimant or by their conduct has led the claimant to act to their disadvantage or led the claimant to an expectation;
- where the deceased has expressly acknowledged to the claimant that they owe responsibility and an obligation towards that person;
- where the doctrine of estoppel arises;
- towards a former spouse/civil partner in certain circumstances and particularly where the financial provision order on the dissolution of the marriage/civil partnership imposes a continuing obligation.

7.6 SIZE AND NATURE OF THE NET ESTATE – I(PFD)A 1975, SECTION 3(1)(E)

For the meaning of 'net estate', see Chapter 9.

The net estate includes the deceased's interest in any foreign property (see *Bheekhun v Williams* [1999] 2 FLR 229). Where the estate is large, there may not be much difficulty in meeting the competing claims of the claimants and the beneficiaries, particularly where the deceased did not owe any obligations or responsibilities to beneficiaries, as where the beneficiary is a charity (*Re Besterman (Deceased), Besterman v Grusin* [1984] Ch 458 (at para 6.2.2) and *Re Debenham (Deceased)* [1986] 1 FLR 404 (at para 6.3) or a remote relative. Where, however, the estate is modest, with insufficient funds available to meet the competing claims, particularly having regard to the cost of litigation, the court will be slow to deprive the testator of their freedom to dispose of their estate as they wish (see *Re Gregory, Gregory v Goodenough* [1970] 1 WLR 1455, where the estate was worth about £2,500 and *Re Harker-Thomas* [1969] P 28, where it was worth about £6,082). However, in some cases, even where the estate is modest, the circumstances may justify the court to attempt to achieve a result which is fair to all the interested parties (*Ball v Ball* [2017] EWHC 1750 (Ch); see, also, *Antonio v Williams* [2022] EWHC 2383 (Ch)). Difficulties may also arise where it is not possible to realise the 'book' value of assets, or where an asset is tied, as in the case of the matrimonial home which provides a home for, say, a child. It is therefore important at the earliest opportunity to establish the extent and value of the estate. It is best practice to seek the information and/or disclosure from the personal representatives. If this is not forthcoming, application under the pre-proceeding disclosure procedure should be considered. It is also important to review the valuation at every stage of the proceedings.

7.7 PHYSICAL AND MENTAL DISABILITY OF ANY CLAIMANT OR BENEFICIARY – I(PFD)A 1975, SECTION 3(1)(F)

Good examples of cases in which an award was held to be justified are *Re Debenham (Deceased)* [1986] 1 FLR 404, where the claimant was an epileptic and unable to work (see para 6.3); *Hanbury v Hanbury* [1999] 2 FLR 255, where the deceased's daughter was physically and mentally disabled with a mental age of about 12 and had been cared for by the deceased, but where the deceased had deliberately taken steps to avoid making provision for her (see para 8.5); *Re Wood, Wood v Wood* [1982] LS Gaz R 774, where the claimant was a severely mentally disabled step-child of the deceased for whom he had not made any financial provision; *Millward v Shenton* [1972] 1 WLR 711, where the claimant was suffering from *dystrophia myotonica* and was an invalid; and *Re McNare, McNare v McNare* [1964] 1 WLR 1255, where the applicant was blind and crippled and 71 years of age.

In *Gold v Curtis* [2005] WTLR 673, the mother of the claimant had left the bulk of her estate to her daughter. She had stated that she had been estranged from her son and, in any event, she had given him financial assistance in her lifetime. Some years prior to her death they had become reconciled, but she had failed to alter her will. The claimant suffered from depression and had a mentally disabled child. His income was insufficient to provide the family with a sustainable standard of living, whereas the daughter had substantial assets and her income exceeded her needs. The court struck a balance between the competing claims of both siblings.

In *Myers v Myers* [2004] EWHC 1944 (Fam), [2005] WTLR 851, the daughter of the deceased suffered from depression, mental health problems and a personality disorder. She was unable to find employment. Her claim against her father's estate was allowed.

Old age without more is not considered to be a disability but it may be a relevant factor when applying the s 3 criteria. A long relationship of dependency and contribution and ill health may justify an award being made. *Thompson v Raggett* [2018] EWHC 688 (Ch) and *Cattle v Evans* [2011] EWHC 945 (Ch) provide two examples.

In *Thompson v Raggett* [2018] EWHC 688 (Ch), the deceased and the claimant had cohabited for 42 years. The claimant was 79 years of age and in poor health and requiring assistance with her care when he died. During their cohabitation she had been financially dependent on him, but she had worked on his farm and his business during this period. The deceased left his entire estate valued at £1.5 million to friends and tenants, giving the explanation that the claimant had her own financial resources and that he did not want her children from a previous relationship to benefit from his estate. She was awarded the outright transfer of the cottage, in which they had lived before he died, and a lump sum of £188,844 to cover the cost of renovation to the cottage and ongoing living costs.

In *Cattle v Evans* [2011] EWHC 945 (Ch), the claimant was 60 years of age. She and the deceased had a long-standing relationship, they had cohabited together for about 5 years and although they had been engaged the couple never married. The deceased died intestate. The beneficiaries under the intestacy rules were the deceased's two sons. Although the couple had always kept their monies and assets separate throughout their relationship, the claimant was awarded a life interest in a property to be purchased for her use and held on trust for the deceased's sons.

Inheritance claims, like personal injury claims, should be meticulously prepared, so that the court is provided with all appropriate medical evidence and evidence about the costs of care. Where appropriate, joint medical and employment experts should be instructed to assess the claimant's disability, earning capacity or lack of it and needs where the disability is profound.

7.8 ANY OTHER MATTER INCLUDING CONDUCT – I(PFD)A 1975, SECTION 3(1)(G)

I(PFD)A 1975, s 3(1)(g) provides that the court must take into account any other matter, including the conduct of the claimant and any other person which, in the circumstances of the case, the court may consider relevant. 'Other relevant matters' may include the deceased's reasons for disposing of their estate as they did, the deceased's wishes in respect of their assets, and mutual wills. What is relevant in any case will be very much fact-specific, as demonstrated by the examples set out below.

7.8.1 The deceased's reasons

I(FP)A 1938, s 1(7), as amended, had required the court to consider the testator's reasons 'so far as ascertainable' for making the dispositions contained in their will (if any), for refraining from disposing of their estate, or for not making any provision for a dependant. The court could admit documentary evidence, other evidence of facts, and oral statements by the deceased for the purpose of ascertaining or inferring the deceased's reasons for making or not making financial provision for the claimant. The court was not obliged, however, to comply with the deceased's wishes. This is demonstrated by the following cases, in which the court considered evidence of the deceased's reasons, but rejected them when determining a claim for financial provision from the deceased's estate. The cases may also be a useful guide on the nature of the evidence which may be relied on in claims under the I(PFD)A 1975 where the deceased's reasons are regarded as relevant to the issues before the court.

In *Re Vrint, Vrint v Swain* [1940] Ch 920, the court permitted a document, which had been formulated by the deceased's solicitors and approved by the deceased in connection with his former wife's application for maintenance in the magistrates' court, to be adduced in evidence for the purposes of inferring the deceased's reasons for not making any provision for her.

In *Re Pugh, Pugh v Pugh* [1943] Ch 387, the deceased by his will left his farm, worth £5,000, to his grandson and the residue, valued at about £1,800, to his widow. In support of her claim, the widow sought to rely on the evidence that, about 4 months before his death, the deceased had told his solicitors that he intended to alter his will. Thereafter, he had told the claimant that he intended to leave everything to her. That intention was repeated by him on many occasions, including as he was passing into unconsciousness, just before his death. It was held that the statements amounted to statements of intention and could not be described as the deceased's reasons for not making any further provision.

In *Re Smallwood, Smallwood v Martins Bank* [1951] Ch 369, on the widow's application for financial provision under the I(FP)A 1938, a statement by the son of the deceased about what the deceased had said to him about the claimant was admitted, on the basis that s 1(7) extended to evidence of facts from which the court could infer the deceased's reasons for making or not making any provision.

In *Re Clarke, Clarke v Roberts* [1968] 1 WLR 415, the deceased had agreed with his wife, the claimant, that they would live with his mother as a temporary measure. The mother's conduct, however, forced the claimant to leave the home, but she told the deceased that they ought to have their own home. The deceased did not respond. He died leaving a legacy of £1,000 to the claimant and the residue to his mother. His reasons for not making any further provision for the applicant were that she had agreed that the matrimonial home should be his mother's home, and that she had left and set up home on her own. The court considered those reasons but found that it was the deceased who had broken the terms of the agreement and that the deceased's moral obligation to the claimant as his wife had not ceased.

In *Re Preston, Preston v Hoggarth* [1969] 1 WLR 317, the deceased gave, as his reasons for not making any provision for his wife, the fact that she was responsible for their separation by returning to Australia with her daughter. Notwithstanding the reasons given, the claimant was awarded a lump sum. See, also, *Re Gregory, Gregory v Goodenough* [1970] 1 WLR 1455 (at para 7.6) and *Millward v Shenton* [1972] 1 WLR 711 (at para 7.4.2).

The I(PFD)A 1975, by contrast with the I(FP)A 1938, does not provide that the deceased's reasons for making or not making any provision is a factor to be considered by the court when determining a claim under s 2. Section 3(1)(g), however, requires the court to have regard to 'any matter which in the circumstances of the case the court may consider relevant'. This is wide enough to include the deceased's reasons for making or not making any financial provision in their will for a claimant, but such considerations must be taken in the context of all the circumstances of the case. If the court considers it relevant, it will weigh that evidence against all the other factors which the court is enjoined to take into account.

Goff LJ referred to the deceased's reason as a relevant factor in *Re Coventry, Coventry v Coventry* [1980] Ch 461, in the following terms:

> Indeed I think any view expressed by a deceased person that he wishes a particular person to benefit will generally be of little significance because the question is not subjective but objective. An express reason for rejecting the applicant is a different matter and may be relevant to the problem.

In *Re Leach (Deceased), Leach v Lindeman* [1986] Ch 226, the claimant obtained an award against her deceased's step-mother's estate despite the fact that she had never lived in her step-mother's household and was never maintained either wholly or partly by her. One of the factors in her favour was that there was considerable evidence that the deceased intended to make a will in the step-daughter's favour.

In *Re Hancock (Deceased)* [1998] 2 FLR 346 (at para 7.4), the deceased had recorded that, had there been sufficient funds available, he would have made provision for the claimant, and a clause in the will expressed his wish that his widow should make provision by her will for the claimant. A plot of land forming part of the deceased's estate was sold for development for a substantial sum of money by the beneficiaries under his will. The Court of Appeal accepted the approach adopted in *Re Coventry* by Goff LJ and said:

> That principle of course governs the approach of the court to the assessment required to be made by the court of the reasonableness of the provision or lack of provision. A good reason to exclude a member of the family has to be a relevant consideration. However, in my view, the recognition by the testator of the status of members of his family and his goodwill towards them and in this case towards the plaintiff are factors which it is proper to take into account under s 3(1)(g) and it is for the court to give such weight to those factors as may in the individual case be appropriate.

In *Myers v Myers* [2004] EWHC 1944 (Fam), [2005] WTLR 851, the deceased's reasons that he had not included his daughter in his will because he considered that he had made adequate provision for her during his lifetime were disregarded.

In *Gold v Curtis* [2005] WTLR 673, the deceased's reasons that she had excluded her son and his family as he had had enough during the lifetime of both his parents and that he had been estranged from her were disregarded. In *H v J's Personal Representatives, Blue Cross, RSPB, RSPCA* [2009] EWHC 3114 (Fam), [2010] 1 FLR 1613, the deceased had set out in a letter of her reasons for excluding her daughter from any benefit the fact that she had been estranged from her and expressed the pain that she had been caused by the daughter's conduct. She had also informed her daughter of her decision and the reasons for it and the daughter had not had any expectation of receiving any benefit. The daughter's claim was allowed at first instance but failed on appeal as the testator had clearly expressed her intention and given her valid reasons for so doing. It was not for the court to interfere with those intentions and the testator's right to dispose of her will as she pleased. The court considered the criteria in I(PFD)A 1975, s 3 but, on the facts, came to the conclusion that none of them weighed sufficiently heavily to justify interfering with the deceased's intention. On further appeal, the Court of Appeal reversed the decision and confirmed the decision of the district judge (reported as *Ilott v Mitson* [2011] EWCA Civ 346, [2012] 2 FLR 170).

In *Ilott v The Blue Cross and Others* [2017] UKSC 17, the Supreme Court has confirmed that it does not follow that once there is a qualified claimant and it is demonstrated that the claimant has a need for maintenance, the testator's wishes cease to be of any weight. They may be overridden, but they are part of the circumstances of the case and fall to be assessed in the round together with all other relevant factors (see [47]).

Other examples include the following. In *Thompson v Raggett* [2018] EWHC 688 (Ch) (discussed at para 7.7), where the deceased's reasons for not making any provision for his cohabitant of 42 years was found to be erroneous and his reasons for not wishing her children to benefit from his assets were considered not to be sufficient to justify his action in depriving the claimant from any financial provision and not fulfilling his obligations and responsibilities towards her.

In *Nahajec v Fowle* [2017] EW Misc 11 (CC) (18 July 2017), the reasons given by the deceased for disinheriting his children were found on the evidence to be based on a false premise. Similarly, in *Banfield v Campbell* [2018] EWHC 1943 (Ch), the deceased's note referring to the claimant as a friend was held to be incorrect. The evidence clearly established that the deceased and the claimant had cohabited together and had a close and supportive relationship, and that the claimant had made a will in the deceased's favour.

It is therefore evident that although a statement made by the deceased setting out the reasons for making or not making financial provision is a relevant factor which the court will consider in weighing up all the matters set out in I(PFD)A 1975, s 3 and carrying out a balancing exercise, it will be the subject of careful scrutiny. If evidence adduced clearly shows that the reasons are inaccurate, erroneous or insufficient, the court will disregard them if the claimant succeeds in making out their claim for financial provision.

7.8.2 Claimant's wish to pass assets to beneficiaries of choice

In claims under the I(PFD)A 1975, particularly where the claimant is a surviving spouse/civil partner of the deceased, the claim may seek an award which includes sufficient assets to enable the claimant to bequeath some of it to beneficiaries of their choice. This is not a factor set out in s 3 which the court is required to consider. It is also not a factor which is set out in Matrimonial Causes Act 1973, s 25, but it has been considered as a legitimate issue which the court should take into account (see *Page v Page* [1981] 2 FLR 198, *Preston v Preston* [1982] Fam 17 and *Re Besterman (Deceased), Besterman v Grusin* [1984] Ch 458) and confirmed in the judgment of Lord Nicholls of Birkenhead in *White v White* [2000] UKHL 54, [2000] 2 FLR 981 in the following passage (at [39]–[40]):

> [39] … I agree that a parent's wish to be in a position to leave money to his or her children would not normally fall within paragraph (b) as a financial need, either of the husband or of the wife. But this does not mean that this natural parental wish is wholly irrelevant to the section 25 exercise in a case where resources exceed the parties' financial needs. In principle, a wife's wish to have money so that she can pass some on to her children at her discretion is every bit as weighty as a similar wish by a husband. A *Duxbury* type fund is intended to provide money for living expenses but not more. The amount of the *Duxbury* fund is calculated on the basis that the capital as well as the income will be used. The calculation assumes that nothing will be left when the wife dies. …
>
> [40] In my view, in a case where resources exceed needs, the correct approach is as follows. The judge has regard to all the facts of the case and to the overall requirements of fairness. When doing so the judge is entitled to have in mind the wish of a claimant wife that her award should not be confined to living accommodation and a vanishing fund of capital earmarked for living expenses which would leave nothing for her to pass on. The judge will give to that factor whatever weight, be it much or little or none at all, he considers appropriate in the circumstances of the particular case

Such an award was made in *Adams v Lewis* [2001] WTLR 493. The court made that allowance by applying the test in I(PFD)A 1975, s 1(2)(a), under which there is no requirement that the award be restricted to the reasonable maintenance of the surviving spouse; and on the basis of s 3(2) which requires the court to have regard to the provision which the surviving spouse might have expected to receive if, on the day on which the deceased died, the marriage, instead of being terminated by death, had been terminated by a decree of divorce. The court also considered *White v White* (above), stating that where the estate of the deceased is substantial and there is a surplus of assets, the application of the principles in *White v White* may be appropriate and may not do injustice to those who may have competing claims, but where the estate is modest or small, it would create injustice to do so.

In *Iqbal v Ahmed* [2011] EWCA Civ 900, [2012] 1 FLR 31, the Court of Appeal approved the award made to the widow of a half share in the matrimonial home and the transfer of the residuary estate to her so that the widow would have a 'capital cushion' to meet future eventualities.

It is suggested that these decisions should not be taken as laying down a principle that in claims under the I(PFD)A 1975 in assessing the surviving spouse's/civil partner's claim, this should be taken account of as a rule. It is suggested that it should be an exception and only where the estate is substantial. Consideration has to be given to the fact that, notwithstanding s 3(2), where the marriage has been terminated by divorce, there are only two parties to the proceedings whose interests the court has to consider, subject to the claims of the minor children, if any; and the parties, or one of them, may have the earning capacity to increase the assets from which the payments may be made.

In claims under the I(PFD)A 1975, the assets from which an award may be made are limited to the net estate, and the interests of other beneficiaries have to be considered. Of the criteria set out in s 3, no one factor has greater significance or priority than any other. The court's duty is to strike a balance between the competing claims of the surviving spouse; any other claimants, who may be minor children of the deceased; a cohabitant of the deceased; disabled children, both adult and minor; and other beneficiaries. It is not the court's function to rewrite the deceased's will nor to make what it considers to be an equitable distribution of the estate. To use the divorce comparison, particularly where the estate is modest, would, it is submitted, be inappropriate (see *Fielden and Graham v Cunliffe* [2005] EWCA Civ 1508, [2006] 1 FLR 745 and *P v G, P and P (Family Provision: Relevance of Divorce Provision)* [2004] EWHC 2944 (Fam), [2006] 1 FLR 431 (see para 7.10)).

7.8.3 Conduct

I(PFD)A 1975, s 3(1)(g) specifically refers to conduct of the parties as a relevant factor. The 'conduct' under the Act does not have the same meaning as it did under the Matrimonial Causes Act 1973 (before its amendment by the Divorce Dissolution and Separation Act 2020, which came into force on 6 April 2022). In relation to a claim made by a surviving spouse/civil partner, conduct cannot be relied on as part of the 'divorce comparison'. In *Miller v Miller; McFarlane v McFarlane* [2006] UKHL 24, [2006] 1 FLR 1186, it was held that it was not open to the courts to redraw the line in relation to conduct under the guise of having regard to all the circumstances of the case. It could only become relevant if the circumstances were such that it would be regarded as inequitable to disregard it. Baroness Hale said that it would only be taken into account if one party has been very much more to blame than the other and it was both 'obvious and gross' (see, also, *Barron v Woodhead* [2008] EWHC 810 (Ch), [2009] 1 FLR 747).

Examples of cases where 'conduct' has been considered a relevant factor include:

- *Talbot v Talbot* [1962] 1 WLR 1113, where the claimant had given birth to a child after the termination of her marriage, her unchastity was considered a relevant though not a decisive factor. It is questionable whether this would now be considered as a relevant factor.

- *Re W* (1975) 119 Sol Jo 439, where after obtaining a divorce on the ground of desertion the wife had not applied for maintenance as the husband had been secretive about his financial position. On his death, the wife was in receipt of state benefits and dependent on charity. The deceased had left his residual estate to two female friends in equal shares. Rees J took account of the deceased's secretive conduct; the fact that he had accumulated capital at the expense of the claimant; the claimant's precarious financial position; and the effect on her of the breakdown of her marriage. Her claim succeeded. In *Re Harker-Thomas* [1969] P 28, the wife had concealed her financial position and had continued to receive maintenance at a higher level than that to which she would have been entitled (see, also, *Re Basham* [1986] 1 WLR 1498). In *Re Rowlands* [1984] FLR 813, the widow's separation for a period of about 48 years was regarded as conduct which was relevant to diminish her entitlement.
- *Ghandi v Patel* [2002] 1 FLR 603, where although the surviving widow's claim failed on the issue of the validity of the marriage, the court observed that had the claim succeeded the court would not have considered the deceased to have made reasonable financial provision for the claimant, but that there was a possibility that the award she would have received would have been reduced by reason of the allegations of unsatisfactory conduct in her relationship with the deceased. Conduct after the death of the deceased and in relation to proceedings may nevertheless be relevant.
- *Baynes v Hedger and Others* [2008] EWHC 1587 (Ch), [2008] 2 FLR 1805, where the court at first instance took into account the claimant's conduct towards the deceased in pressurising the deceased with financial demands which led to the deceased making payments to the claimant of £171,000 during the 4 years immediately preceding her death. On appeal, it was observed that conduct alone should not exclude an otherwise meritorious claim.
- The issue of conduct was considered at all levels in *Ilott v The Blue Cross and Others* (above), which took the form of a long and complete estrangement of the relationship between the mother and her daughter. The Supreme Court has now held that these matters of conduct were not irrelevant, but care must be taken to avoid making awards under the I(PFD)A 1975 primarily as rewards for good behaviour on the part of the claimant or penalties for bad on the part of the deceased. The conduct of both the claimant and the deceased is a relevant factor amongst all the other factors under s 3 and must be taken account of in claims under the Act.
- An adult child is not entitled as of right to an inheritance from their parents even if the estate is substantial. In *Wellesley v Wellesley* [2019] EWHC 11 (Ch), a daughter's claim under the Act, notwithstanding the fact that she had been left a legacy of £20,000, failed by reason of her conduct in remaining estranged from her father for a long period and the fact that she

had not previously relied on him to support her and had been able to live within her means. She was also capable of working.

7.8.4 Proprietary estoppel

The conduct of the deceased in encouraging the claimant to believe that the claimant would acquire an interest in the deceased's estate and thereby, upon that belief, to act to their detriment, can give rise to estoppel upon which a claim may be based. Over the years case law has set out the evidential requirements to establish a claim relying on the doctrine of proprietary estoppel of which the oft cited test is the one set out in *Re Basham (Deceased)* [1986] 1 WLR 1498, namely that the claimant must prove:

(1) that the claimant had a belief at all material times that they would receive the property which is the subject of the action;
(2) that that belief was encouraged by the deceased; and
(3) that, in reliance on that belief and assurance, the claimant acted to their detriment.

Since then there have been three further cases, where this basic test to establish the doctrine of estoppel and the legal principles that apply have been elaborated and clarified, the most significant being that set out in *Davies v Davies* [2014] EWCA Civ 568.

In *Benchdollar Ltd v Revenue and Customs Commissioners* [2009] EWHC 1310 (Ch), [2010] 1 All ER 174, it was held that:

(1) it was not enough that the common assumption was understood by the parties; it had to be expressly shared between them;
(2) the expression of the common assumption by the party alleged to be estopped had to be such that he might properly have assumed some responsibility for it and in conveying to the other party an understanding that he expected the other party to rely on it;
(3) the other party must have relied upon the common assumption to a sufficient extent;
(4) that reliance had to have occurred in connection with some subsequent dealings between the parties; and
(5) the person alleging the estoppel must have acted upon and suffered some detriment or some benefit thereby must have been conferred on the person alleged to have been estopped. The benefit must be sufficient to establish that it would be unjust or unconscionable for that person to assert his legal position.

In *Thorner v Major and Others* [2009] UKHL 18, [2009] 3 All ER 945, the House of Lords (now the Supreme Court) set out the conditions which must be satisfied before a claim based on proprietary estoppel could succeed. These are:

(1) the relevant assurances must be clear and unequivocal and must appear to have been intended to be taken seriously and might reasonably be expected to be relied upon by the person to whom they were made;
(2) the assurances given to the claimant whether expressly or impliedly or tacitly should relate to identified property owned by the defendant.

The most recent guidance which considers earlier decisions has been set out in *Davies v Davies* [2014] EWCA Civ 568, namely:

> 29. …
>
> > '… the doctrine is based on three main elements, although they express them in slightly different terms: a representation or assurance made to the claimant; reliance on it by the claimant; and detriment to the claimant in consequence of his (reasonable) reliance (see Megarry & Wade, *Law of Real Property*, 7th edition (2008) para 16-001; Gray & Gray, *Elements of Land Law*, 5th edition (2009) para 9.2.8; *Snell's Equity*, 31st edition (2005) paras 10-16 to 10-19; Gardner, *An Introduction to Land Law* (2007) para 7.1.1).'
>
> 30. Whilst these three elements are useful for the purposes of analysis and structured decision-making, they are not to be treated as watertight compartments. As Robert Walker LJ (as he was then) said in *Gillett v Holt* [2001] Ch 210:
>
> > '… although the judgment is, for convenience, divided into several sections with headings which give a rough indication of the subject-matter, it is important to note at the outset that the doctrine of proprietary estoppel cannot be treated as subdivided into three or four watertight compartments. Both sides are agreed on that, and in the course of the oral argument in this court it repeatedly became apparent that the quality of the relevant assurances may influence the issue of reliance, that reliance and detriment are often intertwined, and that whether there is a distinct need for a "mutual understanding" may depend on how the other elements are formulated and understood. Moreover the fundamental principle that equity is concerned to prevent unconscionable conduct permeates all the elements of the doctrine. In the end the court must look at the matter in the round.'
>
> 31. Robert Walker LJ went on to explain at page 232 D–E that the concept of detriment for the purposes of this doctrine is not a narrow or technical one. He said:
>
> > 'The detriment need not consist of the expenditure of money or other quantifiable financial detriment, so long as it is something substantial. The requirement must be approached as part of a broad inquiry as to whether

repuditation of an assurance is or is not unconscionable in all the circumstances.'

32. Two further principles emerge clearly from that case. Firstly, whether the claimant has suffered detriment must be judged at the point where the person who gave the assurance seeks to go back on it. Secondly, whether the detriment is sufficiently substantial must be judged by whether it would be unjust or inequitable to allow the assurance to be disregarded: *Gillett v Holt* (above) at 232E–F.
33. Whether there is detrimental reliance in any given case is an evaluative judgment on the facts, which normally lies within the exclusive province of the trial judge. This court can only interfere with the judge's assessment of that issue if it is perverse or clearly wrong: *Suggitt v Suggitt* [2012] EWCA Civ 1140 per Arden LJ at [37].

Applying these principles in *Anaghara v Anaghara* [2020] EWHC 3091 (Ch), the court helpfully enumerated these principles (at [18]) as follows:

i) Deciding whether an equity has been raised and, if so, how to satisfy it is a retrospective exercise looking backwards from the moment when the promise falls due to be performed and asking whether, in the circumstances which have actually happened, it would be unconscionable for a promise not to be kept either wholly or in part: *Thorner v Major* [2009] UKHL 18; [2009] 1 WLR 776 at [57] and [101].
ii) The ingredients necessary to raise an equity are (a) an assurance of sufficient clarity (b) reliance by the claimant on that assurance and (c) detriment to the claimant in consequence of his reasonable reliance: *Thorner v Major* at [29].
iii) However, no claim based on proprietary estoppel can be divided into watertight compartments. The quality of the relevant assurances may influence the issue of reliance; reliance and detriment are often intertwined, and whether there is a distinct need for a 'mutual understanding' may depend on how the other elements are formulated and understood: *Gillett v Holt* [2001] Ch 210 at 225; *Henry v Henry* [2010] UKPC 3; [2010] 1 All E.R. 988 at [37].
iv) Detriment need not consist of the expenditure of money or other quantifiable financial detriment, so long as it is something substantial. The requirement must be approached as part of a broad inquiry as to whether repudiation of an assurance is or is not unconscionable in all the circumstances: *Gillett v Holt* at 232; *Henry v Henry* at [38].
v) There must be a sufficient causal link between the assurance relied on and the detriment asserted. The issue of detriment must be judged at the moment when the person who has given the assurance seeks to go back on it. The question is whether (and if so to what extent) it would be unjust or inequitable to allow the person who has given the assurance to go back on it. The essential test is that of unconscionability: *Gillett v Holt* at 232.
vi) Thus the essence of the doctrine of proprietary estoppel is to do what is necessary to avoid an unconscionable result: *Jennings v Rice* [2002] EWCA Civ 159; [2003] 1 P. & C.R. 8 at [56].

vii) In deciding how to satisfy any equity the court must weigh the detriment suffered by the claimant in reliance on the defendant's assurances against any countervailing benefits he enjoyed in consequence of that reliance: *Henry v Henry* at [51] and [53].

viii) Proportionality lies at the heart of the doctrine of proprietary estoppel and permeates its every application: *Henry v Henry* at [65]. In particular there must be a proportionality between the remedy and the detriment which is its purpose to avoid: *Jennings v Rice* at [28] (citing from earlier cases) and [56]. This does not mean that the court should abandon expectations and seek only to compensate detrimental reliance, but if the expectation is disproportionate to the detriment, the court should satisfy the equity in a more limited way: *Jennings v Rice* at [50] and [51].

ix) In deciding how to satisfy the equity the court has to exercise a broad judgmental discretion: *Jennings v Rice* at [51]. However the discretion is not unfettered. It must be exercised on a principled basis, and does not entail what HH Judge Weekes QC memorably called a 'portable palm tree': *Taylor v Dickens* [1998] 1 F.L.R. 806 (a decision criticised for other reasons in *Gillett v Holt*).

A summary of the facts of the following cases illustrates the points raised above.

Although the case of *Re Basham (Deceased)* [1986] 1 WLR 1498 was not a claim under the I(PFD)A 1975, it concerned the question of family provision, the conduct of the deceased and the assurances he gave during his lifetime. The circumstances and the result of the case, however, may be of relevance in claims under the Act. The claimant was the step-daughter of the deceased. She had lived with the deceased from the age of 15 when her mother married the deceased, and, together with the claimant's husband, they had formed a very closely knit family. The claimant, her husband and their children had assisted the deceased in his business and had worked for the deceased for no reward. The deceased had given the claimant assurances that he would leave her all his estate and that she and her family should have no worries about money. Her understanding was that she would inherit his property. When the claimant's husband wished to move to Lincolnshire to a better job, he was persuaded not to do so by the deceased. He was also persuaded by the deceased not to apply for planning permission on a plot of land he owned with a view to selling it. The claimant also cooked and cleaned for the deceased for the rest of his life and spent a considerable amount of time and money on him. The claim was allowed.

The doctrine of proprietary estoppel was applied in *Wayling v Jones* [1995] 2 FLR 1029 (CA), where the claimant had been in a same sex relationship with the deceased over a long time and had worked for the deceased on the assurance that he would inherit the deceased's estate (see, also, *Greasley v Cooke* [1980] 3 All ER 710).

In *Negus v Bahouse* [2007] EWHC 2628 (Ch), [2008] 1 FCR 768, in a claim under the I(PFD)A 1975 the claimant, who had been in a relationship with the deceased for 12 years, failed to establish that she had a beneficial interest in the property she had lived in with the deceased and owned by him on the ground of proprietary estoppel. The court held that the fact that the deceased had told her that she could live in his home was not in itself sufficient to establish an agreement in relation to the property. The claimant, however, succeeded in establishing that the deceased had not made reasonable financial provision for her maintenance. The court ordered that the flat should be transferred to the claimant free of mortgage and awarded her a lump sum to enable her to provide a pension policy for herself (see *Walsh v Singh* [2009] EWHC 3219 (Ch), [2010] 1 FLR 1658).

In contrast, in *Taylor v Dickens* [1998] 1 FLR 806, the court applied a stricter test to a claim by the claimant for a declaration that he was entitled to the residuary estate of the deceased or, alternatively, damages. The facts were that the claimant had worked for an elderly widow, who had told him that she would leave her house to him. On this basis, the claimant had not charged her for his services. She made a will which accorded with the assurances that she had given him. However, as she became frailer, she needed the services of other carers. She subsequently changed her will, leaving the house to one of the carers, but did not tell the claimant of the change. The court refused his claim and held that, in order to found a case on estoppel, the claimant had to show that the deceased had created a belief or expectation on the part of the claimant that the deceased would not withdraw from the agreement. It was also held that there was no contract between the deceased and the applicant that she would not change her will. The agreement was that she would make a will in the claimant's favour, which she had done. Furthermore, the agreement was a contract relating to land and as such would have had to be in writing. The court thus drew a distinction between a case where the promise was to make a will and no such will is made, and those cases where a will is made, but subsequently the will is changed, and the deceased has not created and encouraged a belief by the applicant that they would not change the will. It is submitted that the distinction made is an artificial one, and the court in making that distinction gave greater weight to the procedural aspect than to the substance and nature of the promise, understanding or assurance given by one person which has encouraged the belief in another, and leads that other to act to their detriment. The test laid down in *Re Basham* and applied in *Wayling v Jones* is to be preferred. See, also, the judgment in *Gillett v Holt* [2000] EWCA Civ 66, [2000] 2 All ER 289, where the decision in *Taylor v Dickens* was criticised, and *Jennings v Rice* [2002] EWCA 159, [2002] WTLR 367.

In *Evans v HSBC Trust Co (UK) Ltd* [2005] WTLR 1289, two brothers claimed the whole of the estate of the deceased, who was unrelated to them, but whom she had treated as if they were her grandchildren. They relied upon the principle of proprietary estoppel to support their claim. They maintained that she had also repeatedly given them assurances that they would inherit the whole of her estate, and they had acted to their detriment on those assurances by purchasing property which they would not have purchased but for the assurances given to them, and had also incurred liabilities. The court found that, in the circumstances, it would be unconscionable to revoke those assurances. However, the court took account of the fact that the deceased was survived by three blood relatives, and adjusted the claim to make allowances for them.

In *Q v Q* [2008] EWHC 1874 (Fam), [2009] 1 FLR 935, in a claim for ancillary relief, the court applied the strict test and found that the husband and wife had acted to their detriment in reliance on the agreement between the father of the husband and the husband's brother, by investing both capital and their efforts on renovating the property on the assurance that the property would become theirs. The shared intentions of all the relevant parties had been clear from the agreement and the supporting documents, which showed that the husband or the husband and wife were to receive the beneficial interest in the property.

Stallion v Albert Stallion Holdings (Great Britain) Limited [2009] EWHC 1950 (Ch), [2010] 2 FLR 78 concerned a divorced woman who had agreed not to contest the divorce proceedings and not to seek ancillary relief, in return for her husband's promise that she would have the right for life to live rent-free in property owned by her husband's company, to have secure employment with his company and the use of a car. The agreement also provided that if her husband were to die and the property had to be sold or she was required to vacate the property, she would be entitled to receive £55,000 from the estate. When the husband died, the company sought to evict her. On the facts, it was held that no representation or assurance had been made to the claimant that she would have exclusive rights to possession of the property, and that she had not enjoyed such rights. However, she had been induced to consent to the divorce and not to claim ancillary relief on the basis of the agreement, and she had acted upon that agreement as a result of which she had not pursued a claim for financial relief and had thus suffered considerable detriment in not applying for an order. The court, in those circumstances, had to stand back and consider whether in all the circumstances it would be 'unconscionable' for the estate to avoid the representations made to her and upon which she had acted to her detriment. On the facts, the court held that, given that the claimant had occupied the property rent-free for about 15 years, and having regard to the circumstances of the other parties to the dispute, it would be unconscionable if the agreement was avoided. Furthermore, the evidence did not establish that events referred to in the saving clause contained in the agreement had arisen. Therefore, until such an event or events occurred, the claimant was entitled to remain at the property.

In *McDonald v Frost* [2009] EWHC 2276 (Ch), the deceased's two daughters brought a claim in estoppel against the estate of their deceased father. They had each been making monthly payments to him and his first wife of £100 and each received money and property worth £20,000 from him. After the deceased's first wife died, he remarried, but the daughters continued to make the monthly payments. In his will, the deceased left his entire estate to his second wife. The daughters brought a claim against the estate asserting that the deceased had repeatedly assured them that they would benefit from his estate. The court dismissed the claim on the grounds that, on the evidence, there had not been any express assurances or promises after the deceased remarried. There was also no particular reason for the deceased to have made such promises.

Issues on estoppels may also arise in businesses operated as a partnership or a family company. This is illustrated in *Shirt v Shirt* [2012] EWCA Civ 1029 and *Shield v Shield* [2014] EWCA Civ 1136. In *Shirt*, the dispute arose between father and son, who were in a farming partnership with the farm being registered in the father's name. Some 10 years later, they fell out and then pursued their own separate business. Many years later, the son claimed a beneficial interest in the farm on the basis that the father had made representations when they had operated the business together. His claim was dismissed, as was his appeal. In *Shield*, the issues related to beneficial interests of a couple's son in a family company in which they all had shares. The couple had intended to leave their shares in the company to their son and executed wills to reflect their joint intentions. The couple separated and, in divorce proceedings, the wife claimed financial remedy. The son intervened, claiming that there was a common intention between his parents which gave rise to a constructive trust or estoppels in his favour. His claim was dismissed and, on dismissing his appeal, the Court of Appeal ruled that for an equity-based claim for estoppel to arise, not only must there be a representation, promise or agreement, but it must also be demonstrated that the person who made the representation or promise has failed to keep it. Since the husband was still alive, it could not be said that he had failed to keep his promise; therefore, the son's claim could not bar the wife's claim for financial relief.

Two further farming cases of relevance are *Suggitt v Suggitt* [2011] EWHC 903 (Ch) and *Davies v Davies* [2014] EWCA Civ 568. *Suggitt v Suggitt* was a case under the I(PFD)A 1975 concerning a farming estate worth £4 million. The deceased had two children – a daughter who was industrious and a son who did not pull his weight. The deceased made a will leaving the estate to his daughter, but on condition that should the son demonstrate his ability to manage the farm, the daughter should transfer the farm to him. The son did well at college, assisted the deceased and was supported by him. The court found that the deceased had sufficiently expressed his intentions in his will and that it was more likely than not that he had given assurances to his son, upon which the son had relied, and had assisted his father without payment on the expectation that he would inherit the farm. However, in a claim under the Act, the court had to make an award which was fair to other beneficiaries. The son was, therefore, granted the farmland and a home, but no other part of the estate.

In *Davies v Davies* [2014] EWCA Civ 568, the claim was made by a daughter that she was entitled to an interest in her parents' pedigree dairy farm on which she had lived and worked with her parents for most of her adult life, for which she had received no payment, but had been told that the farm would be hers one day and had been asked to sign and had signed a partnership agreement by her parents. Unknown to her, however, her parents did not sign the agreement. She succeeded in her claim. The parents' appeal against the decision on the issue of estoppel was dismissed, but the award made to the daughter was adjusted.

See, also, *Southwell v Blackburn* [2014] EWCA Civ 1347, which was a dispute between a cohabiting couple, where the Court of Appeal stated (at [17]) that:

> 17. … Even in cases not concerned with a quasi-matrimonial relationship between promisor and promise, it is clear that where the detriment to the promise is not exclusively financial, its evaluation is not an exercise in financial accounting ... The same is obviously true of benefit. Cases involving couples living together as husband and wife lend themselves still less readily to an arithmetical accounting exercise ...

On the issue of unconscionability, the court ruled (at [20]) that:

> 20. … The detriment to the Respondent was not that she embarked upon a relationship with the Appellant but that she abandoned her secure home in which she had invested and invested what little else she had in a home to which she had no legal title. It is the detrimental reliance which makes the promise irrevocable and leads to the conclusion, at the end of a broad enquiry, that repudiation of the assurance is unconscionable.

In *Habberfield v Habberfield* [2018] EWHC 317 (Ch), the claimant had worked long hours for low wages for over 30 years on her parents' farm on their promise that she would inherit the dairy farm. The estate was valued at £2.5 million. She succeeded in establishing her claim on proprietary estoppel but the court limited her claim to the dairy farm only and not, as she claimed, to the entire farm. She was awarded £1.7 million because the promise relied upon was limited to the dairy farm and not to what she expected to inherit. On appeal when dismissing the appeal the court approved and applied earlier decisions, and in particular referred to the ruling in *Jennings v Rice* [2002] EWCA Civ 159 that where the court is satisfied that the claimant has a genuine claim but is not satisfied that the high level of the claimant's expectations is fairly derived from the assurances given, the court may still take the claimant's (or the upper end of any range of) expectations as a starting point. The court must then look at the circumstances to decide in which way equity can be satisfied while also doing justice to the defendants. It follows that the claimant's expectation is not the basis on which relief is granted but what is equitable from the combination of expectations, detrimental reliance and the unconscionableness of the person who gave those assurances or promises to go back on them. See, also, *James v James* [2018] EWHC 43 (Ch) and *Guest v Guest* [2022] UKSC 27 (see below).

The issue of whether the estate of the donee who predeceases the donor is entitled to make a claim in estoppel for the benefit of the donee's estate remains to be decided. It was an issue raised in *Hughes v Pritchard* [2022] EWCA Civ 386 but the Court of Appeal did not rule on it because the case was remitted for the issue of detriment and appropriate remedy to be considered.

The test to be applied for the approach for granting relief under the doctrine of proprietary estoppel was considered and reset by the Supreme Court in *Guest v Guest* [2022] UKSC 27. Lord Briggs, having reviewed past cases, rejected the theory that the aim of the remedy of proprietary estoppel is entirely detriment based; stated that the concept of the proportionality test is simply a useful cross-check and that the remedy should not without some good reason be out of all proportion to the detriment suffered if it can be readily identified. If it cannot then the proportionality test is unlikely to be of much use. Lord Briggs went on to observe that where the reliant detriment had life-long consequences a detriment valuation will not be useful. A detriment valuation analysis will be useful only where the detriment is specific and short lived and readily identified. The test of proportionality should not be carried out on the basis of financial compensation. He went on to set out (at [71]–[80]) the approach which the court should adopt for granting relief under the doctrine of proprietary estoppel, as follows:

- 'The first stage (which is not in issue in this case) is to determine whether the promisor's repudiation of his promise is, in the light of the promisee's detrimental reliance upon it, unconscionable at all.'
- 'The second (remedy) stage will normally start with the assumption (not presumption) that the simplest way to remedy the unconscionability constituted by the repudiation is to hold the promisor to the promise' but the court may have to consider the promisor's (or his executor's) reasons why something less than full performance will negate the unconscionability.
- The court may then need to consider an alternative remedy such as 'the transfer of less property than promised or the provision of a monetary equivalent in place of it, or a combination of the two' where a transfer would not provide a fair result and cause injustice to the promisor or a third party.
- 'If the promisor asserts and proves, the burden being on him for this purpose, that specific enforcement of the full promise, or monetary equivalent, would be out of all proportion to the cost of the detriment to the promisee, then the court may be constrained to limit the extent of the remedy' and consider how best to limit the remedy.

- 'This does not mean that the court will be seeking precisely to compensate for the detriment as its primary task, but simply to put right a disproportionality which is so large as to stand in the way of a full specific enforcement doing justice between the parties.'
- Where the repudiation occurs during the lifetime of the promisor and the date of performance lies in the future and thus involves an acceleration of the promise. Cases which involve an acceleration of the promise are likely to be the most difficult in terms of finding an appropriate remedy, especially where the parties' relationship has broken down and a clean break is suggested as an alternative. 'A clean break does not necessarily require an acceleration of the promised benefit, or at least not of the whole of it. But if it does, with an early proxy for performance, it is likely to require an appropriate discount for accelerated receipt.'
- The court may be faced with the difficulties an early acceleration may cause to the promisor but 'In the end the court will have to consider its provisional remedy in the round, against all the relevant circumstances, and ask itself whether it would do justice between the parties, and whether it would cause injustice to third parties. The yardstick for that justice assessment will always be whether, if the promisor was to confer that proposed remedy upon the promisee, he would be acting unconscionably. "Minimum equity to do justice" means, in that context, a remedy which will be sufficient to enable that unconscionability question to be answered in the negative.'

7.8.5 Constructive trust

A claim may be made against the estate of the deceased on the basis of constructive trust where the deceased had entered into an arrangement or agreement with another under which property which forms part of the deceased's estate is held in trust for the claimant. Disputes may arise regarding the extent of the beneficial interest (if any) of the claimant to property owned jointly or in the sole name of one of the parties. Where the property is bought in joint names, there is a presumption that the parties hold the property as joint tenants at common law and in equity with the parties having an equal beneficial interest unless it is established that the parties had intended otherwise. Whether the presumption is displaced will depend on the evidence adduced on the common intention of the parties at the time of purchase or subsequently. Most disputes in relation to the parties' beneficial interests arise in the context of family relationships, but disputes can also arise between friends and where the property was purchased as an investment (see *Marr v Collie (Bahamas)* [2017] UKPC 17).

Two leading Supreme Court cases of *Stack v Dowden* [2007] UKHL 17 and *Jones v Kernott* [2011] UKSC 53 set out the principles that apply in such cases.

Where a property is owned jointly without an express declaration of the owners' beneficial interest, the presumption is that they own the property in equal shares, notwithstanding the fact that the contribution made by each of them may have been unequal until the contrary is proved. Where there is no clear evidence from which the parties' intentions can be ascertained the court will impute or infer the appropriate intention. In *Jones v Kernott*, the Supreme Court set out the following principles (at [51]):

> 51. In summary, therefore, the following are the principles applicable in a case such as this, where a family home is bought in the joint names of a cohabiting couple who are both responsible for any mortgage, but without any express declaration of their beneficial interests.
>
> (1) The starting point is that equity follows the law and they are joint tenants both in law and in equity.
> (2) That presumption can be displaced by showing (a) that the parties had a different common intention at the time when they acquired the home, or (b) that they later formed the common intention that their respective shares would change.
> (3) Their common intention is to be deduced objectively from their conduct: 'the relevant intention of each party is the intention which was reasonably understood by the other party to be manifested by that party's words and conduct notwithstanding that he did not consciously formulate that intention in his own mind or even acted with some different intention which he did not communicate to the other party' (Lord Diplock in *Gissing v Gissing* [1971] AC 886, 906). Examples of the sort of evidence which might be relevant to drawing such inferences are given in *Stack v Dowden*, at para 69.
> (4) In those cases where it is clear either (a) that the parties did not intend joint tenancy at the outset, or (b) had changed their original intention, but it is not possible to ascertain by direct evidence or by inference what their actual intention was as to the shares in which they would own the property, 'the answer is that each is entitled to that share which the court considers fair having regard to the whole course of dealing between them in relation to the property': Chadwick LJ in *Oxley v Hiscock* [2005] Fam 211, para 69. In our judgment, 'the whole course of dealing … in relation to the property' should be given a broad meaning, enabling a similar range of factors to be taken into account as may be relevant to ascertaining the parties' actual intentions.
> (5) Each case will turn on its own facts. Financial contributions are relevant but there are many other factors which may enable the court to decide what shares were either intended (as in case (3)) or fair (as in case (4)).

Where the property is transferred into the sole name of one of the parties, the Supreme Court ruled that the starting point is different. The first issue will be whether it was intended that the other party should have any beneficial interest in the property at all. If it was, the second issue is what that interest is. There is no presumption of joint beneficial ownership, but their common intention has, once again, to be deduced objectively from their conduct. If the evidence establishes that their common intention was to share beneficial ownership, but does not show what shares were intended, the court will proceed as set out under paras (4) and (5) above (see *Barnes v Phillips* [2015] EWCA Civ 1056 and *Staden v Jones* [2008] EWCA Civ 936).

These principles were also applied to a situation where the two friends bought a property together, but one party's contribution to the deposit and the mortgage instalments was greater than the others. The Court of Appeal held that they had intended their beneficial ownership to reflect their respective financial contribution (see *Thompson v Hurst* [2012] EWCA Civ 1752).

However, where a family home has been purchased in joint names with no express declaration of trust and the parties subsequently orally agree to alter their respective interest without complying with the formalities for a transfer of title or an express declaration, the issue may arise whether in order to establish a constructive trust it is necessary to establish detrimental conduct in order for there to be a variation of the beneficial interest between the parties. In *Hudson v Hathway* [2022] EWHC 631 (QB), Kerr J, in determining whether the claimant's interest in the property had been transferred to Ms Hathway, held that there was no mention of the need for reliance or change of position in *Stack v Dowden* [2007] UKHL 17 or *Jones v Kernott* [2011] UKSC 53, and that had they considered this element to be crucial it is unlikely that the court would have omitted any reference to it as a relevant principle. Kerr J held (at [79]) that in the domestic context:

> an express agreement as to beneficial interest, provided it is not a unilateral oral declaration of trust making the putative beneficiary merely a volunteer, can itself supply the necessary detriment or … satisfy the requirement of unconscionability without the need to establish separately that the beneficiary has acted in detrimental reliance on or changed her position in reliance of the promise.

On further appeal, the Court of Appeal disagreed with Kerr J on the issue of the requirement of detriment as an element and confirmed that a party who claims a subsequent agreement in relation to the parties' initial beneficial interests must show that they acted to their detriment. On the facts, the court held that by agreeing to take on a less lucrative career to take care of the parties' children and on separation by giving up her claim to a share in Mr Hudson's shares and pension rights, which both parties had considered to be joint assets, and taking on the mortgage payments, Ms Hathway had established that she had acted to her detriment to establish a constructive trust in her favour.

Since 1 April 1985, where property is transferred into joint names it is possible to set out the nature and extent of the beneficial interests of the parties on Form TR1. In relation to transfers which occurred before April 1985 or where Form TR1 has not been completed or does not expressly declare the beneficial interests, there is a presumption that the parties hold the property as joint tenants in law and in equity unless the contrary is proved. In *Cameron v Cameron* [2021] EWHC 229 (Ch) on the evidence, the court found that Form TP1 effectively transferred the deceased's property so that the beneficial interest in it was held jointly by the deceased and her daughter as joint tenants. However, the circumstances in which Form TR1 was executed failed to validly and effectively transfer the whole of the deceased's interests to her daughter. Form TR1 was set aside. This applies in relation to both domestic property and commercial or investment properties and between parties who are business partners. For example, in *Rowland v Blades* [2021] EWHC 426 (Ch), the property in issue was not a family home (see, also, *Jones v Kernott* [2011] UKSC 53.

Where Form TR1 or other clear evidence of intention is not available, the issue will depend on whether the parties' intention can be inferred or imputed from the circumstances and relationships between the parties at the time and since the purchase of the property. It may be possible to establish an appropriate inference from the conduct of, and dealing between, the parties. The court may also impute an intention on the evidence adduced on what is fair and equitable between the parties having regard to the course of dealings between them in relation to the property in issue (for an example of inference/ imputation, see *Oxley v Hiscock* [2004] EWCA Civ 546).

Where Form TR1 has been executed setting out the common intention that the parties were to hold the properties jointly and subsequently, a power of attorney gives one of them control over the beneficial interests in any property and the donee of the power is not permitted to act in conflict with the personal interest of the donor. The donee must at all times act in good faith and account to the donor so that if the property is sold by the donee they must account to the donor for their share of the proceeds of sale (see *Aldoukhi v Abdullah* [2021] EWHC 3086 (Fam)).

Where the property is acquired in the sole name of a party who has not made any financial contribution towards the purchase price, nor in any other way, and they have not discussed their respective interest in the property, it might be possible for a common intention to be inferred that the person who funded the purchase should have an interest deduced objectively from the course of dealings between them (see *Capehorn v Harris* [2015] EWCA Civ 955 and *Constandas v Lysandrou* [2018] EWCA Civ 613). The issue of quantifying their respective interest may, however, prove difficult (see *Aspden v Elvy* [2012] EWHC 1387

(Ch)). In *Liden v Burton* [2016] EWCA Civ 275, the claimant was not able to establish either a common intention or a course of dealings from which the parties' intention could be implied. For a case where the purpose of acquiring the property in the sole name of one of the parties was an illegal one, see *O'Kelly v Davies* [2014] EWCA Civ 1606.

Where property is held in joint names, the burden of proof is on the party seeking to claim that the parties had intended the beneficial interests to be different. The financial arrangements and an accounting process between the parties may be relevant (see *Hudson v Hathway* [2022] EWHC 631 (QB) (discussed above)). In relation to property held in the sole name of one party, the issue on what was the parties' common intention will depend on the strength of the evidence adduced about what was agreed at the time of the purchase, and any change in the parties' relationship and conduct at the time and subsequently, assessed objectively. Where the evidence establishes a common intention for both parties to have a beneficial interest in the property but it is not clear what, if any, agreement was reached or inferred with regard to the extent of each party's interest, the court will look to provide what is fair between the parties having regard to the circumstances of the case. This is particularly relevant where the property is purchased in the sole name of one party, who made no financial or other contribution to the purchase, and the party seeking relief was solely responsible for all the financial payments made at the time and/or since the purchase (see *Culliford v Thorpe* [2018] EWHC 426 (Ch) and *Pickering v Hughes* [2021] EWHC 1672 (Ch), where the claimant had acted to their detriment; for earlier cases, see *Agarwala v Agarwala* [2013] EWCA Civ 1763 and *Wodzicki v Wodzicki* [2017] EWCA Civ 95).

However, in determining what is fair between the parties, the court is not concerned with redistributing property interests or some form of redistributive justice (see *Graham-York v York (Personal Representative of the Estate of Norton Brian York)* [2015] EWCA Civ 72).

7.8.6 Rule in *Rochefoucauld v Boustead*

The case of *Rochefoucauld v Boustead* [1897] 1 Ch 196 established the principle that where a property is transferred gratuitously to one person (A) on the basis of an oral agreement that A will hold it in trust for another person (B), A will not be permitted to rely on the absence of a formal written deed of trust as required under Law of Property Act 1925, s 53(1) to deny B's beneficial interest in the property. This principle was considered in *De Bruyne v De Bruyne* [2010] EWCA Civ 519 and applied in *Archibald v Alexander* [2020] EWHC 1621 (Ch), but see, also,

Solomon v McCarthy [2020] All ER (D) 112 (Jan), where the same result was arrived at on the basis of a resulting trust.

7.8.7 Doctrine of mutual wills

The doctrine of mutual wills applies only where the agreement to enter into mutual wills is reinforced by undertakings that the wills shall not be revoked. Mutual wills must not be confused with mirror wills, where two people make wills in substantially identical form each benefiting the other. However, the existence of a mirror will may be relevant to support the claim that they were intended to have the same effect as mutual wills where there is other evidence to substantiate the claim. The mere existence of mirror wills without more is not sufficient to prove that the wills were intended to be mutual. For a claim on the doctrine of mutual wills to apply, the evidence must be sufficient to establish a contract in law so that if the first testator dies having made a will in compliance with the agreement, the agreement becomes binding on the second testator, and gives rise to an equitable obligation to give effect to the mutually agreed disposition(s). A 'floating trust' is created, and the personal representatives of the second testator are obliged to administer it.

The legal principles which apply to mutual wills were considered in *Charles v Fraser* [2010] EWHC 2154 (Ch), and the law was summarised as follows (at [59]):

> 59. I take the law on mutual wills to be as follows:
>
> (i) Mutual wills are wills made by two or more persons, usually in substantially the same terms and conferring reciprocal benefits, following an agreement between them to make such wills and not revoke them without the consent of the other.
> (ii) For the doctrine to apply there has to be what amounts to a contract between the two testators that both wills will be irrevocable and remain unaltered. A common intention, expectation or desire is not enough.
> (iii) The mere execution of mirror or reciprocal wills does not imply any agreement either as to revocation or non-revocation.
> (iv) For the doctrine to apply it is not necessary that the second testator should have obtained a personal financial benefit under the will of the first testator (albeit that in the present case Ethel had, of course, done so).
> (v) It is perfectly possible for there to have been an agreement preventing revocability as to part of the residuary estate only, in which case the doctrine only applies to that part.
> (vi) The agreement may be incorporated in the will or proved by extraneous evidence. It may be oral or in writing.

(vii) The agreement must be established by clear and satisfactory evidence on the balance of probabilities.

(viii) The agreement is enforced in equity by the imposition of a constructive trust on the property which is the subject matter of the agreement. The beneficiaries under the will that was not to be revoked may apply to the Court for an order that the estate is held on trust to give effect to the provisions of the old will.

(ix) The action relates only to the disposative part of the will. The new will is fully effective to deal with non-disposative matters, such as the appointment of Executors. Accordingly where the doctrine applies the Executors appointed under the final will hold the assets of the estate on trust to give effect to the earlier will.

Where the legal formalities relating to mutual wills have not been complied with, but the parties believed that they had created mutually binding wills, a constructive trust is implied to prevent the second testator from dealing with the deceased's assets in a way which is incompatible with the agreement (see *Healey v Brown* [2002] EWHC 1405 (Ch)). The cases of *Re Goodchild, Goodchild v Goodchild* [1997] 1 WLR 1216 and *Birch v Curtis* [2002] EWHC 1158 (Ch) illustrate the practical difficulties which arise in relation to such wills. In both cases the claim failed. More recently, in *St Clair v King and Another* [2022] EWHC 40 (Ch), having considered all the evidence and applying the civil standard of proof, the court held that an agreement in respect of making mutual wills had not been concluded. In contrast, in *Olins v Walters* [2008] EWCA Civ 782 the claim was allowed. The Supreme Court in *Marley v Rawlings* [2014] UKSC 2, where each party signed the wrong will, overcame the problem by ruling that the will should be treated as a commercial contract and that the mistake should be regarded as a clerical error capable of rectification.

It is therefore important for practitioners who are instructed to draw up wills in identical terms to ensure that their clients have been clearly informed of the legal implications and differences between making a mirror will and one that is mutual, and in particular the effect it may have if a claim is made under the I(PFD)Act 1975. If the clients' intention is to make mutual wills so that each agrees to make a will in the same terms and not to revoke it without the consent of the other, this should be clearly stated on the face of both wills or in some other formal document (see, further, *Snell's Equity* (Thomson Reuters, 34th edn, 2021)).

In view of the difficulties that have arisen in relation to whether the parties intended that their respective wills should be treated as binding on each other mutually or whether the surviving testator holds the property they receive on an implied or constructive trust, the Law Commission has included it in its *Twelfth Programme of Law Reform*, Law Com No 354 (HMSO, 2014).

7.9 FACTORS RELEVANT TO A SURVIVING SPOUSE, FORMER SPOUSE, CIVIL PARTNER AND COHABITANTS

7.9.1 Age

The age of a surviving spouse/civil partner is relevant in assessing their earning capacity. Also relevant is whether and, if so, the extent to which, the surviving spouse is caring for a minor child. If the surviving spouse/civil partner was not gainfully employed during the marriage/civil partnership, age will be relevant in considering whether that person could train or retrain so as to earn an income to meet some or all of their own needs. In such a case, provision may be made for a modest sum to enable the spouse to adjust to the new situation and to take up or resume gainful employment. Cases decided under the Matrimonial Causes Act 1973 should be considered as examples of how the courts have dealt with this issue. For example, in *Khan v Khan* [1981] 2 FLR 131, an order limited in time was made while the wife trained and obtained employment; and in *Attar v Attar (No 2)* [1985] FLR 653, a wife was given a lump sum representing 2 years' maintenance. Where the surviving spouse/civil partner is middle-aged or elderly, it will be relevant whether or not that spouse/civil partner has lost the potential to earn income or is disadvantaged in the labour market (see *Robertson v Robertson* (1983) 4 FLR 387, where a wife had not lost the potential to work). In *Fielden and Graham v Cunliffe* [2005] EWCA Civ 1508, [2006] 1 FLR 745, the age of a widow was a relevant consideration in assessing her ability to gain and remain in full-time employment and obtain pension rights and meet her needs.

7.9.2 Duration of marriage/civil partnership and cohabitation

The duration of marriage is a significant relevant factor in assessing what is reasonable financial provision for the surviving spouse/civil partner. Where the marriage/civil partnership has lasted a long time, with the parties living together and bringing up a family, a substantial award may be justified. Where the surviving spouse/civil partner is not young, although the marriage/civil partnership may have been short, the effect on the spouse/civil partner is relevant in assessing an award which is just in all the circumstances of the case. The surviving spouse/civil partner may have given up their own secure accommodation and employment or lost pension rights and other benefits in order to care for the deceased or the parties' children. The housing needs and the contribution the claimant has made to the family will be relevant considerations (see *Iqbal v Ahmed* [2011] EWCA Civ 900, [2012] 1 FLR 31, *Ames v Jones and Others* [2016] EW Mis B67 and *Kaur v Singh* [2023] EWHC 304 (Fam)).

Where the surviving spouse/civil partner is young and the marriage/civil partnership was short, whether or not there are children, the short duration of the marriage/civil partnership is a relevant consideration. Premarital cohabitation and any contribution made during that period should also be taken into account. Conversely, any period during which the spouses/civil partners were separated may also be relevant in calculating the length of the marriage and the contribution made by the claimant. Much will depend on the facts of the individual case, the competing claims of any beneficiaries and the size and nature of the deceased's estate.

Where the marriage is long but the parties had lived separately and apart with both following separate lives, although not divorced, the period of separation will be a relevant factor (see *Re Rowlands deceased* [1984] FLR 813, where the separation had lasted 43 years). In *GW v RW* [2003] EWHC 611 (Fam), [2003] 2 FLR 108, a period of pre-marriage cohabitation and a period of estrangement during the marriage were both taken into account in calculating the length of the marriage; it was stated that a 12-year period of marriage with two children could not be regarded as a long marriage, but a 20-year marriage would fall into that category. Pre-marriage cohabitation is as relevant as cohabitation after marriage. In *Co v Co (Ancillary Relief: Pre-marriage Cohabitation)* [2004] EWHC 287 (Fam), [2004] 1 FLR 1095, it was held that to ignore pre-marriage cohabitation would be to fly in the face of the principal statutory duty of the court to have regard to all the circumstances of the case in exercising its powers. In that case Coleridge J said:

> Committed, settled relationships which often endure for years in the context of cohabitation (often but not always with children) outside marriage must, I think, be regarded as every bit as valid as those where parties have made the same degree of commitment but recorded it publicly by civil registration, ie by marriage. This has nothing to do with striving to achieve financial fairness as between a couple at a particular stage in society's development.

See, also, *K v L* [2011] EWCA Civ 550, where the period of cohabitation before marriage and during the marriage, which was found to be invalid, was taken into account with the duration of the subsequent valid marriage. The same approach will also be relevant in claims made by cohabitants and those in same sex relationships, who have lived together before entering into a civil partnership or same sex marriage.

In *Fielden and Graham v Cunliffe* [2005] EWCA Civ 1508, [2006] 1 FLR 745, Wall LJ (as he then was) approached the case with a 'divorce comparison' and considered the interplay between the provision of the Matrimonial Causes Act 1973 and the provisions of I(PFD)A 1975, s 3(2), and the application of the principles laid down in *White v White* [2000] UKHL 54, [2000] 2 FLR 981 and its relevance when the marriage was a short one. His Lordship observed that in such cases caution had to be exercised when applying the principles laid down in *White v White* to a case under the Act, and drew a distinction between the two principles as follows:

(1) Divorce involves two living former spouses to each of whom the provisions of Matrimonial Causes Act 1973, s 25(2) apply whereas in cases under the I(PFD)A 1975, a deceased spouse who leaves a widow is entitled to bequeath his estate to whomsoever he pleases; his statutory obligation is to make reasonable financial provision for his widow. In such cases, depending on the value of the estate, the concept of equality may bear little relation to such provision.
(2) Divorce involves a conscious decision by one or both of the spouses to bring the marriage to an end. That process leaves two living former spouses, each of whom has resources, needs and responsibilities. In such a case, the length of the marriage and the parties' respective contribution to it assume a particular importance when the court is striving to reach a fair financial outcome. Where a marriage is dissolved by death, the widow is entitled to say that she entered into it on the basis that it would be of indefinite duration and in the expectation that she would devote the remainder of the parties' joint lives to being his wife and caring for him. The fact that the marriage has been prematurely terminated by death after a short period may, therefore, render the length of the marriage a less critical factor than it would be in the case of a divorce.
(3) There is a clear difference between a widow who had been married for many years and who had made an equal contribution to the family of the deceased and one who like the claimant had been married only a year and who had not made such a contribution. Therefore, the duration of a marriage/civil partnership or even cohabitation before marriage/civil partnership and the 'divorce comparison' is likely to be relevant in considering housing needs.

In *Aston v Aston* [2007] WTLR 1349, in a claim brought by the widow of the deceased, the court held that the 'divorce fiction' referred to in I(PFD)A 1975, s 3(2) was relevant to the specific facts of the case because the marriage had effectively ended well before the death of her husband. She was thus better off than she would have been on a divorce as she had received a lump sum under an insurance policy; she had an earning capacity of £18,000 plus benefits; and a civil service pension as the deceased's widow. Her claim for half the share in the home and half the capital in the estate was refused.

The House of Lords' decision in *Miller v Miller; McFarlane v McFarlane* [2006] UKHL 24, [2006] 1 FLR 1186 considered the approach to be adopted in short marriage cases in the context of a divorce. The former wife in *McFarlane v*

McFarlane where the marriage had lasted for only 2½ years received a substantial award. The House of Lords did not follow the pre-*White* line of cases which confined the former wife to her needs, but Lord Nicholls of Birkenhead observed that in big money cases the court should decide what would be a fair division of the available assets having regard to their financial needs, the need for compensation and all the circumstances of the case, and consider whether there are good reasons for departing from equality. In a short marriage, there will often be a good case for departing substantially from equality with regard to non-matrimonial property. In a short and childless marriage, where both parties worked with a degree of separation of their finances, fairness may require a reduction in the equal sharing principle. In relation to a short marriage, non-matrimonial or inherited assets will be less likely to be shared, but consideration may have to be given on whether some maintenance allowance should be made for a short period to assist the claimant to achieve an independent life (see, further, *Sharp v Sharp* [2017] EWCA Civ 408, *XW v XH* [2019] EWCA Civ 2262 and *E v L* [2021] EWFC 60 on the approach adopted in financial relief application in respect of a short marriage following a divorce).

It should be noted that the cases of *Miller v Miller* and *McFarlane v McFarlane* were not claims under the I(PFD)A 1975 and since the emphasis in a claim under the Act is to achieve fairness, the application of the general principle will depend on the facts of the individual case. In every case, therefore, the result will be very much fact specific, and this is particularly the case in claims under the Act. In every case, the court strives to achieve a fair outcome having regard to the facts and it is more likely than not, particularly where the estate is modest in size and there are competing claims of other claimants and beneficiaries to be taken into account, that equality cannot be achieved so the stakes should not be raised too high. In *Lilleyman v Lilleyman* [2012] EWHC 821 (Ch), Briggs J (as he then was) dealt with the issue of the 'divorce cross-check' as follows (at [60]):

> 60. I must finally mention *P & P* [2006] 1 FLR 431, a decision of Black J in December 2004, in which the divorce cross-check was closely analysed in the context of an Inheritance Act claim by a widow. Her conclusion, with which I agree, is that the cross-check should be treated neither as a floor nor a ceiling in relation to the relief available under the Inheritance Act, nor as something which requires a meticulous quasi-divorce application to be analysed side by side with the application of the separate provisions in Section 3 of the Act. The divorce cross-check is just that, a cross-check, no more and no less. It is, like all the other matters to be taken into account under Section 3, of infinitely variable weight on the facts of each particular case.

I(PFD)A 1975, s 3(2) in its amended form now provides that nothing requires the court to treat the cross-check provision as setting an upper or lower limit on the provision which may be made by an order under s 2 in relation to a spouse/civil partner of the deceased. In any event, in an application under the Act the court will have to adjust the provision it makes to ensure that it is a fair outcome for everyone who may be affected by the order (see *A v L (Departure from Equality)* [2011] EWHC 3150 (Fam), *R v R (Financial Remedies: Needs and Practicalities)* [2011] EWHC 3093 (Fam), [2013] 1 FLR 120, and *Wooldridge v Wooldridge (Case No 3CL1022132)* [2016] Fam Law 451, where the widow's claim was dismissed).

In the case of cohabitants (whether in same sex or opposite sex relationships), the length of the period of cohabitation will be as relevant as it is in marriage/civil partnership cases, particularly where there are children as a result of the relationship and it is established that the cohabitant and the children were wholly or substantially maintained by the deceased, i.e. that they were dependent on the deceased. Evidence of the nature and extent of that dependency and the standard of living enjoyed by the family will be essential to establish a case for an award (see *Negus v Bahouse* [2007] EWHC 2628 (Ch), [2008] 1 FLR 381). In *Webster v Webster* [2008] EWHC 31 (Ch), [2009] 1 FLR 1240, the court applied the case of *Negus*. There the parties had lived together for 27 years and had two children. The home in which they lived was in the man's sole name and he paid the mortgage, whilst the claimant paid some of the outgoings of the home. Both parties worked, but the man earned substantially more than the woman. The man died intestate. The estate fell to be divided under the intestacy laws between his children from his former marriage and the two children from his relationship with the claimant. She made a claim under the I(PFD)A 1975 for an interest in the family home and the company shares in the man's name. On the facts and the evidence adduced before the court in respect of the claimant's circumstances at the date of the hearing, the court transferred the home to her outright and ordered the estate to pay the mortgage on the property. The award combined with the sums already paid to the claimant out of the estate amounted to about the same as a *Duxbury* capitalisation of an income of £1,500 per annum, which was equivalent to the fall in the amount of the family income consequent on the death of the man.

See Law Commission Consultation Paper No 191, *Intestacy and Family Provision Claims on Death* and the report, *The rights of cohabiting partners*, published on 4 August 2022 by the Women and Equalities Committee (a cross-party group of MPs) referred to in Chapter 1.

7.9.3 Claimant's contribution to the welfare of the family

The contribution made by a spouse/civil partner and cohabitants by looking after the home and caring for the family is given as much weight as that of the spouse/civil partner who goes out to work. Greater value should not be placed on the contribution of the breadwinner than that of the homemaker as a reason for an unequal division of assets between the spouses/civil partners. Sterile suggestions that the breadwinner's contributions were greater than the homemaker's should be avoided. The nature of the contributions made by each party may be different and incommensurable, and each should be recognised as of no less value than the other (see *White v White* [2000] UKHL 54 and *Lambert v Lambert* [2002] EWCA Civ 1685, [2003] 1 FLR 139). In the majority of cases since then, where special contribution has been raised to seek an upward adjustment of the assets, the claim has been rejected (see *K v L (Non-Matrimonial Property: Special Contribution)* [2011] EWCA Civ 550, *Gray v Work* [2015] EWHC 834 (Fam) and *Chai v Peng* [2017] EWHC 792 (Fam)). Cases where 'special contribution' was considered to be a relevant factor include *Charman v Charman* [2007] EWCA Civ 503 and *RC v JC* [2020] EWHC 466 (Fam). Contribution made by a party to a marriage, civil partnership or by a cohabitant to the business of the other spouse civil partner or cohabitant which assisted in making the business prosperous must be given due weight (see *Conran v Conran* [1997] 2 FLR 615). Note, however, that the above cases all relate to applications for financial relief following a divorce or in civil proceedings based on constructive trust (*Hudson v Hathway* [2022] EWHC 631 (QB) is a recent example), where the parties to the dispute are only the couple concerned, whereas in claims under the I(PFD)A 1975 the court has to consider the interests of other beneficiaries.

See the recommendation of the Law Commission's Consultation Paper No 191, *Intestacy and Family Provision Claims on Death*, and those made in the report, *The rights of cohabiting partners*, published on 4 August 2022 by the Women and Equalities Committee (a cross-party group of MPs) referred to in Chapter 1 and available at https://publications.parliament.uk/pa/cm5803/cmselect/cmwomeq/92/report.html and the government's response to the report.

7.9.4 Financial contribution

I(PFD)A 1975, s 3 does not refer to financial contribution, but in cases decided under the Matrimonial Causes Act 1973, financial contribution made by a spouse/civil partner has been a relevant factor in so far as a party seeking to receive an uplift in the award made on the ground that the contribution was exceptional (see *Conran v Conran* (above)). The court has also departed from the concept of equality where the husband's/civil partner's special contribution to the marriage/civil partnership was as a result of the exceptional business acumen, which, in *Sorrell v Sorrell* [2005] EWHC 1717 (Fam), [2006] 1 FLR 497, was referred to as amounting to genius, and it was held that it would be unfair not to recognise this special contribution in the final division of the family assets. It was also indicated that the case of *Lambert v Lambert* (above) did not establish any new test in relation to special circumstances. The decision in *Lambert* has tightened the criteria to the 'most exceptional and limited circumstance', but it has not provided or suggested any guidelines on the issue. Some guidance on the approach which the courts should adopt when assessing financial contribution as a factor can be found in the judgment of Lord Nicholls of Birkenhead in *Miller v Miller; McFarlane v McFarlane* [2006] UKHL 24, [2006] 1 FLR 1186, where he said (at [67]), 'Parties should not seek to promote a case of "special contribution" unless the contribution is so marked that to disregard it would be inequitable. A good reason for departing from equality is not to be found in the minutiae of married life.'

Baroness Hale supported this interpretation to some extent when she said that Matrimonial Causes Act 1973, s 25(2)(f) (at [148]):

> does *not* refer to the contribution which each has made to the parties' *accumulated wealth*, but to the contribution they have made (and will continue to make) to the *welfare of the family*. Each should be seen as doing their best in their own sphere. Only if there is such a disparity in their respective contributions to the *welfare of the family* that it would be inequitable to disregard it should this be taken into account in determining their shares. (original emphasis)

It will, however, be observed that the emphasis of the two judgments is on different issues on what should be considered as sufficient to justify a departure from the principle of equality, so although some guidance may be obtained, it is not clear how the issue will be approached in future.

In the majority of cases since then, where special contribution has been raised to seek an upward adjustment of the assets the claim has been rejected (see *K v L (Non-Matrimonial Property: Special Contribution)* [2011] EWCA Civ 550, *Gray v Work* [2015] EWHC 834 (Fam) and *Chai v Peng* [2017] EWHC 792 (Fam)). Cases where 'special contribution' was considered to be a relevant factor include *Charman v Charman* [2007] EWCA Civ and *RC v JC* [2020] EWHC 466 (Fam).

In *McCartney v Mills McCartney* [2008] EWHC 401 (Fam), [2008] 1 FLR 1508, however, where the marriage was short and the assets had been in the main acquired by the husband before the marriage, the court departed from the equality principle and in arriving at its decision applied the 'needs' test as a relevant and important factor.

Pre-nuptial agreements

Where the parties have entered into a pre-nuptial agreement to protect assets acquired before the marriage, the Supreme Court in *Radmacher (formerly Granatino) v Granatino* [2010] UKSC 42, [2011] 1 All ER 373 held that it is for the court to determine the appropriate financial relief to be awarded on the breakdown of a marriage and the parties cannot by agreement oust the jurisdiction of the court, but the court should consider and determine what weight should be attached to such an agreement and whether it was fair or just to depart from it. The court should give effect to a nuptial agreement that is freely entered into by each party with a full appreciation of its implications unless in the circumstances prevailing it would not be fair to hold the parties to their agreement. The agreement must, therefore, have been entered into without undue influence or pressure and with knowledge of its implications. It was important that the parties had disclosure of all the relevant material to enable them to make an informed decision and to seek advice before making the decision, and that both parties understood and intended that the agreement should govern the financial consequences in the event of the marriage coming to an end. Factors such as duress, fraud and misrepresentation or undue influence or unacceptable pressure would negate the agreement (see *NA v MA* [2006] EWHC 2900 (Fam) and *KA v MA (Pre-nuptial Agreement: Needs)* [2018] EWHC 499 (Fam)). Quaere whether one party's controlling and coercive behaviour towards the other party would be sufficient to negate the agreement. Unconscionable conduct would also be likely to have an adverse effect. Other relevant factors which may reduce or eliminate the weight to be attached to the agreement include conduct such as exploitation, unfair advantage, the parties' emotional state, the circumstances of the parties at the time of the agreement and the question whether the marriage would have gone ahead without the agreement. In *Z v Z (Financial Remedy: Marriage Contract)* [2011] EWHC 2878 (Fam) the agreement was upheld although full disclosure of the parties' assets had taken place because the evidence established that the wife had been indifferent to what the husband was worth when she entered into the agreement. Nevertheless, based on the 'needs' factor the court made an award to the wife which was greater than was set out in the agreement on the grounds that if the pre-marital assets were excluded in accordance with the agreement the wife's needs would not be met. As regards the principles which apply to nuptial agreements and 'needs' cases, see the judgment of Holman J in *Luckwell v Limata* [2014] EWHC 502 (Fam) at [155]–[158]. See, also, *Ipekçi v McConnell* [2019] EWFC 19. Reliance on pre-nuptial agreements has not been upheld where legal advice and full disclosure had not taken place or where there has been undue influence or duress (see *Kremen v Agrest (No 1) (Financial Remedy: Non-disclosure: Post-Nuptial Agreement)* [2012] EWHC 45 (Fam)). However, where the agreement was entered into in a foreign country which provides the option for parties to a marriage to enter into 'community of property' or 'separation of property' agreements, it is unlikely for the court in England and Wales not to uphold the agreement even where the parties failed to take legal advice or provide full disclosure (see *Versteegh v Versteegh* [2018] EWCA Civ 1050; see, also, *AH v PH (Pre-Marital Agreement; Compensation)* [2013] EWHC 3873 (Fam)).

These principles also apply to agreements made before same sex couples enter into a civil partnership or marriage.

Once the court is satisfied that the agreement was entered into freely, it would then have to consider whether it was just and fair to hold it as binding. That issue would be dependent on the facts of the particular case. The Supreme Court gave some guidance on the issue of fairness as follows:

- a nuptial agreement could not be allowed to prejudice the reasonable requirements of any children of the family;
- the court should accord respect to the decision of a married couple as to how they wished to regulate their financial affairs;
- the distinction between matrimonial and non-matrimonial property was significant and the preservation of non-matrimonial property may be justified;
- a significant change in the parties' circumstances may make it unfair to hold the parties to their agreement;
- needs and compensation were the strands that could most readily render the agreement unfair, but where these considerations did not apply, fairness might not require a departure from the agreement. It was in relation to the sharing principle that the court would be most likely to make an order in the terms of the nuptial settlement in place of the order that it would otherwise have made.

Brack v Brack [2018] EWCA Civ 2862 is a good example where the court, on reviewing case law on nuptial agreements since the decision in *Radmacher (formerly Granatino) v Granatino* (above), held that even where a party has contracted out of a division of assets the court nevertheless is obliged to take account of all the factors set out in Matrimonial Causes Act 1973, s 25(2), especially in relation to the welfare of any children, even if this results in the court having to make an order for the wife in excess of her needs contrary to the terms of the agreement (at [103]).

The Supreme Court disapproved the decision of the Privy Council in *Macleod v Macleod* [2008] UKPC 64, [2009] 1 FLR 641, which distinguished between pre-nuptial agreements and post-nuptial agreements, and suggested that there should not be any difference between them. It concluded that post-nuptial agreements were contracts and were thus not contrary to public policy and that the same principle should apply to both types of agreements. Both agreements should be enforceable.

The court went on to state that the test for varying a maintenance agreement under Matrimonial Causes Act 1973, s 3 and that in *Edgar v Edgar* [1981] 2 FLR 19 were appropriate for a separation agreement, but not necessarily so for post-nuptial agreements.

The decision in *Radmacher (formerly Granatino) v Granatino* (above) was a majority decision of the Supreme Court and hence it is important to refer in summary to the dissenting judgment of Baroness Hale.

Lady Hale in her dissenting judgment took the view that:

- pre-nuptial agreements were not legally enforceable contracts;
- it was for Parliament with the help of the Law Commission to review and reform the law and not for the court to hold that such agreements are legal contracts and enforceable;
- the test applied by the majority was an impermissible gloss on the courts' statutory duties in that it introduced a presumption or starting point;
- the test should be 'Did each party enter into an agreement, intending it to have legal effect and with a full appreciation of its implication? If so, in the circumstances as they now are, would it be fair to hold them to their agreement?';
- the husband's appeal should have been allowed as, although there was nothing in the circumstances which rendered the agreement unfair, the husband's role as father to the children was a relevant factor even though the children had attained the age of majority to justify providing a home for him for life;
- the Court of Appeal had erred in principle in treating a parent who had been married to the other parent as they would treat a parent who had not.

Since the decision in *Radmacher (formerly Granatino) v Granatino*, pre-nuptial agreements have been entered into more frequently, even in cases where the assets are not substantial, and more particularly where the parties are entering into a second or third marriage. Reference should be made to case law in financial remedy proceedings for further guidance on the impact of *Radmacher*.

The Law Commission in its report, *Matrimonial Property Needs and Agreements*, Law Com No 343) (TSO, February 2014) sets out the criteria which should be met for a valid 'qualifying nuptial agreement' and includes a Draft Bill. Further information on the contents of the report and its recommendation is available at www.lawcom.gov.uk/app/uploads/2015/03/lc343_matrimonial_property.pdf.

As regards nuptial agreements entered into by couples and civil partners in European countries where cross-border issues arise, as from 29 January 2019 the provisions of Council Regulation (EU) 2016/1104 of 24 June 2016 implementing enhanced cooperation in the area of jurisdiction, applicable law and the recognition and enforcement of decisions in matters of the property consequences of registered partnerships may also come into play as between the states that have ratified the Regulation.

7.10 WHAT THE SURVIVING SPOUSE/CIVIL PARTNER MIGHT REASONABLY HAVE EXPECTED TO RECEIVE ON DIVORCE/DISSOLUTION – DIVORCE COMPARISON TEST

I(PFD)A 1975, s 3(2) provides that, in a claim by a surviving spouse/civil partner of the deceased, the court should, unless at the date of death a judicial separation order/decree of judicial separation was in force and the separation was continuing, have regard to the provision which the claimant might reasonably have expected to receive if, on the day on which the deceased died, the marriage, instead of being terminated by death, had been terminated by divorce. This implies an exercise under Matrimonial Causes Act 1973, s 25, although this provision is not the only, or the paramount, factor to be considered by the court. It is one of eight other factors among all the other circumstances of the individual case. The House of Lords' decisions in *White v White* [2000] UKHL 54, [2000] 2 FLR 981 and *Miller v Miller; McFarlane v McFarlane* [2006] UKHL 24, [2006] 1 FLR 1186 set out the principles which now form the basis of the court's approach to applications for financial relief under the Matrimonial Causes Act 1973, although it should be noted that both cases were 'big money cases' and the principles set out there should not be applied inflexibly, but tailored to the individual circumstances of each case and to the value of the assets available for distribution. This is particularly significant in cases under the I(PFD)A 1975. The general principles which emerge from these decisions, bearing in mind that in these cases the assets substantially exceeded the needs, and the court's observations were made in that context, are:

(1) the objective of the court is to achieve a fair outcome;
(2) in seeking to achieve a fair outcome, there is no place for discrimination between husband and wife and their respective roles. Whatever the division of labour between the spouses, fairness requires that this should not prejudice or advantage either party;
(3) the non-financial contributions made to the welfare of the family and the loss of opportunity to acquire and develop money-earning qualifications and skills should be recognised;
(4) where the wife has made a non-financial contribution to the family she is entitled to a fair settlement which is not confined to her reasonable needs;
(5) the '*Duxbury* calculations' (see *Duxbury v Duxbury* [1992] Fam 62) are not always a reliable guide and do not take account of the parental wish to pass money to the next generation;
(6) property acquired before marriage, inherited property or property acquired from sources external to the marriage should be treated differently from assets acquired by the joint efforts of the spouses, referred to as 'matrimonial property';

(7) a presumption of equal division would not be an impermissible judicial gloss on the statute;
(8) equality of division should be the yardstick and, as a general rule, should be departed from only if there are good reasons for doing so. Good reasons for departing from equality should be articulated;
(9) a pre-nuptial agreement freely entered into with full appreciation of its implications should be given effect unless it would not be fair to do so.

Since these decisions, further guidance on the interpretation of these principles has been given in a number of cases. In *Dharamshi v Dharamshi* [2001] 1 FLR 736, the wife received between 35 per cent and 41 per cent of the assets. In *H v H* [2001] EWCA Civ 653, she received 42 per cent. In *D v D (Lump Sum: Adjournment of Application)* [2001] 1 FLR 633, the principles in *White* were applied. In *N v N (Financial Provision: Sale of Company)* [2001] 2 FLR 69, the court ordered the sale of the husband's business, which was an income-producing asset. In *Foster v Foster* [2003] EWCA Civ 565, [2003] 2 FLR 299, the Court of Appeal upheld the district judge's attempts to give back to the parties what they had brought into the marriage at the value at the date of the marriage, and divide equally the proceeds generated during the marriage from property dealings. In *GW v RW* [2003] EWHC 611 (Fam), [2003] 2 FLR 108 (see para 7.8.2), a period of cohabitation before the marriage was treated as equivalent to marriage; it was accepted that some departure from equality was justified as the husband had brought to the marriage a developed career and high earnings capacity, which was unmatched by anything the wife had contributed, and the husband's assets had grown during the separation. The wife was awarded 40 per cent of the assets.

The equality principle has been applied in a number of other cases, but in each of these cases the assets were substantial. These cases may be relevant in cases under the I(PFD)A 1975 where the estate is large and there is a surplus available. Where the estate includes assets acquired before the marriage, or acquired by inheritance or sources outside the marriage, applying *White v White* (above), such assets ought to be treated differently from 'matrimonial assets'. Where the estate is sufficiently large it may be appropriate to apply this principle, but where the funds are insufficient to meet the claims, it may not be.

All the above cases relate to decisions made following the breakdown of the marriage. There are, however, two cases which were dealt with under the I(PFD)A 1975 where the 'divorce comparison test' was considered. In *Fielden and Graham v Cunliffe* [2005] EWCA Civ 1508, [2006] 1 FLR 745, Wall LJ (as he then was) said (at [19]–[21]):

> 19. The correct approach for the court to adopt, following the decision of the House of Lords in *White v White* … is to apply the statutory provisions to the facts of the individual case with the objective of achieving a result which is fair, and

non-discriminatory. Having undertaken that exercise, a way of assessing the fairness and non-discriminatory nature of the proposed result is to check it against the yardstick of equality of division. There is, however, no presumption of equal division of assets, but as a general guide, in the words of Lord Nicholls of Birkenhead, 'equality should be departed from, only if, and to the extent that, there is a good reason for doing so'. He added: 'The need to consider and articulate reasons for departing from equality would help the parties and the court to focus on the need to ensure the absence of discrimination …'.

20. With appropriate adjustments based on the different statutory provisions, I see no reason, in principle, why the *White v White* approach to marital financial claims should not be applied to proceedings under the 1975 Act brought by a widow, not least because, in any case brought under section 1(1)(a) of the 1975 Act, section 3(2) imposes a statutory cross-check of its own to the provision which Mrs Cunliffe might reasonably have expected to receive if on the day on which the deceased died the marriage, instead of being terminated by death, had been terminated by a decree of divorce. This sub-section assumes a particular importance in the instant case due to the brevity of the marriage.

21. Caution, however, seems to me necessary when considering the *White v White* cross-check in the context of a case under the 1975 Act. Divorce involves two living former spouses, to each of whom the provisions of section 25(2) of the Matrimonial Causes Act 1973 apply. In cases under the 1975 Act, a deceased spouse who leaves a widow is entitled to bequeath his estate to whomsoever he pleases: his only statutory obligation is to make reasonable financial provision for his widow. In such a case, depending on the value of the estate, the concept of equality may bear little relation to such provision.

In that case, the court considered this factor with all the others set out in I(PFD)A 1975, s 3, particularly the short length of the marriage, which the court considered was a powerful argument against an equal division (see above), the claimant's housing, her earning capacity and financial needs, and in this context found the *Duxbury* approach a useful guide. Wall LJ (as he then was) advised that caution should be given in following the case of *Re Besterman*, and the 'cushion' advocated to be provided for the claimant, as it predates the changes brought about by *White v White* and *Duxbury v Duxbury*.

In *P v G, P and P (Family Provision: Relevance of Divorce Provision)* [2004] EWHC 2944 (Fam), [2006] 1 FLR 431, Black J (as she then was) observed that there is an uneasy interplay between the obligation of the court under I(PFD)A 1975, s 3(2) which required the court to have regard to the provision which the claimant might reasonably be expected to receive if the marriage had been terminated by divorce rather than death, and the obligation to take account of the facts as they are known at the hearing. In relation to the valuation of assets, she did not consider that the intention of the statute was that the court should embark on a 'most sterile and wasteful of exercises in which valuations of assets in an Inheritance Act claim by a spouse should be carried out on two bases' with the resulting costs of valuers and accountants. As regards the factors set out in Matrimonial Causes Act 1973, s 25, she said that an ancillary relief judge having considered these would have used equality of division as his cross-check for fairness. She did not think that:

> it is helpful to go further with the divorce fiction and to attempt to translate the percentage division of the categories of asset into more precise figures. One has only to begin upon the process, as I have done before abandoning it, to realise that any appearance of accuracy and precision in such an exercise is spurious; an over-exact approach to s 3(2) would provide a thoroughly undesirable opportunity to spend the assets of the estate on litigation rather than on provision for the family without, I think materially assisting the court in its task under the I(PFD)A 1975.

The learned judge concluded:

> Ultimately I have concluded that what the statute contemplates in a case such as this is not that the entire fictional ancillary relief case should be played out within the Inheritance Act claim but that the court should simply reach sufficient of a conclusion about how it would have been resolved to take that factor into account in considering what would be reasonable financial provision under the 1975 Act.

However, in considering the authorities which refer to the difference between divorce where there are two surviving spouses for whom to make provision, and death where there is only one, Black J (as she then was) said:

> it seems to me probable that this difference will not infrequently be reflected in greater provision being made under the 1975 Act than would have been made on divorce and that this may legitimately be so even where the estate is a relatively large one, as it is here. In saying this I have not ignored the importance of testamentary freedom. The wish to be in a financial position to make provision by will for adult children, whilst not a financial need as such for the purposes of s 25 of the Matrimonial Causes Act 1973, was recognised in *White v White* as a valid consideration where resources exceed need.

See, also, para 7.9.2.

In *Clarke v Allen* [2019] EWHC 1193 (Ch), the widow was awarded £731,000 from the estate worth £1.38 million, to cover the costs of her care in a nursing home, necessitated as a result of her suffering a stroke following her husband's death, notwithstanding the fact that it was a short marriage and the deceased's assets had been acquired before the marriage.

It is clear that in a claim under the I(PFD)A 1975 the court is not required to carry out a detailed and precise inquiry to assess what relief the claimant would have received. The approach should be to consider that in matrimonial proceedings the court seeks to achieve a result that is fair and non-discriminatory and tests that against the yardstick of equality of division and applies a similar approach in I(PFD)A 1975 claims, subject to the fact that there is no presumption of an equal division and the fact that the court in a claim under the Act is required to carry out a balancing exercise between different factors and the claims of others. The precise extent of the division must still be decided on a case-by-case basis.

Where the estate is small or modest it is difficult to see how the 'divorce comparison' test can provide a fair result if it outweighs the needs of other claimants and beneficiaries. It can only be considered as one of the many factors which the court is required to take into account. It is suggested that in claims under the I(PFD)A 1975 the court should first consider whether, viewed objectively, the provision made is unreasonable. If the court finds that it is, it should then go on to consider what would be a reasonable provision for the claimant applying the criteria set out in s 3 and consider what a family judge would have ordered if divorce instead of death had separated the couple and what in the circumstances is reasonable, viewed objectively. It is not for the court to interfere with the disposition so as to make an equitable distribution of the estate. *Iqbal v Ahmed* [2011] EWCA Civ 900, *Kaur v Bolina* [2021] EWHC 2894 (Fam), *Re Bhusate (Deceased)* [2020] EWHC 52 (Ch) and *Kaur v Singh* [2023] EWHC 304 (Fam) illustrate how the court has applied the 'deemed divorce' test with the issue of access to housing for the surviving spouse, especially where the marriage has lasted a long time, being recognised as central to the decision. Similarly, in relation to non-matrimonial assets and inherited wealth, this is likely to carry little weight where the claimant's needs cannot be met without recourse to this asset, see for example *Clarke v Allen* [2019] EWHC 1193 (Ch) (discussed above) and *Lilleyman v Lilleyman* [2012] EWHC 821 (Ch), where the marriage was the deceased's second marriage, had subsisted for just over 2 years and the estate was valued at £6 million.

7.11 FACTORS WHICH APPLY TO A FORMER SPOUSE/ CIVIL PARTNER OR COHABITANT

In the case of a claim by a former spouse/civil partner or cohabitant, the matters to which the court must have regard are, save for the deemed marriage issue, the same as for a surviving spouse/civil partner (see above). Where a 'clean break' settlement was made, it will be rare for a claim under the I(PFD)A 1975 to be made or, if made, to succeed, unless there is a continuing liability, or a secured provision order has been made, or there are exceptional circumstances (see *Barrass v Harding* [2001] 1 FLR 138). See, also, *Parnall v Hurst and Others* [2003] WTLR 997, where a former wife, whose marriage to the deceased was dissolved after 29 years and the deceased was ordered to make periodical payments of £500 per year, issued a claim under the I(PFD)A 1975. An application to strike out was refused as the claim was not regarded as 'doomed' to fail.

Where the claimant is able to establish that, following an ancillary relief order, the parties had entered into an agreement that, in return for the wife forgoing her periodical payments, the husband would forgo his charge on the matrimonial home and that she had thus acted to her detriment, a case for constructive trust/proprietary estoppel may be made out (see *S v S and M* [2006] EWHC 2892 (Fam), [2007] 1 FLR 1123). See, also, *Stallion v Stallion Holdings Ltd* [2009] EWHC 1950 (Ch), [2010] 2 FLR 78, in which the parties had, following their divorce, agreed that the wife could live rent-free at a particular property and on that basis she had not proceeded with her application for ancillary relief. It was held that she had thereby acted to her detriment and was entitled to remain in the property as agreed.

In the case of a cohabitant of the deceased, the age of the claimant and the length of period of cohabitation will be relevant factors, as will the contribution made by the claimant to the welfare of the family. The nature of the arrangements between the parties will not necessarily undermine the claim (*Lindop v Agus* [2009] EWHC 1795 (Ch), [2010] 1 FLR 631).

7.11.1 Matrimonial proceedings and disentitlement orders under I(PFD)A 1975, sections 15, 15ZA, 15A and 15B

I(PFD)A 1975, s 15 provides that where a court in England and Wales makes a divorce order/a decree of divorce, a nullity of marriage order/decree of nullity of marriage or a judicial separation order/decree of judicial separation, it may, either then, or at any time thereafter, if it considers it just to do so, exclude the right of the parties to apply for an order under s 2.

The order under s 15 may be made before or after the divorce or nullity order has been made final/decree is made absolute. If it is made before the order has been made final/decree has been made absolute, it does not take effect until the order has been made final/decree has been made absolute (I(PFD)A 1975, s 15(2)).

In the case of an I(PFD)A 1975, s 15 order made on the making of a judicial separation order/decree of judicial separation, with respect to any party to a marriage, then if the other party dies while the order/decree is in force and the separation is continuing, the court cannot entertain any application for an order under s 2 by the surviving party.

Thus, where, on an application for ancillary relief in matrimonial proceedings, a 'clean break' provision is made, consideration should be given to whether an order, disentitling the parties from making any claim for an order under I(PFD)A 1975, s 2 against the estate of the other, would also be appropriate.

CPA 2004, s 71, Sch 4, Part 2, para 21 has extended this restriction to a dissolution, nullity order, separation order or presumption of death order to civil partners with the same consequences by inserting in the I(PFD)A 1975 an additional s 15ZA.

MFPA 1984, s 25 amended the I(PFD)A 1975 by inserting s 15A which gives the court power to make an order similar to that under s 15 to marriages which have been dissolved or annulled overseas; where the parties have been legally separated; and where a court in England and Wales has made an order for ancillary relief under MFPA 1984, s 17. On the making of an order under MFPA 1984, s 17 in respect of a marriage which has been dissolved or annulled overseas, or where there has been a judicial separation order/decree of judicial separation, the court, if it considers it just to do so, may, on the application of either or both parties to the marriage, order that the other party to the marriage shall not, on the death of the other, be entitled to apply for an order under I(PFD)A 1975, s 2.

Where an order under I(PFD)A 1975, s 15, s 15ZA, s 15A or s 15B has been made, with respect to any party to a marriage/civil partnership, then on the death of the other party to that marriage/civil partnership, the court cannot entertain any application under s 2 against the estate of the deceased by the surviving spouse/civil partner.

There are two conflicting decisions of the Court of Appeal on how the court should approach an application for an order under any of the above sections of the I(PFD)A 1975. In *Re Fullard (Deceased)* [1982] Fam 42, when considering the implications of I(PFD)A 1975, s 15 in an application under the Act, Ormrod LJ stated:

> I regard section 15 as a form of insuring against applications under the 1975 Act which some people may very reasonably wish to do, having made financial provision of a capital nature for the former spouse. People obviously have other commitments – second wives (or husbands) and children and so on. I do not regard section 15 as materially affecting the question the court has to answer as the condition precedent to these applications.

In *Whiting v Whiting* [1988] 2 FLR 189, however, following the divorce of the parties, a consent order was made for financial provision for the wife and children. Subsequently the husband applied, under Matrimonial Causes Act 1973, s 31(7), for a variation of the order for periodical payments for the wife and for an order under I(PFD)A 1975, s 15(1). His application was dismissed. On appeal it was held that, before the court can consider it just to make an order, it must be presented with some indication of what the estate is likely to consist of and some details of the person(s) whom the applicant considers to have a prior claim on the estate. Balcombe LJ said:

> For the court to make an order under section 15(1) it must consider it just to do so. In my judgment, before the court can consider it just to make an order depriving a divorced spouse of an opportunity to claim financial provision from the estate of the other spouse, it should be given some indication of what that estate is likely to consist of and some details of the persons whom the applicant considers to have a prior claim on his estate in the event of his decease. I am prepared to accept that the husband's capital asset is his interest in his present house and that this is likely to be the only asset of substance in his estate. It is a reasonable inference that he considers his present wife and, presumably his children, to have a prior claim on his estate in the event of his death, but nowhere in his evidence does he say so. The whole of his evidence is directed towards supporting his application for a discharge of the 1979 order, and he (or those advising him) appear to have assumed that his application under section 15 of the 1975 Act will stand or fall with that other application. In these circumstances it is hardly surprising that the judge made no mention of this limb of the husband's application. For my part, I would dismiss the appeal on the simple ground that the husband has not made out a case to support his application under section 15 of the 1975 Act. That is not to say that he may not be able to do so, and accordingly I would dismiss this part of the appeal without prejudice to the husband's right to renew the application under section 15.

It is suggested that, of the two decisions, that of Ormrod LJ in *Re Fullard* is to be preferred. The decision in *Whiting* fails to take account of social changes, including the increasing independence of women, the growing divorce rate and the fact that divorcing couples tend to be young and move on to form other relationships and have second families. It also disregards the concept of a final and clean break settlement on divorce. It is unrealistic, in the majority of cases, to expect divorcing couples to be able to give the details described in *Whiting*. To require an applicant under I(PFD)A 1975, s 15 to provide details of those they consider would have a prior claim to their estate on their death some decades in the future is almost impossible to fulfil; if such a requirement were to be applied strictly, the provision would, in time, become redundant.

Practitioners should, nevertheless, ensure that there is full and frank disclosure where the court is considering financial provision, particularly where a clean break settlement is sought. If an order is made under I(PFD)A 1975, s 15, s 15ZA, s 15A or s 15B and it is subsequently challenged on the basis that the court did not have the required information when it made the order; or if, in the absence of such an order, a claim is made under s 2, it does not follow that the claim under s 2 will necessarily succeed, because the claimant will still have to satisfy the court that the requirements under the Act are met. Where a former wife's/civil partner's claims under Matrimonial Causes Act 1973, ss 23 and 24 or CPA 2004, Sch 5 have been fully considered and a final order has been made, it is unlikely, save in exceptional circumstances, that a claim for an order under I(PFD)A 1975, s 2 would succeed (for an example of exceptional circumstances, see *Re Fullard* (above)).

This issue was raised in *Cameron v Treasury Solicitor* [1996] 2 FLR 716, where, on the claimant's divorce, a clean break order was made by consent, requiring the deceased to pay the claimant a lump sum of £8,000. About 20 years later, the husband died intestate. His estate, amounting to about £7,677, passed as *bona vacantia* to the Crown. The former wife applied for an order under I(PFD)A 1975, s 2. She was then suffering from ill-health and was in very straitened circumstances; there were no competing claims. At first instance, it was held that the fact of the clean break did not preclude her from making the claim and she was awarded the whole of the net estate. On appeal, it was held that the first task of the claimant in such cases is to make out a case that she is entitled to some relief under the Act. To do this she must satisfy the court that the disposition of the deceased's estate, effected by the law of intestacy in this case, was not such as to make a reasonable financial provision for her. In the present case, a clean break order had been obtained by consent some 19 years before; the deceased had not since then offered any financial support to the claimant; there were no grounds to show that he owed her a moral obligation; nor were there any special circumstances to establish entitlement to an order. The court also expressed the view that it is now the practice of the court to include a s 15 direction in all clean break orders, and an order which did not include such a direction would suggest a fundamental error in drafting.

Parties are likely to be legally represented in applications for financial relief following the breakdown of their marriage/civil partnership when final orders are made. There is provision for a full disclosure of information within those proceedings. Where there is a clean break order which includes a direction under any of the above sections, then that order should be respected. Where such a direction is not included, there is usually a good reason for its absence from the order.

Where the I(PFD)A 1975, s 15 or s 15ZA direction is not made, it should not be assumed that its absence is an error. The court should consider any claim for an order under s 2 on its merits. Since the claimant has to establish that the disposition of the deceased's estate is not such as to make reasonable financial provision within the meaning of s 1(2)(b), the circumstances at the time the financial relief order was made and the circumstances since then would have to be considered in the light of the factors the court is required to have regard to under s 3. The claimant would have to jump over several hurdles to succeed. In some cases, a trial of the preliminary issue may in the long run avoid delay and expense. Furthermore, although the decision in *Cameron v Treasury Solicitor* seems to suggest that a ss 15 and 15ZA direction is inserted in all clean break orders as a matter of practice, the reality is that, although such a direction is usually considered seriously by practitioners who advise divorcing or separating couples, the court has to approve any settlement of the matrimonial proceedings which includes such an order. A claimant who seeks to challenge a s 15 or s 15ZA order in a claim under the Act would need to establish some very exceptional circumstance in order to succeed.

It should also be noted that the provisions of I(PFD)A 1975, ss 15(3) and (4), 15ZA(3) and (4), 15A(2) and (3), and 15B(2) and (3) are all mandatory. It would therefore be open to the court, of its own motion, or on application by a defendant in a claim under the Act, to strike out the claim on the basis that the court does not have the power to entertain the claim by virtue of the aforesaid provisions.

In summary, case law suggests that the following matters are relevant to a claim under the I(PFD)A 1975 by a former spouse/civil partner:

(1) a clean break settlement where there is no continuing obligation;
(2) whether there was a relationship between the deceased and the former spouse/civil partner since the divorce which could suggest a moral obligation to provide for them;
(3) special or exceptional circumstances;
(4) the time that has elapsed since the parties separated and since the divorce and the final settlement;
(5) whether there is any evidence to suggest that a full and frank disclosure was not made, or that the deceased has been secretive about their financial affairs which led the former spouse/civil partner to receive less than they might have received;
(6) whether a s 15, s 15ZA, s 15A or s 15B order has been made in ancillary relief proceedings.

The following have been found not to amount to special circumstances or reasons to allow a claim:

(1) that the former spouse/civil partner received less under different legislation than they might have received when the deceased died;
(2) that the deceased's estate is substantial;
(3) that the former spouse/civil partner is in straitened circumstances or suffering ill-health.

7.12 CLAIM BY SURVIVING HUSBAND/COHABITANT

The I(PFD)A 1975 makes no distinction between a claim by a surviving husband and a claim by a surviving wife/civil partner. In the early cases, however, the courts appeared to be disinclined, save in exceptional circumstances, to grant relief where the claim was made by a surviving husband. This is illustrated by two cases in particular. In *Re Sylvester, Sylvester v Public Trustee* [1941] Ch 87, the parties were married in 1931. The husband subsequently gave up his employment and thereafter did all the housework and nursed his wife during her illness. The wife had her own income. The husband had none. She died in 1940. She bequeathed to him an annuity of £525 per annum and gave her residuary estate to a number of charities. The husband made a claim against the estate for his maintenance under the I(FP)A 1938. Farwell J, in allowing the husband's claim and awarding him 3 shillings a week, stated:

> I do not consider that, in the ordinary way, applications by husbands for this sort of assistance should be readily entertained. Prima facie a husband should be able to maintain himself, and ought not to ask the court to give him, out of his wife's estate, more than she thought fit to provide for him. There are, of course, exceptional cases in which such an application may be justified, but personally I should not be very willing to assist husbands in cases of this sort, unless the circumstances were indeed exceptional.

In *Re Styler, Styler v Griffiths* [1942] Ch 387, the deceased had made an agreement with her second husband that, on his making a will in her favour, she would make a will leaving the income of her estate to him for life. They both made wills in accordance with the agreement. Subsequently, the wife made another will leaving all her estate to her daughter by her first marriage. On the wife's death, the husband applied for reasonable provision. In refusing his application, Morton J approved the judgment of Farwell J in *Re Sylvester* (above) and criticised his own decision in *Re Pointer* [1941] Ch 60. He stated:

> Having now had more experience of administering the Act since I decided that case, I do not think that I should now make any provision, as I did there for a husband with a pension of £180 a year, an annual income of £124 from investments and £25 a year net from property, unless the circumstances were exceptional.

The case of *Lewis v Warner* [2016] EWHC 1787 (Ch) is a recent example where an order for financial provision was made in a claim by a male cohabitant of the deceased in the form of giving him an option to purchase the matrimonial home at a specified price (see, also, para 8.4).

See, also, *White v White* [2000] UKHL 54, [2000] 2 FLR 981 and *Cowan v Cowan* [2001] EWCA Civ 679, [2002] Fam 97. In *White v White*, Lord Nicholls of Birkenhead stated, 'There is one principle of universal application which can be stated with confidence. In seeking to achieve a fair outcome, there is no place for discrimination between husband and wife and their respective roles'. This principle applies as much to claims under the Act as it does in matrimonial proceedings.

7.13 CLAIMS BY CHILD OF THE DECEASED AND A PERSON TREATED AS A CHILD OF THE FAMILY – I(PFD)A 1975, SECTION 1(1)(C) AND (D)

I(PFD)A 1975, s 3(3) requires the court where the deceased stood in the role of a parent to the claimant to have regard to: (1) whether the deceased maintained the claimant who was not his biological child, and if so, the length of time for which and the basis on which the deceased did so, and the extent of the contributions made by way of maintenance; (2) whether and, if so, to what extent the deceased assumed responsibility for the maintenance of the applicant; (3) whether in maintaining or assuming responsibility for maintaining the applicant the deceased did so knowing that the applicant was not his own child; (4) the liability of any other person to maintain the applicant. Where appropriate, the court is also required to take account of the manner in which the child of the deceased and a child for whom he had assumed responsibility was being, or in which they might expect to be, educated or trained: see also under para 7.15.

It should be noted that a person treated by the deceased as a child of the family is not entitled to inherit on the deceased's intestacy, but they can make a claim for financial provision under the Act (see *Higgins v Morgan* [2021] EWHC 2846 (Ch)).

7.14 CLAIMS BY PERSON MAINTAINED BY THE DECEASED – I(PFD)A 1975, SECTION 1(1)(E)

There are three factors which the court is required to consider in relation to those claimants who allege that they were being maintained by the deceased immediately before their death. These are:

(1) the extent to which the deceased assumed responsibility for the claimant;
(2) the basis on which the deceased assumed responsibility for the maintenance of the claimant; and
(3) the length of time for which the deceased discharged that responsibility.

See, further, paras 4.9.2 and 7.5, *Baynes v Hedger and Others* [2009] EWCA Civ 374, [2009] 2 FLR 767, *Bouette v Rose* [2001] 1 FLR 363, *Malone v Harrison* [1979] 1 WLR 1353 and *Graham v Murphy* [1997] 1 FLR 860 as examples of where these issues were dealt with.

7.15 ASSUMPTION OF RESPONSIBILITY BY THE DECEASED – I(PFD)A 1975, SECTION 3(3) AND (4)

In relation to an application by a child of the deceased and a person treated as a child of the family, s 3(3) requires the court in addition to matters set out in s 3(1)(a)–(f) to have regard to the manner in which the applicant was being or in which he might expect to be educated or trained. However, in relation to an application by a person treated by the deceased as a child of the family, s 3(3) requires the court when determining a claim under s 1(1)(e) to have regard to: (1) the length of time and the basis on which the deceased maintained the applicant and the extent of the contribution made by way of maintenance; and (2) whether and, if so, to what extent the deceased assumed responsibility for the maintenance of the applicant. This provision must be read alongside the provision of s 1(3).

The court is also required to take into account the applicant's earning capacity and their obligations and responsibilities.

As a general rule, the fact that the claimant was being maintained by the deceased under an arrangement subsisting at the time of the deceased's death and the deceased was making a substantial contribution in money or money's worth to the reasonable needs of the claimant will raise an inference that the deceased had undertaken to maintain the claimant and had assumed responsibility for the maintenance of the claimant. In such circumstances, there would be no need to establish any other overt act to demonstrate the 'assumption of responsibility'. All the contributions made, whether in kind or otherwise, will be taken into account.

In *Jelley v Iliffe* [1981] Fam 128, Griffiths LJ in his judgment said:

> the court must use common sense and remember that the object of Parliament in creating this extra class of persons who may claim benefit from an estate was to provide relief for persons of whom it could truly be said that they were wholly or partially dependent on the deceased.

And:

> Each case will have to be looked at carefully on its own facts to see whether common sense leads to a conclusion that the applicant can fairly be regarded as a dependant.

The court will consider, for example:

- the circumstances of the claimant and to what extent the contribution made by the deceased affected those circumstances and how it affected the claimant's position (see *Rees v Newbery and Institute for Cancer Research* [1988] 1 FLR 1041);
- the extent to which the claimant had altered their situation based on the actions taken and the contribution made by the deceased (see *Re Wilkinson (Deceased), Neale v Newell* [1978] Fam 22);
- whether the deceased had made any promises, given assurances and/or whether there had been any agreement between the parties;
- whether the deceased had expressed their motives or intention, the circumstances of the claimant and the deceased and the nature of their relationship (e.g. as in *Bouette v Rose* [2001] 1 FLR 363 and *Bishop v Plumley* [1991] 1 All ER 236);
- the extent of the contribution made by the deceased, which has to be substantial. This may not necessarily be quantification in monetary terms. It may involve considering the circumstances of the claimant and the difference the contribution made to the claimant's family, social, working and financial life. The assessment will be made not on a fine arithmetical computation but on a broad common-sense approach. If contributions were made both by the claimant and the deceased, the court will consider the extent of the contributions in the light of each party's circumstance and the effect on both of the overall arrangement.

See, further, paras 4.9 and 4.9.3–4.9.5.

Chapter 8

Powers of the Court to Make Orders

8.1 INTRODUCTION

Once the court is satisfied that the claimant is eligible to make a claim under the I(PFD)A 1975 and that the disposition of the deceased's estate effected by their will or the law of intestacy, or the combination of their will and that law, is not such as to make reasonable financial provision for the claimant, the court must decide the extent and nature of the financial provision which should be provided for the claimant.

The orders which the court may make are set out in I(PFD)A 1975, ss 2, 5, 6–11 and 16–19. The court's powers relate not only to making financial provisions, but also include the power to make orders for the purpose of facilitating the making of those provisions. These specific powers empower the court to make orders for property to be brought into the estate so that it is available for the necessary financial provisions to be made. The Act has also been amended to include the changes brought about as a result of the provisions of the CPA 2004 as from 5 December 2005 and the Marriage (Same Sex Couples) Act 2013. Section 2(1)(g) has been amended to enable the court to vary any settlement made during the subsistence of a civil partnership formed by the deceased or in anticipation of the formation of such a partnership. Sections 16–18 have been amended to take account of orders that can be made in relation to maintenance agreements between civil partners or former civil partners and following the dissolution of a civil partnership.

This chapter deals with the powers set out in I(PFD)A 1975, ss 2, 5, 6, 7 and 16–19. Chapter 10 deals with the orders which relate to making property available where the estate is insufficient to make the necessary provision or where the deceased had disposed of property during their lifetime for the purpose of defeating or reducing a possible claim under ss 10–13.

I(PFD)A 1975, s 2 empowers the court to make any one or more of the following orders:

(1) an order for the making to the applicant, out of the net estate of the deceased, of such periodical payments and for such term as may be specified in the order;
(2) an order for the payment to the applicant, out of that estate, of a lump sum of such amount as may be specified;
(3) an order for the transfer to the applicant of such property comprised in that estate as may be specified;
(4) an order for the settlement, for the benefit of the claimant, of such property comprised in that estate as may be specified;
(5) an order for the acquisition, out of property comprised in that estate, of such property as may be specified and for the transfer of the property so acquired to the applicant, or the settlement thereof for their benefit;
(6) an order varying any ante-nuptial or post-nuptial settlement (including such a settlement made by will) made on the parties to a marriage to which the deceased was one of the parties, the variation being for the benefit of the surviving party to that marriage, or any child of that marriage, or any person who was treated by the deceased as a child of the family in relation to that marriage;
(7) an order varying any settlement made:

    (a) during the subsistence of a civil partnership formed by the deceased, or
    (b) in anticipation of the formation of a civil partnership by the deceased,

(8) an order varying for the applicant's benefit the trusts on which the deceased's estate is held (whether arising under the will, or the law relating to intestacy or both).

In certain circumstances, the court may make an interim order for periodical payments and a lump sum out of the net estate (I(PFD)A 1975, s 5). The financial provisions to meet any interim orders may be made out of the net estate as defined in s 25(1) including property which forms part of the net estate pursuant to orders made under ss 8–12.

8.2 PERIODICAL PAYMENTS – I(PFD)A 1975, SECTION 2(1)(A)

An order for periodical payments must specify the term for which the order is to run (I(PFD)A 1975, s 2(1)).

When making a periodical payment, the court may (I(PFD)A 1975, s 2(2)):

(1) specify in the order the amount to be paid;
(2) express the amount to be paid to be such sum as is equivalent to the whole, or a specified portion, of the income of the net estate;
(3) direct that a specified part of the net estate be appropriated or set aside for meeting periodical payments, and express the amount of such periodical payments to be equivalent to the whole of the income of such part of the net estate.

No larger part of the net estate than is sufficient, at the date of the order, to produce the income required may be set aside or appropriated (I(PFD)A 1975, s 2(3)). The power of appropriation is in addition to any power conferred by the deceased's will or given by the court to the personal representatives under its jurisdiction to make consequential orders and give directions. Alternatively, the court may provide for the amount of the periodical payments, or any of them, to be determined in any other way as the court thinks fit (s 2(2)).

8.2.1 Commencement date

There are three possible dates from which an order for periodical payments can commence:

(1) the date of the deceased's death, when the right to make the claim accrued;
(2) the date when proceedings were commenced, when the right to make the claim was exercised;
(3) the date the order is made, when the court finally determines the merit of the claim.

There is no rule that an order for periodical payments must be backdated to commence from the date of the deceased's death. I(PFD)A 1975, s 19(1) provides that, where an order is made under s 2 then, for all purposes, including the purposes of the enactments relating to inheritance tax, the will or the law of intestacy, or both the will and the law relating to intestacy, as the case may be, shall have effect and be deemed to have had effect as from the deceased's death subject to the provisions of the order.

The commencement date of a periodical payment order or any other order is in the discretion of the court. In the absence of exceptional circumstances, the court will be reluctant to backdate the order to a date earlier than the date the proceedings were commenced. Even when backdating is considered appropriate, the court would be mindful not to backdate the order to such an extent that it results in a substantial lump sum having to be paid.

In order to obviate the need to backdate an order for periodical payments, the court may consider it appropriate to make an order for a small capital sum to be paid (see *Re Debenham (Deceased)* [1986] 1 FLR 404 and *Re Farrow (Deceased)* [1988] 1 FLR 205). Where the claimant has no financial resources and is in receipt of state benefits, it is a matter for the court's discretion whether or not to backdate the order. Each case turns on its own facts, but orders have been made notwithstanding the fact that the claimant was in receipt of state benefits and may have had to pay back the benefits received. The case of *Lusternik v Lusternik* [1972] Fam 125 is an example where an order was backdated although the claimant had been in receipt of state benefits. In that case, the deceased and the claimant were divorced and an order for periodical payments of £6 per week was made following the divorce. The claimant continued to maintain both a social and a business relationship with the deceased. The deceased made a will in 1960 leaving his share in a company to the claimant for life. Six weeks before his death in December 1964, he revoked his will by codicil and left her a legacy of £500 and the residue to his executrix. The net estate was valued at £10,000. When the claimant made her application, she was unable to work and in ill-health. When her appeal was heard, she was in receipt of retirement pension and supplementary benefit of £9.60 per week. The trial judge made an order in her favour of £6 per week backdated to February 1970. On appeal, the order was increased to £8 per week. On the issue of backdating, Cairns LJ said:

> As to backdating, I do not accept the contention of counsel for the applicant that there is any rule that *prima facie* the payments should be backdated to the death. This was certainly not laid down as a rule in the case he cited, *Askew v Askew*. There Marshall J held that it was a matter of discretion in each case; and indeed I think that is the necessary wording of the Act. Where an applicant has not brought proceedings until several years after probate was granted, I should not, in the absence of very special circumstances consider it right to backdate the order to a date earlier than that of the originating summons. And again where, as here, the proceedings have extended over some four years from the date of the originating summons to that of the order, I should not consider it right to backdate the order to the date of the summons unless it is shown that there had been some deliberate obstruction by the respondent in the course of the proceedings. One should I think guard against backdating the order for periodical payments to such an extent as in effect to add to it a lump sum order substantial in relation to the size of the estate. In this case, if there had been no provision at all for the applicant in the will, I should have been disposed to backdate the order for two years or perhaps two and a half years. But taking account of her legacy of £500, I think that the registrar and the judge were right here in choosing the shorter period. By my reckoning, the arrears calculated (now) at £8.00 per week and making an allowance for the interim payments which were ordered and which I understand were made

> between February and May 1971, will be about £480, payable within a week or two, and I do not think it would be fair to the respondent to increase that sum.

In *Askew v Askew* [1961] 1 WLR 725, the court was directly concerned with the question of whether the fact that the former wife had been receiving state benefits afforded a ground for postponing the commencement date of the payments ordered. Marshall J said:

> It falls to the court to consider whether in the section itself there is any indication or guide to the proper date from which the payments should be made out of the estate. The right which the former wife has established is described in s. 3(1) as a right of 'reasonable provision for her maintenance after his death' and I have no doubt whatever that a court in its discretion would if the circumstances of any particular case warrants it, make an order that there is a right arising immediately after death in all circumstances. In my judgment this section gives the court a discretion, and it would be incumbent on the court to consider all the factors in the case before deciding on any date from which the first payment under the section should be made.

In *Re Goodwin (Deceased), Goodwin v Goodwin* [1969] 1 Ch 283, however, the court, in exercising its discretion, considered the matter on the basis that if the will had made reasonable provision, that provision would have taken effect from the testator's death. Accordingly, the court ordered that payments should commence from the death of the testator. The court treated any state benefits which were received by the claimant as a matter which was extraneous to the issue before the court. See, also, *Stead v Stead* [1985] FLR 16, where payments were backdated to the day after the testator's death; and *Re Farrow (Deceased)* [1988] 1 FLR 205, where, in backdating the payments, the court took into account all the relevant factors.

The decision in *Re Goodwin* was not cited in *Lusternik v Lusternik* and appears to suggest that, generally speaking, the discretion should be exercised in favour of backdating the order to the date of death. Since, however, the I(PFD)A 1975 is silent on the date from which an order for periodical payments should commence, and the court's power is any event discretionary, it is suggested that, in exercising its discretion, the court should have regard to all the circumstances of the case, including any delay in issuing proceedings; any delay resulting from deliberate obstruction by the respondent to the claim; any payments made to the claimant under an interim order; and any benefits received by the claimant under the will. The provision which the will should have made is, and should be, one of the considerations, and not the premise from which the court ought to start. The alternative is for the court to make a lump sum order (which may not be equal to the total in periodical payments that the claimant would have received had the order been backdated) to compensate the claimant.

When an immediate order is not required, but it is anticipated that provision will be required in the future, the court may adjourn the application (see *Re Franks, Franks v Franks* [1948] Ch 62).

8.2.2 Setting aside and appropriation of property – I(PFD)A 1975, section 2(3)

I(PFD)A 1975, s 2(3) gives the court power to direct that such part of the net estate as may be specified be set aside or appropriated for the making, out of the income from such property, of the payments ordered by the court. However, the section also restricts the court's power to anticipate the future needs of the claimant, in that it prohibits setting aside or appropriating any part of the net estate larger than would be sufficient at the date of the order to produce, from the income thereof, the amount ordered by the court. The future needs of the claimant must, therefore, be dealt with by an application for variation of the periodical payments order (see para 8.11), but when varying the order, the court has no power to bring in new property to meet any increase.

Thus the court may order that part of the net estate be set aside for the making of the payments out of the income it produces or, should the payments ordered fall into arrears, they can be discharged from the property/capital ordered to be set aside (see para 8.2.4). Note, however, the restriction imposed by this provision that the court cannot set aside any part of the net estate larger than is necessary to meet the needs of the claimant at the date when the order is made. The court cannot, therefore, anticipate the future needs of the claimant and set aside funds to meet those future needs. In order to assess the value of the sum which should be set aside to produce the income to meet the payments, it may be useful to use capitalisation tables such as *Duxbury* Tables which are widely used in financial relief claims in matrimonial proceedings (see, further, under para 8.3).

8.2.3 Supplementary orders and conditions

By virtue of I(PFD)A 1975, s 2(4), the court may make such consequential and supplementary provisions to an order as it thinks necessary or expedient for the purposes of giving effect to the order, or for securing that the order operates fairly as between the beneficiaries of the estate of the deceased.

The court may attach conditions to an order for periodical payments, as it did in *Re Lidington, Lidington v Thomas (No 2)* [1940] Ch 927, where, on making provision for periodical payments for the widow of the deceased, the court required her to undertake to maintain the children during their minority. In *Re Pointer,*

Shonfield v Edwards [1941] Ch 60, the court awarded the daughter of the deceased the income of one fifth of the residuary estate or the sum of 30 shillings per week, whichever was the smaller, during her life, subject to I(FP)A 1938, s 1(2)(b), namely in the particular circumstances of her disability ceasing, but subject to the condition that her daughter should inform the trustees if she received at any time a sum in excess of 200 shillings from any source.

8.2.4 Secured periodical payments order

Matrimonial Causes Act 1973, s 23(1)(b) makes provision for a periodical payments order to be secured for such term as may be specified in the order. The I(PFD)A 1975 does not specifically make any provision for a secured periodical payments order. However, I(PFD)A 1975, s 2(4) confers on the court unlimited power to make such other consequential and supplemental provisions for the purpose of giving effect to its order and for the purpose of securing that the order operates fairly. It is suggested that, as in matrimonial financial relief applications, a secured periodical payments order could be made if the court considers it is justified, necessary or expedient to make those provisions to ensure that payments under the order will be met. It is also suggested that in appropriate cases, the court may consider making provision for an annuity to be set up. See under para 8.12 for variation of a secured periodical payments order made under the Matrimonial Causes Act 1973.

8.2.5 Duration of periodical payments order

The order for periodical payments should specify the term for which the order is to run. In the case of an order or interim order in favour of a former spouse/civil partner of the deceased or where there is a judicial separation order or separation order in force, I(PFD)A 1975, s 19(2) provides that:

> Any order made under section 2 or 5 of this Act in favour of—
>
> (a) an applicant who was the former spouse or former civil partner of the deceased, or
>
> (b) an applicant who was the husband or wife of the deceased in a case where the marriage with the deceased was the subject of a judicial separation order [a decree of judicial separation] and at the date of death the order [decree] was in force and the separation was continuing, or
>
> (c) an applicant who was the civil partner of the deceased in a case where, at the date of death, a separation order under Chapter 2 of Part 2 of the Civil Partnership Act 2004 was in force in relation to their civil partnership and the separation was continuing,
>
> shall, in so far as it provides for the making of periodical payments, cease to have effect on the formation by the applicant of a subsequent marriage or civil partnership, except

> in relation to any arrears due under the order on the date of the formation of the subsequent marriage or civil partnership.

Two matters arise from this provision. First, it appears that although the order will automatically cease on the formation of a subsequent marriage/civil partnership of a former spouse/civil partner, the I(PFD)A 1975 is silent in relation to the former spouse/civil partner forming a subsequent relationship which leads to cohabitation. Second, the Act does not make any like provision for the termination of the order in the case of the formation of a subsequent marriage/civil partnership by a surviving spouse/civil partner or the cohabitation of the spouse/civil partner with another person.

Matrimonial Causes Act 1973, s 28(2) provides for a periodical payments order or secured periodical payments order in favour of a party to the marriage to cease on the remarriage of or formation of a civil partnership by that party except in relation to any arrears due under it on the date of the remarriage or formation of the civil partnership. The order is usually expressed to last 'during the parties' joint lives or the petitioner's earlier remarriage or further order'. It is also now the practice, on the making of an order for periodical payments in matrimonial proceedings, to provide that the order will cease on the cohabitation of the recipient of the payment with another person. It is therefore suggested that an order for periodical payments made under the I(PFD)A 1975 in favour of a widow(er) or the surviving civil partner should likewise provide for such a cut-off date, i.e. on the formation of a subsequent marriage/civil partnership. It should also provide that the order in favour of the surviving spouse, civil partner, former spouse/civil partner should also cease on the spouse/civil partner's cohabitation with another.

In relation to an order in favour of a child, the I(PFD)A 1975 does not specifically provide the maximum term for which the order should last. Matrimonial Causes Act 1973, s 29(1) provides that no financial order and no order for a transfer of property shall be made in favour of a child beyond the age of 18 unless the child remains in education or training or there are special circumstances which justify the order lasting beyond the age of 18 years (s 29(3)). Special circumstances may arise for example where the child suffers from physical or mental incapacity. The order in favour of a child is expressed to last 'until the said child attains the age of 17 or ceases full-time (secondary/tertiary) education, whichever is the later'. It is suggested that, when making an order under the I(PFD)A 1975, the court should follow the same principle. This would ensure that distribution of the estate can take place without delay. The Act makes provision for an application for a variation of the order to be made if the circumstances justify this (for variation and suspension of orders see, further, para 8.11).

8.3 LUMP SUM ORDER – I(PFD)A 1975, SECTION 2(1)(B)

An order for a specified lump sum to be paid out of the net estate may be made on a claim under the I(PFD)A 1975. It can also be made on an application under s 6 for the variation or discharge of an order for periodical payments (see para 8.11.2). A lump sum ordered under s 6, however, may be made only out of any 'relevant property', to the original claimant or to any such person who has applied or would, but for s 4, be entitled to apply for an order under s 2.

In claims under the I(PFD)A 1975, it is more common for the court to award a lump sum payment rather than periodical payments. This is because a lump sum provides finality for both the claimant and the other beneficiaries, and allows the personal representatives to administer the estate without the additional costs of operating trusts, which would have to be created to provide income to meet a periodical payments order.

8.3.1 Instalment order

Pursuant to I(PFD)A 1975, s 7(1), where a lump sum is ordered under s 2(1)(b) or s 6(2)(b), the court has power to order that the lump sum be paid by instalments of such amount as may be specified in the order. Where an instalment order is proposed, in appropriate cases and on the basis of fairness and justice, it may be prudent also to ask the court to consider directing that interest be paid on the lump sum pursuant to its powers under s 2(4) to make consequential and supplemental provisions.

8.3.2 Variation of order

The court also has power to vary a lump sum order, whether made under I(PFD)A 1975, s 2 or s 6, but the power is limited in that the order may be varied only on the application of:

(1) the person to whom the lump sum is payable;
(2) the personal representatives of the deceased; or
(3) the trustees of the property out of which the lump sum is payable.

Further, the order may be varied only by altering:

(1) the number of instalments payable;
(2) the amount of any instalment; and
(3) the date on which any instalment becomes payable (I(PFD)A 1975, s 7(2)).

8.3.3 Assessing amount to be awarded

The factors taken into account in arriving at the amount to be awarded under a lump sum order depend on the circumstances of each case, and in particular the matters set out in I(PFD)A 1975, s 3 (see Chapter 7).

Where a capital sum is provided to produce an income, an important factor to be taken into account in assessing the amount to be awarded is the fact that the claimant is forgoing the right to apply for variation; an adjustment in favour of the claimant should therefore be made to compensate for the loss of that right. This is particularly likely to be the case where the estate is large. Other factors for which the court should make allowance are inflation and future contingencies. In the words of Oliver LJ in *Re Besterman (Deceased), Besterman v Grusin* [1984] Ch 458:

> ... houses decay, circumstances change, the cost of living increases and the value of money falls, or certainly the history of the last ten years leads us to believe. Furthermore, although, happily, the plaintiff appears in good health, there is an inevitable health hazard with advancing age, and having regard to the fact that this lady is the widow of a more than ordinarily wealthy man, reasonable provision would in my judgment require that she should have access to a sufficient sum of money to ensure beyond any reasonable doubt that she is relieved of any anxiety for the future. It is a criticism of the annuity purchase approach to the problem that the income which it is intended to provide is provided only if an annuity is actually purchased which is not, in general, a course which a prudent adviser would advise in an age of inflation and that postulates that there can be no resort to capital in the event of emergency ... The relevant consideration is the extent of the lump sum and that ought (at any rate where as here the estate is ample for the purpose and scarcity of funds is not an inhibiting factor) to take account of the fact that the plaintiff is (whether or not of her volition) giving up the right to return to the court for a variation of the provision in the event of unforeseen contingencies. I think that the absence, which is inherent in a lump sum order, of an opportunity to return to the court does mean that, in assessing the lump sum, the court must take rather greater account than might otherwise be the case of contingencies and inflation. I accept the submission of junior counsel for the plaintiff that reasonable provision, in the case of a very large estate such as this and [a] wholly blameless widow who is incapable of supporting herself, should be such as to relieve her of anxiety for the future. I say 'in the case of a very large estate' not because there is any difference in principle but simply because the existence of a large estate makes that which is desirable also practically possible. It has been pointed out more than once that the calculation in cases of this sort is, of necessity, not one where any precision is possible, but for my part I take the view that reasonable provision in this case would dictate that in addition to the secure roof over her head, the widow should have available to her a capital sum of sufficient size not simply to enable her to purchase an adequate annuity according to her present needs but to provide her with the income which she needs and a cushion in the form of available capital which will enable her to meet all reasonable foreseeable contingencies. What that sum is, is a matter for

> judgment but I think that in it we are entitled to take into account that, though the plaintiff is quite content with her present residence it is in fact somewhat more modest than she might be thought to be entitled to expect to be provided for her by a husband in the financial position of the deceased.

The fact that a lump sum may enable the claimant to provide for someone else should not govern the amount ordered to be paid. In *Preston v Preston* [1982] Fam 17 (a case under the Matrimonial Causes Act 1973), Brandon J said that the lump sum awarded to the wife should not include an amount for the future maintenance of her son (see para 7.8.2).

In assessing the amount of the lump sum to be awarded, the court has sometimes capitalised periodical payments which it has awarded. In *Malone v Harrison* [1979] 1 WLR 1353, the court used a multiplier and multiplicand as applicable in personal injuries actions. In *Re Besterman (Deceased) Besterman v Grusin* [1984] Ch 458, the court used the amount of capital which would be needed to generate the income required to satisfy the claimant's needs. See, also, *Re Bunning (Deceased), Bunning v Salmon* [1984] Ch 480. If the circumstances justify it, it may be appropriate to apply the *Duxbury* Tables (see *Duxbury v Duxbury* [1992] Fam 62) or the Ogden Tables (Michael Ogden, *Actuarial Tables with Explanatory Notes for Use in Personal Injury and Fatal Accident Cases* (Stationery Office Books, 1994)) to achieve the right result.

It should be borne in mind that no hard-and-fast rule has been applied and there is no case which sets out any guidelines. The court's decision turns on the particular facts of the case before it and the application of the principles set out in I(PFD)A 1975, s 3.

8.4 TRANSFER OF PROPERTY ORDER – I(PFD)A 1975, SECTION 2(1)(C)

I(PFD)A 1975, s 2(1)(c) empowers the court to order the transfer to the claimant of such property comprised in the net estate as may be specified in the order. 'Property' is defined in s 25(1) to include 'any chose in action'. This power is similar to that contained in Matrimonial Causes Act 1973, s 24. As in matrimonial proceedings, there is no power to order a transfer of property on an application for periodical payments, but on a variation of a periodical payments order the court may order a transfer of property under s 6(2)(c) (see, further, para 8.11.2).

Where an order for transfer of property in favour of a claimant is justified, but would mean that the needs of the other beneficiaries would not be met because the other assets are insufficient, the court may order the transfer subject to a legacy in favour of a beneficiary or subject to a charge over the property or a life interest.

Martin v Williams [2017] EWHC 491 (Ch) is an example where on appeal by the widow against the transfer of the deceased's share in the property owned jointly by the deceased and the claimant, the court allowed the appeal and ordered that a life interest in the deceased's half share should be vested in the claimant. In *Rajabally v Rajabally* [1987] 2 FLR 390, the testator, who was survived by his widow, their two sons and a son of his first marriage, left his estate, consisting of the former matrimonial home, to his widow and the three children in equal shares. The widow lived in the house with two of her sons. The eldest son suffered from mental illness, lived in council accommodation and his only source of income was state benefits. The widow made a claim under the I(PFD)A 1975. During the proceedings, the eldest son was prepared to take the provision made under the will by being bought out at a valuation. The two younger children were prepared to give assurances that they would not insist on their rights under the will. The court took the view that the widow should be provided with real security in the house, but that account had to be taken of the limited means and uncertain future of the eldest son. The balance was struck by transferring the house to the widow absolutely, but subject to a legacy in favour of the eldest son to be raised by a mortgage on the property. See, also, *Re Christie (Deceased), Christie v Keeble* [1979] Ch 168. More recent examples where a transfer of property order was made are *Williams v Martin* [2016] WTLR 1075 and *Lewis v Warner* [2016] EWHC 1787 (Ch). In *Williams v Martin*, the claimant had lived with the deceased for 18 years in a committed relationship and they had bought a property jointly but as tenants in common. The deceased, however, although separated from his wife, remained married to her. On his death, he failed to make appropriate provision for the claimant, with the result that his half share passed to his widow, leaving the claimant without a home. She applied for an order for financial provision under the I(PFD)A 1975. The widow's challenge to the claim failed and she was ordered to pay £100,000 in costs. The court ordered the transfer of the deceased's half share to the claimant.

In *Lewis v Warner*, the deceased and Mr Warner had been living together for 20 years and Mr Warner had contributed to the outgoings of their home. Mr Warner was 91 years of age. The deceased did not make any provision for Mr Warner and left her estate, which included the home in which she had lived with Mr Warner, to her daughter who sought possession of the property. Mr Warner applied for financial provision. The judge at first instance made an order which gave Mr Warner an option to purchase the property at a price which was higher than the valuation given by the jointly instructed expert and for the property to be transferred to Mr Warner. An appeal by the daughter failed. The court held that it was open to the judge at first instance in exercising the powers under s 2 to compel the daughter to transfer the property.

8.5 SETTLEMENT OF PROPERTY ORDER – I(PFD)A 1975, SECTION 2(1)(D)

The power to order property comprised in the net estate to be settled for the benefit of the claimant is derived from I(PFD)A 1975, s 2(1)(c). There is no power to vary or discharge such an order once made. If it is envisaged that the purpose of the settlement may alter in the future, powers of appointment and variation, and the power to invest and purchase property, can be provided. The deed of trust should be tailored to meet the particular circumstances of the case and the deed should be drafted with care to cover contingencies and changes of circumstances which may occur in the future. Where the interests of others need to be protected it would be advisable for the deed of trust or settlement to be drafted by experienced Chancery lawyers.

The nature of the settlement which the court may order will depend on the circumstances of the case. Where the settlement is in favour of a child, it will provide for the needs of the child during their minority. In the case of a widow/widower, it could be limited until such time as they remarry or cohabit with another person. In the case of a civil partner, it would be limited until a subsequent partnership is formed by the surviving partner.

The power to settle property is particularly useful where the deceased did not make provision for a mentally disabled child, particularly an adult child, in the belief that the child would be adequately provided for by the state. In view of the policy of providing care in the community for those who are disabled, a financial provision order in the form of a settlement would provide for a better quality of life within the community than would otherwise be possible. In such cases, the court should consider making a settlement of property order; and, if necessary, an order for the acquisition of property and its settlement upon a discretionary trust so as to permit the whole or any part of the income from the trust fund to be applied for the maintenance, care and benefit of the claimant as the trustees in their discretion deem fit.

In *Hanbury v Hanbury* [1999] 2 FLR 255, the deceased's daughter was physically and mentally disabled, with a mental age of about 12. She was living with and cared for by her mother, supported by social services. At the time of his death, the deceased was making maintenance payments under a court order to the daughter, but he had, from choice, not had any contact with her since she was 4 years old. Having sought legal advice on how to defeat his daughter's claim, the deceased had transferred his property into, and acquired investments in, the joint names of himself and his second wife and had arranged for investment trust holdings to be bought in the second wife's sole name. Applying the powers it had under I(PFD)A

1975, ss 9 and 10, the court treated the severable share of the jointly owned property as part of the net estate of the deceased and took the net estate to include a one half share of the investment holding and of the joint accounts. The court took into account the fact that the daughter's needs would eventually be met by placement in a residential home. It ordered the costs of such placement to be met by settling £39,000 in a discretionary trust, with the daughter as principal beneficiary, so that her state benefits by way of income support would not be prejudiced.

Re Abrams (Deceased) [1996] 2 FLR 379 is another case where the court used the power to settle property to make appropriate provision for a claimant out of the net estate. In *Re Abrams*, at the date of the hearing, the claimant's business had failed and he had entered into an individual voluntary arrangement under Insolvency Act 1986, Part VIII. It was a term of the individual voluntary arrangement that any capital sum received by the claimant's estate should be paid to the creditors. The claimant's home had been repossessed and he was unemployed. To ensure that the provision ordered by the court was received by the claimant, the court ordered a settlement to be effected under I(PFD)A 1975, s 2(1)(d) whereby 50 per cent of the estate would be settled on the claimant for life on protective trusts, the life interest importing the statutory trusts under Trustee Act 1925, s 33, so that the income would be paid to the claimant for life; but if he became bankrupt or sought to alienate his interest, the life interest would be determined and replaced by a discretionary trust for the claimant and his immediate family.

In *Iqbal v Ahmed* [2011] EWCA Civ 900, [2012] 1 FLR 31, the deceased bequeathed to his wife £8,000 and a right to occupy the former matrimonial home rent free, but her right of occupation was made subject to the condition that she was to be liable for some of the outgoings of the home, its maintenance and the repairs and decorations which amounted to in excess of £30,000. The property was left to their son together with the residual estate of £28,000. The widow made a claim under the I(PFD)A 1975 and was granted a life interest in the property with an entitlement to half the proceeds of sale and the whole of the residuary estate, with the additional provision that the outgoings of the property were to be met by both the widow and the son jointly in equal shares. The son's appeal against the order failed (see, also, *Churchill v Roach* [2002] EWHC 3230 (Ch), [2004] 2 FLR 989).

8.6 ACQUISITION OF PROPERTY ORDER – I(PFD)A 1975, SECTION 2(1)(E)

I(PFD)A 1975, s 2(1)(e) gives the court power to make an order for the acquisition of property comprised in the net estate, and for the acquired property to be transferred to the claimant; or for the settlement of such property for the benefit of the claimant. Once made the order may not be varied (s 6(9)). This power can be useful where the claimant is a person who suffers from physical or mental disability (see Chapter 4) or is a child and needs a home. Where this power is used, the order may also provide for the settlement of the acquired property for the benefit of the claimant. There is no restriction on the type of property which may be acquired but it is likely to be one that satisfies the needs of the claimant.

8.7 VARIATION OF NUPTIAL SETTLEMENT – I(PFD)A 1975, SECTION 2(1)(F) AND (G)

I(PFD)A 1975, s 2(1)(f) provides that the court may vary any ante-nuptial or post-nuptial settlement (including such a settlement made by will) made on the parties to a marriage to which the deceased was one of the parties, the variation being for the benefit of the surviving spouse to that marriage, or any child of that marriage, or any person who was treated by the deceased as a child of the family in relation to that marriage.

Similar provision is made in I(PFD)A 1975, s 2(1)(g), giving the court power to vary any settlement made during the subsistence of a civil partnership formed by the deceased or in anticipation of the formation of a civil partnership by the deceased for the benefit of the surviving civil partner or any child of both the civil partners, or any person who was treated by the deceased as a child of the family in relation to that civil partnership.

As a result of the recommendation made by the Law Commission, provision is now made pursuant to Inheritance and Trustees' Powers Act 2014, s 6, Sch 2, where the deceased died on or after 1 October 2014, giving the court power to make an order varying for the applicant's benefit the trusts on which the deceased's estate is held, whether arising under the will, or the law relating to intestacy or both (I(PFD)A 1975, s 2(1)(h) as amended).

These provisions mirror those which are set out in Matrimonial Causes Act 1973, s 24(1)(c) and in CPA 2004, Sch 5, para 7.

As with variation of settlement orders in the context of divorce and nullity of marriage proceedings and the dissolution and nullity of civil partnerships, the I(PFD)A 1975 requires any settlement to be varied to have a 'nuptial' element and the court's power to vary such a settlement is limited to:

(1) a party to a marriage/civil partnership;
(2) a child of that marriage or a child of both the civil partners; or

(3) a child who was treated by the deceased as the child of the family in relation to that marriage/civil partnership.

8.7.1 Has there been a settlement?

In considering whether to exercise its powers under this provision, the court will first need to determine whether there has been a settlement. The I(PFD)A 1975 does not define an ante-nuptial or post-nuptial settlement. In the case of an ante-nuptial settlement, the agreement to settle property must have been made prior to that marriage/civil partnership. In the case of a post-nuptial settlement, it may result from an agreement made before or after the marriage/civil partnership, but settled after the marriage/civil partnership has taken place. In *Hargreaves v Hargreaves* [1926] P 42, such a settlement was defined as one which was made 'in contemplation of, or because of, marriage and with reference to the interests of married people and their children'.

The term 'settlement', in most cases, has been given a wide meaning. In *Brooks v Brooks* [1995] 2 FLR 13, Lord Nicholls of Birkenhead said:

> The authorities have consistently given a wide meaning to settlement in this context, and they have spelled out no precise limitations. This seems right, because this approach accords with the purpose of the statutory provision. Financial provision that is appropriate so long as the parties are married will often cease to be appropriate when the marriage ends. In order to promote the best interests of the parties and their children in the fundamentally changed situation, it is desirable that the court should have power to alter the terms of the settlement. The purpose of the section is to give the court this power. The object does not dictate that settlement should be given a narrow meaning. On the contrary, the purpose of the section would be impeded, rather than advanced, by continuing its scope. The continuing use of the archaic expression 'ante-nuptial' and 'post nuptial' does not point in the opposite direction. These expressions are apt to embrace all settlements in respect of the particular marriage, whether made before or after the marriage. In this connection, it should be noted in passing that a settlement may be made in respect of a particular marriage even though in certain circumstances the wife or husband by a subsequent marriage might be the person to take. *Lort-Williams v Lort-Williams* [1951] P395 affords an illustration of this.

In *Ben Hashem v Al Shayif* [2008] EWHC 2380 (Fam), Munby J (as he then was) stated that (at [235]):

> one of the classic statements of what is meant by a nuptial settlement for this purpose is to be found in the judgment of Hill J in *Prinsep v Prinsep* [1929] P 225 at 232:
>
> > 'Is it upon the husband in the character of husband or in the wife in the character of wife, or upon both in the character of husband and wife? If it is, it is a settlement on the parties within the meaning of the section. The particular form

> of it does not matter. It may be a settlement in the strictest sense of the term, it may be a covenant to pay by one spouse to the other, or by a third person to a spouse. What does matter is that it should provide for the financial benefit of one or other or both of the spouses as spouses and with reference to their married state.'

Thus, the settlement need not be a classic marriage settlement, nor is it necessary for the settlement to be expressed to be a marriage settlement. It is the substance of the settlement which is significant. The particular form of the settlement does not matter as long as it provides for the financial benefit of one or other of the spouses/civil partners as spouses/civil partners with reference to their married/civil partnership relationship.

It is also irrelevant who the settlor of the settlement is or what the motive of the settlor was when the settlement was made (see *Prescott (formerly Fellowes) v Fellowes* [1958] P 260). What matters is the substance of the arrangements and whether it related to that marriage/civil partnership, not marriage/civil partnership generally, and whether it made continuing provision for the husband, the wife, the civil partners and/or their child or a child of the family. (See, also, *N v N and F Trust* [2005] EWHC 2908 (Fam), [2006] 1 FLR 856 and *C v C (Ancillary Relief: Nuptial Settlement)* [2004] EWCA Civ 1030, [2005] Fam 250, *sub nom Charalambous v Charalambous* [2004] 2 FLR 1093.) In *K v K (Ancillary Relief: Deed of Appointment)* [2007] EWHC 3485 (Fam), [2009] 2 FLR 937, the court on the facts adopted a more restrictive approach. In *K v K*, the trust had been settled by the husband's mother for the benefit of her two children and remoter issue and their spouses, widows and widowers. The trustees had an overriding power of appointment. At a later date, the trust was varied by two deeds of appointment, both revocable with the prior consent of the husband, which excluded the husband's brother and his issue. Both at the time of the original trust and the two subsequent deeds of appointment, the husband was single. He married the woman with whom he had been in a relationship for 24 years after his mother, the settlor, died, so that the children of their relationship could be legitimated and included as beneficiaries under the trust. After the marriage, another deed of appointment was executed by the trustees, again excluding the husband's brother and his family as beneficiaries. The marriage broke down and the wife sought a variation of the trust contending that it was a post-nuptial settlement. The court held that the sole purpose of the deed made after the marriage was an administrative exercise to ensure that the husband's brother and his family could never benefit from the trust and, therefore, he had not revoked the deed made before the marriage and there was nothing in the deed to suggest that there had been any intention to confer an irrevocable benefit on the wife.

The acquisition by a husband and wife or civil partners of a matrimonial home in their joint names constitutes a post-nuptial settlement, but a disposition which confers 'an immediate and absolute interest in an item of property does not constitute a settlement of that property' (see *Brooks v Brooks* (above) and see, also, *Thompson v Thompson* [1986] Fam 38 and *Dinch v Dinch* [1987] 1 WLR 252 (HL)). In *E v E (Financial Provision)* [1990] 2 FLR 233, during the course of the marriage, a property for which the husband's father had provided the funds was settled on discretionary trusts of which the husband and the wife were beneficiaries; it was held that the settlement constituted a post-nuptial settlement. For a review of what constitutes settlement, see *Ben Hashem v Al Shayif* [2008] EWHC 2380 (Fam).

To determine whether a nuptial settlement has been made, the court will take into account all the relevant facts to identify the substance of the transaction, and whether such a settlement was made will depend very much on the facts of the individual case.

8.7.2 How should the court exercise its discretion?

Once it is confirmed that a settlement is a 'nuptial' settlement, the court will then need to identify the property comprised in the settlement/trust and consider how it should exercise its discretion.

In *Dixit v Dixit*, CAT, 23 June 1988 (CA), the testator made no provision in his will for his widow or for the children of his second marriage. There was, however, an investment property, which was held in trust, the effect of which was to give the widow a life interest in one half and, contingent on their attaining the age of 18 years, the other half to the two children of the testator's second marriage. Waite J gave the widow a full life interest in the property and provided for the children by granting them an interest in another property which passed under the will of the deceased. The Court of Appeal held that the order made by the judge could not stand as he had failed to consider the tax implications, but did not decide whether Waite J had power under I(PFD)A 1975, s 2(1)(f) to 'switch' the trusts. This appears to be the only case under the Act on the point.

In general, the power of variation will be exercised to benefit the surviving spouse/civil partner provided the settlement related to that marriage/civil partnership.

In *Ben Hashem v Al Shayif* [2008] EWHC 2380 (Fam), Munby J (as he then was), when dealing with the variation of a settlement under Matrimonial Causes Act 1973, s 24(1)(c), held that:

- The court has unfettered and in theory unlimited discretion, as between husband and wife, to rearrange the 'family assets', but 'there is no such general jurisdiction to take away – in plain language to confiscate – the children's property, let alone the step-children's property to meet claims brought by a wife.

- The court should have regard to all the circumstances and in particular to the matters listed in s 25 with the objective so far as it is possible to make it, to achieve a result which is fair to both parties looking to the effect of the order considered as a whole.
- The court ought to be very slow to deprive innocent third parties of their rights under the settlement. If their interests are to be adversely affected then the court, looking at the wider picture, will normally ensure that they receive some benefit, which, even if not pecuniary, is approximately equivalent, so that they do not suffer substantial injury.
- If and in so far as the variation would affect the interests of the child, it should be permitted only if, after taking into account all the terms of the intended order, all monetary considerations and any other relevant factors, however intangible, it can be said, on the whole, to be for the benefit or, at least, not to their disadvantage.
- The court when exercising its discretion in favour of the spouse/civil partner and contemplating depriving a third party and particularly a child to meet the claims of a spouse/civil partner, should look for fairness and justice and ask itself why a third party and more particularly a child should be deprived of their interest in order to meet the claims of a spouse/civil partner.

Where the marriage or the civil partnership has been dissolved, but the provisions of I(PFD)A 1975, s 14 apply (see paras 4.4.2–4.5.2), the court has power under s 14 to treat the former spouse/civil partner of the deceased in the same category as a surviving spouse and to vary an appropriate settlement for that claimant's benefit.

It should be noted, however, that the class of persons who are eligible to apply for a variation of a nuptial settlement is limited to those referred to at the start of this section.

Where the settlement involves offshore trusts or an international element it is essential to examine the terms of the settlement to ascertain whether it includes a clause giving exclusive jurisdiction to the courts of the state/country where the trust was created, or any other restrictions relating to any variations of its terms. If it does, it may result in difficulties in enforcing any orders made by a court in England and Wales. Problems may also arise in relation to securing disclosure of information relating to the trust, such as trust accounts. Examples of the nature and extent of the problems which may arise are provided in ancillary relief applications in matrimonial proceedings, such as *Charman v Charman* [2005] EWCA Civ 1606, where the trust was originally situated in Jersey but later transferred to Bermuda. The court held that a request for the production of documents and for inspection could not lawfully be made if they represented a 'fishing expedition', and gave guidance on when it would be appropriate to order disclosure, document inspection or an inspection appointment. Other cases include *Tchenguiz-Imerman v Imerman* [2013] EWHC 3627 (Fam), *Re H Trust* [2006] JLR 280, *Re B Trust* [2006] JLR 185, *Mubarak v Mubarik* [2007] EWHC 220 (Fam) and *BJ v MJ* [2011] EWHC 2708 (Fam).

It is also essential, when a variation of settlement is sought, to scrutinise the circumstances in which the trust was created to establish whether it is a 'sham trust', where although the assets are transferred to a third party they effectively remain under the control of the settlor, or is in effect a settlement for the benefit of the settlor and therefore creates a resulting trust (see *Prest v Petrodel Resources Ltd and Others* [2013] UKSC 34). The issues raised in such cases and the principles of law which apply to both sham trust and resulting trust have been considered in numerous cases, of which the most significant is *A v A* [2007] EWHC 99 (Fam), in which Munby J analysed previous relevant authorities and provided guidance (see [32]–[58]). This decision has been applied subsequently in *M v M* [2013] EWHC 2534 (Fam) and *ND v SD* [2017] EWHC 1507 (Fam) (see, also, para 9.3). These cases illustrate the complexity of the issues involved and is therefore beyond the remit of this publication. In either case it is often difficult to adduce sufficient evidence to establish whether it is a sham trust or a genuine resulting trust, and the whole exercise of proving it could lead to satellite litigation, which is therefore costly. This is more relevant in claims made under the I(PFD)Act 1975 because of its impact on the interests of other beneficiaries and its effect in reducing the value of the net estate.

In proceedings for ancillary relief following a dissolution of a marriage/civil partnership the court can, pursuant to the provisions of the Matrimonial Causes Act 1973, as amended by Welfare Reform and Pensions Act 1999, Sch 3, para 3, make a pension sharing order, but there is no such power in respect of a claim under the I(PFD)A 1975. It has been suggested that the decision in *Brooks v Brooks* [1996] 1 AC 375 could be applied to a claim under the Act, but there is no direct authority on the subject.

The Law Commission in its Consultation Paper No 191, *Intestacy and Family Provision Claims on Death*, considered the issue of pension assets and its unavailability in proceedings under the I(PFD)A 1975. The view expressed at para 7.80 was that 'resort to pension assets should in practice be limited to those cases, where there are insufficient other assets in the estate from which provision can be made for deserving applicants for family provision', but the Commission invited further responses on whether this was a serious problem that needed to be addressed and whether there were any technical implications. The Consultation

Paper asked consultees to consider whether they would favour reform of the Act to the effect that benefits from a pension fund, whether lump sums or periodical payments, could be the subject of family provision orders made by the court and whether legal or practical difficulties would result if benefits from a pension fund could be the subject of a family provision order and, if so, what these might be. Although the response from many consultees was positive, this was not included in the Inheritance and Trustees' Powers Act 2014.

8.8 CONSEQUENTIAL AND SUPPLEMENTAL ORDERS – I(PFD)A 1975, SECTION 2(4)

When making any of the orders referred to under I(PFD)A 1975, s 2(1), the court also has power, under s 2(4), to make such consequential and supplemental provisions as it thinks necessary or expedient for the purposes of:

(1) giving effect to the order;
(2) securing that the order operates fairly as between one beneficiary of the deceased and another.

There are no limitations on the very wide scope which the court has under this provision. Without in any way restricting the court's power under this sub-section, I(PFD)A 1975, s 2(4) particularises three specific orders which the court can make under this provision, namely:

(1) to order any person who holds any property which forms part of the net estate of the deceased to make such payment, or transfer such property, as may be specified in the order;
(2) to vary the disposition of the deceased's estate effected by the will or the law of intestacy, or by both the will and the law relating to intestacy, in such manner as the court thinks fair and reasonable having regard to the provisions of the order and all the circumstances of the case;
(3) to confer on the trustees of any property which is the subject of an order under s 2 such powers as appear to the court to be necessary or expedient.

The powers given under this provision can be used to impose conditions on a substantive order made under I(PFD)A 1975, s 2 to define, restrict or regulate the order made. For instance, where a periodical payments order is made the court may direct the claimant to inform the personal representatives of any change in the financial circumstances of the claimant, or it may grant the claimant the right to occupy a property subject to making payment for use and occupation. The specific power under s 2(1)(d) enables the court to extend the authority given to trustees under the will to meet the particular requirements of the case.

The court's power under I(PFD)A 1975, s 2(4) to make consequential directions for the purpose of giving effect to the order, or to secure that the order operates fairly between the beneficiaries, enables the court to apportion the incidence of any orders between different classes of beneficiary or between the same class. Usually, the awards are made out of the residuary estate, but where this is not possible the court is likely to apportion the burden between pecuniary legatees and residuary legatees (see *Bunning (Deceased), Bunning v Salmon* [1984] Ch 480 and *Malone v Harrison* [1979] 1 WLR 1353).

The court is not bound by any express declaration of the deceased as to how an award should be borne; although awards are usually made out of the residuary estate this is not always the case. In *Re Preston, Preston v Hoggarth* [1969] 1 WLR 317, the testator provided in his will that in the event of his widow making a claim, it was his wish that the award should be discharged out of the provision made for his grandchildren. The court held that it had power not only to apportion the burden of the award as regards respective classes of beneficiary, but also to throw the burden unequally between beneficiaries in the same class.

In exercising its discretion, the court should have regard to the claims of beneficiaries who would be claimants under the I(PFD)A 1975 and those who do not qualify. It should also have regard to the intention of the deceased, whether expressed or presumed (see *Re Simson, Simson v National Provincial Bank* [1950] Ch 38). Lastly, the court should have regard to the matters which influence the court in deciding whether or not the deceased has made reasonable financial provision for the claimant.

In addition to these wide powers the court also has the powers it can exercise under CPR Part 25, to preserve any property until the conclusion of the proceedings, to grant injunctions and freezing orders and orders to prevent the dissipation of assets or disposition of property intended to defeat or reduce a claim under the I(PFD)A 1975, see, for example, *Antonio v Williams* [2022] EWHC 2383 (Ch), where the court made an interim injunction restraining any registered disposition of two of the properties which formed part of the deceased's estate.

The court may also make orders for the disclosure of information under CPR r 25.1(1)(g) directing a party to provide information about the location of relevant property or assets or to provide information about relevant property or assets which are or may be the subject of an application for a 'freezing order'. Practitioners are advised to consider the orders which are available under the CPR. An application for disclosure of information may also be sought before proceedings are begun under CPR r 31.16 and for a direction for accounts or inquiries to be undertaken or made under Part 24, PD 24, para 6.

8.9 INTERIM ORDERS – I(PFD)A 1975, SECTION 5

On an application under I(PFD)A 1975, s 2 the court has power to order interim payments to be made, out of the net estate, of such sum or sums, and if more than one, at such intervals, as the court thinks reasonable.

8.9.1 Conditions precedent

Before the court can make an interim order it must be satisfied that:

(1) the claimant is in immediate need of financial assistance but it is not yet possible to determine what order (if any) should be made under s 2 (see e.g. *Smith v Smith* [2011] EWHC 2133 (Ch), and see, also, *M v M* [2011] EWHC 3574 (Fam) where 'immediate' was held to mean 'current' not 'urgent'); and
(2) property forming part of the net estate of the deceased is or can be made available to meet the needs of the claimant.

Since the power to make the order is discretionary, the claimant must also prove that it would be just in all the circumstances of the case for the court to exercise its discretion. For a case where both a periodical payments order and a lump sum order were made on an interim application, see *Re Besterman (Deceased), Besterman v Grusin* [1984] Ch 458.

In *Re Ralphs, Ralphs v District Bank* [1968] 1 WLR 1522, the deceased's second wife had left him after a marriage which had lasted about 9 years. By his will, the deceased left her the income from a sum of £8,000. To his daughter he left an income of £13,000 and capital of £3,000, and the residue he left to his son. The daughter was destitute. The second wife applied for financial provision. An interim order was made in her favour, the court holding that in the great majority of cases where some benefit is given to the claimant by the will, there can be no good reason for withholding it pending the hearing of the summons.

8.9.2 Matters to be considered

I(PFD)A 1975, s 5(3) provides that in determining what order, if any, should be made under the section, the court shall, so far as the urgency of the case admits, have regard to the same matters as those to which the court is required to have regard under s 3 (see Chapter 7). In exercising its discretion, the court has regard to the fact that the purpose of any order it makes is to hold the situation as reasonably and fairly as possible until the determination of the final application.

8.9.3 Orders that can be made

The court's power to make interim orders is limited to ordering such sum or sums as the court thinks reasonable. This would include an order for periodical payments and a lump sum order, but not a property transfer order. The court may, however, make an order for a lump sum payment to enable the claimant to purchase a home, as occurred in *Re Besterman* (above). The court may impose conditions and restrictions, and determine the duration of any interim orders it may make. It may order that any sum paid to the claimant shall be treated, to such an extent and in such manner as may be provided, as having been paid on account of any payment provided for by that order (I(PFD)A 1975, s 5(4)). When making an interim order, therefore, the court may seek an undertaking that if, say, the claimant's financial circumstances change, the claimant should notify the personal representatives so that an application for variation of an interim order can be applied for.

If an interim periodical payments order is made, the court may specify its duration in the order or make it last until the final determination of the substantive application, i.e. until an order under I(PFD)A 1975, s 2 is made. Section 5 makes no provision for repayment of any sums paid under the interim order in a case where either the final order is made in favour of the claimant or the order made falls short of the payments made under the interim order.

It would seem that because the court has the power to make orders for 'such sum or sums' as it thinks reasonable, there is no reason why the court should not entertain more than one application. I(PFD)A 1975, s 5(1) empowers the court to make the order subject to such condition or restrictions, if any, and to any further order of the court. This implies that the court has the power to vary any interim order it has made.

By virtue of I(PFD)A 1975, s 5(2), when making an interim order, the court may provide for:

(1) payments of such amount as may be specified in the order;
(2) payments equal to the whole of the income of the net estate or of such portion thereof as may be specified;
(3) payments equal to the whole of the income of such part of the net estate as the court may direct to be set aside or apportioned for the making out of the income thereof of interim payments, or may provide for the payments or any of them to be determined in any other way as the court thinks fit.

8.9.4 Personal representatives and interim orders – I(PFD)A 1975, section 20(2)

I(PFD)A 1975, s 20(2) provides that where the personal representative of a deceased person pays any sum directed by an order under s 5 to be paid out of the net estate, they should not be under any liability by reason of the estate's not being sufficient to make the payment, unless at the time of making the payment they had reasonable cause to believe that the estate was not sufficient. In *Re Ralphs, Ralphs v District Bank* [1968] 1 WLR 1522, Cross J laid down the following guidelines for personal representatives faced with an application for an interim order:

> They should form their own view, with the assistance, of course, of their legal advisers, as to the payments which can properly be made, and if they are not prepared to make such payments on their own responsibility they should ask the parties who might conceivably be affected – whether applicant or residuary legatee – for their consent. If such consent is not forthcoming the executors can apply to the court for leave to make the payment in question and the court, if it thinks that any withholding of consent was unreasonable, could throw the costs of the application on the party to blame.

8.10 INJUNCTIONS

In *Andrew v Andrew* [1990] 2 FLR 376, it was held that the court does not have power to restrain tortious conduct in relation to an application under the I(PFD)A 1975. The substantive issues raised in the proceedings were not for assault, trespass or any other cause of action based on tort or an invasion of a legal right; therefore the applicant was not, under County Courts Act 1984, s 38, entitled to any injunctive relief. Section 38 has since been amended by the Courts and Legal Services Act 1990 to confer wide injunctive powers on the county court. It now provides that, subject to certain exceptions, a county court may make any order which could be made by the High Court if the proceedings were in the High Court. Any such order may be made either unconditionally or on such terms and conditions as the court thinks just.

In addition, the CPR now govern practice and procedure across all jurisdictions and the procedural rules in relation to claims made under the I(PFD)A 1975 are governed by those rules. The court, therefore, is empowered to make such orders as may be appropriate under CPR Part 25, to preserve any property until the conclusion of the proceedings, to grant injunctions and freezing orders, and to grant orders to prevent the dissipation of assets or disposition of property intended to defeat or reduce a claim under the I(PFD)A 1975.

The provisions of I(PFD)A 1975, s 2(4) (see para 8.8) are wide enough to empower the court to grant injunctions. Hence, in order to preserve the property or other assets which are likely to be the subject of a s 10 application, it would be prudent to seek interim remedies such as freezing injunctions, injunctions to restrain disposal or transfer or other dealings with the property, disclosure orders and, where appropriate, to join the third party as a party to the proceedings (if not already so joined), in order to enable the third party to advance their case and for the court to be presented with all the available relevant evidence. Failure to do so is likely to result in breach of that person's Art 6 rights under the Human Rights Convention. For an example where the court made an order restraining the disposal of the disputed properties, see *Antonio v Williams* [2022] EWHC 2383 (Ch).The court may also make orders for the disclosure of information under CPR r 25.1(1)(g) directing a party to provide information about the location of relevant property or assets in the form of a mandatory injunction which may be enforced, if necessary, by a committal order provided the order has been endorsed with a penal notice and is personally served on the person to whom it is directed. It may also order pre-action disclosure against any person who is likely to be a respondent in the substantive application pursuant to CPR r 31.16 (see, further, *Black v Sumitomo Corp* [2001] EWCA Civ 1819 for guidance on how the court is likely to deal with such an application).

Furthermore, in *Burris v Azadani* [1995] 1 WLR 1372, it was held that both the High Court and county courts have jurisdiction to grant injunctions in wide terms to restrain conduct that was not in itself tortious or otherwise unlawful if such an order was reasonably regarded as necessary for the protection of a claimant's legitimate interests.

Since the I(PFD)A 1975 provides for a transfer of property order, the court would have jurisdiction to make any orders to prevent any dealing with property and to make any orders which would ensure that property is preserved until the claim before the court is finally disposed of. Before making such an order, the court will need to be satisfied that the claimant has an arguable case for an order under s 2, and that it would be just in all the circumstances of the case to exercise the court's discretion.

8.11 VARIATION, DISCHARGE, SUSPENSION AND REVIVAL OF ORDERS – I(PFD)A 1975, SECTION 6

Where the court has made an order for periodical payments under I(PFD)A 1975, s 2(1)(a) (the 'original order'), it has power to vary or discharge that order; to suspend any provision of it temporarily; and to revive the operation of any provision so suspended (s 6(1)). An application to vary an order may be made only in respect of a periodical payments order. Section 7 makes provision for a lump sum order to be varied but only in respect of instalments (see para 8.3.2). For variation of orders made under the Matrimonial Causes Act 1973, see ss 16–18, paras 8.12–8.14. An order varied once may be varied again (see *Fricker v Personal Representatives of Fricker* (1982) 3 FLR 228).

8.11.1 Who may apply?

An application under I(PFD)A 1975, s 6 for variation, discharge, suspension or revival of an order for periodical payments may be made by any one of the following persons (I(PFD)A 1975, s 6(5)):

(1) a person who has applied for an order under s 2, or who would have been entitled to apply for an order under s 2 were it not for the time limit for applications imposed by s 4;
(2) the personal representatives of the deceased;
(3) the trustees of any 'relevant property' (see *Fricker v Personal Representatives of Fricker* (above));
(4) any beneficiary of the estate of the deceased.

8.11.2 Orders that can be made – I(PFD)A 1975, section 6(2)–(4)

On an application for variation of the original order the court may:

(1) provide for the making, out of any relevant property, of such periodical payments and for such term as may be specified in the order, to any person who has applied, or would but for I(PFD)A 1975, s 4 be entitled to apply, for an order under s 2 (whether or not, in the case of any claim, an order was made in favour of the claimant);
(2) provide for the payment, out of any relevant property, of a lump sum of such amount as may be specified, to the original recipient or to any such person as is mentioned in (1) above;
(3) provide for the transfer of the relevant property, or such part thereof as may be specified, to the original recipient or to any such person as is referred to in (2) above (s 6(2));
(4) make orders under s 6(3) (see below);
(5) give consequential directions as it thinks necessary and expedient having regard to the provisions of the order (s 6(8)).

There is no power, on an application for variation under I(PFD)A 1975, s 6, to make any of the following orders:

(1) a settlement of property under s 2(1)(d);
(2) an order for the acquisition of specified property out of the net estate (s 2(1)(e));
(3) a variation of an ante-nuptial or post-nuptial settlement (s 2(1)(f));
(4) dealing with the deceased's severable share of property on a joint tenancy under s 9;
(5) dealing with dispositions intended to defeat applications for financial provision under s 10;
(6) under s 11 in respect of contracts to leave property by will.

Where an order for periodical payments is to cease:

(1) on the occurrence of an event (other than the remarriage of a former spouse) specified in the order, or
(2) on the expiration of a period specified in the order,

and no application for variation has been made before the occurrence of the specified event or the expiration of the specified period, as the case may be, then if, before the end of the period of 6 months from the date of the occurrence of that event or of the expiration of that period, an application is made for variation, discharge, suspension or revival, the court may make any order which it would have had power to make if the application had been made before that date. Note that the limitation period for making the application in these circumstances is 6 months. The court has no powers to extend this period (see under para 8.11.5).

Where an application is made within the limitation period of 6 months the order in such an instance may be made in favour of:

(1) the original recipient;
(2) any other person who has applied for an order under s 2; or
(3) any person who would have been entitled to apply for an order under s 2 were it not for the time limits for application imposed by s 4.

The case of *Taylor v Bell* [2015] EW Misc B3 (CC) is a good example of the wide powers that the court has to vary an order it has previously made. In *Taylor v Bell*, a periodical payments order was made in favour of the deceased's son who was 17 years of age and for whom the deceased had not made any provision, although the estate was worth £2 million. The son was a talented singer, but had learning difficulties. Before a consent order under the I(PFD)A 1975 was made, the son suffered a major road traffic accident for which he continued to receive treatment for a long period. These difficulties led to a delay in his university education. The consent order set out in detail the maximum amount of the payments that were to be made and to last until August 2014. The sum of £210,000 was set aside to meet these payments. The claimant was not able to complete his education by 2014, but it was anticipated he would be able to do so by August 2015. Thereafter, he wished to pursue a postgraduate course for 2 years. By the trial date, only £112,433 of the total of £210,000 had been utilised. The claimant applied for a further £90,000. The executors contested the application. The court nevertheless varied the order to provide for him to receive £6,100 per annum for the year 2015 and thereafter £7,500 per annum for the next 2 years, on the condition that the claimant attended the full-time postgraduate course.

It appears from I(PFD)A 1975, s 6(3) and (5) that a person who was debarred from making an application under s 2 by reason of the limitation period imposed by s 4, or a person whose original application was unsuccessful, may nevertheless apply for the variation of an order made in favour of another.

In an application falling within I(PFD)A 1975, s 6(3), the court has power to make any order which it would have had power to make if the application had been made in time. An order varying the original order may be made only within the limits of the 'relevant property' available. It follows that an increase in periodical payments or other variation can occur only in limited circumstances, such as:

(1) if there is an increase in income available from the relevant property;
(2) if another recipient dies, thus releasing the payments in respect of them; or
(3) there is a reduction in payments to another recipient.

8.11.3 Meaning of 'relevant property'

I(PFD)A 1975, s 6(6) defines 'relevant property' as follows:

> (a) property the income of which is at the date of the order applicable wholly or in part for the making of periodical payments to any person who has applied for an order under this Act, or
> (b) in the case of an application under subsection (3) above in respect of payments which have ceased to be payable on the occurrence of an event or the expiration of a period, property the income of which was so applicable immediately before the occurrence of that event or expiration, as the case may be …

8.11.4 Matters to be considered

In exercising the power to vary, the court must have regard to all the circumstances of the case, including any change in those circumstances and any change in the matters to which the court was required to have regard under I(PFD)A 1975, s 3 when making the original order (s 6(7)).

Lewis v Lewis [1977] 1 WLR 409 concerned the construction of Matrimonial Causes Act 1973, s 31, which gives the court power to vary or discharge a periodical payments order in divorce proceedings. It was held that, in considering an application for variation, the court is not confined to looking at any change in the means of the parties since the original order was made, but is required to look at the actual means of the parties as they stand at the time when the case is before the court, and to approach the matter as if it were fixing the payment *de novo*.

An order can be varied to take account of inflation (see *Fricker v Personal Representatives of Fricker* (1982) 3 FLR 288).

8.11.5 Time limits

Save for the limitation in I(PFD)A 1975, s 6(3), an application for the variation, discharge, suspension or revival of the original order may be made at any time. Section 6(3) relates to periodical payments which are to cease on the occurrence of an event or the expiry of a specified period. An application relating to such an order must be made within 6 months of the event's occurring or the expiry of the specified period. There is no power to extend this period. In all other cases, however, the court is entitled to consider any delay which has occurred in making the application. Some or all of the matters set out in Chapter 3 may be relevant where the application is made by a person who has failed to apply within the time limit set out in s 4. It is unlikely that a claimant who has been refused leave to apply out of time will succeed in bringing a claim by using this provision unless there are exceptional reasons.

8.11.6 Commencement of the order

An order made by virtue of I(PFD)A 1975, s 6(3) may be directed to take effect from:

(1) the date of the occurrence of the specified event;
(2) the expiration of the specified period; or
(3) such later date as may be specified by the court.

8.12 VARIATION AND DISCHARGE OF SECURED PERIODICAL PAYMENTS ORDERS MADE UNDER MATRIMONIAL CAUSES ACT 1973 – I(PFD)A 1975, SECTION 16

Matrimonial Causes Act 1973, s 31(6) provides that, where a person liable to make payments under a secured periodical payments order has died, an application relating to that order (and to any order made under s 24A(1) which requires the proceeds of sale of property to be used for securing those payments) may be made by the person entitled to payments under the periodical payments order or by the personal representatives of the deceased person, for variation or discharge of the order, or the suspension of the order temporarily, or to revive the operation of any provision so suspended. Such an application must be made within a period of 6 months from the date on which representation in regard to the estate of the deceased person is first taken out unless the court grants permission to make the application out of time.

CPA 2004, Sch 5, para 60 includes a similar provision in relation to a secured periodical payments order made following the dissolution of a civil partnership.

I(PFD)A 1975, s 16 incorporates a similar provision, enabling an application by the person entitled to secured periodical payments, or the personal representatives of the deceased, to apply to vary or discharge that periodical payments order or to revive the operation of any provision thereof which has been suspended under Matrimonial Causes Act 1973, s 31 or under CPA 2004, Sch 5. The powers exercisable by the court under this section in relation to an order are also exercisable in relation to any instrument executed in pursuance of the order (I(PFD)A 1975, s 16(3)). The personal representatives of the deceased will not be liable for distributing the estate prior to an application being made, if it is made after the 6-month time limit has elapsed.

It should be noted, however, that where an order has been made under I(PFD)A 1975, s 15 restricting the right to an application to be made for financial provision under the I(PFD)A 1975, then on the death of the payer the application for the court to vary, etc, a secured periodical payments order should be made under Matrimonial Causes Act 1973, s 31. Note also that an application under Matrimonial Causes Act 1973, s 31(6) or CPA 2004, Sch 5 must be made within 6 months of the date on which representation in regard to the estate of the deceased is first taken out, unless the court grants permission thereafter.

In *Re Eyre* [1968] 1 WLR 530, although the court was not directly concerned with the provisions of I(PFD)A 1975, s 16, it took into account the fact that there was an order in favour of the applicant, who was the former spouse of the deceased, for secured periodical payments. On the facts, it was concluded that, 'an order for secured maintenance should not properly be treated as a pre-determination of what a survivor is to receive after the death of a former spouse, although it is necessarily an important factor to be considered in every application under section 26'. (Note that this was a pre-I(PFD)A 1975 decision.)

8.12.1 Who may apply?

Under Matrimonial Causes Act 1973, s 31(6), CPA 2004, Sch 5, para 60 and I(PFD)A 1975, s 16, the application may only be made by:

(1) the person entitled to the secured provision;
(2) the personal representatives of the deceased.

Time limit

The application must be made within 6 months of the date on which representation with regard to the estate was taken out, unless the court extends that time limit.

Note, however, that an application under I(PFD)A 1975, s 16 may not be made if the original order made in matrimonial proceedings included an order under s 15 or s 15ZA of that Act. In such cases the relief sought may only be made under Matrimonial Causes Act 1973, s 31(6) or s 36 provided that the application is brought within 6 months of the grant of representation.

Matters to be considered

In exercising its powers under I(PFD)A 1975, s 16, the court must have regard to all the circumstances of the case, including any order which the court proposes to make under s 2 or s 5 and any change (whether resulting from the death of the deceased or otherwise) in any of the matters to which the court is required to have regard when making a secured periodical payments order (s 16(2)).

Orders that can be made

The court may make the following orders under I(PFD)A 1975, s 18(2):

- Where an application is made under Matrimonial Causes Act 1973, s 31(6) for a variation or discharge of the secured periodical payments order or for the revival of the operation of any provision of that order which has been suspended, the court has power to direct that the application made under s 31(6) is deemed to have been accompanied by an application for an order under I(PFD)A 1975, s 2.
- On the making of the order that the application under Matrimonial Causes Act 1973, s 31(6) be deemed to be accompanied by an application for financial provision under the I(PFD)A 1975, the court may give such directions as it has power to make under the Act as if the application had been made jointly with an application for an order for financial provision under I(PFD)A 1975, s 2.

- The court also has power to give such consequential directions as may be necessary for enabling it to exercise any of the powers available to it under the I(PFD)A 1975 (see paras 7.9 and 7.11).
- The court has similar powers in relation to civil partnerships.

8.12.2 Provisions of Children Act 1989, Schedule 1

Children Act 1989, Sch 1, para 7 makes comparable provisions whereby secured periodical payments orders in favour of children which continue after the death of the payer may be varied after the death of the payer, on the application of the surviving parent or guardian of the child or any person in whose favour a care arrangement order/residence order in respect of the child is in force. The personal representatives of the deceased also have a right to apply.

In exercising its powers the court must have regard to all the circumstances of the case, including the changed circumstances resulting from the death of the payer (Children Act 1989, Sch 1, para 7(5)).

8.13 VARIATION AND REVOCATION OF MAINTENANCE AGREEMENTS – I(PFD)A 1975, SECTION 17

Matrimonial Causes Act 1973, s 35 and CPA 2004, Sch 5, para 73 provide for either party to a marriage or a civil partnership (as the case may be) to apply for a maintenance agreement reached between parties to a marriage to be varied. Where a maintenance agreement provides for continuation of payments after the death of one of the parties and that party dies domiciled in England and Wales, the surviving party or the personal representatives of the deceased party may apply to the court for the agreement to be varied or revoked (Matrimonial Causes Act 1973, ss 35 and 36 and CPA 2004, Sch 5, para 73(4)) provided it is made within 6 months from the date on which representation in regard to the estate of the deceased is first taken out. Similar provisions are set out in CPA 2004, Sch 5, in relation to civil partners.

In addition, where a claim for an order under I(PFD)A 1975, s 2 is made to the court by any person who was, at the time of the death of the deceased, entitled to payments from the deceased under a maintenance agreement which continues after the death of the deceased, the court has power to vary or revoke the agreement if an application is made under s 17 by either the payee or the personal representatives (s 17(1)). This sub-section identifies the persons who may apply for an order under this section namely:

(1) the payee; and
(2) the personal representatives.

8.13.1 Meaning of 'maintenance agreement'

'Maintenance agreement' is defined in Matrimonial Causes Act 1973, s 34 as an agreement in writing between the parties to a marriage which contains: (1) financial arrangements whether made during the continuance or after the dissolution of the marriage; or (2) a separation agreement which contains no financial arrangements in a case where no other agreement in writing between the same parties contains such an arrangement. In relation to civil partnership, a similar provision is set out in CPA 2004, Sch 5, para 67.

'Financial arrangements' is defined as:

> provisions governing the rights and liabilities towards one another when living separately of the parties to a marriage (including a marriage which has been dissolved or annulled) in respect of the making or securing of payments or the disposition or use of any property, including such rights and liabilities with respect to the maintenance or education of any child, whether or not a child of the family.

Similar provisions are contained in CPA 2004, Sch 5, para 67 in relation to civil partners.

Note the time limit of 6 months from the grant of representation unless the court extends this period.

An application for variation or revocation of a maintenance agreement can also be made within an application under the I(PFD)A 1975. I(PFD)A 1975, s 17(4), as amended, now takes account of those who are in a civil partnership relationship and defines 'maintenance agreement' as follows:

> In this section 'maintenance agreement' in relation to a deceased person means any agreement made, whether in writing or not whether before or after the commencement of this Act, by the deceased with any person with whom he formed a marriage or civil partnership, being an agreement which contained provisions governing the rights and liabilities towards one another when living separately of the parties to that marriage or of the civil partners (whether or not the marriage or civil partnership has been dissolved or annulled) in respect of the making or securing of payments or the disposition or use of any property, including such rights and liabilities with respect to the maintenance or education of any child, whether or not a child of the deceased or a person who was treated by the deceased as a child of the family in relation to that marriage or civil partnership.

To fall within the definition, the agreement must be one made between parties to a marriage/civil partnership.

Children Act 1989, Sch 1, para 10 contains provisions whereby a maintenance agreement in favour of a child, which provides for the continuation of payments after the death of one of the parties, may be varied or revoked by the High Court or the county court on the application of the surviving party or the personal representatives of the deceased. The application must not, however, except with the leave of the court, be made after the end of the period of 6 months beginning with the day on which representation in regard to the estate of the deceased is first taken out (Sch 1, para 11(3)). A grant limited to settled land or to trust property is left out of account when calculating when representation was first taken out, unless a grant limited to the remainder of the estate has previously been made or is made at the same time (Sch 1, para 11(2)).

8.13.2 Orders that can be made

I(PFD)A 1975, s 17(1) limits the court's power where an application is made under s 17 to:

- vary the agreement;
- revoke that agreement.

Where the court decides to vary the agreement, it has wide powers to make such other orders as it considers fit. This includes making provision for periodical payments or secured periodical payments. The court can also make any other order under I(PFD)A 1975, s 2.

8.13.3 Criteria to be applied by the court

I(PFD)A 1975, s 17(2) requires the court in exercising its powers under s 17 to have regard to all the circumstances of the case, including any order the court proposes to make under s 2 or s 5, and any change (whether resulting from the death of the deceased or otherwise) in any of the circumstances in the light of which the agreement was made.

8.13.4 Effect of the order

If the maintenance agreement is varied by the court under I(PFD)A 1975, s 17 the effect of the variation will be 'as if the variation had been made immediately before the death of the deceased by agreement between the parties and for valuable consideration' (s 17(3)).

8.14 COURT'S POWERS IN RELATION TO APPLICATIONS UNDER MATRIMONIAL CAUSES ACT 1973, SECTIONS 31 AND 36 AND CPA 2004, SCHEDULE 5, PARAGRAPHS 60 AND 73 – I(PFD)A 1975, SECTION 18

Where on the death of a person against whom a secured periodical payments order was made under the Matrimonial Causes Act 1973, an application is made under s 31(6) for the variation or discharge of that order or for the revival of the operation of any provision thereof which has been suspended or where a party to a maintenance agreement within the meaning of s 34 dies, then if the agreement provided for the continuation of payments under the agreement after the death of one of the parties and an application is made under s 36 for the alteration of the agreement under s 35, the court has power to direct that the application made under s 31(6) or s 36(1) is deemed to have been accompanied by an application for an order under I(PFD)A 1975, s 2 (I(PFD)A 1975, s 18(1)(a) and (b)).

Similar provisions apply in relation to an application made under CPA 2004, Sch 5, paras 60 and 73.

Where the court gives a direction under I(PFD)A 1975, s 18(1)(a) or (b) that the application under the Matrimonial Causes Act 1973 or the CPA 2004 is deemed to be accompanied by an application for an order under I(PFD)A 1975, s 2, it has power, in the proceedings on the application under Matrimonial Causes Act 1973, s 31(6) or s 36(1), or CPA 2004, Sch 5, to make any order which the court would have had power to make under the I(PFD)A 1975 if the application under s 31(6) or s 36(1), or CPA 2004, Sch 5, paras 60 and 73 had been made jointly with an application for an order under I(PFD)A 1975, s 2. The court also has power to give such consequential directions as may be necessary for enabling the court to exercise any of the powers available to the court under the I(PFD)A 1975 in the case of an application under s 2 (I(PFD)A 1975, s 18(2)).

However, it does not have the power to direct that an application under Matrimonial Causes Act 1973, ss 31(6) and 36(1) or CPA 2004, Sch 5, paras 60 and 73 is deemed to have been accompanied by an application for an order under I(PFD)A 1975, s 2 if an order under s 15(1) is in force with respect to a marriage (I(PFD)A 1975, s 18(3)) (see Chapter 7).

8.14.1 Time limit

The application must not, except with the leave of the court, be made after the end of the period of 6 months beginning with the day on which representation in regard to the estate of the deceased is first taken out (Matrimonial Causes Act 1973, ss 31(6)–(9) and 36(2)–(6) and CPA 2004, Sch 5).

8.15 EFFECT, DURATION AND FORM OF ORDERS – I(PFD)A 1975, SECTION 19

I(PFD)A 1975, s 19(2) makes provisions for any order made under s 2 or s 5 for the making of periodical payments in favour of an applicant who was the former spouse/civil partner of the deceased or where the marriage/civil partnership was the subject of a judicial separation, or separation order as the case may be, and the order was in force at the date of death and the separation was continuing at the date of death of the deceased, to cease to have effect on the remarriage or subsequent formation of a civil partnership (see, further, para 8.2.5).

I(PFD)A 1975, s 19(4) provides that every order made under the Act other than an order made under s 15(1) or s 15ZA(1) (see para 7.11.1) must be sent to the Principal Registry of the Family Division for entry and filing, and a memorandum of the order must be endorsed on, or permanently annexed to, the probate or letters of administration under which the estate is being administered.

Chapter 9

The Net Estate

9.1 INTRODUCTION

I(PFD)A 1975, s 2 gives the court power to make orders for financial provision out of the net estate of the deceased. The definition of 'net estate' under the Act is set out in s 25(1) and replicates the definition in I(FP)A 1938, s 5(1), but is wider in scope in three respects (I(PFD)A 1975, ss 10 and 11):

(1) any property may be treated as part of the net estate if the court considers it just so to order;
(2) 'net estate' includes property held on a joint tenancy which can be treated as forming part of the net estate by the court, overriding the law of survivorship (s 9); and
(3) the court may order that 'net estate' also includes any property which forms part of a transaction intended to defeat an application for financial provision.

I(PFD)A 1975, s 25(1) nevertheless restricts the meaning of 'net estate'. This chapter deals with the definition of 'net estate' in s 25(1), and the provisions which permit the court to treat certain property as part of the net estate if necessary to make an award for financial provision under the Act. These include nominated property and *donatio mortis causa* which comes within the definition of net estate by virtue of s 8, and property held jointly by the deceased and another which is included in the net estate pursuant to s 9. Any property which may be included in the net estate by reason of the deceased disposing of it with a view to defeating or decreasing a claim is dealt with in Chapter 10.

9.2 DEFINITION – I(PFD)A 1975, SECTION 25(1)–(3)

I(PFD)A 1975, s 25(1) defines the 'net estate' from which any order for financial provision may be made as follows:

(a) all property which the deceased had power to dispose of by his will (otherwise than by virtue of a special power of appointment), less his funeral, testamentary and administration expenses, debts and liabilities, including any inheritance tax payable out of his estate on his death;
(b) any property in respect of which the deceased held a general power of appointment (not being a power exercisable by will) which has not been exercised;
(c) any sum of money or other property which is treated for the purposes of the Act as part of the net estate of the deceased by virtue of section 8(1) or (2) of this Act;
(d) any property which is treated for the purposes of this Act as part of the net estate of the deceased by virtue of an order made under section 9 [see para 9.8];
(e) any sum of money or other property which is, by reason of a disposition or contract made by the deceased, ordered under section 10 or 11 of this Act to be provided for the purpose of the making of financial provision under this Act [see Chapter 10].

'Property' is defined as including any chose in action. It would also appear that cryptocurrencies and other forms of crypto-assets are also likely to be included within this definition (see the *Legal Statement on Cryptoassets and Smart Contracts*, published on 18 November 2019 by the UK Jurisdiction Taskforce, chaired by Sir Geoffrey Vos, available at judiciary.uk/the-chancellor-of-the-high-court-sir-geoffrey-vos-launches-legal-statement-on-the-status-of-cryptoassets-and-smart-contracts/; see, also, *AA v Persons Unknown* [2019] EWHC 3556 (Comm) and *Wang v Darby* [2021] EWHC 3054 (Comm) and *Tulip Trading Ltd (a Seychelles company) v Van der Laan and Others* [2022] EWHC 667 (Ch)). There are some useful publications which provide detailed legal implications of such assets which should be consulted, and where appropriate it is suggested that expert evidence on the issue should be obtained.

9.3 PROPERTY WHICH THE DECEASED HAD POWER TO DISPOSE OF BY WILL

This category corresponds to that set out in I(FP)A 1938, s 5(1). It will include payments payable to the deceased under life insurance policies or outstanding debts which were due to the deceased before death, such as lump sums due on early retirement or damages awarded in civil litigation. Note also that under I(PFD)A 1975, s 25(1) under para (a) of the definition of 'net estate', liabilities and debts and expenses due are excluded. Creditors take priority over beneficiaries and dependants. Property subject to a special power of appointment is excluded.

I(PFD)A 1975, s 25(2) provides that, for these purposes, a person who is not of full age and capacity is treated as having power to dispose by will of all property of which they would have had power to dispose by will if they had been of full age and capacity.

I(PFD)A 1975, s 25(3) provides that any reference in the Act to provision out of the net estate of a deceased person includes a reference to provision extending to the whole of that estate.

Any property which the deceased owned but which was disposed of during their lifetime in order to avoid a claim under the I(PFD)A 1975 or to avoid a claim by a third party during the deceased's lifetime may be brought into question and included into the net estate by challenging the validity of such a disposition as is possible in proceedings under the Matrimonial Causes Act 1973.

This may raise questions to what extent the court is entitled to inquire into transactions or arrangements entered into by the deceased which may be sham, as occurs in matrimonial proceedings. Much will depend on whether or not the evidence establishes that the deceased completely divested themselves of the ownership of the assets or whether they continued to have control over the property for their benefit, for example, where property is transferred to a company. In a claim for financial remedy within matrimonial proceedings, the court has taken into account assets to include company property from which the claim may be satisfied in limited and exceptional circumstances. The issue of whether and, if so, when the court may 'pierce the corporate veil' has now been settled by the Supreme Court's decision in *Prest v Petrodel Resources Ltd and Others* [2013] UKSC 34, [2013] 2 FLR 732, in which Lord Sumption concluded that (at [35]):

> ... there is a limited principle of English law which applies when a person is under an existing legal obligation or liability or subject to an existing legal restriction which he deliberately evades or whose enforcement he deliberately frustrates by interposing a company under his control. The court may then pierce the corporate veil for the purpose, and only for the purpose, of depriving the company or its controller of the advantage that they would otherwise have obtained by the company's separate legal personality. The principle is properly described as a limited one, because in almost every case where the test is satisfied, the facts will in practice disclose a legal relationship between the company and its controller which will make it unnecessary to pierce the corporate veil. Like Munby J in *Ben Hashem*, I consider that if it is not necessary to pierce the corporate veil, it is not appropriate to do so, because on that footing there is no public policy imperative which justifies that course.

See, also, [25], where approving the test applied by Munby J (as he then was) in *Ben Hashem v Al Shayif* [2008] EWHC 2380 (Fam), Lord Sumption said that the corporate veil can be pierced only if: (1) there was impropriety; (2) the impropriety in question is linked to the use of the company structure to avoid or conceal liability; and (3) there is both control of the company by the wrongdoer and misuse of the company as a device or facade to conceal the wrongdoing.

In short, therefore, the person seeking to pierce the corporate veil would need to establish that: (1) a party has deliberately entered into the transaction to avoid an obligation or liability; or (2) the company in reality holds the assets on trust for the benefit of that party.

After a review of case law and applying these principles in *M v M and Others* [2013] EWHC 2534 (Fam), it was held that the proper approach in law was (at [210]):

> i) Whether assets legally vested in a company are beneficially owned by its controller is a highly fact-specific issue.
> ii) The court must search for *evidence of the subjective intention of the transferor (Lord Philips)* or *evidence of actual intention.*
> iii) In determining the intention of the parties the courts may, where appropriate draw adverse inferences against the parties, either in respect of their failure to give or call evidence to rebut the presumption, or by their failure to make proper disclosure within the proceedings.
> iv) Only in the absence of evidence of intention will the law of presumption apply, which presumption will be easily rebutted by evidence of the transferor's intention to make an outright transfer.
> v) Where the company in whose name the property in question is held is owned by the same individual who asserts that he has retained the beneficial interest by virtue of a resulting trust, there is less room for such a resulting trust to be established by a presumption in the absence of evidence of intention however:
>
> > a) The burden remains on the transferee to rebut the presumption
> > b) Positive evidence of the source from which the purchases are funded establishes the ordinary inference that the provider of the funds is the beneficial owner of the property absent any evidence to rebut that ordinary presumption of equity.
>
> vi) In the case of the matrimonial home the facts are quite likely to justify the inference that the property was held on trust for a spouse who owned and controlled the company. (original emphasis)

On the facts in *M v M*, the court found that the husband was a shadow director, and his will and intention were the will and intention of the company. He had intended to, and did, retain beneficial interest in the properties. However, see *Li Quan v Bray* [2014] EWHC 3340 (Fam), where the issue for determination was whether a charitable trust relating to the protection of tigers was, in fact, a post-nuptial settlement capable of variation. The issues involved the court inquiring into the circumstances in which trusts were set up, the purposes of the trusts, whether they could be considered nuptial, the availability of funds to the parties and whether the funds within the trust could only be used for tiger conservation. Coleridge J found that during the exhaustive examination of the actions of two main trusts, since their creation he did not come across any behaviour or actions by either the husband or the wife which in any way caused him concern that they might be improper from a UK charitable perspective (see, also, *ND v SD* [2017] EWHC 1507 (Fam) and para 8.7.2).

Whether the same principle could be applied in claims under the I(PFD)A 1975 to bring within the net estate assets held by a third party or company will depend on the facts and the strength of the evidence available to challenge what would otherwise appear to be a lawful transaction.

9.4 PROPERTY UNDER GENERAL POWER OF APPOINTMENT

Where the deceased had a general power of appointment which they could have exercised by will, and either they did not exercise the power, or did so by will, in either case, the property subject to the power forms part of the net estate of the deceased. Note, however, that in I(PFD)A 1975, s 25(1) under the definition of 'net estate', the deceased's interest in a special power of appointment is excluded.

9.5 WHAT MAY BE DEDUCTED FROM THE NET ESTATE?

The following may be deducted from the net estate:

- Funeral expenses.
- Testamentary and administrative expenses.
- Debts and liabilities.
- Inheritance tax.

I(PFD)A 1975, s 2 has been amended by the Inheritance and Trustees' Powers Act 2014 to provide in s 2(3A) that 'in assessing for the purposes of an order under this section the extent (if any) to which the net estate is reduced by any debts or liabilities (including any inheritance tax paid or payable out of the estate), the court may assume the order has already been made'.

The debts and liabilities in most cases will not be too difficult to ascertain and agree, but in some instances could be problematic. Disputes may arise between siblings and/or the surviving spouse/civil partner regarding funeral testamentary and administrative expenses. Tension and conflicts are often heightened where the deceased had a number of relationships and children from those relationships.

A classic example of these disputes which then give rise to uncertainty about the amount of the expenses and the values of the assets comprising the estate and liabilities due to creditors is provided by the case of *Musa v Holliday* [2012] EWCA Civ 1268, [2013] 1 FLR 806. There were major disputes in relation to the valuation of companies and the impact of the investigation by HM Revenue and Customs (HMRC). The total liabilities suggested was of up to £500,000 plus fines and penalties consequent upon the HMRC investigation and therefore until the investigation had been concluded 'it would be very difficult to sell the shares for anything like their proper value, whatever that might be' (at [41]). There were also possible issues as to the amount of inheritance tax and the administration costs. In the event, the trial judge had to establish a figure for the net estate as best she could and then decide what financial provision it would be reasonable in all the circumstances of the case for the applicant to receive.

9.6 NOMINATED PROPERTY – I(PFD)A 1975, SECTION 8(1)

I(PFD)A 1975, s 8(1) provides that where a deceased person has, in accordance with the provision of any enactment, nominated any person to receive any sum of money or other property on their death, and that nomination is in force at the time of their death, that sum of money, after deducting any inheritance tax payable thereon, or that property to the extent of the value thereof at the date of death of the deceased after deducting any inheritance tax payable, is treated as part of the net estate of the deceased.

I(PFD)A 1975, s 8(1) also provides that nothing in the section renders any person liable for having paid that sum or transferred that property to the person named in the nomination in accordance with the directions given in the nomination. This provision exempts from liability the person transferring property on a nomination, but such transfer should not be made until 6 months after the grant was first taken out.

Two conditions apply to any nomination made by the deceased before it can be treated as forming part of the net estate. These are that the nomination must be in force at the time of the deceased's death and must be in accordance with the provision of any enactment.

The scope of this section was raised in *Goenka v Goenka* [2014] EWHC 2966 (Ch), in which the issue for determination was whether a nomination of a person to receive the lump sum payable where a National Health Service employee dies in pensionable employment made in accordance with the National Health Service Pension Scheme Regulations 1995 (SI 1995/300) (which were themselves made under powers conferred by the Superannuation Act 1972) was a nomination made 'in accordance with the provisions of an enactment'. It also raised issues as to the correct approach to apply to a claim by a spouse under the I(PFD)A 1975. Judge Hodge QC, sitting as a Judge of the High Court, ruled (at [57]) that he could see no reason why Parliament should have wished to discriminate between nominations made in accordance with the provisions of primary legislation and those made under the provisions of secondary legislation. He also stated that there is nothing within the I(PFD)A 1975 which would justify such a limitation upon the scope of the section. He therefore concluded that since the nomination was made pursuant to rules made by way of statutory instrument made under a power conferred by a statute the nomination should, within the meaning of I(PFD)A 1975, s 8(1), be regarded as one made 'in accordance with the provisions of any enactment'. He therefore held that the lump sum death in service payment fell to be treated as part of the deceased's 'net estate' (at [59]).

9.6.1 Insurance policies and pension schemes

A nominated policy under an insurance scheme which is effected pursuant to a contract does not form part of the net estate. Under such a policy, a member of the scheme may nominate a beneficiary, within a designated class of permitted beneficiaries, to whom the benefit is payable on the member's death. The nominations under these schemes are not effected pursuant to any statute, and the benefits payable therefrom fall outside the definition of net estate. If the benefits under such a scheme automatically fall into the estate of the deceased, they form part of the net estate. If the pension benefits automatically pass to the deceased's widow or widower they are not included in the net estate.

Private occupational pension schemes are not operated pursuant to any enactment and so fall outside I(PFD)A 1975, s 8. It is debatable whether public sector schemes fall within the ambit of s 8. Any capital or income, however, which is paid to a beneficiary in consequence of a pension scheme will be considered by the court when it takes into account the financial resources and financial needs of a beneficiary of the estate.

This point was raised in *Re Cairnes (Deceased), Howard v Cairnes* [1983] FLR 225. The preliminary issue was whether, on the true construction of I(PFD)A 1975, s 25(1), a death benefit fell within the meaning of net estate. The claimant was the deceased's mistress. The defendant and the deceased were married in 1954. They were divorced in 1976. After the divorce, the deceased lived, on and off, with his former wife and with the claimant, until his death. On the divorce, the deceased had agreed with his wife that he would give her £80 per month and that he would share the household expenses of the matrimonial home while he lived there. In addition, he gave her £18 per week and paid the hire instalments on the television and the washing machine. The deceased's employment was pensionable. Under the terms of the pension scheme, a member could nominate a beneficiary, within a designated class, to whom benefits would accrue on the member's death. The designated classes were:

(1) a member's wife; and
(2) any person who, in the opinion of the insurance company, was, immediately prior to the member's death, in receipt of any regular weekly or monthly voluntary payment from the member for the ordinary necessities of life.

The deceased had nominated his wife as beneficiary. The nomination of the beneficiary or its cancellation required the trustees' consent, as did any variation of the nominated beneficiary.

On the deceased's death, the claimant, the deceased's mistress, applied for an order under the I(PFD)A 1975. She contended that the proper time for determining whether a beneficiary fell within the designated class was at the time of death, and therefore the nomination of the former wife as beneficiary was no longer effective and the fund fell into the residuary estate. Further, in any event, under the terms of s 25(1), the words 'net estate' were to be construed as widely as possible. The court rejected these submissions on the grounds that:

(1) even if the entitlement to the death benefit vested only at the testator's death, the former wife was still within the designated class of beneficiary because she was receiving regular payments from the deceased and was dependent upon him, within (2) above;
(2) the death benefit did not come within para (a) of the definition of 'net estate' in s 25(1) because the power of the testator to dispose of the death fund was circumscribed. He did not have the power to dispose of the fund which was in the control of the trustees;
(3) the death benefit could not be construed as part of the net estate within para (c) of the definition because s 8(1) required the nomination to be 'in accordance with the provision of any statute'.

Accordingly, on the preliminary issue, it was held that the death benefit was not part of the net estate.

Monies due under a life insurance policy of the deceased or under a pension scheme are not excluded and form part of the net estate.

9.7 DONATIO MORTIS CAUSA – I(PFD)A 1975, SECTION 8(2)

I(PFD)A 1975, s 25(1)(c) provides an order to be made for financial provision from any sum of money or other property which is treated for the purposes of the

Act as part of the net estate of the deceased by virtue of s 8(2). Section 8(2) provides as follows:

> (2) Where any sum of money or other property is received by any person as a *donatio mortis causa* made by a deceased person, that sum of money, after deducting therefrom any inheritance tax payable thereon, or that other property, to the extent of the values thereof at the date of the death of the deceased after deducting therefrom any inheritance tax so payable, shall be treated for the purposes of this Act as part of the net estate of the deceased ...

9.7.1 What is *donatio mortis causa*?

Donatio mortis causa is a gift made by a person in contemplation of death but which does not take effect until the death of the donor.

For a gift to be regarded as *donatio mortis causa*, four conditions need to be satisfied:

(1) the gift must be made in contemplation of the death of the donor;
(2) the gift must be made on condition that it becomes absolute and irrevocable only on the death of the donor;
(3) the subject matter of the gift, or something that represents the gift, must have been delivered to the donee or someone on their behalf, with the intention of parting with it;
(4) the property must be capable of passing by *donatio mortis causa*. Any property which can be transferred by delivery or some suitable document can be given.

Donatio mortis causa of land is now possible (see *Sen v Headley* [1991] Ch 425). The above principles were set out in *Sen v Headley*. These were approved in *Vallee v Birchwood* [2013] EWHC 1449 (Ch). However, in *King v Dubrey* [2014] EWHC 2083 (Ch), the Court of Appeal ruled that *Vallee v Birchwood* had been wrongly decided. It set out the following principles that must be satisfied for the gift to amount to a *donatio mortis causa*:

(1) the donor must be contemplating impending death in the near future for a specific reason, for example, the deceased is in hospital and seriously ill or is terminally ill or has good reason to anticipate death in the near future;
(2) the gift must be conditional on that contemplated death and, until then, may be revoked at will and in any event will be ineffective if the donor does not die soon enough; and
(3) the donor must part with control over the subject matter of the gift – this means physical possession of the subject matter or some means of

accessing the subject matter (such as the key to a box) or the documents evidencing entitlement of the title of the subject matter (at [55]–[60]).

The court also ruled that these conditions must be complied with strictly and that since the doctrine is open to abuse the court should require strict proof of compliance with the above requirements. The evidence in support must be unequivocal.

These principles were applied in *Davey v Bailey* [2021] EWHC 445 (Ch), where on the facts the court held that the case based on *donatio mortis causa* had not been made out.

If the gift is made unconditionally, it does not form part of the net estate unless it can be proved that it was made with the intention of defeating a claim for financial provision under the I(PFD)A 1975 (see Chapter 10).

I(PFD)A 1975, s 8(2) exempts from liability any person who has paid a sum of money or transferred property in order to give effect to the *donatio mortis causa*.

I(PFD)A 1975, s 20 absolves the personal representatives from liability for having distributed any part of the estate of the deceased after 6 months from the date of the grant. By analogy it could be submitted that the same principle applies where payment is made or property transferred in accordance with a nomination or *donatio mortis causa*. It would, however, be advisable for the persons responsible for giving effect to the *donatio mortis causa* or the nomination to ensure that a grant has been obtained and that there is no potential claim under the I(PFD)A 1975 before making the payment.

9.8 PROPERTY HELD ON JOINT TENANCY – I(PFD)A 1975, SECTION 9

I(PFD)A 1975, s 9(1) in its original form provided that where a deceased person was immediately before their death beneficially entitled to a joint tenancy of any property, then if, before the end of the period of 6 months from the date on which representation with respect to the estate of the deceased was first taken out, an application is made for an order under s 2, the court for the purposes of facilitating the making of financial provision for the applicant under the Act may order that the deceased's severable share of that property, at the value thereof immediately before their death, shall, to such extent as appears to the court to be just in all the circumstances of the case, be treated for the purposes of the Act as part of the net estate of the deceased.

As from 1 October 2014, I(PFD)A 1975, s 9 has been amended by Inheritance and Trustees' Powers Act 2014, s 6, Sch 2, para 7 to provide as follows:

> (1) Where a deceased person was immediately before his death beneficially entitled to a joint tenancy of any property, then, if an application is made for an order under section 2 of this Act, the court for the purpose of facilitating the making of financial provision for the applicant under this Act may order that the deceased's severable share of that property shall, to such extent as appears to the court to be just in all the circumstances of the case, be treated for the purposes of this Act as part of the net estate of the deceased.
>
> (1A) Where an order is made under subsection (1) the value of the deceased's severable share of the property concerned is taken for the purposes of this Act to be the value that the share would have had at the date of the hearing of the application for an order under section 2 had the share been severed immediately before the deceased's death, unless the court orders that the share is to be valued at a different date.
>
> (2) In determining the extent to which any severable share is to be treated as part of the net estate of the deceased by virtue of any order under subsection (1) above, the court shall have regard to any capital transfer tax payable in respect of that severable share.
>
> (3) Where an order is made under subsection (1) above, the provisions of this section shall not render any person liable for anything done by him before the order was made.
>
> (4) For the avoidance of doubt it is hereby declared that for the purposes of this section there may be a joint tenancy of a chose in action.

There are a number of matters which must be considered if an application under I(PFD)A 1975, s 9 is intended to be made:

(1) What is the time limit for making the application and does the court have power to extend the time limit?
(2) What does 'property' include?
(3) Was the property held by the deceased *jointly* with another immediately before their death?
(4) In what circumstances will the court consider it appropriate to make an order under s 9?
(5) What criteria will the court apply when considering such an application?
(6) What is meant by the term 'at the value thereof immediately before his death'?
(7) The valuation of the deceased's severable share.

9.8.1 Time limit

Before 1 October 2014, an application under I(PFD)A 1975, s 9 had to be made 'before the end of the period of six months from the date on which representation with respect to the estate of the deceased was first taken out'. Unlike the provision of s 4, the court did not have any power to extend this time limit. So practitioners had to be on guard to avoid falling into what was referred to as 'the section 9 trap' and finding out that it was too late to bring in to the net estate possible assets which would have made the difference to the extent of the family provision which the court may order. This time limit has now been removed. An application under s 9 may be made where death has occurred on or after 1 October 2014, even where the s 4 limitation period applies, but with the court having a discretion to extend time. However, since a substantive claim can now be made before the grant, the application for a s 9 order should be included in the substantive application rather than making the application later in the proceedings, particularly where it appears that the size and nature of the estate may be either small or modest, in order to prevent any dealings with the property in question. If, when disclosure has taken place, the issue is not relevant, the application may be withdrawn. On the other hand, if an issue arises on whether there is any merit in pursuing the application, this may be dealt with as a preliminary issue. The advantage of dealing with this issue at an early stage is that until the matter can be resolved, interlocutory orders or undertakings may be sought to preserve the assets in question. It also puts on notice any person who has an interest in the jointly owned property not to dispose of it until the court has ruled on it. Where there are limited assets, the merit of the s 9 application may be argued on the basis of the s 3 criteria and the fact that one of the factors that the court has to consider under s 3 is the nature and size of the net estate and therefore this additional asset in appropriate cases cannot be ignored and must be preserved until the substantive application is determined.

Another reason for taking this step is the fact that I(PFD)A 1975, s 9(3) specifically provides that the person dealing in any way with such an asset is not liable for anything done by them before the order was made.

9.8.2 Meaning of 'property'

I(PFD)A 1975, s 9(4) provides that there may be a joint tenancy of a chose in action. 'Property' therefore includes not only real property but also monies held in a joint account (see *Powell v Osbourne* [1993] 1 FLR 1001), a joint insurance policy and other joint investments.

Issues may arise with regard to whether the property was, in fact, jointly owned or owned by the deceased and another as tenants in common. Issues under I(PFD)A 1975, s 9 can only arise in relation to property jointly owned. In the case where property has been transferred into joint names after April 1998 it is possible to set out the nature and extent of the beneficial interests in Form TR1, which contains an express declaration of the beneficial interest. It is also possible for the joint owners to express a declaration of their respective beneficial interests or subsequently to vary their interests by a deed or completing Form TP1. A declaration in these forms or in the conveyance or transfer or in some other way that the property was held by the parties jointly, should be conclusive (see *Goodman v Carlton* [2002] EWCA Civ 545, [2002] 2 FLR 259). In the case of transfer of property in joint names prior to April 1998, there is a presumption in the domestic context that the beneficial interests were to be held jointly in equal shares. If no such evidence exists and there is a dispute as to ownership or the extent of the parties' interests in the property, it may become necessary for the court to determine the issue if a challenge is made. There is a presumption that the beneficial entitlement follows the legal title, but if this is in dispute it will be for the party who makes the challenge to prove otherwise. *Laskar v Laskar* [2008] EWCA Civ 347 is an example of a case where the presumption was held not to apply. There the mother and daughter bought property in joint names as an investment. The evidence clearly established that the parties had led separate lives. The court found that the property was held on a resulting trust with each party entitled to the percentage of their original contribution and no more (see, also, *Adekunle and Others v Ritchie* [2007] EW Misc 5 (CC), [2007] WTLR 1505). Where the deceased and the claimant were cohabiting, the starting point is that the beneficial entitlement follows the legal title, as was the case in *Gibson v Revenue and Customs Prosecution Office* [2008] EWCA Civ 645. A challenge to the presumption is usually based on the grounds that the transfer was achieved by the surviving joint tenant exercising undue influence or other forms of abuse and coercive behaviour or misrepresentations or fraud or that the deceased did not fully understand the legal implications, such as to impact on the free will of the deceased (see, for instance, *Cameron v Cameron* [2021] EWHC 229 (Ch)). However, these allegations may be rebutted by evidence such as from the lawyer who was instructed to draw up the conveyance that the deceased had sought legal advice and/or had been advised of the legal implications of the transfer and had freely chosen to act as the deceased did (see *Brindley v Brindley* [2018] EWHC 157 (Ch)).

Similar principles apply to life insurance policies (see *Holland v Murphy* [2003] EWCA Civ 1862 and *Lim v Walia* [2014] EWCA Civ 1076). As regards bank accounts held jointly by the deceased and a third party, similar principles may apply, but a challenge could be raised as to whether the parties genuinely held the monies jointly or whether the deceased was entitled to the entire sums in the account and the other party was merely a nominee. This could be the position where the account was opened and/or operated in joint names solely for convenience. As an example, see *Drakeford v Cotton* [2012] EWHC 1414 (Ch), where the deceased transferred her accounts into joint names of herself and one of her daughters. She subsequently made statements confirming that she intended to make an immediate gift of the sums held in the accounts to her daughter. On her death, one of the other three daughters claimed that the sums held in the accounts should be divided in equal shares between the three daughters, in accordance with the dispositions made in the deceased's will made in 1997 before she had made the gift. On the evidence, the court held that the deceased had clearly intended and had formed a settled intention for the money held in the accounts to pass to her daughter who was the joint account holder and that she had expressed that intention to all her children. *Whitlock v Moree* [2017] UKPC 44 is an example where a joint bank account was opened by two friends with only one of them providing the funds deposited into the account, but the documents which they both signed when the account was opened clearly set out their respective beneficial interests.

9.8.3 Severance

I(PFD)A 1975, s 9 applies only to property which is subject to a joint tenancy at the date of the deceased's death. If the joint tenancy was severed before death then the provisions of s 9 do not apply. A joint tenancy may be severed by notice in writing or by any act done which has the effect of severing the joint tenancy. The question of whether or not the joint tenancy has, in fact, been severed may be raised as an issue. The following cases are provided as illustrations of the evidence needed to establish severance.

In *Hawkesley v May* [1956] 1 QB 304, a settled fund was held on a trust which provided that, on attaining the age of 21, the applicant and his sister would become absolutely entitled to the fund as joint tenants. The question was whether the joint tenancy had been severed, and the sister's share transferred to her, when she wrote a letter requesting that the dividends be paid into her bank account. Holding that the tenancy had been severed, Havers J stated:

> there are a number of ways by which a joint tenancy may be severed. In *Williams v Hensman* [1861] Sir W Page Wood VC in the course of his judgment said 'a joint tenancy may be severed in three ways: in the first place, an act of any one of the persons interested operating upon his own share may create severance as to that share. The right of each tenant is a right by survivorship only in the event of no severance having taken place of the share which is claimed under the *jus accrescendi*: each one is at liberty to dispose of his own interest in such manner as to sever it from the joint fund – losing, of course, at the same time, his own right by survivorship. Secondly, a joint tenancy may be severed by mutual agreement. And in the third place, there may be severance by any course of dealing sufficient to intimate that the interests of all were mutually treated as constituting a tenancy in common. When a severance depends on an inference of this kind without any express act of severance it will not suffice to rely on an intention, with respect to the particular share, declared only behind the backs of the other persons interested. The first method indicated, namely an act of any one of the persons interested operating upon his own share, obviously includes a declaration of intention to sever by one party.

In *Re Draper's Conveyance, Nihan v Porter* [1969] 1 Ch 486, property was conveyed to a husband and wife as joint tenants in October 1951. The parties divorced and the decree absolute was made in March 1966. On 11 February 1966, the wife issued proceedings under Married Women's Property Act 1882, s 17 for an order for sale of the property and the division of the net proceeds. It was held that the joint tenancy was severed by the issue of the proceedings, coupled with the affidavit in support of it which clearly evinced an intention on the part of the wife to sever the tenancy.

In *Harris v Goddard* [1983] 1 WLR 203, the issue was whether a prayer in a petition for divorce for a property adjustment order operated as a notice in writing to sever the joint tenancy. Before the application was heard the husband died in a road traffic accident. The executors and the children of the deceased's first marriage sought a declaration that the tenancy had been severed and that they were entitled to one half of the net proceeds of sale. In holding that the prayer in the petition did not take effect as a severance notice, Lawton LJ said:

> When notice in writing of a desire to sever is served pursuant to s 36(2) [of the Law of Property Act 1925], it takes effect forthwith. It follows that a desire to sever must evince an intention to bring about the wanted result immediately. A notice in writing which expresses a desire to bring about the wanted result at some time in the future is not, in my judgment, a notice in writing within s 36(2). Further, the notice must be one which shows an intent to bring about the consequences set out in section 36(2), namely that the net proceeds of the statutory trust for sale shall be held upon trust which would have been requisite for giving effect to the beneficial interests if there had been an actual severance. I am unable to accept the submission of counsel for the plaintiffs that a notice in writing which shows no more than a desire to bring the existing interest to an end is a good notice. It must be a desire to sever which is intended to have the statutory consequences. Paragraph 3 of the prayer of the petition does no more than invite the court to consider at some future time whether to exercise its jurisdiction under section 24 of the 1973 Act, and if it does, to do so in one or more of three different ways. Orders under section 24(1)(a) and (b) could bring co-ownership to an end by ways other than by severance.

Dillon LJ stated:

> Joint ownership is a form of co-ownership or concurrent ownership of property. Its special feature is the right of survivorship, whereby the right to the whole of the property accrues automatically to the surviving joint tenant or joint tenants on the death of any one joint tenant. Severance is, as I understand it, the process of separating off the share of a joint tenant, so that the concurrent ownership will continue but the right of survivorship will no longer apply. The parties will hold separate shares as tenants in common. The joint tenancy may come to an end through other acts which destroy the whole ownership e.g. if one joint tenant acquires the entire beneficial interest of the

> other joint tenant(s) so as to become solely and absolutely entitled beneficially to the property, or by all the joint tenants joining in resettling the property on other trusts not involving concurrent ownership; but such acts do not involve severance and would not be called severance of the joint tenancy. In *Draper's Conveyance* the relief claimed by the originating summons which had been issued and by the affidavit in support included, as Lawton LJ has pointed out, a claim that the property might be sold and the proceeds be divided equally in accordance with the rights of the parties. This plainly involved severance of the beneficial joint tenancy as I understand the term 'severance'. In the present case, however, paragraph 3 of the prayer in the petition merely seeks relief in the most general and unparticularised terms under Matrimonial Causes Act 1973, s 24. Apart from the fact that any relief for Mrs Harris under s 24 lay in the future and was contingent on the court exercising its discretion under the section in her favour, she had not yet specified what she desired by the time Mr Harris died, and the general prayer in her petition could have been satisfied by relief which did not involve severance, eg an order extinguishing Mr Harris's interest in the property and directing that the property be vested in Mrs Harris as sole absolute beneficial owner, or an order directing a resettlement of the property on Mr and Mrs Harris successively and not as concurrent owners. Therefore the petition in this case cannot be notice of a desire to sever the joint tenancy.

Where on an application for ancillary relief following a divorce or dissolution order an agreement is reached between the parties for the sale of the former matrimonial home and the division of the proceeds of sale, the joint tenancy is severed so that if one of the parties dies before the agreement is approved by the court and an order made, the joint tenancy remains severed by the agreement. The agreement does not have to be enforceable provided it indicated a common intention to sever (see *Hunter v Babbage* [1994] 2 FLR 806).

Where during divorce proceedings a settlement is reached between the parties, their course of conduct, such as putting a jointly owned property up for sale, surrendering an endowment policy and dividing the proceeds between them on legal advice taken by both parties, can be sufficient to sever the tenancy (see *Davis v Smith* [2011] EWCA Civ 1603, [2012] 1 FLR 1177, where the wife died on the day she was due to sign the notice of severance).

A similar situation may arise between parties who are not married, as occurred in *Quigley v Masterson* [2011] EWHC 2529 (Ch). In that case, when the relationship between the unmarried couple broke down, the solicitors for the man attempted to sever the joint tenancy of the house in which they had lived by giving written notice. The man subsequently became incapacitous and his daughter applied to the Court of Protection for authorisation to sell the house. The woman in the relationship took part in the proceedings and sought the sale of the property and the division of the proceeds of sale. Before an order was made, the man died. It was held on appeal that the notice served on the daughter by the woman indicating her agreement to the sale and the division of the proceeds was sufficient notice of severance within Law of Property Act 1925, s 36(2).

Where a deceased person's estate is found to be insolvent, administration takes place under Insolvency Act 1986, s 421 and the matter is governed by the Insolvent Estates of Deceased Persons Order 1986 (SI 1986/1999). However, the making of an insolvency administration order does not relate back to sever the deceased's beneficial interest in property owned by the deceased and his wife immediately before the deceased's death as the deceased's interest in the property passes to the widow by survivorship at the moment of death (see *Re Palmer (A Debtor)* [1994] 2 FLR 609 (CA)).

9.8.4 Circumstances in which an order will be considered

The court is given a discretion to consider bringing into the net estate the severable share of a jointly owned asset. It can, however, use its discretion only for the purposes of facilitating the making of financial provision for the claimant. This will usually occur where the net estate is insufficient to meet the claims made by the claimant(s) as well as honour the wish of the deceased expressed in their will towards other beneficiaries.

9.8.5 Criteria which will be applied

I(PFD)A 1975, s 9(1) and (2) refers to four factors which the court should take into account when dealing with an application under s 9 for the severance of the deceased's share in jointly owned property. These are:

- The court should exercise its discretion only to the extent as appears to be just in all the circumstances.
- Whether it is necessary to facilitate the making of financial provision for the claimant.
- The value of the asset.
- In determining the extent to which any severable share is to be treated as part of the estate, the court must have regard to any inheritance tax payable in respect of the severed share (s 9(2)).

9.8.6 Facilitating the making of financial provision/and appears to be just

The language of I(PFD)A 1975, s 9 is so broadly phrased that it gives the court a very wide discretion in respect of the matters it may take into account when determining the issue. The objective is to ensure that justice is done. This must mean justice not only to the claimant(s), but also to other beneficiaries and any other respondent who may have an interest in the asset. If severance would lead to hardship to the surviving joint owner, in order to deal with the application justly the court will need to balance the needs of the claimant against those of the other party. Although the provisions of the section appear not to refer to any other criteria, in order to determine whether severance is necessary and just, it would appear that the court will have to consider the s 3 factors (see Chapter 7 and below).

The court may only exercise its discretion if it is satisfied that it is necessary for the purposes of facilitating the making of financial provision and then only to the extent that it appears to the court to be just in all the circumstances of the case. The severance may relate to part of the severable share of the deceased in the assets and not the whole. Whether or not the court exercises its discretion, the factors which will weigh in that exercise and the extent to which that discretion is exercised will depend on the circumstances of the individual case. The following cases may offer some guidance on the criteria used by the court when determining an application for a s 9 order.

In *Kourkgy v Lusher* (1983) 4 FLR 65, Wood J stated that the words 'facilitating and making financial provision for the applicant' should not be understood to narrow the broad discretionary power given by s 9. In considering the application the court will necessarily take into account the financial needs and resources of the parties. With the increase in divorce and cohabitation, it seems inevitable that the courts will be concerned with cases where the property which is the subject matter of the application provides a home for the deceased's families, or with assets which provide, as far as possible, financial security for such families and step-families. Since the court's duty when exercising its discretion is to impart justice having regard to all the circumstances of the case, it seems unlikely that the courts will take from Peter to give to Paul where the assets are inadequate. The discretion is to be exercised at each stage of the proceedings applying the provisions of the section (see *Kourkgy v Lusher* (1983) 4 FLR 65, 80 and 81 and *Re Crawford* (1983) 4 FLR 273, 280 (both judgments of Eastham J)).

In *Re Crawford (Deceased)* (1983) 4 FLR 273 (see para 6.2.4), the court applied the provisions of I(PFD)A 1975, s 3 and took into account financial benefits to the beneficiaries under the will of the deceased. In *Kourkgy v Lusher* (above), Wood J approached the exercise of discretion by considering the matters set out under Matrimonial Causes Act 1973, s 25. Although those matters resemble those under I(PFD)A 1975, s 3, they are not identical in all respects. It is submitted that it is questionable whether it is appropriate to introduce the provisions of the Matrimonial Causes Act 1973, which concern matters following the breakdown of a marriage, to claims for financial provision under the I(PFD)A 1975, where the circumstances are necessarily different, and the statutory bases for determining the applications are set out in different enactments.

In *Jessop v Jessop* [1992] FLR 591, the property was owned jointly by the deceased and his mistress. The value of the property had risen considerably between the death of the deceased and the date of the final hearing. Although the value to be taken into account is the value immediately before the death, in determining the claim, Nourse J took into account the income, expenditure and capital resources of the parties when making an order for the payment of £10,000 to the deceased's widow. Where the court is asked to take into account the deceased's severable share in any property, it does not follow that the whole of the property will be treated as part of the net assets of the deceased. Whether the court will treat the severable share as part of the net estate and, if so, to what extent will depend on the particular circumstances and what appears, in those circumstances, to be just. In some cases part of the value may be sufficient to meet the justice of the case. In others, as in *Hanbury v Hanbury* [1999] 2 FLR 255 (see para 8.5), the whole of the share may be treated as part of the net estate.

Where the deceased had an interest in property abroad, much will turn on the laws of succession of the country in question, and whether the deceased made a valid will according to the law of that country or died intestate. Where the property is overseas, the court does not have jurisdiction over it unless the property is brought within the jurisdiction of the court or the person who has control over the property is within the jurisdiction which would then enable the court to direct any order it makes to that person.

9.8.7 Meaning of 'at the value thereof'

Before I(PFD)A 1975, s 9 was amended by the Inheritance and Trustees' Powers Act 2014, the relevant date for evaluating the value of any jointly held property was immediately before the deceased's death. This issue was considered by the Court of Appeal in *Zulekha Bibi Dingmar v Dingmar* [2006] EWCA Civ 942, [2007] Ch 109, where the appellant widow of the deceased had appealed against the decision of the trial judge who had awarded her one half of the value of the matrimonial home as at the date of death. The property had been owned jointly by the appellant's husband and a third party, who became the sole owner of the property by survivorship when the husband died in 1977. After his death, the widow continued to live in the property until her two children reached majority in 2004, when the third party claimed possession, about 7 years after her husband's death. The widow then obtained letters of administration and made a claim under the I(PFD)A 1975 for financial provision and an application under s 9 for the deceased's severable share in the property to be treated as part of his net estate. It was agreed that, at the date of death, the house was valued at £40,000, but its value had increased to £95,000 when the application was heard. She was awarded one half of the value at the date of death. The widow appealed on the grounds that the words of s 9 should not be taken to restrict the court's discretionary power to make reasonable financial provision for her. Ward and Jacob LJJ gave different reasons for allowing the appeal. Jacob LJ considered three different interpretations and concluded that 'value' does not refer to monetary value, but to a proportionate value of the property as this interpretation fits in best with the purpose of the Act. He opined that to view otherwise would lead to irrationalities, and Parliament could not have intended the irrational. His Lordship also stated that another possible explanation may lie in tax consideration and the words are there to define the value for tax reasons and to inform that the value to be assessed for tax purposes is the value at the date of death.

This issue has now been resolved with the amendments made to I(PFD)A 1975, s 9 by the Inheritance and Trustees' Powers Act 2014 with effect for deaths occurring after 1 October 2014. The relevant date for valuation is now the date of the hearing of the application.

Since, when dealing with an application under the I(PFD)A 1975, the court has to consider the circumstances of the parties at the date of the hearing and one of the factors under s 3 that is relevant to the determination of the application is the size and nature of the net estate, an up-to-date valuation of all property which is the subject of the proceedings must be provided. Valuation of the property at the time of death will be relevant to assess the inheritance tax payable on such property to obtain the net value and then the valuation at the date of the application and at the date of the hearing will be an important consideration to determine what would be reasonable financial provision for the claimant, as occurred in *Jessop v Jessop* [1992] FLR 591 (see above).

Where the property is subject to a charge, the value of the outstanding debt/mortgage must be deducted from the valuation, but if the charge/mortgage was protected by a collateral endowment policy, the value of that policy at the time immediately before the death must be accounted for and set off against debt. See *Powell v Osbourne* [1993] 1 FLR 1001 (CA), where the deceased and his wife were divorced, but the decree nisi (now a conditional divorce order) had not been made absolute (now final) as there were pending ancillary relief proceedings. The deceased lived with his mistress. About 2 months before the deceased's death, he and his mistress purchased a property as beneficial joint tenants. The property was subject to a substantial mortgage. There was also a joint collateral endowment policy. The house was the only property out of which any provision for the widow could be made. It was argued that, immediately before the death of the deceased, the policy had no surrender value. It acquired a value on death and therefore should be disregarded in valuing the deceased's assets. The Court of Appeal rejected this argument, holding that the value on death should be taken into account and set off against the collateral mortgage secured on the jointly owned property. Any liabilities or debts of the deceased secured against the property will need to be deducted in assessing the value.

It follows from this decision that the value of the property for the purposes of making an order under I(PFD)A 1975, s 2 will be assessed after setting off the value of the policy at death against the mortgage debt on the property.

I(PFD)A 1975, s 9(2) also specifically provides for the inheritance tax payable on the values of the severable share to be taken into account.

9.9 FOREIGN PROPERTY

The issue of whether an order may be made against foreign property involves complex issues relating to jurisdiction, succession laws which apply in the foreign jurisdiction and whether and, if so, how any orders made by the court can be enforced in the foreign country. A general overview, including a summary of EU Regulation 650/2012, is set out below, but practitioners should in such cases obtain expert advice.

9.9.1 Jurisdiction

If there is a person against whom an order made in relation to property outside the jurisdiction can be enforced, the court may consider making an order (see *Goyal v Goyal* [2016] EWFC 50, where Mostyn J made an order in financial remedy proceedings). Where there is property overseas, it would be advisable to identify those assets and the person who is entitled, or likely to be entitled, to the property. If the person so entitled is within the jurisdiction, the court may be invited in the first instance to grant an injunction preventing the person from disposing of or dealing with the property (see *Bheekun v Williams* [1999] 2 FLR 229).

9.9.2 Law of succession

Under English law, the law of the country where the property is sited will govern immoveable property. This applies whether or not the deceased died testate or intestate. Moveables are governed by the law of the deceased's domicile, i.e. England and Wales, subject to succession rules which may govern the rights of married couples. Where there are no heirs or next of kin, the succession rules of the country where the moveables are situated will apply.

9.9.3 EU Regulation 650/2012

As regards jurisdiction and succession rules in relation to those who have assets in EU Member States, practitioners will need to be familiar with EU Regulation 650/2012, which came into force on 17 August 2015, except for Arts 77 and 78 which apply from 16 January 2014, and Arts 79–81 which came into force on 5 July 2012. Article 77 sets out the obligations imposed on Member States to make information available to the public and to provide the Commission with a short summary of the national legislation and procedures to succession, and Art 78 requires the Member States to communicate information referred to in the Article to the Commission. Articles 79–81 deal with administrative matters. The Regulation is not retrospective and applies only in respect of those dying on or after that date. Note, however, that the United Kingdom has not signed up to this Regulation.

In view of the open border policy within the European Union, the aim of EU Regulation 650/2012 is to ensure the proper administration of justice within the Union and to ensure a 'genuine connection factor exists between the succession and the Member State in which jurisdiction is exercised'. The Regulation therefore provides that the applicable law should be the habitual residence of the deceased at the time of death. It is for the authority dealing with the succession to determine habitual residence, having regard to the circumstances of the life of the deceased during the years preceding their death and at the time of death and, having regard to all the 'relevant factual elements, in particular the duration and regularity of the deceased's presence in the Member State concerned and the conditions and reasons for that presence' (Art 4 and Recital, para 23).

Where the deceased has been living abroad for a long period of time, but has maintained a close and stable connection with the country of their origin, depending on the circumstances, it may be considered that their habitual residence is in the state of their origin 'in which the centre of interests of their family and their social life was located'. Where the deceased led a peripatetic life, then if they were a national of one of those states or had all their main assets in one of those states, their nationality or the location of those assets could be a special factor in the overall assessment of the factual circumstances (Recital, para 24 of EU Regulation 650/2012). In exceptional cases (Recital, para 25):

> in exceptional cases – where, for instance, the deceased had moved to the State of his habitual residence fairly recently before his death and all the circumstances of the case indicate that he was manifestly more closely connected with another State – arrive at the conclusion that the law applicable to the succession should not be the law of the State of the habitual residence of the deceased but rather the law of the State with which the deceased was manifestly more closely connected. That manifestly closest connection should, however, not be resorted to as a subsidiary connecting factor

> whenever the determination of the habitual residence of the deceased at the time of death proves complex.

EU Regulation 650/2012, however, gives the deceased the option to choose the law to govern his succession as a whole, the law of a state of which they were a national at the time they make the choice or at the time of their death. In the case where they possess multiple nationalities, they may choose the law of any of the states whose nationality they possess at the time of making the choice or at the time of death. The choice must be made expressly in a declaration in the form of a disposition of property upon death or must be demonstrated by the terms of such disposition (see Art 22 for details). Thus a choice made that only deals with assets in the European Union, but not those outside the Union would be invalid because it would not govern the succession of the *whole* of the estate. To err on the side of caution, therefore, it would be safer to make the choice of law in one's will and/or expressly provide to be effective in relation to the whole of their estate wherever the assets may be located. Note, however, that the Regulation applies only to disposition and choice made after 17 August 2015. The courts of a Member State whose law has been chosen by the deceased to govern their succession may decline jurisdiction if they consider that the court of another Member State is better placed to rule on the succession, for example, habitual residence of the parties and the location of the assets or if the parties to the proceedings have agreed to confer jurisdiction on the court of another Member State (see Arts 5–7, and Arts 9–11, 17 and 18 for other instances when jurisdiction may be exercised). Thus these provisions will be relevant to a testator who is habitually resident in a Member State and has assets there at the time of death, notwithstanding the fact that they may be a national of another state unless the testator comes within the exception or makes a choice pursuant to Arts 7 and 22 (see, also, below).

As regards succession, the starting point is that the law applicable to the succession as a whole will be the state in which the deceased had his habitual residence at the time of death, unless it is clear from all the circumstances of the case that at the time of death the deceased was manifestly more closely connected with another state (Art 21 of EU Regulation 650/2012). However, the testator has a right to choose the law which should govern his succession – the law of any state whose nationality they possess at the time of making the choice or at the time of death. In the case where the testator has multiple nationalities, they may choose the law of any of the states whose nationality they possess at the time of making the choice or at the time of death, provided the choice is made expressly in a declaration in the form of a disposition of property upon death or is demonstrated by the terms of such disposition (see Art 22). The issues which will be governed by the law of the deceased's habitual residence or the choice of law they make are set out in Art 23.

Any disposition made by the testator as to succession must be governed as to its admissibility and validity in accordance with the law, which under EU Regulation 650/2012 applies to such disposition if they had died on the day on which the disposition was made, unless they have chosen the law of another state to govern the disposition of property upon their death (Art 23). These include capacity, any bar to the disposition of the property or on the person receiving it, admissibility of representation, interpretation of the disposition and issues of fraud, duress and any other question relating to the consent or intention of the testator or their capacity to vary or revoke the disposition (Art 26). These factors are not dissimilar to those which apply under the Wills Act 1837.

The formal validity of a disposition of property upon death (i.e. validity of a will) must comply with the law:

(1) of the state in which the disposition was made or the agreement as to succession concluded;
(2) of the state whose nationality the testator or at least one of the persons whose succession is concerned, by an agreement as to succession possessed, either at the time when the disposition was made or the agreement concluded, or at the time of death;
(3) of the state in which the testator or at least one of the persons whose succession is concerned by an agreement as to succession had their domicile either at the time when the disposition was made or the agreement concluded or at the time of death. In this case the issue of domicile must be governed by the law of that state; or
(4) of the state in which the testator or at least one of the persons whose succession is concerned by an agreement as to succession had his habitual residence, either at the time when the disposition was made or the agreement concluded, or at the time of death; or
(5) in so far as immoveable property is concerned, of the state in which that property is located (Art 27 of EU Regulation 650/2012).

These provisions also apply to any variation or revocation of the will. This Article also provides that any limitations on the form of disposition of property on death by reference to age, nationality or other personal conditions of the testator or of the persons whose succession is concerned must conform to the form and of the qualifications to be possessed by the witness required for the validity of the disposition of property on death. These rules relate to the execution of the disposition (i.e. the will), so it is important to ensure when faced with a foreign will that the will has been made and executed in accordance with the law of the relevant Member State.

Special rules on the appointment and powers of an administrator of the estate are set out in Art 29 of EU Regulation 650/2012. Where the laws of the state, in which certain immoveable property, enterprises or other special categories of assets are located, contain special rules which impose restrictions, those rules will apply to the succession (Art 30). The *commorientes* rule in Art 32 provides that in cases where the death of two or more persons occurs in circumstances in which it is not known or there is uncertainty as to in what order their death occurred and where those laws provide differently or make no provision for it at all, none of the deceased persons have any rights to the succession of the other or others. This differs from the position under English law which, in Law of Property Act 1925, s 184, provides that in all cases where two or more persons have died in circumstances rendering it uncertain which of them survived the other or others, such death shall (subject to an order of the court) for all purposes affecting the title to property, be presumed to have occurred in order of seniority and, accordingly, the younger shall be deemed to have survived the elder. Article 33 provides for the estate to pass to the state (*bona vacantia*) where there is no heir or legatee for any assets under a will or intestacy subject to the right of creditors to be met out of the estate.

The doctrine of *renvoi* is dealt with under Art 34 of EU Regulation 650/2012, and will continue to be relevant where the law which applies to the deceased's estate under the Regulation is that of a non-Regulation state. It is not clear whether or not it applies to the United Kingdom, but it would seem that it does not apply to Member States not bound by the Regulation, and therefore there is to be no *renvoi* from the United Kingdom to other Member States. The option which should be considered by a testator when making a will is for the testator with a connection to the United Kingdom, whose succession rights may be subject to *renvoi* back to a Member State subject to the Regulation, to consider making a choice of applicable law pursuant to Art 22 (see above).

The provisions in relation to recognition, enforceability and enforcement of decisions and the procedure to be adopted are set out in Chapter IV, Arts 39–58 of EU Regulation 650/2012. Chapter V deals with the authentication of instruments and enforceability of court settlements. Chapter VI sets out the provisions for the creation of a European Certificate of Succession: its purpose; the procedure for making an application for a certificate and its issue; the contents of the certificate; its effect, rectification, variation and withdrawal.

It will be apparent from the above that in order to deal with claims under the I(PFD)A 1975, the issues covered by EU Regulation 650/2012 will need to be considered. For example, it will be necessary to ascertain whether the estate comprises foreign property in a Member State; if so, whether it is moveable or immoveable; to identify who is entitled under the applicable law to the assets under any disposition made by the testator or the succession laws; whether the personal representatives of the deceased's estate in England and Wales are also responsible for the administration of the foreign assets. It will also be necessary to ascertain whether the deceased has made a valid will disposing of their foreign assets in accordance with the law which applies in the state where the deceased was habitually resident or domiciled or a national, as the case may be, and in relation to where the asset is located; whether the deceased has exercised their right of choice under the provisions of Art 22 and, if so, has jurisdiction been declined or do circumstances exist where the *lis pendens* principle applies; and whether there is any limitation imposed on the testator's freedom to dispose of their property. Quantifying the amount of inheritance tax or death duties under the foreign applicable law will also be relevant to determine 'net estate'.

These matters raise complex issues, and it is suggested that expert advice, including advice from experienced lawyers in the appropriate Member State(s), should be obtained in cases where they arise.

Chapter 10

Dispositions Intended to Defeat Financial Provision

10.1 INTRODUCTION

Provision is made in the I(PFD)A 1975 to prevent a person from defeating, frustrating or reducing claims made under the Act on their death by making dispositions of their assets during their lifetime or contracting to do so after their death. The powers of the court in respect of such evasion or avoidance, and the duties of personal representatives and the protection afforded to them, are set out in ss 10–13. Section 10 deals with disposition made during the lifetime of the deceased and s 11 with contracts made to bequeath property in a will. Section 12 makes supplementary provisions relating to applications made under ss 10 and 11, which include how the court can determine the intention to defeat an application under the Act and any consequential order it can make when dealing with issues arising from applications made under either s 10 or s 11. Section 13 deals with powers of the court to make orders against trustees who have received money or such property.

The provisions under I(PFD)A 1975, ss 10 and 11 may be invoked only if the court is satisfied that the exercise of its powers under s 10 would facilitate the making of financial provision for the claimant.

10.2 INTER VIVOS DISPOSITION

Where a claim for financial provision is made under I(PFD)A 1975, s 2, the claimant in those proceedings may apply to the court for an order under s 10(2) that the donee of an *inter vivos* disposition (whether or not at the date of the order they hold any interest in the property disposed of to them or for their benefit by the deceased) provide, to the claimant, for the purposes of making that financial provision, such sum of money or property as may be specified in the order. Thus any order made by the court will be directed to the donee to provide the 'money or other property'.

10.2.1 Condition precedent for an order

Before the court may make an order under I(PFD)A 1975, s 10(2), it must be satisfied that:

(1) less than 6 years before the date of the deceased's death, the deceased, with the intention of defeating an application for financial provision under the Act, made a disposition;
(2) full valuable consideration for that disposition was not given by the donee to whom, or for the benefit of whom, the disposition was made, or by any other person; and
(3) the exercise of the power conferred by s 10 would facilitate the making of financial provision for the claimant under the Act.

10.2.2 Meaning of 'disposition'

The section is wide in its terms. I(PFD)A 1975, s 10(7) defines 'disposition' to include:

> any payment of money (including the payment of a premium under a policy of assurance) and any conveyance, assurance, appointment or gift of property of any description, whether made by an instrument or otherwise.

On the other hand, the I(PFD)A 1975 specifically excludes:

(1) any provision in a will, any such nomination as is mentioned in s 8(1) (see para 9.6) or any *donatio mortis causa* (see para 9.7); or
(2) any appointment of property made, otherwise than by will, in the exercise of a special power of appointment.

The transactions under point (1) (above) are excluded because they form part of the 'net estate' pursuant to other provisions in the I(PFD)A 1975. Property which is the subject of a special power of appointment and is disposed of *inter vivos* is excluded by reason of the fact that it was never part of the deceased's 'net estate'.

In *Clifford v Tanner*, unreported, CAT, 10 June 1986, the deceased had a right under a covenant to occupy a house belonging to his daughter. He released the right to his daughter without full valuable consideration. It was held that the release of the right to occupy came within the definition of disposition, as a 'gift of property of any description'.

I(PFD)A 1975, s 10(8) also excludes any disposition made in respect of any property before the commencement of the Act on 1 April 1976.

10.2.3 Full valuable consideration

I(PFD)A 1975, s 25(1) provides that 'valuable consideration does not include marriage or a promise of marriage'. A civil partnership or a promise to enter into a civil partnership will now also be excluded.

The consideration need not, however, have been provided by the donee. It could have been provided by 'any other person' (I(PFD)A 1975, s 10(2)(b)).

The consideration has to be 'full', i.e. not nominal or at a value well below the market price. See, for example, *Dawkins v Judd* [1986] 2 FLR 360, where a disposition made by the deceased to his daughter for £100 was held not to have been made for full consideration (at para 10.2.4).

10.2.4 Intention of defeating a claim

For a disposition to come within the provisions of I(PFD)A 1975, s 10 the claimant must satisfy the court that, in making the disposition, the deceased had the intention of defeating a claim for financial provision under the Act (s 10(2)). Section 12(1) of the Act provides that this condition should be fulfilled if the court is of the opinion that, on a balance of probabilities, the intention of the deceased (though not necessarily their sole intention) in making the disposition was to prevent an order for financial provision being made under the Act, or to reduce the amount of the provision which might otherwise be granted.

Three issues are highlighted by taking the provisions of I(PFD)A 1975, ss 10(2) and 12(1) together. These are that:

- the intention to defeat a claim need not be the sole intention but there must be some evidence of an intention to defeat a claim for financial provision under the Act;
- the standard of proof is the civil standard of proof, namely 'the balance of probabilities';
- the intention of the deceased in making the disposition was either:
  - to prevent an order for financial provision being made, or
  - to reduce the amount of the provision which might be granted.

Proving the necessary intention is a question of fact. In matrimonial proceedings under the Matrimonial Causes Act 1973, the test to be applied has been referred to as 'a deliberate or reckless dealing with assets rather than some random event unconnected to the motives of the respondent' (Mostyn J in *UL v BK (Freezing Order: Safeguards: Standard Examples* [2013] EWHC 1735 (Fam)).

The issues raised above can be illustrated by the following cases.

The intention to defeat a claim need not be the sole intention, but there must be some evidence of an intention to defeat such a claim. The intention also need not necessarily be in relation to a claim under the I(PFD)A 1975. In *Re Kennedy (Deceased), Kennedy v Official Solicitor* [1980] CLY 2820, the deceased transferred his house to his mistress in consideration of natural love and affection. The deceased's wife issued proceedings for divorce in which she indicated her intention to apply for ancillary relief, but before the decree nisi (now a conditional divorce order) was pronounced, he died. A few months later the mistress also died. It was held that it was not essential to show that the Act or its provisions were present in the mind of the deceased when he entered into the transaction which was called into question, but there had to be evidence that he intended to defeat a claim made after his death against the estate.

In *Dawkins v Judd* [1986] 2 FLR 360, the deceased had transferred the matrimonial home to his daughter by his first marriage for £100, a year before he indicated to his wife that he wanted a divorce. He left a will leaving his entire estate to the daughter. He died 2 years after making the transfer. Evidence was adduced that the deceased had sought legal advice on how he could preserve the property for his daughter in the event of his death. Bush J had no difficulty, when applying the test set out in I(PFD)A 1975, s 12, in reaching the conclusion that the sale of the house to the daughter was entered into with the intention, though not necessarily the sole intention, of defeating a claim for financial provision.

In *Hanbury v Hanbury* [1999] 2 FLR 255, having sought legal advice on how to defeat his disabled daughter's claim under the I(PFD)A 1975, the deceased transferred his property into the joint names of himself and his second wife and arranged for investments to be bought in the sole name of his second wife (see Chapter 8). Intention to defeat was proved by disclosure given during the proceedings of the legal advice the deceased had sought. (For further information on disclosure, see CPR Part 31.)

The court's power to avoid transactions made or entered into to defeat a claim under the I(PFD)A 1975 are similar, but not on exactly the same terms as those set out in Matrimonial Causes Act 1973, s 37. Subject to the differences between the provisions in the 1975 Act and Matrimonial Causes Act 1973, s 37, case law under s 37 may be relevant in cases under the 1975 Act, for example, see *Kremen v Agrest* [2010] EWHC 2571, [2011] 2 FLR 478 and *AC v DC and Others (Financial Remedy: Effect of s 37 Avoidance Order)* [2012] EWHC 2032 (Fam),

[2013] 2 FLR 1483. These differences were referred to in *Dellal v Dellal and Others* [2015] EWHC 907 (Fam), which was an application to strike out or grant summary judgment in relation to a claim under the I(PFD)A 1975. The applicant contended that: (1) no disposition was identified within the 6-year period required under s 10; (2) there was insufficient evidence of ill motive on the part of the deceased; (3) the widow had substantial assets of her own to satisfy her needs; (4) the defendants were outside the jurisdiction and any order made by the court would be ineffective.

Mostyn J stated (at [9]–[11]):

> 9. Section 10 is similar in its language to section 37 of the Matrimonial Causes Act 1973 although there are real conceptual and structural distinctions between the two provisions. I endeavoured to explain these differences in my decision of *AC v DC & Ors (Financial Remedy: Effect of s37 Avoidance Order) (No 1)* [2012] EWHC 2032 (Fam), [2013] 2 FLR 1483. The effect of an order under section 37 is to annul or 'avoid' the transaction under attack. Moreover, the bad intention to defeat the principal ancillary relief claim is presumed for transactions done within the three year period before the avoidance claim. There is no time limit on attackable transactions. A transaction done 20 years earlier is, at any rate in theory, capable of being annulled. By contrast, a claim under section 10 of the 1975 Act does not affect the validity of the disposition under attack. If relief is granted then it takes the form of a money judgment against the disponee to pay a specified sum to the estate. There is no presumption as to the necessary bad intention and there is a six year time limit on attackable transactions. If the disponee is a trustee then by section 13 the money judgment cannot exceed the value of the disposition left in the hands of the trustee.
> 10. In this case the six year period began on 28 October 2006.
> 11. Accordingly if the claimant is to succeed in her application under section 10 she will have to show at trial the following as against each separate defendant:
>
>   i) At least one disposition was made by Jack in favour of the defendant in question after 28 October 2006.
>   ii) For these purposes a disposition is an outright transfer of the beneficial ownership of the transferred thing done otherwise than for full valuable consideration. A transfer to a person to hold the thing as agent or nominee or bare trustee is not within the section. A transfer to a person as trustee presupposes that the trust is more than just a bare trust.
>   iii) Where it is said that the disposition was to a trustee that the trustee actually holds some money or property deriving from the disposition.
>   iv) The disposition was done by Jack with the intention of defeating the claimant's claim for financial provision under section 2 of the 1975 Act. The motive does not have to be the dominant motive in the transaction; if it is a subsidiary (but material) motive then that will suffice: see *Kemmis v Kemmis Welland and Others Intervening); Lazard Brothers and Co (Jersey) Ltd v Norah Holdings Ltd and Others* [1988] 1 WLR 1307, CA.

v) A payment order would facilitate the making of an award for financial provision under the 1975 Act in favour of the claimant.
vi) Where the defendant is out of the jurisdiction that the order for payment would be enforceable in the foreign land: see Hamlin v Hamlin [1986] Fam 11, CA, at 18 per Kerr LJ.
vii) The court should exercise its discretion to make an order for a payment to the estate.

In relation to the defendants' claim to strike out the application, Mostyn J concluded that their application did not in any respect meet the standards specified in CPR r 3.4(20)(a) or (b) and, accordingly, he dismissed that part of the application (at [65]). As to summary judgment, he ruled that the claim was not speculative and any determination on this issue should be on an informed basis. He therefore gave directions on disclosure (at [66]). As regards the applicant's wealth, he took the view that this in itself did not make her claim hopeless (at [73]).

To summarise:

- The evidence of such an intention therefore need not be in writing.
- It may be by way of oral statements made by the deceased or evidence of the legal advice sought or it can be derived from the circumstances of the disposition.
- The following matters are relevant and must be taken into account:
  - the value of the property in issue at the time of the disposition;
  - the value of any consideration given for the property; and
  - the relationship between the deceased and the donee.

10.2.5 Matters the court will take into consideration

In determining whether to exercise its powers under I(PFD)A 1975, s 10(2), and in what manner to exercise its powers, the court must have regard to the following matters (I(PFD)A 1975, s 10(6)):

(1) the circumstances in which the disposition was made;
(2) the valuable consideration which was given;
(3) the relationship, if any, of the donee to the deceased;
(4) the conduct of the donee;
(5) the financial resources of the donee; and
(6) all the other circumstances of the case.

The cases set out at para 10.2.4 illustrate how the court has determined the issue of 'intention'. It should also be noted that the court is under a duty to have regard to and consider the above factors when an issue of intention to defeat a claim arises in an application under the I(PFD)A 1975. The provision of s 10(6) is mandatory.

10.2.6 Orders that can be made

If the conditions referred to above are satisfied, and subject to the provisions of I(PFD)A 1975, ss 12 and 13, the court's order will be directed to the donee to provide the asset, be it money or property, to meet the financial provision the court makes in favour of the claimant. The court may order the donee of an *inter vivos* disposition to provide such money or other property as may be specified for the purposes of making financial provision for the claimant, whether or not, at the date of the order, the donee retains any interest in the property disposed of to them or for their benefit by the deceased (s 10(2)).

If the donee of the *inter vivos* disposition is dead, the court can proceed to make the appropriate orders in like manner against the personal representatives of the donee (I(PFD)A 1975, s 12(4)).

It will be seen that the provisions of I(PFD)A 1975, s 10 affect the donee, not the property given to the donee. If the donee is dead, the action can be made or continued against their estate. The court does not, however, have power to make any orders under s 10 in respect of any property which has been distributed by the personal representatives. Furthermore, a personal representative is not liable for having distributed any such property before they have had notice of the making of a claim under the Act in which an application is made under s 10, on the grounds that they ought to have taken into account the possibility that such an application would be made (s 12(4)).

I(PFD)A 1975, s 10(3) provides that where an order is made under s 10(2), as respects any disposition which consisted of the payment of money to or for the benefit of the donee, the amount of any sum of money or the value of any property ordered to be provided must not exceed the amount of the payment made by the deceased, after deducting any inheritance tax borne by the donee in respect of that payment.

Where the disposition consisted of the transfer of property (other than a sum of money) to or for the benefit of the donee, the amount of any sum of money under I(PFD)A 1975, s 10(2) must not exceed the value, at the date of the death of the deceased, of the property disposed of by them to, or for the benefit of, the donee (or if that property has been disposed of by the person to whom it was transferred by the deceased, the value at the date of disposal thereof), after deducting any inheritance tax borne by the donee in respect of the transfer of that property by the deceased (s 10(4)).

Thus, if the donee purchases property or shares with the money paid to them, neither the increase in the value of the property or shares, nor the income from the investment, would need to be accounted for (I(PFD)A 1975, s 10(3)). The value will be the value at the date of disposal or at the death of the deceased, after the deduction of inheritance tax. The value of the property is the capital value and does not include income from the property which may have accrued since the disposition was made to the donee. The donee will have to provide only such sum of money or property as will meet the financial provision order made by the court in favour of the claimant.

If the donee has disposed of the asset, they will have to provide a sum equivalent to that which satisfies the sum ordered to be made available by the court.

The court is given wide powers under I(PFD)A 1975, s 12(3) to give such consequential directions including directions requiring the making of any payment or transfer of any property, as it thinks fit for giving effect to its order or for securing a fair adjustment of the rights of the person affected.

10.2.7 Donee's right to apply

By virtue of I(PFD)A 1975, s 10(5), if an application is made for an order under s 10(2), the donee of the property in question can apply for the court to substitute, for the disposition which is the subject of the application, another disposition made to them by the deceased. Certain preconditions must be fulfilled. Section 10(5) provides that where an application (the 'original application') is made for an order in relation to such a disposition, then if on application under s 10(5) the court is satisfied of certain matters, the court may exercise, in relation to the person to whom or for whose benefit that other disposition was made, the powers which the court would have had under s 10(2) if the original application had been made in respect of that other disposition. The matters of which the court must be satisfied are that:

(1) less than 6 years before the date of the death of the deceased, the deceased, with the intention of defeating an application for financial provision under the Act, made a disposition other than the disposition which is the subject of the original application; and
(2) full valuable consideration for that other disposition was not given by the person to whom, or for the benefit of whom, that other disposition was made or by any other person.

Where the claim includes an application for an order under I(PFD)A 1975, s 10, it is desirable to give notice of the proceedings to the donee, so that the donee has the opportunity to apply to be joined as a party to the proceedings and to be heard before decisions are made which affect them and their rights and interests. The bona fides of the donee can be dealt with as a preliminary point in appropriate cases. This course would also be beneficial to the claimant because it would enable the claimant to seek disclosure from the donee and, if necessary, preserve the property until the determination of the claim, by obtaining an undertaking or an order prohibiting the disposal, transfer or other dealing with the property.

10.3 CONTRACTS TO LEAVE PROPERTY BY WILL

I(PFD)A 1975, s 11 gives the court jurisdiction to order any sum of money or other property bequeathed in a will by virtue of a contract to make a will, to be made available for the purposes of facilitating the making of a financial provision order, provided that the conditions in s 11 are satisfied.

10.3.1 Condition precedent for an order

Before the court can make any of the orders under I(PFD)A 1975, s 11(2) in respect of a contract to leave property by will to another, it must be satisfied that:

(1) the deceased made a contract by which they agreed to leave by their will a sum of money or other property to any person, or by which they agreed that a sum of money or other property would be paid or transferred to any person, out of their estate;
(2) the deceased made this contract with the intention of defeating an application for financial provision under the Act;
(3) when the contract was made, full valuable consideration for that contract was not given or promised by the person with whom or for whose benefit the contract was made ('the donee') or by any other person; and
(4) the exercise of the powers conferred by s 11 would facilitate the making of financial provision for the claimant under the Act.

10.3.2 Contract

The I(PFD)A 1975 is silent on the meaning of 'contract', and therefore the assumption is that the word must be given its ordinary legal meaning. It could, however, be argued that the Act did not intend the term 'contract' to have the ordinary legal interpretation because the provisions of s 12(2) envisage a situation where 'no valuable consideration' is given. Thus, where the deceased made a promise or representation to leave property by will, and as a result the promisee or representee acted to their detriment, there may not be an enforceable contract, but if the evidence suggests that the doctrine of proprietary estoppel arises, there may be an enforceable claim against the estate. The same may be so if a constructive trust is implied by the agreement.

In *Irani v Irani* [2006] EWHC 1811(Ch), Lightman J considered the issue of whether the deceased who had died intestate had entered into an agreement with his former wife to leave by his will property in equal shares to three of their children and an informally adopted child. The evidence before Lightman J consisted of contemporaneous correspondence and documents, witness statements and oral evidence. Lightman J was satisfied that such a contract had been entered into by the deceased. Of particular significance was the fact that the evidence clearly showed that the deceased believed that he had made a valid will and that its execution constituted the fulfilment of his obligations. As regards its enforceability, as a matter of law if an offer is made in writing and is accepted orally, that contract is in law a valid contract in writing as required by Law of Property Act 1925, s 40 (see *Tiverton Estates Ltd v Wearwell Ltd* [1975] Ch 146). See, also, *Soulsbury v Soulsbury* [2007] EWCA Civ 969, [2008] 1 FLR 90, where the issue on appeal was whether the personal representative of the estate of the deceased former husband of the claimant was liable to pay her £100,000, which the deceased had promised he would ensure she would receive on his death if she did not enforce an order for periodical payments in her favour or seek an order for ancillary relief against him. The court held that there was a valid and enforceable contract. On the other hand, in *St Clair v King and Farrell* [2022] EWHC 40 (Ch), on the facts the court ruled that a valid enforceable contract had not been established.

I(PFD)A 1975, s 11 extends to a contract by which the deceased agreed that their personal representatives would pay a sum of money or transfer other property out of their estate. Contracts to leave property by mutual wills (see para 7.8.2) will also fall within the provisions of s 11.

The I(PFD)A 1975 did not come into force until 1 April 1976 and therefore does not apply to contracts made before that date. Unlike the provisions of s 10, where only dispositions made less than 6 years before the date of death may be subject to an order, there are no time limits in respect of contracts to leave property by will. Time may, however, be relevant to the issue of the deceased's intention in making the contract.

Any arrangement which applies in the case of intestacy falls outside I(PFD)A 1975, s 11, because the section refers to a contract by which the deceased agreed to leave a sum of money or other property 'by will'.

10.3.3 Intention to defeat a claim

The claimant must satisfy the court that, in making the contract, the deceased had the intention of defeating a claim by the claimant for financial provision out of the estate under the I(PFD)A 1975. Certain circumstances or conduct will be presumed as indicating the required intention unless evidence proving the contrary is adduced by the donee.

I(PFD)A 1975, s 12(2) provides that, with respect to any contract made by the deceased where no valuable consideration is given or promised by any person, then it is to be presumed, unless the contrary is shown, that the deceased made the contract with the intention of defeating a claim for financial relief under the Act (cf s 10 where no such provision applies). Section 25(1) provides that 'valuable consideration' does not include marriage or a promise of marriage. It should now also exclude a civil partnership or a promise to enter into a civil partnership.

The statutory presumption is rebuttable by the donee on production of evidence to show that the deceased did not have the intention to defeat any claim for financial provision by the claimant, but that their motives were sincere and genuine.

The intention to defeat a claim implies a fraudulent dealing and the question then arises whether the standard of proof required to prove such intention should be that applicable where fraud is alleged; but I(PFD)A 1975, s 12(1) states that the standard to be applied is that of the 'balance of probabilities'. In some respects, the donee is at a disadvantage because in most cases the motives of the deceased cannot be tested by direct evidence from the deceased, by contrast with the position in applications under Matrimonial Causes Act 1973, s 37.

As in cases under I(PFD)A 1975, s 10, the test that the court would need to apply is whether the intention of the deceased (though not necessarily their sole intention) in making the contract was to prevent an order for financial provision being made under the Act, or to reduce the amount of the provision which might otherwise be granted (s 12(1)). It would seem that the court, in applying the test, would be concerned with the deceased's intention subjectively; and that, in determining whether the required intention existed, the deceased would be taken to intend the natural consequences of their acts. All facts, statements and declarations made before, after or at the time the act occurred are relevant in determining the state of mind of the deceased.

10.3.4 Full valuable consideration

The meaning of 'full valuable consideration' is that provided in I(PFD)A 1975, s 25(1):

- it 'does not include marriage or a promise of marriage';
- it need not have been provided by the donee as long as it was provided at the time the contract was made;
- it could have been provided by any other person on the donee's behalf (s 11(2)(c)).

In view of the changes made by the CPA 2004, it should also exclude a civil partnership or a promise to enter into a civil partnership.

10.3.5 Matters to be considered by the court

The court has a discretion whether or not to make an order under I(PFD)A 1975, s 11. In determining whether or not to exercise its powers and, if so, in what manner to exercise them, the court must have regard to the following matters (s 11(4)):

(1) the circumstances in which the contract was made;
(2) the relationship, if any, of the donee to the deceased;
(3) the conduct of the donee;
(4) the financial resources of the donee; and
(5) all the circumstances of the case.

10.3.6 Orders that can be made under I(PFD)A 1975, section 11

If the conditions outlined above are satisfied, the court may make any one or more of the following orders to facilitate the making of financial provision under I(PFD)A 1975, s 2 for the claimant (s 11(2)):

(1) if any money has been paid, or any other property has been transferred to or for the benefit of the donee in accordance with the contract, an order directing the donee to provide, for the purposes of the making of that financial provision, such sum of money or other property as may be specified in the order;
(2) if the money or all the money has not been paid, or the property or all of the property has not been transferred, in accordance with the contract, an order directing the personal representatives not to make any further payment or transfer any property or further property, as the case may be,

or directing the personal representatives to make such payment or transfer such property only as may be specified in the order.

The court may also give such consequential directions as it thinks fit (including directions requiring the making of any payments or the transfer of any property) for giving effect to the order or for securing a fair adjustment of the rights of the persons affected thereby (I(PFD)A 1975, s 12(3)).

The orders referred to in points (1) and (2) above are considered at paras 10.3.7 and 10.3.8.

10.3.7 Where money has been paid

Where the personal representatives of the deceased have made payment of money or transferred property to the donee in accordance with the contract, the court can order the donee to provide such sums of money or transfer such property as will facilitate the making of a financial provision order. The order does not attach to the specific sum of money or property that had been transferred.

10.3.8 Where money has not been paid

If the terms of the contract have not been fulfilled (whether wholly or partially) by the personal representatives, the court may forbid them from making payment and from transferring such of the money or the property as may be specified in the order. If the donee of the contract by will has died, the court can proceed to make the appropriate orders against the personal representatives of the donee (I(PFD)A 1975, s 12(4)). The court cannot, however, make any of the orders set out in s 11 in respect of any property which has been distributed by the personal representatives. Nor are the personal representatives liable for having distributed any such property before they had notice of the making of the claim which included an application for an order under s 11, on the ground that they ought to have taken into account the possibility that such an application would be made (s 12(4)).

10.3.9 Position of donee who is a trustee

The court's power to make any orders under I(PFD)A 1975, ss 10 and 11 against a trustee is limited to such sum as is, at the date of the order, in the hands of the trustee, or the value at that date of any property which represents that money. In the case of any property transferred, it is limited to so much of that property as is, at the date of the order, in the hands of the trustee and the value at that date of any property (s 13(1)).

As in the case of the personal representatives of the donee, the trustee is exempt from liability for having distributed any money or other property on the ground that they ought to have taken into account the possibility that such an application would be made (I(PFD)A 1975, s 13(2)).

10.3.10 Restrictions on the court's powers

The court may exercise its powers in relation to any contract made by the deceased only to the extent that the court considers that the amount of any sum of money paid or to be paid, or the value of any property transferred or to be transferred in accordance with the contract, exceeds the value of any valuable consideration given or to be given for the contract.

The property transferred or to be transferred under the contract is to be valued at the date of the hearing.

10.3.11 Rights of persons to enforce the contract

I(PFD)A 1975, s 11(5) provides that where the court makes an order under s 11(2) in relation to any contract, the contractual rights of the donee to enforce that contract or to recover damages, or to obtain other relief for the breach, is subject to any adjustment made by the court under s 12(3). The contractual relief is available to the extent only as is consistent with the court's order.

Chapter 11

Personal Representatives and Trustees

11.1 INTRODUCTION

The personal representatives of a deceased person are under a duty to collect and get in the real and personal estate of the deceased and administer it according to law. When required to so by the court, they must provide, on oath, a full inventory of the estate and, if required by the court, render an account of the administration of the estate to the court (Administration of Estates Act 1925, s 25).

The personal representatives are liable for any waste to the estate or the conversion of the real or personal estate of the deceased. Where it is apparent that a claim may be made under the I(PFD)A 1975, the personal representatives must ensure that nothing is done by them to prejudice the claim. Where a personal representative is also a beneficiary, they and their legal advisers must ensure that there is no conflict of interest between their role as a personal representative of the estate and as a beneficiary under the will and/or intestacy. If there is a likelihood of a conflict it is better to err on the side of caution and step down. An application should be made under Administration of Justice Act 1985, s 50 and the appointment of a replacement should be made if this is considered necessary. Similarly, if a sole personal representative is likely to be a claimant, consideration should be given as to whether it is possible to continue fairly in the two capacities without seemingly appearing to be prejudiced in the execution of the duties imposed on a personal representative. Where there is more than one personal representative, there should be no difficulty in the others continuing to act on behalf of the estate as defendant(s) whilst the person who is likely to be the claimant is pursuing their claim (see, also, para 11.3).

The I(PFD)A 1975 provides that any claim against the estate must be begun within 6 months from the date when the grant of representation was taken out. If the personal representatives have not, on the expiry of the time limit, received any notice of a claim, they are free to distribute the estate. Again, however, to err on the side of caution, if there is any inkling of a possible claim under the Act, it would be advisable to give notice of the intention to distribute the estate to any potential claimant(s). Where the personal representatives have notice of a claim, it is their duty to ensure that no steps are taken which will have the effect of prejudicing the claim. Where distribution has taken place, it is still possible for the court to direct the beneficiary/beneficiaries to meet any financial provision order it makes in favour of the claimant.

The I(PFD)A 1975 makes provisions which are aimed at providing protection to the personal representatives from liability after the end of the period of 6 months from the date when a grant has been obtained in some circumstances. These are dealt with below.

11.2 LIABILITIES UNDER THE I(PFD)A 1975

The I(PFD)A 1975 extends the categories of persons to whom personal representatives owe a duty, but also provides certain protection from liability. A successful claimant is regarded in law as a person interested in the will or intestacy and is thus in the same position vis-à-vis the personal representatives as a beneficiary and has the same rights of action against them.

The personal representatives are liable to the beneficiaries and creditors for any loss of assets of the estate or breach of any trust contained in the will. Personal representatives may apply to the court for relief under Trustee Act 1925, s 61 where they have made an interim distribution of the estate without a court order. Personal representatives may be faced with the difficult situation that beneficiaries are suffering hardship because distribution has been delayed by the inheritance proceedings, while at the same time the personal representatives have a duty to the claimant to preserve property. In *Re Simson, Simson v National Provincial Bank Ltd* [1949] 2 All ER 826, Vaisey J expressed the view that it was the duty of executors faced with a claim for financial provision to make no distribution until the hearing of the claim, and to preserve the estate intact for the court to deal with. On the other hand, in *Re Ralphs, Ralphs v District Bank* [1968] 1 WLR 1522, Cross J took a different view. He advocated that executors should:

> form their own view, with the assistance of their legal advisers, as to payments which can properly be made, and if they are not prepared to make such payments on their own responsibility they should ask the parties who might conceivably be affected for their consent. If such consent was not forthcoming they could apply to the court for leave to make the payment in question. If the court finds that consent was unreasonably withheld it can penalise the party responsible in costs.

11.3 PROTECTION AFFORDED BY I(PFD)A 1975, SECTION 20

I(PFD)A 1975, s 20 makes special provision in relation to the liabilities of personal representatives in the following circumstances:

- Section 20(1) provides that personal representatives are not liable for having distributed any part of the estate of the deceased, after the end of the period of 6 months from the date on which representation with respect to the estate of the deceased is first taken out, on the ground that they ought to have taken into account the possibility:

  - that the court might permit the making of an application for an order under s 2 after the end of that period (i.e. extend the time for making the application); or
  - that, where an order has been made under s 2, the court might vary the order in exercise of the powers conferred on it by s 6.

  This provision, however, does not prejudice any power to recover, by reason of the making of an order under the Act, any part of the estate which has been distributed.
- Section 20(2) protects personal representatives from liability for having made interim payments directed by the court to be paid by an order under s 5 out of the net estate of the deceased, and thereby leaving the estate insufficient to make the payments, unless at the time of the making of the payments they have reasonable cause to believe that the estate is not sufficient.
- Section 20(3) empowers the personal representatives to postpone the payment of money or the transfer of property out of the estate of the deceased which the deceased had agreed by contract to leave by their will, where the personal representatives have reason to believe that the deceased entered into the contract with the intention of defeating an application for financial provision under the Act, until the expiry of 6 months from the date on which representation with respect to the estate of the deceased is first taken out or, if during that period, an application is made for an order under s 2, until the determination of that application.

These provisions protect the personal representatives who distribute the assets after the period of 6 months from the grant of representation. They should, therefore, avoid any distribution which might prejudice the claim within 6 months from the grant. Where they have notice of a possible claim, they should wait until the 6 months from the grant of representation have expired, and then give notice of their intention to distribute. If they distribute the whole or a part of the assets, notwithstanding the fact that they were notified of a possible claim, they will be liable personally (see *Lane v Cullen Solicitors and Others* [2011] EWCA Civ 547, in which the court applied the principles set out in *Guardian Trust and Executors Co of New Zealand Ltd v Public Trustee of New Zealand* [1942] AC 115).

However, they are protected if they pay any sum directed to be paid by the court by way of interim payments under I(PFD)A 1975, s 5, unless, at the time of making the payments, they had reasonable grounds for believing that the estate was insolvent.

In any case where the personal representatives are uncertain about the circumstances or have doubts about how they should act, they should avoid any risk of impropriety by applying to the court for directions.

Protection is also provided where the personal representatives make a distribution under a contract which might be caught under I(PFD)A 1975, s 11, provided they did not make any payment of money or transfer any property until after the expiry of 6 months from the date on which representation was taken out. If a claim is pending, the personal representatives must postpone any distribution until the final determination of the claim. Where they have notice of a possible claim, it would be desirable to give notice to the claimant(s) or their legal advisers of the intention to distribute before doing so.

In relation to any application under I(PFD)A 1975, s 10 (see Chapter 10), if the donee of an *inter vivos* disposition is dead, the court can proceed to make the appropriate order in like manner against the personal representatives of the donee under s 10. The court does not, however, have the power to make any of the orders under s 10 in respect of any property which has been distributed by the personal representatives. Further, the personal representatives are not liable for having distributed any such property before they have notice of the making of an application under s 10 on the grounds that they ought to have taken into account the possibility that such an application would be made (s 12(4)).

Personal representatives do not have, in relation to claims under I(PFD)A 1975, protection equivalent to that provided by Trustee Act 1925, s 27. Section 27 protects personal representatives from liability to any beneficiary who does not respond in time to an advertisement notifying the personal representatives' intention to distribute the estate. If there is any doubt about whether or not the estate may be distributed, an application should be made to the court for a direction.

A personal representative who is also a beneficiary must ensure that the two capacities are kept separate. In some circumstances it may be prudent for a claimant under the I(PFD)A 1975 to apply to the court, under Administration of Justice Act 1985, s 50, to replace that personal representative.

Where, on the death of the deceased, it appears that the person appointed executor might also be a possible claimant under the I(PFD)A 1975, it may be advisable that the grant is not taken out by that person unless that person is one of a number of personal representatives appointed.

11.3.1 Responsibilities and duties after proceedings have been issued

CPR Part 57 sets out the personal representatives' duties once proceedings have been issued under the I(PFD)A 1975. These and other matters which relate to the claim are set out in Chapter 12.

11.4 TRUSTEES

I(PFD)A 1975, s 13 imposes limitations on the court's powers under ss 10 and 11. Section 13 applies where an application is made for:

(1) an order under s 10 in respect of a disposition made by the deceased to any person as a trustee;
(2) an order under s 11 in respect of any payment made or property transferred in accordance with a contract made by the deceased, to any person as a trustee.

In these cases, the powers of the court under I(PFD)A 1975, ss 10 and 11 to order the trustee to provide a sum of money or other property from which the award to the claimant is to be met, are subject to limitation. The limitation is, in the case of an application under s 10, additional to any provision regarding the deduction of inheritance tax. The limitation is that the amount of any sum of money or the value of any property ordered to be provided:

(1) in the case of an application in respect of a disposition which consisted of the payment of money, or an application in respect of the payment of money in accordance with a contract, may not exceed the aggregate of so much of that money as is at the date of the order in the hands of the trustee and the value at that date of any property which represents that money, or is derived therefrom, and is at that date in the hands of the trustee;
(2) in the case of an application in respect of a disposition which consisted of the transfer of property (other than a sum of money) or an application in respect of the transfer of property (other than a sum of money) in accordance with a contract, shall not exceed the aggregate of the value at the date of the order of so much of that property as is at that date in

> the hands of the trustee and the value at that date of any property which represents the first mentioned property, or is derived therefrom, and is at that date in the hands of the trustee.

Where any application is made in respect of a disposition made to any person as a trustee, or in respect of any payment made or property transferred in pursuance of a contract to any person as a trustee, the trustee is not liable for having distributed any money or other property on the ground that they ought to have taken into account the possibility that such an application would be made (I(PFD)A 1975, s 13(2)).

Where any such application is made in respect of a disposition made to any person as a trustee, or in respect of any payment made or property transferred in accordance with a contract to any person as a trustee, any reference in I(PFD)A 1975, s 10 or s 11 to the donee is to be construed as including a reference to the trustee or trustees for the time being in question, and any reference to a trustee is to be construed in the same way (s 13(3)).

Chapter 12

Procedure

12.1 INTRODUCTION

All applications under the I(PFD)A 1975 may be made in the Chancery Division or the Family Division of the High Court, with limited jurisdiction in the county court (see below). The procedure is governed by CPR Part 57 as amended and the Practice Direction which supplements Part 57 irrespective of whether the application is issued in the Chancery Division or the Family Division of the High Court or is transferred to the Family Division (CPR r 57.15(2)). However, if the application is issued in the Family Division or is transferred there, the requirements as to bundles and preliminary documents set out in FPR 2010, PD 27A should be followed (see *Re XY Application of PD 27A, Claims under the Inheritance (Provision for Family and Dependants) Act 1975* [2019] EWHC 1610 (Fam)). The rules now provide uniform practice and procedure in both the High Court and the county courts. In addition to Part 57, the CPR generally apply to claims under the I(PFD)A 1975, for example 'the overriding objective', the need to comply with the *Chancery Guide 2022* (Courts and Tribunals Judiciary, 2022), the General Pre-Action Conduct and Protocols Practice Direction and recourse to alternative dispute resolution, service and costs.

The county courts' jurisdiction to entertain a claim under the I(PFD)A 1975 was limited to estates not exceeding £30,000. This limit was removed by Courts and Legal Services Act 1990, ss 1 and 120, and the High Court and County Courts Jurisdiction Order 1991 (SI 1991/724).

12.2 PRE-ACTION PROTOCOL

The CPR impose a duty on the parties and the court to ensure that the General Pre-Action Conduct and Protocols Practice Direction is followed. Although there is no specific Protocol that applies to claims under the I(PFD)A 1975, CPR r 3.1(4) requires the court when giving directions to take into account whether or not a party has complied with the General Pre-Action Conduct and Protocols Practice Direction and any other Pre-Action Protocol (for which, see the *White Book Service* (Sweet & Maxwell, 2022)). CPR r 3.1(5) gives the court power to order a party to pay a sum of money into court if that party has, without good reason, failed to comply with a relevant protocol. The court is also required, when dealing with any application for relief from sanctions imposed for non-compliance with any rule, practice direction or order, to consider the extent to which the party in default has complied with any relevant Pre-Action Protocol.

In addition, when deciding what order to make on costs, one of the factors which the court has to take into account is the conduct of the parties and this includes conduct before as well as during the proceedings, and in particular the extent to which the parties followed any relevant General Pre-Action Conduct and Protocols Practice Direction (CPR r 44.3(5)(a)) and the *Chancery Guide 2022*, and in particular those set out in Chapter 23 relating to applications under the I(PFD)A 1975). It is, therefore, essential to follow the General Pre-Action Conduct and Protocols Practice Direction before commencing any proceedings under the I(PFD)A 1975. It may also be useful to follow the guidance given by the Association of Contentious Trust and Probate Specialists in their ACTAPS Code (which includes claims under the I(PFD)A 1975), where appropriate (see Appendix A11).

12.3 VENUE

Proceedings may be commenced in the High Court or a county court. Proceedings in the High Court are assigned to the Chancery Division – Business and Property Courts of England and Wales (Property, Trusts and Probate List) and the Family Division of the High Court (CPR r 57.15). Note, that the Family Court does not have jurisdiction to hear claims under the I(PFD)A 1975 because The President's Guidance, *Jurisdiction of the Family Court: Allocation of Cases within the Family Court to High Court Judge Level and Transfer of Cases from the Family Court to the High Court*, of 24 May 2021, para 13 and Sch, Part A (5) specifically confirm that the Family Court does not have jurisdiction and that proceedings under the I(PFD)A 1975 must be commenced in the Family Division. Masters of the Chancery Division and district judges of the Family Division also have jurisdiction to hear claims issued in their respective divisions. The choice of division is a matter of discretion for the claimant. Where there have been matrimonial proceedings affecting the claimant or any of the parties to the proposed action, the court in which the matrimonial proceedings were heard would be the appropriate court in which to make a claim under the I(PFD)A 1975 if the passage of time between the previous proceedings and the proceedings under the Act is not long. The *Chancery Masters' Guidelines for the Transfer of Claims* issued by the Chief Master at para 14 states that, 'Inheritance Act Claims by a spouse will usually be suitable for transfer to the

Family Division'. See also para 30 of the *Business and Property Courts Advisory Note* issued by the Chancellor of the High Court on 13 October 2017.

County courts where there is a Chancery District Registry (CPR PD 57.2) have jurisdiction to hear and determine any application for an order under I(PFD)A 1975, s 2, including any application for permission to apply for such an order, and any application made in the proceedings for an order under any other provision of the Act (County Courts Act 1984, s 25). The county court in which the proceedings are commenced will be the county court for the district in which the defendants or one of the defendants live(s) or carry/carries on business, or where the subject matter of the claim is situated.

The decision on venue is made on the basis of the nature and complexity of the case. If there is an overseas aspect to the case, or if the claim or the estate is particularly large, it would be advisable to commence the proceedings in the High Court.

Since claims under the I(PFD)A 1975 are commenced in accordance with CPR Part 8, and are treated as being allocated to the multi-track (see below and r 8.9(c), and PD 2B, the Masters in the Chancery Division or the district judges in the provincial Chancery District Registries, and district judges in the Family Division have jurisdiction to hear claims under the I(PFD)A 1975 and to approve agreements reached in such claims. Pursuant to CPR PD 2B, and in particular para 1.1C, district judges (including district judges of the Principal Registry of the Family Division) have jurisdiction to hear and dispose of proceedings under the I(PFD)A 1975 subject to any Directions given by the President of the Family Division.

In proceedings in the Chancery Division, a Master or a district judge has jurisdiction to approve compromises on behalf of a person under disability where that person's interest in a fund in an application made under the I(PFD)A 1975 exceeds £100,000 (CPR PD 2B, para 7B.2).

As claims under the I(PFD)A 1975 are Part 8 proceedings, a Master or district judge may also try contested or uncontested applications under the Act (CPR PD 2B, para 4.1). Where a case is likely to involve long and complex issues of fact or law, or an issue arises as to jurisdiction or has an international element, it should be issued in the High Court. Where the claim is made by a widow or surviving partner or a former spouse/civil partner to whom I(PFD)A 1975, s 14 applies, it would be desirable to issue the application in the Family Division of the High Court which is accustomed to dealing with the issues which are likely to arise in such cases. Where the application involves complicated accounts, partnerships and business issues, the application should be issued in the Chancery

Division which is perhaps best equipped to deal with such issues, and if commenced in the county court or the Family Division an application should be made for the proceedings to be transferred.

12.4 CLAIM FORM

CPR r 8.1(2) provides that the procedure under Part 8 ('alternative procedure for claims') may be used:

(1) where the court's decision on a question which is unlikely to involve a substantial dispute of fact is sought; or
(2) where a rule or practice direction in relation to a specified type of proceedings requires or permits the use of Part 8 procedure and disapplies or modifies any of the rules set out in Part 8 as they apply to those proceedings.

CPR r 57.16(1) provides that a claim under I(PFD)A 1975, s 1 must be made by issuing a claim form in accordance with Part 8. Part 8 and the Practice Directions under Part 8 therefore also apply to a claim under the I(PFD)A 1975. This provision is mandatory so that the application must be made using the Part 8 claim form, even where it is anticipated that a probate claim may be made or some other relief or claim is made to which Part 7 applies (see, also, the *Chancery Guide 2022*). On this issue of relevance are the observations made by Chief Master Marsh in *Bhusate v Patel* [2018] EWHC 2362 (Ch) at [13]–[17]. See, also, *Churchill v Roach and Others* [2002] EWHC 3230 (Ch). Where there is a probate and/or other civil claim (e.g. proprietary estoppel or concerning beneficial interest in property) in relation to the deceased's estate and a claim under the I(PFD)A 1975, the court should be asked to give directions as to how the two or more sets of proceedings should proceed. Since the contents of the will and, therefore, its validity are crucial to any claim under the I(PFD)A 1975, it is likely that directions will be given that the probate claim should proceed first followed by the claim under the Act.

Where there is more than one claimant, the claimants will usually agree to file a single claim form, but where this is not possible and separate claim forms are issued by each claimant, application should be made for the proceedings to be consolidated under CPR r 3.1(2).

12.4.1 Contents

The claim form must be entitled 'In the estate of [*name*] (deceased)' and 'In the matter of the Inheritance (Family Provision and Dependants) Act 1975'.

CPR r 8.2 requires that the claim form must state:

(1) that Part 8 applies;
(2) the question which the claimant wants the court to decide; or the remedy or relief which the claimant is seeking and the legal basis for the claim to that remedy or relief;
(3) if the claim is being made under an enactment, what that enactment is;
(4) if the claimant is claiming in a representative capacity, what that capacity is; and
(5) if the defendant is sued in a representative capacity, what that capacity is.

Where it is intended to make any other applications for substantive orders under the I(PFD)A 1975, this must be set out in the claim form. These include the following.

12.4.2 Time limits

The claim must be issued within 6 months of the date on which representation is taken out, unless the court grants an extension of time (I(PFD)A 1975, s 4: see Chapter 3). Leave to extend the time limit must be made in the claim form. (For a draft of the order, see Appendix A7.)

12.4.3 Application under I(PFD)A 1975, section 9 for severance of joint tenancy

Where it is intended to make an application under I(PFD)A 1975, s 9, to treat the deceased's severable share of a joint tenancy as part of the net estate (see Chapter 9), for deaths occurring before 1 October 2014 the application had to be made within 6 months of the date on which the grant of representation with respect of the deceased's estate was first taken out. There was no power to extend this time limit (s 9(1)). An application for severance, therefore, had to be made in the claim form and supported by evidence either in the claim form or in the written statement accompanying the claim form. It was essential to identify the property which was intended to be the subject of the application and to ensure that it was indeed in the joint names of the deceased and another as joint tenants and that, if jointly owned initially, that the joint tenancy had not been severed. In respect of deaths after 1 October 2014, the 6-month time limit has been removed by Inheritance and Trustees' Powers Act 2014, Sch 2, para 7. For all applications after 1 October 2014, the time limit for any application under I(PFD)A 1975, s 9 is the same as that for the substantive application and, consequently, the provision of s 4 which gives the court discretionary powers to permit a claim to be made out of time applies (see Chapter 9).

Where the joint tenant is a third party not directly connected with the application and is not a defendant to the application for an order under I(PFD)A 1975, s 2, it will be necessary to seek direction for the person to be joined as a defendant or a respondent only to the s 9 application in order to preserve confidentiality of the claimant and the defendants who have a direct interest in the substantive application. (See, further, CPR r 19 on joinder of parties.)

12.4.4 Application under I(PFD)A 1975, sections 10 and 11 to set aside transactions made by the deceased with the intention of defeating or reducing a claim under the Act

Where it is alleged that the deceased has disposed of assets to a third party or contracted to leave property by will to a third party, with the intention of defeating or reducing a claim under the I(PFD)A 1975 (see Chapter 10), it is essential that the application is made with supporting evidence filed as soon as possible, and preferably when the claim form is issued. This is particularly the case where it is believed that the assets will be dissipated by the third party and there is, therefore, a need to preserve the asset by obtaining an injunction forbidding the disposal or transfer of the asset or any dealing with the asset or part of it, where appropriate, until the determination of the substantive application (see CPR Part 25) or, alternatively, to extract an undertaking from the third party in like terms. Other alternatives to preserve the property until determination of the claim include applying for interim remedies under CPR Part 25, for example, freezing orders and other consequential remedies such as disclosure orders.

For examples of claims which might be included in the claim form, see Appendix A2.

12.4.5 Claimants

The claimant must fall within the classes of person listed under I(PFD)A 1975, s 1(1) as amended (see Chapter 4). If a claim is made jointly by two or more persons, and if it later appears that there is a conflict of interests between claimants (CPR PD 57, para 17):

(1) any claimant may choose to have separate representation or may appear in person;
(2) if the court considers that claimants should be separately represented, it may adjourn the action until they are.

Where separate claims are issued, it is open to apply for the claims to be consolidated under CPR r 3.1(2)(g).

Where a claimant is also a personal representative, provided there is another personal representative, the action may proceed with the claimant continuing as personal representative. Where, however, it appears that there may be a conflict of interests, it would be advisable for the claimant who is a personal representative to stand down.

Where a potential claimant dies before the claim is issued, the claim does not survive for the benefit of their estate, because the claim is personal to the claimant (see *Re Bramwell* [1988] 2 FLR 263 and *Whyte v Ticehurst* [1986] Fam 64). Similarly, where a claim is issued, but the claimant dies before an order is made, the claim dies with the claimant. Where an interim order was made, for example, for the payment of periodical payments, and arrears had accumulated before the claimant's death, the right to enforce those arrears survives.

Where the claimant is a bankrupt, provided the claim is limited to maintenance for the claimant, it seems that the claim can be pursued by the claimant personally, without the leave of the trustee in bankruptcy or permission from the court. Similarly, it seems that CPR r 19.2(4) will not apply where the claimant becomes the subject of a bankruptcy order while the claim is pending and before a final order is made. It would seem that where the claim is not limited to provision for the maintenance of the claimant, but is for a capital sum or property, it could be argued that the trustee in bankruptcy should be brought in (see *Re Abrams* [1996] 2 FLR 379, where a discretionary/protective trust was created in order to avoid the benefits of the order being vested in a trustee in bankruptcy).

12.4.6 Defendants

There are no rules on who should be made a party to the claim. However, note that pursuant to I(PFD)A 1975, s 4 as amended, an application can now be made before grant of representation is taken out, and CPR r 57.16 has been amended to permit a claim to be made without naming the defendant(s) and for an application to be made to the court for directions. The court may also on its own initiative give directions (CPR r 57.16(3B)).

Personal representatives and beneficiaries under the deceased's will or intestacy are obvious defendants. Where there are numerous beneficiaries, it may be desirable first to ascertain the extent of their beneficial interests. If they are entitled to receive small legacies or devises and their interest is not likely to be affected, it should be possible to reach agreement that they should not be made defendants. In any other case, it may be desirable or appropriate to apply for a representation order under CPR r 19.7, or apply for notice to be given to those who form members of a class, under r 19.8A.

Where an order under I(PFD)A 1975, s 8 (property to be treated as part of the net estate) is sought, the appropriate nominee or donee should be made a party.

Where an order under I(PFD)A 1975, s 9 (property held on a joint tenancy) is sought, the person beneficially entitled to the joint tenancy should be made a party or a respondent to the specific application if it is proposed to resolve this as a preliminary issue.

Where it is sought to apply to set aside, under I(PFD)A 1975, s 10, a disposition made by the deceased, the person in whose favour the disposition is made and against whom an order is sought should be made a party, or if it is proposed that this issue should be determined as a preliminary issue, the person concerned will be a respondent to that specific issue only. The same applies where an order is sought under s 11.

Any other person who is alleged to be a constructive trustee of property belonging to the deceased or forming part of the estate should be joined in the claim.

Any other person directed by the court to be added as a defendant under the provisions of CPR r 19.7 must be so added. For example, the court may order the appointment of a person to represent an unborn person, a person who cannot be found or a person who cannot easily be identified. Where the court exercises its powers under this rule, a judgment or order of the court given in the claim, or a settlement approved by the court, is binding on all persons who are interested in or may be affected (CPR r 19.7(6) and (7)).

12.5 CLAIMANT'S WITNESS STATEMENTS/AFFIDAVIT

CPR r 8.5 provides that the claimant may rely on the matters set out in their claim form as evidence under the rule if the claim form is verified by a statement of truth, but see r 8.5(1), which states that if the claimant wishes to rely on written evidence, they should file it when their Part 8 claim form is issued (r 8.8(1)), unless the evidence is contained in the claim form itself. Where a claimant relies on the evidence set out in the claim form, it must be verified with a statement of truth. Information about statements of truth is contained in Part 22 and the Practice Direction which supplements it.

The written statement should contain the witness's own words so far as is practicable. The person taking the statement must not try to persuade the witness of what they should or should not say. See, further, *Aquarius Financial Enterprises Inc v Certain Underwriters at Lloyds* [2001] 2 Lloyd's Rep 542.

Irrespective of whether the evidence is set out in a witness statement verified by a statement of truth or in an affidavit, the format and the procedure for drafting the statement/affidavit must comply with the requirements of CPR Part 32 and PD 32 which supplements it.

In addition, CPR r 57.16(3) requires that the written statement filed and served by the claimant with the claim form must, except in the circumstances specified in para 3A (see below), have exhibited to it an official copy of the grant of probate or letters of administration in respect of the deceased's estate, and of every testamentary document in respect of which probate or letters of administration were granted.

Where no grant has been obtained, a claimant may make an application without naming a defendant, and the written evidence must:

(1) explain the reason why it has not been possible for a grant to be obtained;
(2) be accompanied by the original or a copy (if either is available) of the will or other testamentary document in respect of which probate or letters of administration are to be granted; and
(3) contain the following information so far as known to the claimant:

    (a) brief details of the property comprised in the estate, with an approximate estimate of its capital value and any income that is received from it;
    (b) brief details of the liabilities of the estate;
    (c) the names and addresses of the persons who are in possession of the documents relating to the estate; and
    (d) the names of the beneficiaries and their respective interests in the estate.

There is no other specific requirement in the rules relating to the contents of the claimant's witness statement or affidavit, but it is suggested that the statement or affidavit should contain the following matters in addition to those set out above:

(1) the name of the deceased, the date of their death and the country of their domicile at that date;
(2) a certified copy of the deceased's death certificate;
(3) the date on which representation with respect to the deceased's estate was taken out and the names and addresses of the personal representatives;
(4) the value of the net estate (to the best of the claimant's knowledge and belief). Where possible, brief details of the property comprised in the net estate, with an approximate value and any income received therefrom, and any known liabilities, should be included;
(5) the relationship of the claimant to the deceased, or other qualification of the claimant for making the claim (see I(PFD)A 1975, s 1 and

Chapter 4). In the case of a widow, the marriage certificate should be exhibited. In the case of a judicially separated spouse, the judicial separation order/decree of judicial separation and a copy of any orders for ancillary relief made should be exhibited. In the case of a former spouse, a copy of the decree absolute and any order for ancillary relief made in those proceedings should be exhibited. Similar evidence will need to be provided in the case of civil partners and former civil partners;

(6) particulars of any known proceedings relevant to the claim. Such material is particularly relevant to the question whether a claim which has been commenced in a county court ought to be transferred to the Chancery Division or the Family Division of the High Court;

(7) whether the disposition of the deceased's estate effected by their will or the law relating to intestacy was such as to make any provision for the claimant, and, if so, the nature of the provision;

(8) details of the persons or classes of person interested in the deceased's estate and the nature of their interests;

(9) full particulars of the claimant's present and foreseeable financial resources and financial needs, and any other information which the claimant relies on under s 3 (see Chapter 7 and *Re Smallwood, Smallwood v Martins Bank* [1951] Ch 369). The deceased's reasons, if known, for making or not making a provision should be included. In *Re Blanch, Blanch v Honhold* [1967] 1 WLR 987, Buckley J said:

> In certain cases there are likely to be respects in which the state of the deceased's mind may properly be regarded as relevant and material. For instance, the state of the deceased's mind may be very material to the weight to be attributed to any reasons which he may have given in his lifetime for failing to make provision for a dependant or making such provision as he did make for such a dependant;

(10) where appropriate, a request for the court's permission to make the claim out of time and the grounds for the delay;

(11) the nature of the provision claimed;

(12) details of any orders sought under ss 8–13.

Sample statements are set out in Appendices A3–A6.

12.6 PARTY UNDER DISABILITY

Where a party, whether a claimant or defendant, is a child or a protected person, CPR r 21 must be considered. A child is defined as a person under 18. Rule 21.1(2)(d) defines a 'protected person' as a party, or an intended party, who lacks capacity to conduct the proceedings. A 'protected beneficiary' is defined as a protected person who lacks capacity to manage and control any money recovered by them or on their behalf or for their benefit in the proceedings (r 21.1(2)(e)).

The Mental Capacity Act 2005 (MCA 2005) sets out a definitive test for assessing whether a person has capacity to make a specific decision at the material time. It provides for a two-stage process, namely the diagnostic stage, which is set out in MCA 2005, s 2(1), and a functional test which is set out in s 3.

MCA 2005, s 2(1) states that 'a person lacks capacity in relation to a matter if at the material time he is unable to make a decision in relation to the matter because of an impairment of, or disturbance in, the functioning of the mind or brain'.

It does not matter whether the disturbance is permanent or temporary (s 2(2)).

The functional stage of the test is 'function specific', and it has to be demonstrated that the impairment or disturbance renders the person unable to make the decision in question for themselves. MCA 2005, s 3 sets out the criteria which must be satisfied to demonstrate that a person is unable to make a decision for themselves if they are unable:

(1) to understand the information relevant to the decision;
(2) to retain that information;
(3) to use or weigh that information as part of the process of making the decision; or
(4) to communicate their decision (whether by talking, using sign language or any other means).

MCA 2005, s 1 sets out the fundamental principles which underpin the Act and to which regard must be had in every decision made. These are:

(1) a person must be assumed to have capacity unless it is established that they lack capacity;
(2) a person is not to be treated as unable to make a decision unless all practicable steps to help them to do so have been taken without success;
(3) a person is not to be treated as unable to make a decision merely because they make an *unwise* decision;
(4) an act done, or decision made, under the I(PFD)A 1975 for or on behalf of a person who lacks capacity must be done or made, in their best interests;
(5) before the act is done, or the decision is made, regard must be had to whether the purpose for which it is needed can be as effectively achieved in a way that is less restrictive of the person's rights and freedom of action.

(See, further, Nasreen Pearce and Sue Jackson, *Urgent Applications in the Court of Protection* (Jordan Publishing Ltd, 2014).)

A protected person must have a litigation friend to conduct proceedings on their behalf (CPR r 21.1(1)).

A child must have a litigation friend to conduct proceedings unless the court has made an order under CPR r 21.2(3) permitting the child to conduct proceedings without a litigation friend (r 21.2(2)).

Where a claim is made by or on behalf of a child or a person who lacks capacity, or against a child or a person who lacks capacity, no settlement, compromise or payment and no acceptance of money paid into court will be regarded as valid unless it has been approved by the court (CPR r 21.10(1)). Where a settlement or compromise is reached for or on behalf of a child or person who lacks capacity, or against such a person before a claim is issued, the court procedure is for a claim to be made under Part 8 seeking the court's approval for the settlement or compromise (r 21.10(2)). For this purpose, it is advisable to prepare a case summary and submit a comprehensive opinion of counsel representing the child or patient setting out an analysis of the issues and the basis upon which it is suggested that the settlement is in the interest of the child or patient.

For a draft consent order setting out a compromise in favour of a claimant under disability, see Appendix A7.

12.7 SERVICE

The method of service set out in CPR r 6 and PD 6A must be followed. Service may be effected by:

(1) personal service, in accordance with r 6.5;
(2) first class post, document exchange or other form of service which provides for delivery on the next working day in accordance with PD 6A;
(3) leaving a document at a place specified in rr 6.7–6.10; or
(4) by fax or other means of electronic communication in accordance with PD 6A.

Service by the court is the general rule and service by first class post is the most favoured unless the parties are represented, in which case service is usually effected by document exchange.

CPR rr 6.30–6.33 and PD 6B apply to service outside the jurisdiction. Where a potential defendant is outside the jurisdiction, it should be ascertained whether that person has authorised or instructed another, for example, to accept service on his behalf within the jurisdiction. Where service outside the jurisdiction is necessary, application should be made for permission to do so (see CPR r 6.36 and PD 6B).

12.8 ACKNOWLEDGEMENT OF SERVICE AND DEFENDANT'S EVIDENCE

The provisions of CPR rr 8.3 and 8.5 apply to claims under the I(PFD)A 1975 (r 57.16(2)).

Defendants served within the jurisdiction must file and serve an acknowledgement of service within 21 days after service of the claim form and the supporting evidence (CPR r 57.16(4)). Any written statement in answer must also be filed within 21 days of service unless an extension of time has been agreed or granted by the court (CPR r 8.5(3) and (4)). If the claim form was served out of the jurisdiction under r 6.32 or r 6.33, the period for filing an acknowledgement of service and any written evidence is 7 days longer than the period specified in r 6.35 or PD 6B (r 57.16(4A)).

12.8.1 Position of personal representative who is a defendant

A personal representative who is a defendant and who wishes to remain neutral and abide by the decision of the court should state this in Section A of the acknowledgment of service form (CPR r 57.16(4), PD 57, para 15).

The personal representative must also file and serve a written statement which must set out the information required by CPR PD 57, para 16(1)–(4) (see below) within 21 days of service of the claim form on them.

The written evidence filed by a defendant who is a personal representative must state to the best of that person's ability:

(1) full details of the value of the deceased's net estate, as defined in I(PFD)A 1975, s 25(1);
(2) the person or classes of persons beneficially interested in the estate, and: (a) the names and (unless they are parties to the claim) addresses of all living beneficiaries; and (b) the value of their interests in the estate so far as they are known;

(3) whether any living beneficiary (and if so, naming them) is a child or a person who lacks capacity (within the meaning of the MCA 2005); and
(4) any facts which might affect the exercise of the court's powers under the I(PFD)A 1975.

Unlike the old provisions of Rules of the Supreme Court, Ord 99.5(2)(d), which required a personal representative to state facts known to them to the best of their knowledge and belief, CPR r 57.16(5) and PD 57, para 16, which are both mandatory, require that the evidence filed 'must state to the best of the person's ability' the facts which might affect the court's decision. It would seem, therefore, that the rule, combined with the Practice Direction, imposes on the personal representatives a duty to make inquiries and to provide such facts as may be relevant and which may affect the exercise of the court's discretion.

12.8.2 Other defendants

It is no longer possible for defendants to a claim under the I(PFD)A 1975 to wait until the first directions hearing to file their defence or their evidence. Under CPR r 57.16(4), all defendants are required to file and serve an acknowledgement of service and any written evidence within 21 days after service of the claim form. Their statements must also comply with r 8.5 unless the court otherwise directs under r 8.6(1). It is essential to comply with the timescales in the rules (rr 8.5 and 57.16(4)). Where for some reason there may be difficulty in complying with the time limits, an application should be made for permission to file and serve the evidence out of time or for an extension of time under PD 8, para 7.4. The parties may agree in writing to extend the time for filing and serving evidence under r 8.5(3) or r 8.5(5) (PD 8, para 7.5(1)). However, an agreement extending time for a defendant to file their evidence under r 8.5(3) or r 8.5(5) (PD 8, para 7.5(2)):

(1) must be filed by the defendant(s) at the same time as they file their acknowledgement of service; and
(2) must not extend by more than 14 days after the acknowledgement of service is filed by the defendant(s).

12.8.3 Claimant's reply

The claimant(s) may, within 14 days of service of the defendant's evidence on them, file and serve evidence in reply (CPR r 8.5(5) and (6)).

An agreement extending time for a claimant(s) to file evidence in reply under CPR r 8.5(5) must not extend time to more than 28 days after service of the defendant's evidence on the claimant (PD 8, para 7.5(3)).

12.9 INTERLOCUTORY MATTERS, DIRECTIONS AND CASE MANAGEMENT

The CPR apply to claims under the I(PFD)A 1975. Where there is a risk of the assets being dissipated, particularly where it is sought to apply for an order under ss 8–11, it is important to take steps to preserve the assets. This may be done by obtaining appropriate undertakings; registering the claim as a pending land action where appropriate; applying for an injunction forbidding any dealing with the property; and, in the case of liquid funds, seeking an order freezing such assets. (For an example where an interim order restraining any disposition of relevant properties which was the subject of the proceedings was made, see *Antonio v Williams* [2022] EWHC 2383 (Ch).)

At the directions hearing it will be necessary to consider matters such as disclosure; the need for an expert's report, for example a medical report; valuations; and accounts, as, for instance, in the case of a partnership or a private company.

A chronology, a summary of the facts, and a statement of issues should be provided to the court for the case management conference. It is always prudent to discuss beforehand the directions required and the reasons for them. Serious consideration should also be given to providing the court with a realistic time estimate. The availability of an interpreter, if needed, should be considered. When making a time estimate, account should be taken of the fact that the hearing takes longer when an interpreter is required or one of the parties is in person. Difficult issues – such as whether evidence by video link or other special measures are necessary, where, for example, a witness is vulnerable, or suffers from a disability, or a party is serving a long prison sentence, or is violent or lives overseas – should be addressed. The question of whether the final hearing should take place in public or continue to remain private or whether a reporting restrictions order may be necessary should also be considered (see below).

12.10 DISCLOSURE

The parties' duty to provide disclosure is set out in CPR PD 51U and also in *Chancery Guide 2022*, Chapter 7, which must be complied with. Breach of any of the duties will be treated as a serious matter by the court and may result in sanctions.

The court has wide powers to order disclosure both before and during the proceedings.

Pre-trial disclosure may be applied for under CPR r 31.16 against a defendant who is likely to be a party to proposed proceedings under the I(PFD)A 1975.

Disclosure may also be ordered under CPR r 25.1(1)(g) directing a party to provide information about the location of relevant property or assets or to provide information about relevant property or assets which are or may be the subject of an application for a freezing order. This may be relevant in relation to property or assets which form part or may form part of the net estate, for example property which may be the subject of applications under I(PFD)A 1975, ss 9–11 where it may be necessary to seek orders to bring the asset within the net estate or to freeze the assets so that they are available if needed when the substantive application is heard.

Practitioners should be aware of the provisions in CPR Part 31 and PD 31B which deal with disclosure of electronic material. The Practice Direction was introduced to regulate the approach practitioners should take when considering material relevant to a case which is stored electronically. In particular, it aims to focus the parties on the sources of electronic material and give guidance to those with less experience of dealing with such issues. This will apply to cases that are or likely to be allocated to the multi-track. Rule 31.5(4) requires that where the Electronic Documents Questionnaire has been exchanged, the questionnaire should be filed with the report required under r 31.5(3). This supports the Practice Direction that the questionnaire may be treated as a disclosed document.

The Electronic Documents Questionnaire is set out in the Schedule to PD 31B.

'Electronic document' means any document held in electronic form. It includes, for example, emails and other electronic communication such as text messages and voice mail, word processed documents and databases, and documents stored on portable devices such as memory sticks and mobile phones. In addition, it applies to documents that are readily accessible from computer systems and other electronic devices and media. It includes documents that are stored on servers and backup systems and documents that are deleted. It also includes Metadata and other embedded data which are not typically visible on screen or on a print out.

Where electronic documents exist or are likely to exist, PD 31B, para 9 requires the parties and their legal representatives to discuss the disclosure of electronic documents before the first case management conference, and in more complex cases to begin the discussion before proceedings are commenced. It also sets out the matters which should be included in the discussions. It is therefore advisable to have a joint meeting or conference to discuss how this type of disclosure should be provided so that the information is available at the case management hearing.

12.11 ATTEMPTS/OFFERS TO SETTLE

The CPR apply to claims under the I(PFD)A 1975 and therefore the court will be looking to deal with the case with the overriding objective in mind and in particular the matters set out in CPR r 1.1(2). The parties are required to help the court to further the overriding objective (r 1.3). This means encouraging the parties to make attempts to negotiate and settle the dispute between them by using an alternative dispute resolution procedure. Rule 1.4 also imposes a duty on the court when managing the case to 'encourage the parties to use an alternative dispute resolution procedure if the court considers that appropriate and facilitating the use of such procedure' and to help 'the parties to settle the whole or part of the case' (r 1.4(2)(e) and (f)).

The General Pre-Action Conduct and Protocols Practice Direction requires the parties to explore the option of resolving the dispute by meetings and negotiations and to consider the use of alternative dispute resolution, which includes mediation as a more suitable process than litigation.

Chancery Guide 2022, Chapter 10, paras 10.4 and 10.5 provide that in all cases, legal representatives should consider with their clients and the other parties concerned the possibility of attempting to resolve the dispute or particular issues by alternative dispute resolution and they should ensure that their clients are fully informed about points (a)–(e) of para 10.3. Alternative dispute resolution should be considered before issue and at all stages of a claim. At the case management conference, parties should be prepared for a discussion about what steps have already been taken to try to resolve the claim, and in appropriate cases the parties will be invited to consider whether their dispute, or particular issues in it, could be resolved by alternative dispute resolution, and when that should take place. See, also, the provisions relating to early neutral evaluation at paras 10.17–10.24 and Chancery financial dispute resolution at paras 10.25–10.33.

The General Pre-Action Conduct and Protocols Practice Direction now makes it clear that claims should not be issued prematurely when a settlement is being explored. If a resolution is being explored but there is concern about the s 4 time limit, attempts should be made to agree that the expiry of the time limit will not be raised as an issue. Alternatively, the claim may be issued and then application made as provided for in *Chancery Guide 2022*, Chapter 10, paras 10.6–10.12, for a stay of the proceedings for mediation/ alternative dispute resolution to continue. See, also, *WC v HC* [2022] EWFC 40 which, although a decision in matrimonial financial relief proceedings, held that sensible attempts to settle the case or an unreasonable failure to settle would be a powerful factor when considering costs. Peel J also stated (at [13]) that 'even in needs based claims no litigant is automatically insulated from costs penalties, notwithstanding the possible impact on the intended needs award'.

The General Pre-Action Conduct and Protocols Practice Direction should be used to obtain as much information as possible, including information on the deceased's assets and valuation to enable the parties to identify the issues on which the parties are agreed and those which remain in dispute. Where necessary, an application should be made for pre-action disclosure. If the issues cannot be narrowed before the proceedings are issued, then when all the evidence has been filed and disclosure and valuation have taken place, it is important to take stock, exchange position statements and arrange a joint issue resolution meeting or round table conference to attempt to iron out the outstanding issues.

The court may order early neutral evaluation at a case management conference if it deems this appropriate. This may be ordered even if one or more party does not consent (see, further, *Chancery Guide 2022*, Chapter 10).

12.11.1 CPR Part 36 offer

CPR Part 36 contains a carefully structured and prescriptive set of rules which deal with the procedure for the settlement of disputes and with specific consequences in those cases where an offer is not accepted and the offer fails to do better after a trial. It prescribes in some detail the manner in which an offer should be made and the consequences which flow from accepting or failing to accept it. The offer must comply with the provisions of r 36.5 and the Practice Directions to the rule, and must be made not less than 21 days before the trial date. The offer should be made in writing; state that it is intended to have the consequences of Part 36; specify the period of not less than 21 days within which the offer is to be accepted, which also means that it should be made at least 21 days before the final hearing; and whether it relates to the whole or part of the claim. A Part 36 offer may be made using Form N242A (PD 36, para 1.1; see, also, *Essex County Council v UBB Waste (Essex) Ltd (No 3)* [2020] EWHC 2387 (TCC)). Acceptance of the offer must be made in writing and served on the offeror and filed with the court where the case is proceeding (CPR r 36.11(1), PD 36, para 3.1). If the offer is accepted within the 21-day period or any other period agreed by the parties, the claimant will be entitled to the costs of the proceedings up to the date on which notice of acceptance was served and including pre-action costs (CPR r 36.13). For the costs consequences of unaccepted offers, see CPR rr 36.16–36.17.

If the claimant fails to obtain an award which is more advantageous than the defendant's offer, the court will, unless it considers it unjust to do so, order that the defendant is entitled to the costs from the date when the 21-day period expired with interest on those costs (CPR r 36.17(1)). In relation to any money or money claim or money element of a claim, 'more advantageous' means better in money terms by any sum however small, and 'at least as advantageous' will be construed accordingly (r 36.17(2)).

If the claimant has made an offer and the judgment against the defendant is at least as advantageous to the claimant as the proposal made in the Part 36 offer, the court will, unless it considers it unjust to do so, order that the claimant is entitled to interest on the whole or part of any sum of money (excluding interest) awarded at a rate not exceeding 10 per cent above the base rate for some or all of the period starting with the date on which the 21-day period expired, costs on an indemnity basis from the date on which the 21-day period expired and interest on those costs at a rate not exceeding 10 per cent above the base rate; and an additional sum not exceeding £75,000 based on the percentage of the award on the money claim and/or on the costs awarded by applying the prescribed percentage set out in the rule (CPR r 36.17(4)).

In considering whether it would be unjust to make the order, the court will take account of all the circumstances of the case including: (1) the terms of the Part 36 offer; (2) the stage in the proceedings when the offer is made, including how long before the trial; (3) the information available to the parties when the offer was made; (4) the conduct of the parties with regard to giving or refusing to give information for the purposes of enabling the offer to be made or evaluated; and (5) whether the offer was a genuine attempt to settle the proceedings (CPR r 36.17(4)). The court will also take into account all the matters set out in Part 44. For an example of how this may operate, see *Lilleyman v Lilleyman* [2012] EWHC 1056 (Ch), where, although the claimant succeeded in proving her claim and received a substantial award, the award was less advantageous than the offer that had been made by the defendants. The defendants sought their costs and interest which would have had the effect of reducing the award to the claimant, but not to the extent that it would have left the claimant inadequately provided for. An order for costs against her would not be considered unjust. However, the court also had regard to the defendant's conduct in challenging the claim and, in particular, raising irrelevant issues which had prolonged the case.

In *Carver v BAA* [2008] EWCA Civ 412, [2009] 1 WLR 113, it was held that in determining whether the judgment was more advantageous to the claimant than the Part 36 offer, the court should take into account all aspects of the case including emotional distress. In *Gibbon v Manchester City Council and Another Appeal* [2010] EWCA Civ 726, [2010] 1 WLR 2081, the Court of Appeal took the view that obtaining judgment for an amount greater than a CPR Part 36 offer is likely to outweigh all other factors. In considering the offer made, a party should evaluate it by reference to an assessment of their case including the risk of incurring irrecoverable costs.

In *Gibbon v Manchester City Council and Another*, the Court of Appeal also held that:

- although basic concepts of offer and acceptance clearly underpinned CPR Part 36, it should not be understood as incorporating all the rules of law governing the formation of contracts; rather it should be read and understood according to its terms without importing other rules derived from the general law, save where that was clearly intended. Moore-Bick LJ said that certainty was as much to be commended in procedural as in substantive law, especially, perhaps, in a procedural code which had to be understood and followed by ordinary citizens who wished to conduct their own litigation. Part 36 had been drafted with those considerations in mind and was to be read and understood according to its terms without importing other rules derived from the general law, save where that was clearly intended;

- the offer remains in force until it is withdrawn by service of a notice of withdrawal. Part 36 puts the onus on the maker of the offer to withdraw any existing offer if they do not wish it to be available for acceptance. There is no concept of implied withdrawal. If the maker of the offer wishes to withdraw the offer they must be do so expressly in writing. Although no particular form of notice is required, in order to avoid uncertainty the notice should include a clear reference to the date on which the offer was made and its terms. It should clearly express that the offer has been withdrawn. The offer may be accepted even though a different offer or offers has/have been made by the offeror. If the offeror varies the terms of the original offer, it will continue to remain valid as from the date on which it was originally made (see, also, *C v D* [2011] EWCA Civ 646 and *Howell v Lees-Millais* [2011] EWCA Civ 786).

12.11.2 *Calderbank* offers

A *Calderbank* offer is an offer made in a letter with a view to settling the case. The offer letter is marked 'without prejudice save as to costs'. Sometimes, it is marked 'without prejudice', but clearly stated to be subject to an express reservation of the right to refer to it on the issue of costs. The effect of the order is that if the court's order is more favourable to the party who made the offer, the party to whom the offer is made stands the risk of order for costs being made against them.

Although CPR Part 36 procedure has largely superseded the *Calderbank* offer letter, it still remains preserved, and if an offer is made in such a letter, it will be taken into account when the court considers the issue of costs, but the consequences set out in r 36 will not necessarily follow. It is thus preferable, if the decision is taken to make an offer, to use the Part 36 procedure.

12.12 HEARING

Before the final hearing, the case will be listed for a case management conference. In preparation for that hearing, every effort should be made to ensure that the parties have complied with any directions that the court has previously given. The provisions of CPR Part 29 and PD 29 apply to this hearing as they do to other multi-track cases. The court will review the steps taken by the parties in preparation for the case; decide and give directions to progress the case in accordance with the overriding objective; and ensure as far as it can that all agreements between the parties about the matters in issue and the conduct of the claim have been made. Rule 29.3(2) provides that where a party is legally represented, a representative who is familiar with the case and has sufficient authority to deal with any issues that are likely to arise must attend the case management conference. PD 29, para 5.5(2) requires that the person who attends the hearing should be someone who is personally involved in the conduct of the case and who has authority and information to deal with any matter which may reasonably be expected to be dealt with at such a hearing, including the fixing of the timetable, the identification of issues and matters of evidence. If the person attending the case management conference fails to deal with issues which arise during the hearing or where the inadequacy of that person's instructions leads to an adjournment, the 'court will expect to make a wasted cost order' (PD 29, para 5.2(3)). It is therefore essential that the person who is to attend the hearing is identified in good time so that the person can familiarise themselves with the case and spend time on preparing for the case management conference and, in particular, to consider the topics which the court is likely to raise, which may include:

(1) whether the claim sets out clearly the claim and the order sought;
(2) whether any amendments need to be made to the claim or the evidence filed to support the claim;
(3) whether all the appropriate persons who might be affected by the claim have been made parties to the claim or notified of it so that they can apply to be joined;
(4) whether any further disclosure of documents is necessary;
(5) what expert evidence is reasonably required in accordance with r 35.1, and how and when that evidence should be obtained and disclosed. Expert evidence is more likely to be needed to value property or other assets. It is therefore important that if expert evidence is considered to be necessary, effort is made to agree a joint expert and a letter of instructions for approval by the court. Where an expert has been instructed and has reported, but further questions need to be put to them to clarify issues, how this should be achieved. Practitioners should also consider whether the expert will be required to attend the final hearing or whether their report can be agreed;
(6) the number of witnesses who will be giving oral evidence and therefore the estimated time for the hearing. On this issue, the court will be assisted by a case summary which should set out a brief chronology; the issues which are agreed and those which remain in dispute; and what efforts, if any, have been made to resolve the issues by agreement and through mediation or alternative dispute resolution;

(7) most importantly, it is essential now to provide a costs budget in an approved form under r 3.12. Rule 3.13 requires all parties except litigants in person to file and exchange costs budgets as required by the rules or directed by the court and, in any event, 7 days before the case management conference. Unless the court otherwise directs, failure to file a costs budget will result in the defaulting party to be deemed to have filed a budget comprising only 'the applicable court fees' (r 3.14).

CPR r 39.2 provides that in general a hearing is to be in public, but r 39.2(3) makes provision for a hearing to be conducted in private only if the court is satisfied of one or more of the matters set out in r 39.2(3) and that it is necessary to sit in private to secure the proper administration of justice. The rule now (amended in 2019) clearly sets out that the parties cannot agree that the hearing should take place in private without the court considering whether any one or more of the factors set out in r 39.2(3) are satisfied. The rule was amended to reflect the shift across all jurisdictions for the importance of the principle of open justice, i.e. that justice must be seen to be done.

12.13 ENDORSEMENT OF MEMORANDUM ON GRANT

If the court makes an order under the I(PFD)A 1975, the original grant (together with a sealed copy of the order) must be sent to the Principal Registry of the Family Division for a memorandum of the order to be endorsed on or permanently annexed to the grant in accordance with s 19(3) (CPR PD 57, para 18.2).

In the Family Division, the practice has always been for memoranda of all consent orders in proceedings under the I(PFD)A 1975 to be endorsed on the probate or letters of administration, whether or not the parties are *sui juris*. The practice in the Chancery Division was otherwise. The differences in practice between the two Divisions has been resolved by PD 57, para 18.3, which provides that every final order embodying terms of compromise made in proceedings under the Act whether made with or without a hearing must contain a direction that a memorandum of the order shall be endorsed on, or permanently annexed to, the probate or letters of administration, and a copy thereof shall be sent to the Principal Registry of the Family Division with the relevant grant of probate or letters of administration for endorsement.

12.14 DRAWING UP AND SERVICE OF ORDERS

The provision for drawing up and service of orders made in the Chancery Division is set out in CPR Part 40 and PD 40B, but pursuant to CPR r 57.15(2), the FPR 2010 relating to the drawing and service of orders apply to proceedings brought in the Family Division of the High Court instead of the provisions of CPR Part 40 and its Practice Direction.

12.15 SUBSEQUENT APPLICATIONS

Any subsequent application under the I(PFD)A 1975, for example for a variation of an order, whether made by the claimant or any other party, must be made by issuing an application notice in accordance with CPR Part 23.

The application notice must set out the order(s) sought and the grounds for seeking the order(s). If the applicant intends to rely on matters set out in the notice as evidence, it must be verified by a statement of truth. Where the information set out in the notice of application is inadequate and it is intended to particularise the matters relied on more fully, the notice must be supported by a written statement or affidavit. The statement or affidavit in support must set out in detail the grounds relied on for seeking the order(s) applied for and any other relevant matter. Thereafter, the procedure which applies to the application is the same as for a substantive application under the I(PFD)A 1975.

12.15.1 Procedural guide

Who may apply?	The spouse of the deceased, which includes the surviving spouse of marriage between same sex couples	I(PFD)A 1975, s 1(1)(a) as amended
	The registered civil partner of the deceased, which includes opposite sex civil partners	I(PFD)A 1975, s 1(1)(a); CPA 2004, s 71, Sch 4 as amended
	The former spouse of the deceased who has not remarried	I(PFD)A 1975, s 1(1)(b)
	The former civil partner of the deceased who has not formed a subsequent civil partnership	I(PFD)A 1975, s 1(1)(b); CPA 2004, s 71, Sch 4
	A cohabitant of the deceased	I(PFD)A 1975, s 1(1)(ba), s 1(1A) as amended by the Law Reform (Succession) Act 1995
	A person who lived in the same household as the deceased as their civil partner	I(PFD)A 1975, s 1(1)(ba), s 1(1B); CPA 2004, s 71, Sch 4
	A child of the deceased	I(PFD)A 1975, s 1(1)(c)
	Any person who was treated as a child of the family whether within a marriage or in a civil partnership	I(PFD)A 1975, s 1(1)(d)
	Any other person who immediately before the death of the deceased was being maintained by the deceased	I(PFD)A 1975, s 1; CPA 2004
Which court?	High Court (Chancery (Business and Property Courts – Property, Trusts and Probate List) or Family Division) or county court	CPR r 57.15; County Courts Act 1984, s 25
	Masters/District judges (including district judges of the Principal Registry of the Family Division) have jurisdiction to hear such applications	CPR r 57.15; I(PFD)A 1975, s 22; PD of 22 April 1999

Application	*High Court/county court* By Part 8 Claim Form (N208) which should be entitled: 'In the estate of ... (*name of deceased)* (deceased)' and 'In the matter of I(PFD)A 1975'	CPR rr 57.16, 8.2, PD 8B
Time limit	The claim must be issued before or within 6 months of the date on which representation is taken out (unless extended by the court). Application to extend the time limit must be included in the claim form Note, however, that nothing prevents proceedings to be issued before a grant and this should be done to avoid having to apply for an extension	I(PFD)A 1975, s 4 as amended by Inheritance and Trustees' Powers Act 2014, s 6 (Sch 2)
Documents	The claimant(s) must file with the claim form a witness statement/ affidavit in support exhibiting an official copy of the grant of representation and of every testamentary document admitted to proof. Where no grant has been obtained, the witness statement should set out the information required under CPR r 57.16(3A) and apply for directions under r 57.16(3B)	CPR rr 57.16(3), 8.5(1), (2)
Defendants	Personal representatives Beneficiaries Other persons affected by the claim Any other person directed by the court to be added If a grant has not as yet been obtained, there is no need to name a defendant	CPR r 19.7 CPR r 57.16(3A)

Service	The claim form must be served within 4 months of the date of issue	
	Extension of time must be sought under CPR r 7.6	
	Acknowledgement of service must be filed within 21 days of service of the claim form and served on the claimant and other parties if served within the jurisdiction	
	If served outside the jurisdiction under CPR r 6.32 or r 33 the acknowledgement of service and statement in support is 7 days longer	CPR rr 57.16(4), 57.16(4A)
	For service on children and patients, see CPR r 6.13	
	Otherwise, in accordance with CPR r 57.16(4) and (4A)	CPR r 10.3(2)
Statement/ Affidavit in answer	Must be filed by the personal representatives within 21 days of service of the claim form (it should include the matters set out in CPR PD 57, para 16)	CPR r 57.16(4), (5), PD 57, para 16
	May be filed by other defendants within 21 days after service of the claim form	CPR r 57.16(4)
Service of answer	Every defendant who files any written evidence within 21 days in answer must serve a copy on the claimant and every other defendant (who is not represented by the same solicitor)	CPR r 57.16(4)
Reply	A claimant(s) may serve a statement in reply on all other parties within 14 days of service of the defendant's evidence on them	CPR r 8.5(5), (6)

Directions/case management conference pretrial hearing	At the same time as issuing the claim form a directions hearing may be requested. Where no grant has as yet been obtained when the claim is issued, consider applying for directions under CPR r 57.16(3B). The court may also on its own initiative give directions in such a case	CPR PD 8, paras 6.1–6.4
	The court will in any event give directions after the defendant has filed the acknowledgement of service or after the time for filing it has expired	
	Parties must complete the listing questionnaire in Form N170 and provide an estimate of costs following which the court will consider whether to hold a pre-trial review and set a timetable and fix the date for the trial	CPR rr 29.6–29.8
Fee payable	High Court: £528	Civil Proceedings Fees Order 2008, fee 1.5
	County court: £355	Civil Proceedings Fees Order 2008, fee 1.5
Order	Periodical payments	I(PFD)A 1975, s 2(1)(a)
	Lump sum	I(PFD)A 1975, s 2(1)(b)
	Transfer of property	I(PFD)A 1975, s 2(1)(c)
	Settlement of property	I(PFD)A 1975, s 2(1)(d)
	Acquisition, transfer and settlement of property	I(PFD)A 1975, s 2(1)(e)
	Variation of ante-nuptial and post-nuptial settlement	I(PFD)A 1975, s 2(1)(f)
	Variation or discharge of secured periodical payments	I(PFD)A 1975, s 16
	Variation or revocation of maintenance agreements	I(PFD)A 1975, s 17
	Order setting aside disposition intended to defeat a claim under the I(PFD)A 1975	I(PFD)A 1975, ss 10, 11
	Treatment of deceased's former beneficial interest in joint property as part of their estate and not passing by survivorship	I(PFD)A 1975, s 9
	Interim order	I(PFD)A 1975, s 5
	Consequential orders	I(PFD)A 1975, s 2(4)

Chapter 13

Appeals

13.1 INTRODUCTION

CPR Part 52 and PD 52 apply to all appeals, including those under the I(PFD)A 1975, and provide a uniform procedure for appeals in the county courts, the High Court and the Court of Appeal. The CPR are amended periodically and care should be taken to ensure that the correct rules are followed. It is important that the procedure laid down in the rules and Practice Directions is followed.

This chapter is not intended to provide a detailed commentary on the rules, Practice Directions and case studies. It sets out just the bare bones of the matters that should not be ignored.

13.2 PERMISSION TO APPEAL

Access to Justice Act 1999, s 54 provides that any right of appeal from the county court or the High Court and the Court of Appeal may be exercised only with permission.

CPR r 52.3(1) provides that permission to appeal from the decision of a judge in the county court or the High Court is required in all cases.

An application for permission to appeal should be made orally to the trial judge at the conclusion of the final hearing. If the application is refused or if the application is made subsequently, it should be made to the appeal court in the notice of appeal. If the application for permission is not made at the conclusion of the hearing, the appellant should not seek to apply for leave in the lower court (CPR PD 52A, para 4.1; see, also, para 4.7 and PD 52C, paras 15 and 16 in relation to appeal to the Court of Appeal). When applying for permission to appeal, a reason or explanation for seeking permission to appeal is required.

Useful guidance on the correct procedure for seeking permission to appeal is set out in *McDonald v Rose* [2019] EWCA Civ 4 as follows:

> THE CORRECT PROCEDURE
>
> 21. It is the experience of the Court that the effect of the rules, as expounded in the authorities referred to above, is often not properly understood by would-be appellants. We think there is value in our summarising in this judgment the effect of those authorities and the procedure that ought to be followed in consequence by parties wishing to seek permission to appeal from the lower court (which is good practice though not mandatory). We would set the position out as follows:
>
> (1) The date of the decision for the purposes of CPR 52.12 is the date of the hearing at which the decision is given, which may be *ex tempore* or by the formal hand-down of a reserved judgment: see *Sayers v Clarke* and *Owusu v Jackson*. We call this the decision hearing.
>
> (2) A party who wishes to apply to the lower court for permission to appeal should normally do so at the decision hearing itself. In the case of a formal hand-down where counsel have been excused from attendance that can be done by applying in writing prior to the hearing. The judge will usually be able to give his or her decision at the hearing, but there may be occasions where further submissions and/or time for reflection are required, in which case the permission decision may post-date the decision hearing.
>
> (3) If a party is not ready to make an application at the decision hearing it is necessary to ask for the hearing to be formally adjourned in order to give them more time to do so: *Jackson v Marina Homes*. The judge, if he or she agrees to the adjournment, will no doubt set a timetable for written submissions and will normally decide the question on the papers without the need for a further hearing. As long as the decision hearing has been formally adjourned, any such application can be treated as having been made 'at' it for the purpose of CPR 52.3 (2) (a). We wish to say, however, that we do not believe that such adjournments should in the generality of cases be necessary. Where a reserved judgment has been pre-circulated in draft in sufficient time parties should normally be in a position to decide prior to the hand-down hearing whether they wish to seek permission to appeal, and to formulate grounds and such supporting submissions as may be necessary; and that will often be so even where there has been an *ex tempore* judgment. Putting off the application will increase delay and create a risk of procedural complications. But we accept that it will nevertheless sometimes be justified.
>
> (4) If no permission application is made at the original decision hearing, and there has been no adjournment, the lower court is no longer seized of the matter and cannot consider any retrospective application for permission to appeal: *Lisle-Mainwaring*.
>
> (5) Whenever a party seeks an adjournment of the decision hearing as per (3) above they should *also* seek an extension of time for filing the appellant's notice, otherwise they risk running out of time before the permission decision is made. The 21 days continue to run from the decision date, and

an adjournment of the decision hearing does not automatically extend time: *Hysaj*. It is worth noting that an application by a party for more time to make a permission application is not the only situation where an extension of time for filing the appellant's notice may be required. It will be required in any situation where a permission decision is not made at the decision hearing. In particular, it may be that the judge wants more time to consider (see (2) above): unless it is clear that he or she will give their decision comfortably within the 21 days an extension will be required so as to ensure that time does not expire before they have done so. In such a case it is important that the judge, as well as the parties, is alert to the problem.

(6) As to the length of any extension, Brooke LJ says in *Jackson v Marina Homes* (para. 8) that it should normally be until 21 days after the permission decision. However, the judge should consider whether a period of that length is really necessary in the particular case: it may be reasonable to expect the party to be able to file their notice more promptly once they know whether they have permission.

22. We should add for completeness that the authorities summarised above do not cover a third situation, namely where the judge announces his or her decision, with reasons to follow. That too will start time running, but it should be standard practice, unless there are very unusual circumstances, for the Court to adjourn the decision hearing and extend time under CPR 52.12 (2) (a) until a specified period, normally 21 days, after the reasons are promulgated.

Permission to appeal will be given only where (CPR r 52.6):

(1) the court considers that the appeal would have a real prospect of success; or
(2) there is some other compelling reason why the appeal should be heard.

'Real prospect of success' means a realistic as opposed to a fanciful prospect (see *Swain v Hillman* [2001] 1 All ER 91 and *Tanfern Limited v Cameron-MacDonald (Practice Note)* [2000] 1 WLR 131).

The respondent should not make any submissions on the merits of the application unless requested to do so. (See, further, *Jolly v Jay* [2002] EWCA Civ 277 for guidance on the role of the respondent when permission to appeal is sought.)

If permission to appeal is sought from the appeal court other than the Court of Appeal, the application will be dealt with initially without a hearing. If the application is refused, the person seeking permission may request the decision to be reconsidered at an oral hearing (CPR r 52.4(2)), but note that where permission to appeal without a hearing is refused, the appeal court may, if it considers that the application is totally without merit, make an order that the person seeking permission may not request the decision to be reconsidered at an oral hearing (r 52.4(3)).

Where the application for permission to appeal is made to the Court of Appeal, the Court of Appeal will determine the application on paper. However, the judge considering the application on paper may direct that the application should be determined at an oral hearing and more particularly if the judge is of the opinion that the application cannot be fairly determined on paper without an oral hearing. Where an oral hearing is directed, the court may in particular identify any issue or issues on which the party seeking permission should specifically focus at the oral hearing and direct that the respondent to the appeal serve and file written submission and to attend the oral hearing (CPR r 52.5).

An order giving permission to appeal may limit the issues to be heard and be made subject to conditions, including the provision for security of the costs of an appeal.

13.3 ROUTE OF APPEAL

CPR PD 52A, para 3.3 sets out the court to which an appeal should be made (subject to obtaining any necessary permission) as follows:

Decision of	Appeal made to
District judge of a county court	Circuit Judge
Master or district judge of the High Court	High Court
Circuit Judge	High Court
High Court Judge	Court of Appeal

13.4 TIME LIMITS

The appellant(s) must file their notice of appeal at the Court of Appeal within 21 days of the date of the decision of the lower court, not the date on which the order was drawn up, unless such period has been extended by direction of the lower court. An application for an extension of time should be made at the final hearing, to the trial judge unless the hearing has been adjourned pursuant to PD 52A, para 4.1 (CPR r 52.12(2), PD 52A, para 4.1).

13.5 STAY OF EXECUTION

Unless the appeal court or the lower court otherwise orders a stay, an appeal does not operate as a stay of any order made by the lower court. An application for a stay, if required, should be made at the conclusion of the final hearing, to the trial judge, at the same time as the application for permission to appeal is made (CPR r 52.16). If an application for a stay is not made at the conclusion of the hearing, or is made but refused, a separate application for a stay, supported by evidence, may be made to the appeal court. A court will not grant a stay unless it is satisfied by cogent, full and frank evidence that there is a real risk of injustice to one or more of the parties if it grants or refuses a stay, or there has been a material change in the circumstances since the application for the stay was refused, or that the original refusal was based on a mistake (see *Hall v Elia* [2016] EWHC 1023 (Ch)).

13.6 GROUNDS OF APPEAL

An appeal under the I(PFD)A 1975 may relate to the court's decision on whether or not reasonable financial provision for the claimant was made in the will, and if that has been found proved on the provision made in the order for one or more of the orders the court could have made under I(PFD)A 1975, s 2. For examples of appeals in proceedings under the I(PFD)A 1975 and the approach of the Court of Appeal and the Supreme Court, see *Ilott v Mitson* [2011] EWCA 346, [2015] EWCA Civ 797, *Ilott v The Blue Cross and Others* [2017] UKSC 17, *Iqbal v Ahmed* [2011] EWCA Civ 900, [2012] 1 FLR 31 and *Musa v Holliday* [2012] EWCA Civ 1268.

An appeal will be allowed where the decision of the lower court was (CPR r 52.21(3)):

(1) wrong; or
(2) unjust because of a serious procedural or other irregularity in the proceedings in the lower court.

The effect of point (1) (above) is that the appellant has to satisfy the appeal court that the decision of the lower court was:

(1) against the weight of evidence;
(2) wrong in law; or
(3) an error in the exercise of the court's discretion.

Where an appeal is based on the argument that the decision of the lower court was against the weight of the evidence, the decision on appeal depends on the judge's assessment of the evidence of witnesses, their reliability and credibility; and it is only in exceptional circumstances that such an appeal will succeed.

In an appeal based on a point of law, it must be shown that the judge was plainly wrong on a point of law which was crucial to the decision. For examples, see *Moody v Stevenson* [1992] Ch 486 and *Re Besterman (Deceased), Besterman v Grusin* [1984] Ch 458. In *Ilott v The Blue Cross and Others* [2017] UKSC 17, the

Supreme Court has said that the order made by a judge at first instance ought to be upset only if he has erred in principle or in law, 'An appellate court will be slow to interfere and should never do so simply on the grounds that its judge(s) would have been inclined, if sitting at first instance, to have reached a different conclusion' (at [24]). See, also, *Musa v Holliday* [2012] EWCA Civ 1268, [2013] 1 FLR 806.

To succeed in an appeal based on an erroneous exercise of discretion, the appellant will have to show that the judge had misunderstood the facts; had taken account of irrelevant material; had failed to exercise their discretion; had made a decision that no reasonable judge could have made; or that there was no material before the court to justify the decision the judge took. It has been stated that it must be shown that the decision was plainly wrong since it 'was outside the ambit within which a reasonable disagreement is possible' (see *G v G (Minors)* [1985] 1 WLR 647). See, also, *AEI Ltd v PPL* [1999] 1 WLR 1507, where it was stated:

> Before the court can interfere it must be shown that the judge has either erred in principle in his approach or has left out of account or has taken into account some feature that he should, or should not, have considered, or that his decision was plainly wrong because the court is forced to the conclusion that he has not balanced the various factors fairly in the scale.

In cases under the I(PFD)A 1975, where the judge has clearly gone beyond the s 3 criteria or given it an interpretation which cannot be justified and has re-written the deceased's will, it could be said that the judge has both erred in law and failed to exercise their discretion (see *Barrass v Harding* [2001] 1 FLR 138). In general, where the challenge relates to the exercise of the court's discretion the approach which the appeal court will adopt is best explained by referring to what the Supreme Court stated in *Illot v The Blue Cross and Others* [2017] UKSC 17 when dealing with the two-stage process which the court considers in a claim under the Act:

> 23. It has become conventional to treat the consideration of a claim under the 1975 Act as a two-stage process, viz (1) has there been a failure to make reasonable financial provision and if so (2) what order ought to be made? That approach is founded to an extent on the terms of the Act, for it addresses the two questions successively in, first, section 1(1) and 1(2) and, second, section 2. In re Coventry at 487 Goff LJ referred to these as distinct questions, and indeed described the first as one of value judgment and the second as one of discretion. However, there is in most cases a very large degree of overlap between the two stages. Although section 2 does not in terms enjoin the court, if it has determined that the will or intestacy does not make reasonable financial provision for the claimant, to tailor its order to what is in all the circumstances reasonable, this is clearly the objective. Section 3(1) of the Act, in introducing the factors to be considered by the court, makes them applicable equally to both stages. Thus the two questions will usually become: (1) did the will/intestacy make reasonable

financial provision for the claimant and (2) if not, what reasonable financial provision ought now to be made for him?

24. There may be some cases in which it will be convenient to separate these questions, particularly if there is an issue whether there was any occasion for the deceased to make any provision for the claimant. But in many cases, exactly the same conclusions will both answer the question whether reasonable financial provision has been made for the claimant and identify what that financial provision should be. In particular, questions arising from the relationship between the deceased and the claimant, questions relating to the needs of the claimant, and issues concerning the competing claims of others, are all equally applicable to both matters. The Act plainly requires a broad brush approach from the judge to very variable personal and family circumstances. There can be nothing wrong, in such cases, with the judge simply setting out the facts as he finds them and then addressing both questions arising under the Act without repeating them. Nor should there normally be any occasion for a split hearing. Moreover, Goff LJ's observations ought not to be thought to mean that the approach of an appeal court should differ as between the two parts of the process. Whether best described as a value judgment or as a discretion (and the former is preferable), both stages of the process are highly individual in every case. The order made by the judge ought to be upset only if he has erred in principle or in law. An appellate court will be very slow to interfere and should never do so simply on the grounds that its judge(s) would have been inclined, if sitting at first instance, to have reached a different conclusion. The well-known observations of Lord Hoffmann in *Piglowska v Piglowski* [1999] 1 WLR 1360 esp at 1373–1374 are directly in point. It is to 'kill the parties with kindness' to permit marginal appeals in cases which are essentially individual value judgments such as those under the 1975 Act should be. The present case, as it happens, is an example of much to be regretted prolongation, and presumably expensive prolongation, of the forensic process.

13.7 PROCEDURE

13.7.1 Appellant's notice

Where the appellant seeks permission from the appeal court, the permission must be requested in the appellant's notice in Form N161 (CPR r 52.12(1), PD 52A, para 4.2). The time allowed for filing the notice is 21 days after the date of the decision of the lower court. The filing of the notice should not be delayed until the appellant has received a copy of the transcript of the judgment under appeal. The documents that should be filed with the appeal notice are set out in PD 52B, para 4.2, and para 6.4 sets out a list of documents that should be included in the appeal bundle to be filed when issuing the appeal proceedings or as soon as practicable thereafter. If permission to appeal is sought from the Court of Appeal, the documents set out in PD 52C, para 3 should be filed with the appeal notice. Note also that within 14 days of filing the appeal notice the appellant is required to lodge a core bundle prepared in accordance with PD 52C, para 27 (CPR

PD 52C, para 14). Where the time for filing the notice of appeal has expired, the appellant should file his notice and include in it an application for permission to appeal (if required), and for an extension of time. The appellant's notice must set out the reasons for the delay and the steps taken prior to the application being made (PD 52C, para 4). If the notice includes an application for permission to appeal, the respondent has the right to be heard. The respondent must: (1) be served with a copy of any evidence filed in support of the application; and (2) inform the court in writing of any objections to the grant of the extension of time within 7 days of being served with the appellant's notice. An application for extension of time will be dealt with without an oral hearing unless the court directs otherwise (CPR PD 52C, para 4(3)(c)).

13.7.2 Amendment of appeal notice

An appeal may be amended only with the permission of the court. An application to amend and any opposition to it will normally be dealt with at the hearing, unless such a course would cause unnecessary expense or delay (CPR r 52.17). If that is likely to be the case, the court should be informed and a request made for the application for the amendment to be heard separately and before the substantive hearing (CPR PD 52C, para 30).

13.7.3 Respondent's notice

The respondent may file and serve a respondent's notice. Unless the respondent wishes to cross appeal or wishes to support the lower court's decision for reasons other than those given in the lower court, they do not need to file a notice. A respondent who wishes to vary the order of the lower court in any way must appeal, and permission will be required on the same basis as for an appellant. If the respondent fails to do so, they will not be able to rely on any reason not relied on in the lower court unless the appeal court gives them permission to do. The respondent's notice must be filed within 14 days unless otherwise directed (CPR r 52.13) and a copy sent to the appellant as soon as practicable and, in any event, within 7 days thereafter (r 52.13(6)). Where an extension of time is required, the extension must be sought in the respondent's notice and reasons given for the delay. The respondent's notice of appeal must be accompanied by a skeleton argument and must serve the same on the appellant. If it is not filed with the notice, the skeleton argument must be filed and sent to the appellant within 14 days of the filing of the notice (PD 52C, para 9). If the respondent does not file a respondent's notice, the skeleton argument opposing the appellant's appeal must be filed and sent to the appellant at least 7 days before the appeal hearing. (See, further, Part 1 of the Timetable under PD 52C, para 21 in relation to appeals to the Court of Appeal. As to the requirements of skeleton arguments, see CPR PD 52A, Section V and PD 52C, para 31.)

The matters set out in this chapter are a brief outline of the appeal process. Practitioners and those wishing to appeal are advised to refer to CPR r 52 and the Practice Directions which supplement that rule.

13.8 PROCEDURAL TABLES

Appeal from a county court judge or High Court to the Court of Appeal

Who may appeal?	Any party to the proceedings with permission	Senior Courts Act 1981, s 16 County Courts Act 1984, s 77
Permission to appeal	Application should be made to the trial judge Application should be made to the Court of Appeal if leave is either not made or, if made, is refused	CPR r 52.3(2), (3) CPR PD 52A, paras 4.1, 4.7 PD 52C, paras 15, 16
	Permission to appeal is applied for in the notice of appeal together with an appeal bundle skeleton argument, copy of the transcript of the judgment and the documents set out in CPR PD 52C, para 3	CPR PD 52C, para 3 Civil Proceedings Fees Order 2008 (CPFO 2008), art 13.1(a)
	Court considers the application without a hearing unless a hearing is requested. Respondent to the appeal is notified but does not need to attend unless requested to do so by the court	CPR r 52.5, PD 52C, para 15
Fee payable	£569 on application for permission or extension of time £1,292 if permission is not required £1,292 on filing of appeal questionnaire £569 on filing of respondent's notice £569 on filing of application notice	CPFO 2008, art 13.1
Procedure on appeal	Notice of appeal in Form N161 should be filed within 21 days of the order appealed. It must be served not later than 7 days after filing the notice of appeal. The appellant must file with the notice the documents set out in the PDs	CPR r 52.12 CPR PD 52A, para 4.1, PD 52B, paras 4.2, 6.4, PD 52C, paras 3.14, 27

Service	If permission to appeal is granted the appellant must serve on each respondent a copy of the bundle of documents within 7 days of permission being granted	CPR PD 52C, para 4
Documents to be lodged	Appellant must lodge at the Civil Appeal Registry with his notice: (a) a copy of his notice for each respondent and two further copies for the court (b) a copy of the skeleton argument (c) a sealed copy of the order being appealed with the order giving or refusing permission to appeal together with reasons for the same (d) witness statements and any sworn statements and transcript of judgment or a note of the judgment (e) an appeal bundle (f) any other documents (g) a bundle of authorities must be filed 7 days before the hearing which must comply with the PD	CPR PD 52C, paras 3, 21, 29
Respondent's notice	Respondent may file a notice Respondent must file a notice if they seek to cross appeal or seek to oppose or uphold the decision of the lower court for different reasons within 14 days of service of the notice of appeal and serve it as soon as practicable and in any event within 7 days of filing his notice	CPR r 52.13 CPR PD 52C, paras 8–10, 21
Fee on cross appeal	£569 (see, also, above)	CPFO 2008, art 13.2
Documents to be filed by the respondent	The same as that by the appellant (see above)	

Powers of the Court of Appeal	To affirm set aside or vary any order or judgment made or given by the lower court To refer any claim or issue for determination by the lower court To receive fresh evidence To make any order which the lower court could have made To order a retrial	CPR r 52.20
Further appeal	To the Supreme Court with permission of the Court of Appeal or the Supreme Court if leave is refused by the Court of Appeal	Constitutional Reform Act 2005, s 40(2) Supreme Court Rules 2009 (SCR 2009), r 11(1)

Appeal to the Supreme Court

Permission to appeal is required to appeal from the decision of the Court of Appeal	If an appeal from the Court of Appeal from that court. If permission is refused, then from the Supreme Court with a fee of £1,000	SCR 2009, rr 10, 11 Supreme Court Fees Order 2009 (SCFO 2009), fee 1.1
Time limit	Within 28 days of the decision	SCR 2009, r 11
Documents for permission	Four copies of: (a) application for permission to appeal (b) copy of the order appealed from (c) copy of order refusing permission to appeal (d) transcript of judgment (e) any other orders and judgments given by the court (f) transcript of any unreported authorities (g) a chronology	SCR 2009, rr 11, 14 Supreme Court PD 3.2.1, PD 7

Respondent's objections	Respondent must, within 14 days of being served with the application for permission, file his notice of objection. A fee of £160 is payable	SCR 2009, r 13 Supreme Court PD 3.1.8–3.1.10, PD 7, Form 3 Fee 1.2
Fee for application for permission Fee for filing of notice of objection Fee for filing notice of appeal Fee for filing an acknowledgement of service Fee for filing of relevant statement of facts	£1,000 £160 £1,600 £320 £4,820	SCFO 2009, fee 1.1 SCFO 2009, fee 1.2 SCFO 2009, fee 2.2 SCFO 2009, fee 2.4 SCFO 2009, fee 2.5
Procedure on application for permission	Court will deal with application without a hearing and may: – grant or refuse permission – invite parties to make written submissions within 14 days – direct an oral hearing	SCR 2009, r 16 Supreme Court PD 3.3.1–3.4.8
Procedure if permission is granted	(a) the application for permission will stand as notice of appeal (b) the grounds will be those on which permission was granted and (c) within 14 days of the permission being granted the appellant must file notice of intention to proceed	SCR 2009, r 18
Fee on filing of notice of intention to proceed	£800	SCFO 2009, fee 2.1
Procedure where permission is not required	Notice of appeal must be filed within 42 days of the order appealed from with a copy of the order, order granting permission and fee of £1,600	SCR 2009, r 19 Supreme Court PD 4, PD 7 SCFO 2009, fee 2.2

Respondent's cross appeal	If wishing to participate in the appeal, the respondent must within 14 days of service of notice of intention to proceed file notice in the appropriate form and pay a fee of £320 If the respondent wishes to uphold the decision on different grounds than those given by the lower court, they must clearly state this in the written case Permission to cross appeal is required and SCR 2009, Part 2 applies	SCR 2009, r 21 Supreme Court PD 7, Form 3 SCFO 2009, fee 2.4 SCR 2009, rr 25(2), 10–17 Supreme Court PD 8.3.1–8.3.8
Documents	Within 112 days after filing the notice of intention to proceed or notice of appeal, the appellant must lodge with the court the documents referred to in the Supreme Court PD 5.1.2–5.1.5 with the number of copies referred to and in the order mentioned. All documents must be paginated and an index of contents must be included	SCR 2009, r 22 Supreme Court PD 5.1.2–5.1.5
Fee	Payable on filing statement of relevant facts and appendix of documents: £4,820	SCFO 2009, fee 2.5
Exchange of parties' cases	Appellant and respondent, every intervenor or advocate to the court must exchange and file their respective written cases	SCR 2009, r 22(4) Supreme Court PD 6.3.1–6.3.13
Core volumes	No later than 14 days after the date fixed for the hearing the appellant must file 10 core volumes and 10 volumes of authorities in the order set out in the PD	SCR 2009, rr 23, 24 Supreme Court PD 6.4.1–6.4.4, 6.5.1
Hearing	Is in open court	SCR 2009, r 27
Powers of court	All the powers of the court below. May also: – affirm, set aside or vary the order – remit any issue for determination by the court below – direct a retrial or hearing – order payment of interest – make an order for costs	

Appendices

Precedents

Legislation

Practice Guidance

A1 APPLICATION FOR A POSTAL SEARCH OF THE PROBATE RECORDS OF ENGLAND AND WALES, FORM PA1S

Postal search of the Probate records of England and Wales

PA1S

Complete this form if you want to find a will or 'grant of representation' for someone who died in or after 1858.

A 'grant of representation' gives someone the legal right to deal with a deceased person's estate.

Online search
Use our online service and you can order documents and get them within 10 working days.

www.gov.uk/search-will-probate

If you use our postal service we aim to respond within **four weeks** with your requested copies or a letter to explain that no grant has been issued. Please wait until after the four weeks has passed before contacting us.

What if the person died in the last six months?
If the person died within the last six months, a grant may not have been issued yet. You should check the online search service regulary to see when a grant has been issued. You can then order the documents.

If you are unable to search online, you may apply for a standing search to enable a single copy to be sent to you when the grant issues. The copy will not be sealed.

After a period of six months without result, your standing search will expire. You are able to extend the search for a further six months within one month of the expiry date by sending a further £3.

We will send you a letter telling you the date the standing search was entered.

Your details

Surname

Forenames

Full address

Postcode

DX address (if applicable)

Your reference (if any)

Please send your completed form with payment to:

The Postal Copies and Searches Department
District Probate Registry
York House
31 York Place
Leeds
LS1 2BA

If you use the DX postal service, our address is: **DX 26451 Leeds Park Square**

Please **do not** send a covering letter or staple your cheque, postal order or international money order to this form.

Please complete the rest of the form over the page

Search type

You can only request **one** type of search.

I request a search for:	Only use this search option if
☐ information about an estate or for family history research	you need information about an estate or are doing family history research. We will send you a copy of the will and grant.
☐ a copy to **administer an estate within the UK**	you need to administer an estate in the UK. We will send you sealed copies of the will and grant.
☐ a copy to **administer an estate outside of the UK** Country(ies) of use:	you need to administer an estate outside of the UK. We will send you sealed and certified copies of the will and grant.
☐ a standing search	the person died within the last six months, so a grant may not have been issued yet. A single copy of the grant (including a will, if any) will be sent to you if issued in the next six months.

Details of the deceased person

Surname

Forenames

Alternative names

Date of death

DAY MONTH YEAR

Full address

Postcode

The fee

The fee for a search is **£1.50**. This includes **one copy document** - this includes one copy of the grant and if applicable, one copy of the will. If you need extra copies, there is a fee of **£1.50 per copy document**.

The fee for a standing search (this copy will not be sealed) is **£3.00**.

How many extra copies do you need? ☐

The search fee (where a grant has already been issued)	**£1.50**
Extra copies of the grant (includes the will, if applicable)	£
Total fee to pay	£

Standing search If you don't know a grant has been issued.	**£3.00**

PBA number (if applicable)

Make your cheque, postal order or international money order (in sterling) payable to: 'HMCTS'

Please write the name of the deceased person on the back of your cheque, postal order or international money order.

Before returning your form, please check have you

- completed your details on the front page
- given details of the deceased person
- ticked only one box for the search
- enclosed the correct fee

A2 EXAMPLE CLAIMS TO BE INCLUDED IN THE PART 8 CLAIM FORM

The claimant claims:

1. An order that such reasonable financial provision may be made for the claimant from the estate of [name] deceased as the court thinks just.
2. An order be made for the claimant for such periodical payments and for such term out of the estate of the deceased as may be just.
3. An order for the payment to the claimant of such lump sum[s] out of the estate of the deceased as may be just.
4. The property at [address] or such other property forming part of the estate of the deceased as the court may specify be transferred to the claimant.
5. An order for the settlement for the benefit of the claimant of such property comprised in the estate of [name] the deceased as may be specified by the court and on such terms as the court thinks just.
6. An order for the acquisition out of the property forming part of the net estate of the deceased of such property as may be specified and for the transfer of the property so acquired to the claimant or for the settlement thereof for the benefit of the claimant.
7. An order for the variation of the ante-nuptial settlement [give details of the settlement] for the benefit of the claimant [who must be the surviving spouse of the marriage to whom the settlement related] or [name] the child of the deceased and the claimant.
8. An order pursuant to section 9 of the Inheritance (Provision for Family and Dependants) Act 1975 that the severable share of [name] the deceased at the date of [his] [her] death in the property at [insert address] be treated as forming part of the net estate of the deceased.
9. An order pursuant to section 10 of the Inheritance (Provision for Family and Dependants) Act 1975 that [identify the donee of the disposition] do provide such sum or sums of money or other property for the making of reasonable financial provision for the claimant.
10. An order pursuant to section 11 of the Inheritance (Provision for Family and Dependants) Act 1975 that [name] do provide the following sums of money and property for the purposes of making an order for reasonable financial provision for the claimant:
    (a) the sum of £[ ] contracted to be paid by the deceased to [name];
    (b) [identify any property which was the subject of the contract].

11. An order pursuant to section 11 of the Inheritance (Provision for Family and Dependants) Act 1975 directing the personal representatives of the deceased not to [make any payment] [transfer any property under the contract] [make any further payment] [transfer any further property].

12. An order for the variation of: [set out the details of the orders under the Matrimonial Causes Act 1973 of which variation is sought; see I(PFD)A 1975, ss 16–18].

13. An order pursuant to section 5 of the Inheritance (Provision for Family and Dependants) Act 1975 for interim relief.

14. An order giving permission to issue the claim notwithstanding that more than six months have elapsed from the date on which representation with respect to the estate of the deceased was granted namely since [date] on the grounds set out in the statement of the claimant served with this claim.

15. [Set out details of any injunctive relief sought, for example, a restraining order or a freezing order.]

16. An order that the claimant's cost of this claim be paid out of the deceased's estate.

A3 WITNESS STATEMENT BY THE CLAIMANT (A SURVIVING SPOUSE)

[Set out details of the party making the statement, with date, etc as required under CPR PD 32]

IN THE HIGH COURT OF JUSTICE

CHANCERY DIVISION

BUSINESS AND PROPERTY COURTS OF ENGLAND AND WALES

[PROPERTY, TRUSTS AND PROBATE LIST] CLAIM NO [ ]

[FAMILY DIVISION]

[PRINCIPAL REGISTRY] [DISTRICT REGISTRY]

(*Delete as appropriate*)

In the Matter of the Estate of [ ](*insert name)*, Deceased

And in the Matter of the Inheritance (Provision for Family and Dependants) Act 1975

BETWEEN:

[Name] Claimant

– and –

[Name] First Defendant

(the personal representative of the deceased)

– and –

[Name] Second Defendant

[All interested parties should be made defendants; see Chapter 12.]

WITNESS STATEMENT OF THE CLAIMANT

I, [name] the above named claimant of [address] unemployed will say as follows:

1. I am the widow of [ ], deceased. The deceased and I were married on 10 March 1980. A copy of our marriage certificate is attached to this statement and marked '...'. We have three children, a daughter and two sons.

2. The deceased died on 21 June 2022. A certified copy of his death certificate is attached to this statement marked '...'. The deceased was domiciled in England and Wales.

3. A grant of probate with respect to the deceased's estate was taken out on 14 September 2022 by [names] his executors from the Principal Registry. An official copy of the grant with the deceased's last will dated 12 January 2019 is marked '...'.

4. To the best of my knowledge and belief the net estate is valued at approximately £ [give the value] and consists of:

   [set out the details, or if a schedule has been prepared by the executors and is available, refer to the schedule and exhibit it to the statement].

5. [Set out the history of the marriage and such of the s 3 factors as may be relevant (see Chapter 5); if possible set out a schedule of income from all sources, details of capital and property and a list of expenditure. The information should also include the relevant factors which apply under Matrimonial Causes Act 1973, s 24.]

6. [If an order under ss 9–11 is sought, set out details of the reasons for seeking such an order.]

7. [Set out details of the substantive orders for financial provision sought and reasons for seeking the orders.]

STATEMENT OF TRUTH

[See CPR PD 32, para 20.2, FPR 2010, r 17 and PD 17A]

I believe that the facts set out in this statement are true. I understand that proceedings for contempt of court may be brought against anyone who makes, or causes to be made, a false statement in a document verified by a statement of truth without an honest belief in its truth

Signed: [ ]

A4 WITNESS STATEMENT OF THE PERSONAL REPRESENTATIVE

[Set out details of the party making the statement, with date, etc as required under CPR PD 32]

IN THE HIGH COURT OF JUSTICE CLAIM NO [ ]

CHANCERY DIVISION

BUSINESS AND PROPERTY COURTS OF ENGLAND AND WALES

[PROPERTY, TRUSTS AND PROBATE LIST]

[FAMILY DIVISION]

[PRINCIPAL REGISTRY] [DISTRICT REGISTRY]

COUNTY COURT

(Delete as appropriate)

In the Matter of the Estate of [ ] *(insert name)*, Deceased

And in the Matter of the Inheritance (Provision for Family and Dependants) Act 1975

BETWEEN:

[Name] Claimant

– and –

[Name] First Defendant

(the personal representative of the deceased)

– and –

[Name] Second Defendant

[All interested parties should be made defendants; see Chapter 12.]

WITNESS STATEMENT OF THE FIRST DEFENDANT

I [name] of [address] solicitor will say as follows:

1. I am a solicitor of the Supreme Court and partner in the firm of Messrs [ ].

2. I am one of two executors of the will of the deceased. I have personal and professional knowledge of the deceased and his estate and knowledge derived from my involvement as an executor of the estate.

3. The grant of probate in relation to the deceased's estate was granted to me and [name] out of the District Registry at [ ] on [*insert date*]. A true copy of the grant is attached to my statement marked '...'.

4. The gross value of the deceased's estate was accounted for probate at £ [ ] and the net estate at £ [ ] The estate consists of:

The property at [address] valued at	£550,000
Premium Bonds:	£5,000
National Savings Certificates:	£2,000
Cash at [ ] Bank:	£300
Total	£557,300

[Set out all identifiable assets and values, including any foreign property owned by the deceased, if necessary in a Schedule and the total.]

5. The deceased was entitled to receive a death benefit from his employers under the terms of his employers' pension scheme. The deceased nominated [name] his cohabitee to receive the said benefit. The death benefit amounted to £ [ ] and the said sum was paid to [name] on [date].

6. The liabilities of the deceased at the date of his death were as follows:

   [Set these out, including, for example, credit card debts, utility bills, loans, sums due under HP agreements.]

7. The funeral expenses of the deceased amounted to £ [ ].

8. The whole of the estate was liable to inheritance tax subject to exemptions. Full details of the property comprised in the estate are set out in the Schedule attached to this statement marked '...'.

9. The estate has not yet been administered.

10. [If there has been delay in making the claim and the application for an extension is opposed, set out the reasons for the objection to the application.]

11. [If an order under s 9 is sought by the claimant, set out details of the assets and any other information which may be of assistance to the court; similarly if the claim includes a claim for orders under ss 10 and 11.]

12. The persons beneficially entitled to the deceased's estate are: [set out the names and addresses of all beneficiaries, and if any of the beneficiaries is a child or under a disability, give details].

13. [If there are matters to which the court's attention needs to be drawn these should be dealt with in addition to answering any matter set out in the claimant's statement.]

STATEMENT OF TRUTH

[See CPR PD 32, para 20.2, FPR 2010, r 17 and PD 17A]

I believe that the facts set out in this statement are true. I understand that proceedings for contempt of court may be brought against anyone who makes, or causes to be made, a false statement in a document verified by a statement of truth without an honest belief in its truth

Signed: [ ]

A5 WITNESS STATEMENT BY A COHABITANT OF THE DECEASED

[Set out details of the party making the statement, with date, etc as required under CPR PD 32]

IN THE HIGH COURT OF JUSTICE CLAIM NO [ ]

CHANCERY DIVISION

BUSINESS AND PROPERTY COURTS OF ENGLAND AND WALES

[PROPERTY, TRUSTS AND PROBATE LIST]

[FAMILY DIVISION]

[PRINCIPAL REGISTRY] [DISTRICT REGISTRY]

[COUNTY COURT]

(Delete as appropriate)

In the Matter of the Estate of [ ] *(insert name)*, Deceased

And in the Matter of the Inheritance (Provision for Family and Dependants) Act 1975

BETWEEN:

[Name] Claimant

– and –

[Name] First Defendant

(the personal representative of the deceased)

– and –

[Name] Second Defendant

[All interested parties should be made defendants; see Chapter 12.]

WITNESS STATEMENT OF [THE CLAIMANT]

I [name] of [address] will say:

1. The deceased was married to [name] on [date]. They had no children.

2. I met the deceased in January 2005 and shortly thereafter he left his wife [name] and came to live with me. I was then working and had lived in a flat at [address] which was owned by me. The deceased purchased the property at [address] in which I now live. I sold my flat and the net proceeds of sale were used to pay the deposit on the property. The property was purchased in the sole name of the deceased as I trusted him. The mortgage was also in his sole name. Thereafter we lived in the property as husband and wife.

3. We have two children, a son, Thomas, born on 1 January 2006 and a daughter, Samantha, born on 25 December 2008.

4. When I met the deceased I was working full time as a manager of the local supermarket. The deceased did not like me working and when I became pregnant he asked me to give up work and be a full-time carer of our children. Since then I and my children have been fully dependent on him.

5. Both children have attended public schools and the fees were paid for by the deceased. The deceased provided us with a high standard of living. We had two holidays a year with the children in Europe and sometimes further afield.

6. When the deceased began suffering from ill health I considered taking up employment to help with the finances but he assured me that there was no need for me to do so and that he would ensure that I and the children would be provided for if anything should happen to him. He also assured me that he would arrange for the property to be transferred into my name so that I would not have to worry if anything should happen to him.

7. Before the deceased could attend his solicitor to make a will he died. He was domiciled in England and Wales. A copy of his death certificate is attached to this statement marked '...'.

8. As a result of his failure to make a new will I and the children have been left without support and his widow is the main beneficiary under the will. I produce a copy of the grant taken out by his executors marked '...'.

9. Since the death of the deceased I have had to rely on state benefits. I have been unable to discharge the school fees. I have no other income. [Set out details of the claimant's earning capacity if any.]

10. I have the following outgoings: [list the outgoings or produce a schedule].

11. I am informed that the deceased's widow has insisted that the property in which I live with my children should be sold. If I have to vacate the home I and the children will become homeless. My solicitors have given to the executors and the solicitors acting for the widow all the relevant information and have been trying to negotiate a settlement. Negotiations had been progressing well. My solicitors were urged not to issue proceedings with a view to saving costs particularly as the negotiations had reached the final stages and the agreement was in the process of being drafted. Unfortunately, the widow has withdrawn from the negotiations. I was obliged to apply for

public funding to issue proceedings and this caused some delay. The delay, however, has been minimal. Proceedings were not issued immediately as there appeared to be a realistic hope of reaching an agreement without recourse to litigation. The estate has not yet been administered. No prejudice has been caused to any beneficiary. I therefore request that I be granted permission to pursue my claim notwithstanding the fact that the proceedings were not issued within six months from the date when the grant was taken out.

12. If permission to make the claim is refused I and my children will suffer extreme hardship and an injustice.
13. [Set out in detail the orders sought and the reasons.]

STATEMENT OF TRUTH

[See CPR PD 32, para 20.2, FPR 2010, r 17 and PD 17A]

I believe that the facts set out in this statement are true. I understand that proceedings for contempt of court may be brought against anyone who makes, or causes to be made, a false statement in a document verified by a statement of truth without an honest belief in its truth

Signed: [ ]

[This precedent should be adapted where the claimant is a same sex cohabitant].

A6 WITNESS STATEMENT OF AN ADULT PERSON TREATED AS A CHILD OF THE FAMILY

Set out details of the party making the statement, with date, etc as required under CPR PD 32]

IN THE HIGH COURT OF JUSTICE CLAIM NO [ ]

CHANCERY DIVISION

BUSINESS AND PROPERTY COURTS OF ENGLAND AND WALES

[PROPERTY, TRUSTS AND PROBATE LIST]

[FAMILY DIVISION]

[PRINCIPAL REGISTRY] [DISTRICT REGISTRY]

[COUNTY COURT]

(Delete as appropriate)

In the Matter of the Estate of [ ] *(insert name)*, Deceased

And in the Matter of the Inheritance (Provision for Family and Dependants) Act 1975

BETWEEN:

[Name] Claimant

– and –

[Name] First Defendant

(the personal representative of the deceased)

– and –

[Name] Second Defendant

[All interested parties should be made defendants; see Chapter 12.]

I [name] of [address] will say as follows:

1. I am the deceased's step-son. My mother married the deceased on [date]. A copy of my mother's marriage certificate is attached to this statement marked '...' and a copy of my birth certificate is attached marked '...'.

2. I was fourteen years of age when my mother married the deceased. I lived with them and the deceased treated me as his son. My mother and the deceased had two children from their marriage. They are Solomon born on [date] and Jacob born on [date]. The deceased did not treat me any differently after the birth of my step-brothers. We all went to public schools. The deceased encouraged me to take up medicine. He paid all my college tuition fees and paid all my other expenses.

3. The deceased died domiciled in England and Wales on [date]. Copies of his death certificate and of his will and the grant of representation of the deceased's estate are attached to this statement marked '...', '...' and '...' respectively.

4. I believe that the deceased's estate is valued at £2.5 million. There is no provision made for me in his will although he has made provision for my step-brothers who are also adults and in full-time education.

5. My father has never seen me or maintained me. I am informed by my mother that he had a brief relationship with her when he was serving in the USA forces and was stationed here. When he discovered that she was pregnant he terminated the relationship and returned to the USA. His whereabouts are not known. I always regarded the deceased as my father.

6. [Set out the claimant's financial circumstances and any other matter of relevance under s 3.]

A7 DRAFT ORDERS

The precedents below are intended to be a guide only. The orders made by the court vary depending on the circumstances of each individual case.

IN THE HIGH COURT OF JUSTICE CLAIM NO [ ]

CHANCERY DIVISION

BUSINESS AND PROPERTY COURTS OF ENGLAND AND WALES

[PROPERTY, TRUSTS AND PROBATE LIST]

[FAMILY DIVISION]

[PRINCIPAL REGISTRY] [DISTRICT REGISTRY]

In the Matter of the Estate of [ ], Deceased

And in the Matter of the Inheritance (Provision for Family and Dependants) Act 1975

BETWEEN:

[Name] Claimant

– and –

[Name] First Defendant

(the personal representative of the deceased)

– and –

[Name] Second Defendant

[All interested parties should be made defendants; see Chapter 12.]

UPON HEARING [counsel] [solicitor] for the Claimant and [counsel] [solicitor] for the Defendant[s] and the Third Defendant appearing in person [set out the representations or otherwise of the parties before the court]

AND UPON READING the documents in the court file and the agreed bundle of documents

AND UPON THE COURT being satisfied that the disposition of the estate of the deceased [name] effected by [his/her] [will] [intestacy] is not such as to make reasonable financial provision for the Claimant

IT IS ORDERED pursuant to section 2 of the Inheritance (Provision for Family and Dependants) Act 1975 that:

PERIODICAL PAYMENTS

There be paid out of the estate of the Deceased [name] to the Claimant [name] periodical payments to the Claimant at the rate of £ [ ] per annum payable monthly from 1 February 2010 and thereafter on the first day of each calendar month until [the claimant shall remarry] [the claimant shall cease his/her full time education etc] [if the payments relate to the income from assets, set out the rate which is equal to whole of the income] [or as the case may be] of the estate comprised by [ ].

LUMP SUM

There be paid to the Claimant the lump sum of £ [ ] out of the net estate of the Deceased within [ ] days from the date of this order; or

There be paid to the Claimant the lump sum of £ [ ] out of the estate of the Deceased in four instalments of £ [ ] payable on 31 March 20[ ], 30 June 20[ ], 30 September 20[ ] and 30 December 20[ ] [if the payments are to be made in, for example, 12 equal monthly instalments, state the same or as the case may be.]

TRANSFER OF PROPERTY

There be transferred to the Claimant from the estate of the Deceased within three months from the date of this order the property at [address].

SETTLEMENT OF PROPERTY

The property at [address] forming part of the net estate of the Deceased be settled for the benefit of the Claimant [set out the settlement ordered, e.g. for life] and that the form of the deed of settlement be agreed between the Claimant and the Defendants or in default of agreement be referred to conveyancing Counsel to settle.

ACQUISITION OF ASSETS

From the net estate of the Deceased there be purchased the property at [address] and that [the same be transferred into the name of the Claimant absolutely] [such property be settled for the benefit of the Claimant to the effect that [set out the terms of the settlement]] and that the form of deed of settlement be agreed and in default of agreement be referred to conveyancing Counsel to settle.

VARIATION OF ANTE-NUPTIAL/POST-NUPTIAL SETTLEMENT

The [ante-] [post-] nuptial settlement made between [name] and the Deceased, etc be varied so as to provide as follows: [set out the variation(s)].

ORDER UNDER SECTION 9

The severable share of the Deceased in the property at [address] be treated as part of the estate of the Deceased in [set out the proportions directed] for the purposes of facilitating the making of the financial provision set out in this Order.

ORDER UNDER SECTION 10 OR 11

That pursuant to section [10] [11] of the Inheritance (Provision for Family and Dependants) Act 1975 [name] is directed to provide the sum of £ [ ] to the Claimant [or transfer to the Claimant the property at [address]] [within [ ] days of the making of this order] or [within [ ] days of the receipt of this order by him/her].

ORDER UNDER SECTION 4

Pursuant to section 4 of the Inheritance (Provision for Family and Dependants) Act 1975, IT IS ORDERED THAT the period of six months prescribed by section 4 of the Inheritance (Provision for Family and Dependants) Act 1975 be extended until [ ].

DRAFT CONSENT ORDER SETTING OUT COMPROMISE OF CLAIM AND DECLARATION OF TRUST ON BEHALF OF CLAIMANT UNDER DISABILITY

UPON HEARING Counsel for the parties and reading the consents of the defendants

AND UPON READING the evidence filed and documents recorded in the court file

AND UPON THE COURT being of the opinion that the disposition of the estate of [name] the Testator effected by [his/her] will is not such as to make reasonable financial provision for the maintenance of [name] the Claimant, the Testator's son

AND UPON THE COURT being satisfied that the terms of compromise reached between the parties are for the benefit of the Claimant

THE COURT DOES APPROVE THE SAID TERMS OF COMPROMISE AND IT IS ORDERED THAT:

1. The First Defendant [name] as personal representative of the Testator be at liberty to and so carry the said terms of compromise into effect.

2. Pursuant to section 2(1)(d) of the Inheritance (Provision for Family and Dependants) Act 1975 that the residue of the estate of the said Testator including all accumulations of income [or otherwise identify the property to be settled] shall be settled upon the trusts named in the will for the benefit of the Claimant in accordance with the terms set out in the Schedule hereto.

3. [Set out details of any adjustments which need to be made to any clauses in the will relating to any legacies or bequests.]

4. The costs of the Claimant and the Defendants be referred to a district judge for detailed assessment and paid out of the residuary estate of the Testator [or set out details of the agreement if any on costs].

Dated this [ ] day of [ ] 20[ ]

SCHEDULE

That the Testator's estate shall henceforth be administered as if:

1. The Testator had omitted from his Will Clause 3 and Clause 6(j) therein contained.

2. The Testator had included in his Will the following clause in substitution of Clause 2 as therein contained:

   (a) My trustees shall hold the remainder of the trust fund after payment of the foregoing legacies (hereinafter called 'the discretionary fund') upon the following trusts and with and subject to the following powers:

   (b) (i) During the life of my son [name] (hereinafter 'my said son') my trustees shall have power in their absolute discretion to pay or apply the whole or any part or proportion of the income of the discretionary fund as they think fit to or for the maintenance care or benefit of my said son with power to pay such income to any person or persons responsible for his care without seeing to the application thereof.

   (ii) After expiration of the period of [twelve years] [or insert appropriate term] from my death my trustees shall have the further power in their absolute discretion to pay any income then arising which in their opinion is surplus to the present and future needs of my said son to the persons who would be entitled thereto if he were dead and in equal shares.

   (iii) During the period of [eighteen years] [or insert appropriate term] from my death while my said son is living my trustees shall accumulate the income of the discretionary fund which shall not be paid or applied as aforesaid as an accretion to the capital thereof but shall have power to pay or apply such accumulations to or for the maintenance, care or benefit of my said son during his life as if the same were income of the then current year.

(iv) If my said son is still living at the expiration of the said period of [eighteen years] my trustees shall thereafter during the remainder of his life pay all income then arising which shall not be paid or applied under the foregoing powers to the persons who would be entitled thereto if he were dead and in equal shares.

(c) My trustees being at least two in number or a trust corporation shall have the following powers in addition to those set out in Clause 9 of the Will and the following provisions shall apply [set out the powers, for example:]

(i) power to sell, exchange, convey, lease, mortgage, charge, agree to let, licence or otherwise conduct the management of any land of any tenure that may at any time be subject to the trusts hereof as if my trustees were the sole beneficial owners thereof;

(ii) power to change or vary any property or investments for the time being subject to the trusts hereof;

(iii) power to invest [set out details];

(iv) power to permit my son to have use and enjoyment of any chattel forming part of the discretionary fund in such manner and subject to such conditions (if any) as my trustees may consider reasonable and without being liable to account for any consequential loss;

(v) power to invest the whole or any part of the discretionary fund in the purchase or improvement of any dwelling-house or flat and to permit the same to be used as a residence for my son whether alone or jointly with another person without being required to insist upon the payment by any other person whether or not a joint occupier thereof of a market rent;

(vi) power to apply any part of the capital or income of the discretionary fund towards meeting the cost of –

A altering or adapting any residential accommodation in the ownership of any person or body for the more convenient occupation thereof by my said son as a home;

B purchasing domestic appliances or procuring domestic assistance for my said son;

C holidays for my said son or the expenses incurred by any person with whom he resides to enable such person to accompany him on holiday or to make provision for a carer to care for him.

(d) After the death of my said son my trustees shall stand possessed of the discretionary fund and the income thereof (or so much thereof as may not have been paid or applied under any trust or power affecting the same) in trust for the residuary beneficiaries (that is to say [name them]) in equal shares PROVIDED THAT for the avoidance of doubt should any of those persons entitled to the discretionary fund predecease my said son their share of the discretionary fund shall accrue to their estates AND PROVIDED FURTHER that (notwithstanding the aforementioned trusts) my trustees may pay out of the capital of the discretionary fund such funeral expenses in respect of my said son as they may consider appropriate and reasonable.

(e) Any of my trustees may join in exercising any of the powers under this clause notwithstanding that he/she is one of the beneficiaries and will or may benefit from any such exercise.

(f) Any of my trustees being a solicitor, accountant or other person engaged in any profession or business shall be entitled to be paid all usual professional or proper charges for business transacted time expended acts done by him/her or any partner of his/hers in connection with the trusts hereof including acts which a trustee not being in any profession or business could have done personally.

A8 INHERITANCE (PROVISION FOR FAMILY AND DEPENDANTS) ACT 1975

1 Application for financial provision from deceased's estate.

(1) Where after the commencement of this Act a person dies domiciled in England and Wales and is survived by any of the following persons:—

[(a) the spouse or civil partner of the deceased;
(b) a former spouse or former civil partner of the deceased, but not one who has formed a subsequent marriage or civil partnership;]
[(ba) any person (not being a person included in paragraph (a) or (b) above) to whom subsection (1A) ... below applies;]
(c) a child of the deceased;
(d) any person (not being a child of the deceased) [who in relation to any marriage or civil partnership to which the deceased was at any time a party, or otherwise in relation to any family in which the deceased at any time stood in the role of a parent, was treated by the deceased as a child of the family;]
(e) any person (not being a person included in the foregoing paragraphs of this subsection) who immediately before the death of the deceased was being maintained, either wholly or partly, by the deceased;

that person may apply to the court for an order under section 2 of this Act on the ground that the disposition of the deceased's estate effected by his will or the law relating to intestacy, or the combination of his will and that law, is not such as to make reasonable financial provision for the applicant.
[(1A) This subsection applies to a person if the deceased died on or after 1st January 1996 and, during the whole of the period of two years ending immediately before the date when the deceased died, the person was living—

(a) in the same household as the deceased, and
(b) [as if that person and the deceased were a married couple or civil partners].]

(1B) ...
(2) In this Act "reasonable financial provision"—

(a) in the case of an application made by virtue of subsection (1)(a) above by the husband or wife of the deceased (except where the marriage with the deceased was the subject of a [judicial separation order] and at the date of death [the order] was in force and the separation was continuing), means such financial provision as it would be reasonable in all the circumstances of the case for a husband or wife to receive, whether or not that provision is required for his or her maintenance;

[(aa) in the case of an application made by virtue of subsection (1)(a) above by the civil partner of the deceased (except where, at the date of death, a separation order under Chapter 2 of Part 2 of the Civil Partnership Act 2004 was in force in relation to the civil partnership and the separation was continuing), means such financial provision as it would be reasonable in all the circumstances of the case for a civil partner to receive, whether or not that provision is required for his or her maintenance;]

(b) in the case of any other application made by virtue of subsection (1) above, means such financial provision as it would be reasonable in all the circumstances of the case for the applicant to receive for his maintenance.

[(2A) The reference in subsection (1)(d) above to a family in which the deceased stood in the role of a parent includes a family of which the deceased was the only member (apart from the applicant).]

[(3) For the purposes of subsection (1)(e) above, a person is to be treated as being maintained by the deceased (either wholly or partly, as the case may be) only if the deceased was making a substantial contribution in money or money's worth towards the reasonable needs of that person, other than a contribution made for full valuable consideration pursuant to an arrangement of a commercial nature.]

AMENDMENTS

Section 1(1)(a), (b) substituted by Civil Partnership Act 2004, ss 71, 263(2), Sch 4 para 15(2); Civil Partnership Act 2004 (Commencement No 2) Order 2005 (SI 2005/3175), art 2(1), Sch 1

Section 1(1)(ba) inserted by Law Reform (Succession) Act 1995, s 2(2)

Words in s 1(1)(ba) omitted by virtue of Civil Partnership (Opposite-sex Couples) Regulations 2019 (SI 2019/1458), reg 1(2), Sch 3 para 3(2)(a)

Words in s 1(1)(d) substituted by Inheritance and Trustees' Powers Act 2014, s 12(2), Sch 2 para 2(2) (with s 12(4)); Inheritance and Trustees' Powers Act 2014 (Commencement) Order 2014 (SI 2014/2039), art 2

Section 1(1A) inserted by Law Reform (Succession) Act 1995, s 2(3)

Words in s 1(1A)(b) substituted by Civil Partnership (Opposite-sex Couples) Regulations 2019 (SI 2019/1458), reg 1(2), Sch 3 para 3(2)(b)

Section 1(1B) omitted by virtue of Civil Partnership (Opposite-sex Couples) Regulations 2019 (SI 2019/1458), reg 1(2), Sch 3 para 3(2)(c)

Words in s 1(2)(a) substituted by Divorce, Dissolution and Separation Act 2020, s 8(1), (8), Sch para 44(2)(a), (b); Divorce, Dissolution and Separation Act 2020 (Commencement) Regulations 2022 (SI 2022/283), reg 2

Section 1(2)(aa) inserted by Civil Partnership Act 2004, ss 71, 263(2), Sch 4 para 15(6); Civil Partnership Act 2004 (Commencement No 2) Order 2005 (SI 2005/3175), art 2(1), Sch 1

Section 1(2A) inserted by Inheritance and Trustees' Powers Act 2014, s 12(2), Sch 2 para 2(3) (with s 12(4)); Inheritance and Trustees' Powers Act 2014 (Commencement) Order 2014 (SI 2014/2039), art 2

Section 1(3) substituted by Inheritance and Trustees' Powers Act 2014, s 12(2), Sch 2 para 3 (with s 12(4)); Inheritance and Trustees' Powers Act 2014 (Commencement) Order 2014 (SI 2014/2039), art 2

2 Powers of court to make orders.

(1) Subject to the provisions of this Act, where an application is made for an order under this section, the court may, if it is satisfied that the disposition of the deceased's estate effected by his will or the law relating to intestacy, or the combination of his will and that law, is not such as to make reasonable financial provision for the applicant, make any one or more of the following orders:—

(a) an order for the making to the applicant out of the net estate of the deceased of such periodical payments and for such term as may be specified in the order;
(b) an order for the payment to the applicant out of that estate of a lump sum of such amount as may be so specified;
(c) an order for the transfer to the applicant of such property comprised in that estate as may be so specified;
(d) an order for the settlement for the benefit of the applicant of such property comprised in that estate as may be so specified;
(e) an order for the acquisition out of property comprised in that estate of such property as may be so specified and for the transfer of the property so acquired to the applicant or for the settlement thereof for his benefit;
(f) an order varying any ante-nuptial or post-nuptial settlement (including such a settlement made by will) made on the parties to a marriage to which the deceased was one of the parties, the variation being for the benefit of the surviving party to that marriage, or any child of that marriage, or any person who was treated by the deceased as a child of the family in relation to that marriage.
[(h) an order varying for the applicant's benefit the trusts on which the deceased's estate is held (whether arising under the will, or the law relating to intestacy, or both).]
[(g) an order varying any settlement made—

(i) during the subsistence of a civil partnership formed by the deceased, or
(ii) in anticipation of the formation of a civil partnership by the deceased,

on the civil partners (including such a settlement made by will), the variation being for the benefit of the surviving civil partner, or any child of both the civil partners, or any person who was treated by the deceased as a child of the family in relation to that civil partnership.]

(2) An order under subsection (1)(a) above providing for the making out of the net estate of the deceased of periodical payments may provide for—

(a) payments of such amount as may be specified in the order,
(b) payments equal to the whole of the income of the net estate or of such portion thereof as may be so specified,
(c) payments equal to the whole of the income of such part of the net estate as the court may direct to be set aside or appropriated for the making out of the income thereof of payments under this section,

or may provide for the amount of the payments or any of them to be determined in any other way the court thinks fit.
(3) Where an order under subsection (1)(a) above provides for the making of payments of an amount specified in the order, the order may direct that such part of the net estate as may be so specified shall be set aside or appropriated for the making out of the income thereof of those payments; but no larger part of the net estate shall be so set aside or appropriated than is sufficient, at the date of the order, to produce by the income thereof the amount required for the making of those payments
[(3A) In assessing for the purposes of an order under this section the extent (if any) to which the net estate is reduced by any debts or liabilities (including any inheritance tax paid or payable out of the estate), the court may assume that the order has already been made.]
(4) An order under this section may contain such consequential and supplemental provisions as the court thinks necessary or expedient for the purpose of giving effect to the order or for the purpose of securing that the order operates fairly as between one beneficiary of the estate of the deceased and another and may, in particular, but without prejudice to the generality of this subsection—

(a) order any person who holds any property which forms part of the net estate of the deceased to make such payment or transfer such property as may be specified in the order;
(b) vary the disposition of the deceased's estate effected by the will or the law relating to intestacy, or by both the will and the law relating to intestacy, in such manner as the court thinks fair and reasonable having regard to the provisions of the order and all the circumstances of the case;
(c) confer on the trustees of any property which is the subject of an order under this section such powers as appear to the court to be necessary or expedient.

AMENDMENTS

Section 2(1)(h) inserted by Inheritance and Trustees' Powers Act 2014, s 12(2), Sch 2 para 4(2) (with s 12(4)); Inheritance and Trustees' Powers Act 2014 (Commencement) Order 2014 (SI 2014/2039), art 2

Section 2(1)(g) inserted by Civil Partnership Act 2004, ss 71, 263(2), Sch 4 para 16; Civil Partnership Act 2004 (Commencement No 2) Order 2005 (SI 2005/3175), art 2(1), Sch 1

Section 2(3A) inserted by Inheritance and Trustees' Powers Act 2014, s 12(2), Sch 2 para 4(3) (with s 12(4)); Inheritance and Trustees' Powers Act 2014 (Commencement) Order 2014 (SI 2014/2039), art 2

3 Matters to which court is to have regard in exercising powers under s 2.

(1) Where an application is made for an order under section 2 of this Act, the court shall, in determining whether the disposition of the deceased's estate effected by his will or the law relating to intestacy, or the combination of his will and that law, is such as to make reasonable financial provision for the applicant and, if the court considers that reasonable financial provision has not been made, in determining whether and in what manner it shall exercise its powers under that section, have regard to the following matters, that is to say—

(a) the financial resources and financial needs which the applicant has or is likely to have in the foreseeable future;
(b) the financial resources and financial needs which any other applicant for an order under section 2 of this Act has or is likely to have in the foreseeable future;
(c) the financial resources and financial needs which any beneficiary of the estate of the deceased has or is likely to have in the foreseeable future;
(d) any obligations and responsibilities which the deceased had towards any applicant for an order under the said section 2 or towards any beneficiary of the estate of the deceased;
(e) the size and nature of the net estate of the deceased;
(f) any physical or mental disability of any applicant for an order under the said section 2 or any beneficiary of the estate of the deceased;
(g) any other matter, including the conduct of the applicant or any other person, which in the circumstances of the case the court may consider relevant.

(2) [This subsection applies, without prejudice to the generality of paragraph (g) of subsection (1) above, where an application for an order under section 2 of this Act is made by virtue of section 1(1)(a) or (b) of this Act.]
The court shall, in addition to the matters specifically mentioned in paragraphs (a) to (f) of that subsection, have regard to—

(a) the age of the applicant and the duration of the marriage [or civil partnership];
(b) the contribution made by the applicant to the welfare of the family of the deceased, including any contribution made by looking after the home or caring for the family.

... In the case of an application by the wife or husband of the deceased, the court shall also, unless at the date of death a [judicial separation order] was in force and the separation was continuing, have regard to the provision which the applicant might reasonably have expected to receive if on the day on which the deceased died the marriage, instead of being terminated by death, had been terminated by a [divorce order] [; but nothing requires the court to treat such provision as setting an upper or lower limit on the provision which may be made by an order under section 2.]
[In the case of an application by the civil partner of the deceased, the court shall also, unless at the date of the death a separation order under Chapter 2 of Part 2 of the Civil Partnership Act 2004 was in force and the separation was continuing, have regard to the provision which the applicant might reasonably have expected to receive if on the day on which the deceased died the civil partnership, instead of being terminated by death, had been terminated by a dissolution order [; but nothing requires the court to treat such provision as setting an upper or lower limit on the provision which may be made by an order under section 2.]]
[(2A) Without prejudice to the generality of paragraph (g) of subsection (1) above, where an application for an order under section 2 of this Act is made by virtue of section 1(1)(ba) of this Act, the court shall, in addition to the matters specifically mentioned in paragraphs (a) to (f) of that subsection, have regard to—

(a) the age of the applicant and the length of the period during which the applicant lived [in the same household as the deceased as if the applicant and the deceased were a married couple or civil partners];
(b) the contribution made by the applicant to the welfare of the family of the deceased, including any contribution made by looking after the home or caring for the family.]

(3) Without prejudice to the generality of paragraph (g) of subsection (1) above, where an application for an order under section 2 of this Act is made by virtue of section 1(1)(c) or 1(1)(d) of this Act, the court shall, in addition to the matters specifically mentioned in paragraphs (a) to (f) of that subsection, have regard to the manner in which the applicant was being or in which he might expect to be educated or trained, and where the application is made by virtue of section 1(1)(d) the court shall also have regard—

[(a) to whether the deceased maintained the applicant and, if so, to the length of time for which and basis on which the deceased did so, and to the extent of the contribution made by way of maintenance;
(aa) to whether and, if so, to what extent the deceased assumed responsibility for the maintenance of the applicant;]

(b) to whether in [maintaining or assuming responsibility for maintaining the applicant] the deceased did so knowing that the applicant was not his own child;
(c) to the liability of any other person to maintain the applicant.

(4) Without prejudice to the generality of paragraph (g) of subsection (1) above, where an application for an order under section 2 of this Act is made by virtue of section 1(1)(e) of this Act, the court shall, in addition to the matters specifically mentioned in paragraphs (a) to (f) of that subsection, have [regard—

(a) to the length of time for which and basis on which the deceased maintained the applicant, and to the extent of the contribution made by way of maintenance;
(b) to whether and, if so, to what extent the deceased assumed responsibility for the maintenance of the applicant.]

(5) In considering the matters to which the court is required to have regard under this section, the court shall take into account the facts as known to the court at the date of the hearing.
(6) In considering the financial resources of any person for the purposes of this section the court shall take into account his earning capacity and in considering the financial needs of any person for the purposes of this section the court shall take into account his financial obligations and responsibilities

AMENDMENTS

Words in s 3(2) substituted by Civil Partnership Act 2004, ss 71, 263(2), Sch 4 para 17(2); Civil Partnership Act 2004 (Commencement No 2) Order 2005 (SI 2005/3175), art 2(1), Sch 1

Words in s 3(2)(a) inserted, and the words from "the court shall, in addition" to the end of s 3(2)(b) become the second sentence of the subsection, by virtue of Civil Partnership Act 2004, ss 71, 263(2), Sch 4 para 17(3); (SI 2005/3175), art 2(1), Sch 1

Word in s 3(2) repealed, and the words following it become the third sentence of the subsection, by virtue of Civil Partnership Act 2004, ss 71, 261(4), 263(2), Sch 4 para 17(4), Sch 30; Civil Partnership Act 2004 (Commencement No 2) Order 2005 (SI 2005/3175), art 2(1)(6), Sch 1

Words in s 3(2) substituted by Divorce, Dissolution and Separation Act 2020, s 8(1), (8), Sch para 44(3)(a), (b); Divorce, Dissolution and Separation Act 2020 (Commencement) Regulations 2022 (SI 2022/283), reg 2

Words in s 3(2) inserted by Inheritance and Trustees' Powers Act 2014, s 12(2), Sch 2 para 5(2) (with s 12(4)); Inheritance and Trustees' Powers Act 2014 (Commencement) Order 2014 (SI 2014/2039), art 2

Words in s 3(2) inserted by Civil Partnership Act 2004, ss 71, 263(2), Sch 4 para 17(5); Civil Partnership Act 2004 (Commencement No 2) Order 2005 (SI 2005/3175), art 2(1), Sch 1

Section 3(2A) inserted by Law Reform (Succession) Act 1995, s 2(4)
Words in s 3(2A)(a) substituted by Civil Partnership (Opposite-sex Couples) Regulations 2019 (SI 2019/1458), reg 1(2), Sch 3 para 3(3)
Section 3(3)(a)(aa) substituted for s 3(3)(a) by Inheritance and Trustees' Powers Act 2014, s 12(2), Sch 2 para 5(3)(a) (with s 12(4)); Inheritance and Trustees' Powers Act 2014 (Commencement) Order 2014 (SI 2014/2039), art 2
Words in s 3(3)(b) substituted by Inheritance and Trustees' Powers Act 2014, s 12(2), Sch 2 para 5(3)(b) (with s 12(4)); Inheritance and Trustees' Powers Act 2014 (Commencement) Order 2014 (SI 2014/2039), art 2
Words in s 3(4) substituted by Inheritance and Trustees' Powers Act 2014, s 12(2), Sch 2 para 5(4) (with s 12(4)); Inheritance and Trustees' Powers Act 2014 (Commencement) Order 2014 (SI 2014/2039), art 2

4 Time-limit for applications.

An application for an order under section 2 of this Act shall not, except with the permission of the court, be made after the end of the period of six months from the date on which representation with respect to the estate of the deceased is first taken out [(but nothing prevents the making of an application before such representation is first taken out)].

AMENDMENTS

Words in s 4 inserted by Inheritance and Trustees' Powers Act 2014, s 12(2), Sch 2 para 6 (with s 12(4)); Inheritance and Trustees' Powers Act 2014 (Commencement) Order 2014 (SI 2014/2039), art 2

5 Interim orders.

(1) Where on an application for an order under section 2 of this Act it appears to the court—

(a) that the applicant is in immediate need of financial assistance, but it is not yet possible to determine what order (if any) should be made under that section; and
(b) that property forming part of the net estate of the deceased is or can be made available to meet the need of the applicant;

the court may order that, subject to such conditions or restrictions, if any, as the court may impose and to any further order of the court, there shall be paid to the applicant out of the net estate of the deceased such sum or sums and (if more than one) at such intervals as the court thinks reasonable; and the court may order that, subject to the provisions of this Act, such payments are to be made until such date as the court may specify, not being later than the date on which the court either makes an order under the said section 2 or decides not to exercise its powers under that section.

(2) Subsections (2), (3) and (4) of section 2 of this Act shall apply in relation to an order under this section as they apply in relation to an order under that section.

(3) In determining what order, if any, should be made under this section the court shall, so far as the urgency of the case admits, have regard to the same matters as those to which the court is required to have regard under section 3 of this Act.
(4) An order made under section 2 of this Act may provide that any sum paid to the applicant by virtue of this section shall be treated to such an extent and in such manner as may be provided by that order as having been paid on account of any payment provided for by that order.

6 Variation, discharge etc. of orders for periodical payments.
(1) Subject to the provisions of this Act, where the court has made an order under section 2(1)(a) of this Act (in this section referred to as "the original order") for the making of periodical payments to any person (in this section referred to as "the original recipient"), the court, on an application under this section, shall have power by order to vary or discharge the original order or to suspend any provision of it temporarily and to revive the operation of any provision so suspended.
(2) Without prejudice to the generality of subsection (1) above, an order made on an application for the variation of the original order may—

(a) provide for the making out of any relevant property of such periodical payments and for such term as may be specified in the order to any person who has applied, or would but for section 4 of this Act be entitled to apply, for an order under section 2 of this Act (whether or not, in the case of any application, an order was made in favour of the applicant);
(b) provide for the payment out of any relevant property of a lump sum of such amount as may be so specified to the original recipient or to any such person as is mentioned in paragraph (a) above;
(c) provide for the transfer of the relevant property, or such part thereof as may be so specified, to the original recipient or to any such person as is so mentioned.

(3) Where the original order provides that any periodical payments payable thereunder to the original recipient are to cease on the occurrence of an event specified in the order [(other than the formation of a subsequent marriage or civil partnership by a former spouse or former civil partner)] or on the expiration of a period so specified, then, if, before the end of the period of six months from the date of the occurrence of that event or of the expiration of that period, an application is made for an order under this section, the court shall have power to make any order which it would have had power to make if the application had been made before that date (whether in favour of the original recipient or any such person as is mentioned in subsection (2)(a) above and whether having effect from that date or from such later date as the court may specify).
(4) Any reference in this section to the original order shall include a reference to an order made under this section and any reference in this section to the original

recipient shall include a reference to any person to whom periodical payments are required to be made by virtue of an order under this section.
(5) An application under this section may be made by any of the following persons, that is to say—

(a) any person who by virtue of section 1(1) of this Act has applied, or would but for section 4 of this Act be entitled to apply, for an order under section 2 of this Act,
(b) the personal representatives of the deceased,
(c) the trustees of any relevant property, and
(d) any beneficiary of the estate of the deceased.

(6) An order under this section may only affect—

(a) property the income of which is at the date of the order applicable wholly or in part for the making of periodical payments to any person who has applied for an order under this Act, or
(b) in the case of an application under subsection (3) above in respect of payments which have ceased to be payable on the occurrence of an event or the expiration of a period, property the income of which was so applicable immediately before the occurrence of that event or the expiration of that period, as the case may be,

and any such property as is mentioned in paragraph (a) or (b) above is in subsections (2) and (5) above referred to as "relevant property".
(7) In exercising the powers conferred by this section the court shall have regard to all the circumstances of the case, including any change in any of the matters to which the court was required to have regard when making the order to which the application relates.
(8) Where the court makes an order under this section, it may give such consequential directions as it thinks necessary or expedient having regard to the provisions of the order.
(9) No such order as is mentioned in sections 2(1)(d), (e) or (f), 9, 10 or 11 of this Act shall be made on an application under this section.
(10) For the avoidance of doubt it is hereby declared that, in relation to an order which provides for the making of periodical payments which are to cease on the occurrence of an event specified in the order [(other than the formation of a subsequent marriage or civil partnership by a former spouse or former civil partner)] or on the expiration of a period so specified, the power to vary an order includes power to provide for the making of periodical payments after the expiration of that period or the occurrence of that event.

AMENDMENTS

Words in s 6(3), (10) substituted by Civil Partnership Act 2004, ss 71, 263(2), Sch 4 para 19; Civil Partnership Act 2004 (Commencement No 2) Order 2005 (SI 2005/3175), art 2(2), Sch 1

7 Payment of lump sums by instalments.

(1) An order under section 2(1)(b) or 6(2)(b) of this Act for the payment of a lump sum may provide for the payment of that sum by instalments of such amount as may be specified in the order.

(2) Where an order is made by virtue of subsection (1) above, the court shall have power, on an application made by the person to whom the lump sum is payable, by the personal representatives of the deceased or by the trustees of the property out of which the lump sum is payable, to vary that order by varying the number of instalments payable, the amount of any instalment and the date on which any instalment becomes payable.

Property available for financial provision

8 Property treated as part of "net estate".

(1) Where a deceased person has in accordance with the provisions of any enactment nominated any person to receive any sum of money or other property on his death and that nomination is in force at the time of his death, that sum of money, after deducting therefrom any capital transfer tax payable in respect thereof, or that other property, to the extent of the value thereof at the date of the death of the deceased after deducting therefrom any capital transfer tax so payable, shall be treated for the purposes of this Act as part of the net estate of the deceased; but this subsection shall not render any person liable for having paid that sum or transferred that other property to the person named in the nomination in accordance with the directions given in the nomination.

(2) Where any sum of money or other property is received by any person as a donatio mortis causa made by a deceased person, that sum of money, after deducting therefrom any capital transfer tax payable thereon, or that other property, to the extent of the value thereof at the date of the death of the deceased after deducting therefrom any capital transfer tax so payable, shall be treated for the purposes of this Act as part of the net estate of the deceased; but this subsection shall not render any person liable for having paid that sum or transferred that other property in order to give effect to that donatio mortis causa.

(3) The amount of capital transfer tax to be deducted for the purposes of this section shall not exceed the amount of that tax which has been borne by the person nominated by the deceased or, as the case may be, the person who has received a sum of money or other property as a donatio mortis causa.

9 Property held on a joint tenancy.

(1) Where a deceased person was immediately before his death beneficially entitled to a joint tenancy of any property, then, if ... an application is made for an order under section 2 of this Act, the court for the purpose of facilitating the making of financial provision for the applicant under this Act may order that the deceased's severable share of that property ... shall, to such extent as appears to the court to be just in all the circumstances of the case, be treated for the purposes of this Act as part of the net estate of the deceased.

[(1A) Where an order is made under subsection (1) the value of the deceased's severable share of the property concerned is taken for the purposes of this Act to be the value that the share would have had at the date of the hearing of the application for an order under section 2 had the share been severed immediately before the deceased's death, unless the court orders that the share is to be valued at a different date.]

(2) In determining the extent to which any severable share is to be treated as part of the net estate of the deceased by virtue of an order under subsection (1) above, the court shall have regard to any capital transfer tax payable in respect of that severable share.

(3) Where an order is made under subsection (1) above, the provisions of this section shall not render any person liable for anything done by him before the order was made.

(4) For the avoidance of doubt it is hereby declared that for the purposes of this section there may be a joint tenancy of a chose in action.

AMENDMENTS

Words in s 9(1) omitted by virtue of Inheritance and Trustees' Powers Act 2014, s 12(2), Sch 2 para 7(2)(a), (b) (with s 12(4)); Inheritance and Trustees' Powers Act 2014 (Commencement) Order 2014 (SI 2014/2039), art 2

Section 9(1A) inserted by Inheritance and Trustees' Powers Act 2014, s 12(2), Sch 2 para 7(3) (with s 12(4)); Inheritance and Trustees' Powers Act 2014 (Commencement) Order 2014 (SI 2014/2039), art 2

Powers of court in relation to transactions intended to defeat applications for financial provision

10 Dispositions intended to defeat applications for financial provision.

(1) Where an application is made to the court for an order under section 2 of this Act, the applicant may, in the proceedings on that application, apply to the court for an order under subsection (2) below.

(2) Where on an application under subsection (1) above the court is satisfied—

(a) that, less than six years before the date of the death of the deceased, the deceased with the intention of defeating an application for financial provision under this Act made a disposition, and

(b) that full valuable consideration for that disposition was not given by the person to whom or for the benefit of whom the disposition was made (in this section referred to as "the donee") or by any other person, and
(c) that the exercise of the powers conferred by this section would facilitate the making of financial provision for the applicant under this Act,

then, subject to the provisions of this section and of sections 12 and 13 of this Act, the court may order the donee (whether or not at the date of the order he holds any interest in the property disposed of to him or for his benefit by the deceased) to provide, for the purpose of the making of that financial provision, such sum of money or other property as may be specified in the order.
(3) Where an order is made under subsection (2) above as respects any disposition made by the deceased which consisted of the payment of money to or for the benefit of the donee, the amount of any sum of money or the value of any property ordered to be provided under that subsection shall not exceed the amount of the payment made by the deceased after deducting therefrom any capital transfer tax borne by the donee in respect of that payment.
(4) Where an order is made under subsection (2) above as respects any disposition made by the deceased which consisted of the transfer of property (other than a sum of money) to or for the benefit of the donee, the amount of any sum of money or the value of any property ordered to be provided under that subsection shall not exceed the value at the date of the death of the deceased of the property disposed of by him to or for the benefit of the donee (or if that property has been disposed of by the person to whom it was transferred by the deceased, the value at the date of that disposal thereof) after deducting therefrom any capital transfer tax borne by the donee in respect of the transfer of that property by the deceased.
(5) Where an application (in this subsection referred to as "the original application") is made for an order under subsection (2) above in relation to any disposition, then, if on an application under this subsection by the donee or by any applicant for an order under section 2 of this Act the court is satisfied—

(a) that, less than six years before the date of the death of the deceased, the deceased with the intention of defeating an application for financial provision under this Act made a disposition other than the disposition which is the subject of the original application, and
(b) that full valuable consideration for that other disposition was not given by the person to whom or for the benefit of whom that other disposition was made or by any other person,

the court may exercise in relation to the person to whom or for the benefit of whom that other disposition was made the powers which the court would have had under subsection (2) above if the original application had been made in respect of that other disposition and the court had been satisfied as to the matters

set out in paragraphs (a), (b) and (c) of that subsection; and where any application is made under this subsection, any reference in this section (except in subsection (2)(b)) to the donee shall include a reference to the person to whom or for the benefit of whom that other disposition was made.
(6) In determining whether and in what manner to exercise its powers under this section, the court shall have regard to the circumstances in which any disposition was made and any valuable consideration which was given therefor, the relationship, if any, of the donee to the deceased, the conduct and financial resources of the donee and all the other circumstances of the case.
(7) In this section "disposition" does not include—

(a) any provision in a will, any such nomination as is mentioned in section 8(1) of this Act or any donatio mortis causa, or
(b) any appointment of property made, otherwise than by will, in the exercise of a special power of appointment,

but, subject to these exceptions, includes any payment of money (including the payment of a premium under a policy of assurance) and any conveyance, assurance, appointment or gift of property of any description, whether made by an instrument or otherwise.
(8) The provisions of this section do not apply to any disposition made before the commencement of this Act.

11 Contracts to leave property by will.
(1) Where an application is made to a court for an order under section 2 of this Act, the applicant may, in the proceedings on that application, apply to the court for an order under this section.
(2) Where on an application under subsection (1) above the court is satisfied—

(a) that the deceased made a contract by which he agreed to leave by his will a sum of money or other property to any person or by which he agreed that a sum of money or other property would be paid or transferred to any person out of his estate, and
(b) that the deceased made that contract with the intention of defeating an application for financial provision under this Act, and
(c) that when the contract was made full valuable consideration for that contract was not given or promised by the person with whom or for the benefit of whom the contract was made (in this section referred to as "the donee") or by any other person, and
(d) that the exercise of the powers conferred by this section would facilitate the making of financial provision for the applicant under this Act,

then, subject to the provisions of this section and of sections 12 and 13 of this Act, the court may make any one or more of the following orders, that is to say—

(i) if any money has been paid or any other property has been transferred to or for the benefit of the donee in accordance with the contract, an order directing the donee to provide, for the purpose of the making of that financial provision, such sum of money or other property as may be specified in the order;

(ii) if the money or all the money has not been paid or the property or all the property has not been transferred in accordance with the contract, an order directing the personal representatives not to make any payment or transfer any property, or not to make any further payment or transfer any further property, as the case may be, in accordance therewith or directing the personal representatives only to make such payment or transfer such property as may be specified in the order.

(3) Notwithstanding anything in subsection (2) above, the court may exercise its powers thereunder in relation to any contract made by the deceased only to the extent that the court considers that the amount of any sum of money paid or to be paid or the value of any property transferred or to be transferred in accordance with the contract exceeds the value of any valuable consideration given or to be given for that contract, and for this purpose the court shall have regard to the value of property at the date of the hearing.

(4) In determining whether and in what manner to exercise its powers under this section, the court shall have regard to the circumstances in which the contract was made, the relationship, if any, of the donee to the deceased, the conduct and financial resources of the donee and all the other circumstances of the case.

(5) Where an order has been made under subsection (2) above in relation to any contract, the rights of any person to enforce that contract or to recover damages or to obtain other relief for the breach thereof shall be subject to any adjustment made by the court under section 12(3) of this Act and shall survive to such extent only as is consistent with giving effect to the terms of that order.

(6) The provisions of this section do not apply to a contract made before the commencement of this Act.

12 Provisions supplementary to ss 10 and 11.

(1) Where the exercise of any of the powers conferred by section 10 or 11 of this Act is conditional on the court being satisfied that a disposition or contract was made by a deceased person with the intention of defeating an application for financial provision under this Act, that condition shall be fulfilled if the court is of the opinion that, on a balance of probabilities, the intention of the deceased (though not necessarily his sole intention) in making the disposition or contract was to prevent an order for financial provision being made under this Act or to reduce the amount of the provision which might otherwise be granted by an order thereunder.

(2) Where an application is made under section 11 of this Act with respect to any contract made by the deceased and no valuable consideration was given or promised by any person for that contract then, notwithstanding anything in subsection (1) above, it shall be presumed, unless the contrary is shown, that the deceased made that contract with the intention of defeating an application for financial provision under this Act.
(3) Where the court makes an order under section 10 or 11 of this Act it may give such consequential directions as it thinks fit (including directions requiring the making of any payment or the transfer of any property) for giving effect to the order or for securing a fair adjustment of the rights of the persons affected thereby.
(4) Any power conferred on the court by the said section 10 or 11 to order the donee, in relation to any disposition or contract, to provide any sum of money or other property shall be exercisable in like manner in relation to the personal representative of the donee, and—

(a) any reference in section 10(4) to the disposal of property by the donee shall include a reference to disposal by the personal representative of the donee, and
(b) any reference in section 10(5) to an application by the donee under that subsection shall include a reference to an application by the personal representative of the donee;

but the court shall not have power under the said section 10 or 11 to make an order in respect of any property forming part of the estate of the donee which has been distributed by the personal representative; and the personal representative shall not be liable for having distributed any such property before he has notice of the making of an application under the said section 10 or 11 on the ground that he ought to have taken into account the possibility that such an application would be made.

13 Provisions as to trustees in relation to ss 10 and 11.
(1) Where an application is made for—

(a) an order under section 10 of this Act in respect of a disposition made by the deceased to any person as a trustee, or
(b) an order under section 11 of this Act in respect of any payment made or property transferred, in accordance with a contract made by the deceased, to any person as a trustee,

the powers of the court under the said section 10 or 11 to order that trustee to provide a sum of money or other property shall be subject to the following limitation (in addition, in a case of an application under section 10, to any provision regarding the deduction of capital transfer tax) namely, that the amount of any sum of money or the value of any property ordered to be provided—

(i) in the case of an application in respect of a disposition which consisted of the payment of money or an application in respect of the payment of money in accordance with a contract, shall not exceed the aggregate of so much of that money as is at the date of the order in the hands of the trustee and the value at that date of any property which represents that money or is derived therefrom and is at that date in the hands of the trustee;

(ii) in the case of an application in respect of a disposition which consisted of the transfer of property (other than a sum of money) or an application in respect of the transfer of property (other than a sum of money) in accordance with a contract, shall not exceed the aggregate of the value at the date of the order of so much of that property as is at that date in the hands of the trustee and the value at that date of any property which represents the first-mentioned property or is derived therefrom and is at that date in the hands of the trustee.

(2) Where any such application is made in respect of a disposition made to any person as a trustee or in respect of any payment made or property transferred in pursuance of a contract to any person as a trustee, the trustee shall not be liable for having distributed any money or other property on the ground that he ought to have taken into account the possibility that such an application would be made.
(3) Where any such application is made in respect of a disposition made to any person as a trustee or in respect of any payment made or property transferred in accordance with a contract to any person as a trustee, any reference in the said section 10 or 11 to the donee shall be construed as including a reference to the trustee or trustees for the time being of the trust in question and any reference in subsection (1) or (2) above to a trustee shall be construed in the same way.

Special provisions relating to cases of divorce, separation etc.

14 Provision as to cases where no financial relief was granted in divorce proceedings etc.

(1) Where, within twelve months from the date on which a [divorce order or nullity of marriage order has been made final or a judicial separation order has been made,] a party to the marriage dies and—

(a) an application for a financial provision order under section 23 of the Matrimonial Causes Act 1973 or a property adjustment order under section 24 of that Act has not been made by the other party to that marriage, or

(b) such an application has been made but the proceedings thereon have not been determined at the time of the death of the deceased,

then, if an application for an order under section 2 of this Act is made by that other party, the court shall, notwithstanding anything in section 1 or section 3 of this Act, have power, if it thinks it just to do so, to treat that party for the purposes of that application as if the [divorce order or nullity of marriage order had not been made final or the judicial separation order had not been made,] as the case may be.
(2) This section shall not apply in relation to a [judicial separation order] unless at the date of the death of the deceased [the order] was in force and the separation was continuing.

AMENDMENTS
Words in s 14(1) substituted by Divorce, Dissolution and Separation Act 2020, s 8(1), (8), Sch para 44(4)(a)(i), (ii); Divorce, Dissolution and Separation Act 2020 (Commencement) Regulations 2022 (SI 2022/283), reg 2
Words in s 14(2) substituted by Divorce, Dissolution and Separation Act 2020, s 8(1), (8), Sch para 44(4)(b)(i), (ii); Divorce, Dissolution and Separation Act 2020 (Commencement) Regulations 2022 (SI 2022/283), reg 2

[14A Provision as to cases where no financial relief was granted in proceedings for the dissolution etc. of a civil partnership.
(1) Subsection (2) below applies where—

(a) a dissolution order, nullity order, separation order or presumption of death order has been made under Chapter 2 of Part 2 of the Civil Partnership Act 2004 in relation to a civil partnership,
(b) one of the civil partners dies within twelve months from the date on which the order is made, and
(c) either—

    (i) an application for a financial provision order under Part 1 of Schedule 5 to that Act or a property adjustment order under Part 2 of that Schedule has not been made by the other civil partner, or
    (ii) such an application has been made but the proceedings on the application have not been determined at the time of the death of the deceased.

(2) If an application for an order under section 2 of this Act is made by the surviving civil partner, the court shall, notwithstanding anything in section 1 or section 3 of this Act, have power, if it thinks it just to do so, to treat the surviving civil partner as if the order mentioned in subsection (1)(a) above had not been made.
(3) This section shall not apply in relation to a separation order unless at the date of the death of the deceased the separation order was in force and the separation was continuing.]

AMENDMENTS

Section 14A inserted by Civil Partnership Act 2004, ss 71, 263(2), Sch 4 para 20; Civil Partnership Act 2004 (Commencement No 2) Order 2005 (SI 2005/3175), art 2(1), Sch 1

15 Restriction imposed in divorce proceedings etc. on application under this Act.

[(1) On the [making of a divorce, nullity of marriage or judicial separation order] or at any time thereafter the court, if it considers it just to do so, may, on the application of either party to the marriage, order that the other party to the marriage shall not on the death of the applicant be entitled to apply for an order under section 2 of this Act.

In this subsection "the court" means the High Court or [the family court].]

(2) In the case of a [divorce or nullity of marriage order] an order may be made under subsection (1) above before or [after the divorce or nullity of marriage order is made final, but if it is made before that order is made final it shall not take effect unless that order is made final].

(3) Where an order made under subsection (1) above on the [making of a divorce or nullity of marriage order] has come into force with respect to a party to a marriage, then, on the death of the other party to that marriage, the court shall not entertain any application for an order under section 2 of this Act made by the first-mentioned party.

(4) Where an order made under subsection (1) above on the [making of a judicial separation order] has come into force with respect to any party to a marriage, then, if the other party to that marriage dies while the [order is] in force and the separation is continuing, the court shall not entertain any application for an order under section 2 of this Act made by the first-mentioned party.

AMENDMENTS

Section 15(1) substituted by Matrimonial and Family Proceedings Act 1984, s 8(1)

Words in s 15(1) substituted by Divorce, Dissolution and Separation Act 2020, s 8(1), (8), Sch para 44(5)(a); Divorce, Dissolution and Separation Act 2020 (Commencement) Regulations 2022 (SI 2022/283), reg 2

Words in s 15(1) substituted by Crime and Courts Act 2013, s 61(3), Sch 10 para 36(2); Crime and Courts Act 2013 (Commencement No 10 and Transitional Provision) Order 2014 (SI 2014/954), art 2(d) (with art 3) (with transitional provisions and savings in Crime and Courts Act 2013 (Family Court: Transitional and Saving Provision) Order 2014 (SI 2014/956), arts 3–11)

Words in s 15(2) substituted by Divorce, Dissolution and Separation Act 2020, s 8(1), (8), Sch para 44(5)(b)(i), (ii); Divorce, Dissolution and Separation Act 2020 (Commencement) Regulations 2022 (SI 2022/283), reg 2

Words in s 15(3) substituted by Divorce, Dissolution and Separation Act 2020, s 8(1), (8), Sch para 44(5)(c); Divorce, Dissolution and Separation Act 2020 (Commencement) Regulations 2022 (SI 2022/283), reg 2

Words in s 15(4) substituted by Divorce, Dissolution and Separation Act 2020, s 8(1), (8), Sch para 44(5)(d)(i), (ii); Divorce, Dissolution and Separation Act 2020 (Commencement) Regulations 2022 (SI 2022/283), reg 2

[15ZA Restriction imposed in proceedings for the dissolution etc. of a civil partnership on application under this Act.

(1) On making a dissolution order, nullity order, separation order or presumption of death order under Chapter 2 of Part 2 of the Civil Partnership Act 2004, or at any time after making such an order, the court, if it considers it just to do so, may, on the application of either of the civil partners, order that the other civil partner shall not on the death of the applicant be entitled to apply for an order under section 2 of this Act.

(2) In subsection (1) above "the court" means the High Court or [the family court].

(3) In the case of a dissolution order, nullity order or presumption of death order ("the main order") an order may be made under subsection (1) above before (as well as after) the main order is made final, but if made before the main order is made final it shall not take effect unless the main order is made final.

(4) Where an order under subsection (1) above made in connection with a dissolution order, nullity order or presumption of death order has come into force with respect to a civil partner, then, on the death of the other civil partner, the court shall not entertain any application for an order under section 2 of this Act made by the surviving civil partner.

(5) Where an order under subsection (1) above made in connection with a separation order has come into force with respect to a civil partner, then, if the other civil partner dies while the separation order is in force and the separation is continuing, the court shall not entertain any application for an order under section 2 of this Act made by the surviving civil partner.]

AMENDMENTS

Section 15ZA inserted by Civil Partnership Act 2004, ss 71, 263(2), Sch 4 para 21; Civil Partnership Act 2004 (Commencement No 2) Order 2005 (SI 2005/3175), art 2(1), Sch 1

Words in s 15ZA(2) substituted by Crime and Courts Act 2013, s 61(3), Sch 10 para 36(3); Crime and Courts Act 2013 (Family Court: Transitional and Saving Provision) Order 2014 (SI 2014/956), art 2(d) (with art 3) (with transitional provisions and savings in Crime and Courts Act 2013 (Family Court: Transitional and Saving Provision) Order 2014 (SI 2014/956), arts 3–11)

[15A Restriction imposed in proceedings under Matrimonial and Family Proceedings Act 1984 on application under this Act.

(1) On making an order under section 17 of the Matrimonial and Family Proceedings Act 1984 (orders for financial provision and property adjustment

following overseas divorces, etc.) the court, if it considers it just to do so, may, on the application of either party to the marriage, order that the other party to the marriage shall not on the death of the applicant be entitled to apply for an order under section 2 of this Act.

In this subsection "the court" means the High Court or [the family court].

(2) Where an order under subsection (1) above has been made with respect to a party to a marriage which has been dissolved or annulled, then, on the death of the other party to that marriage, the court shall not entertain an application under section 2 of this Act made by the first-mentioned party.

(3) Where an order under subsection (1) above has been made with respect to a party to a marriage the parties to which have been legally separated, then, if the other party to the marriage dies while the legal separation is in force, the court shall not entertain an application under section 2 of this Act made by the first-mentioned party.]

AMENDMENTS

Section 15A inserted by Matrimonial and Family Proceedings Act 1984, s 25(3)

Words in s 15A(1) substituted by Crime and Courts Act 2013, s 61(3), Sch 10 para 36(4); Crime and Courts Act 2013 (Family Court: Transitional and Saving Provision) Order 2014 (SI 2014/956), art 2(d) (with art 3) (with transitional provisions and savings in Crime and Courts Act 2013 (Family Court: Transitional and Saving Provision) Order 2014 (SI 2014/956), arts 3–11)

[15B Restriction imposed in proceedings under Schedule 7 to the Civil Partnership Act 2004 on application under this Act.

(1) On making an order under paragraph 9 of Schedule 7 to the Civil Partnership Act 2004 (orders for financial provision, property adjustment and pension-sharing following overseas dissolution etc. of civil partnership) the court, if it considers it just to do so, may, on the application of either of the civil partners, order that the other civil partner shall not on the death of the applicant be entitled to apply for an order under section 2 of this Act.

(2) In subsection (1) above "the court" means the High Court or [the family court].

(3) Where an order under subsection (1) above has been made with respect to one of the civil partners in a case where a civil partnership has been dissolved or annulled, then, on the death of the other civil partner, the court shall not entertain an application under section 2 of this Act made by the surviving civil partner.

(4) Where an order under subsection (1) above has been made with respect to one of the civil partners in a case where civil partners have been legally separated, then, if the other civil partner dies while the legal separation is in force, the court shall not entertain an application under section 2 of this Act made by the surviving civil partner.]

AMENDMENTS

Section 15B inserted by Civil Partnership Act 2004, ss 71, 263(2), Sch 4 para 22; Civil Partnership Act 2004 (Commencement No 2) Order 2005 (SI 2005/3175), art 2(1), Sch 1

Words in s 15B(2) substituted by Crime and Courts Act 2013, s 61(3), Sch 10 para 36(5); Crime and Courts Act 2013 (Family Court: Transitional and Saving Provision) Order 2014 (SI 2014/956), art 2(d) (with art 3) (with transitional provisions and savings in Crime and Courts Act 2013 (Family Court: Transitional and Saving Provision) Order 2014 (SI 2014/956), arts 3–11)

16 Variation and discharge of secured periodical payments orders made under Matrimonial Causes Act 1973.

(1) Where an application for an order under section 2 of this Act is made to the court by any person who was at the time of the death of the deceased entitled to payments from the deceased under a secured periodical payments order made under the Matrimonial Causes Act 1973 [or Schedule 5 to the Civil Partnership Act 2004], then, in the proceedings on that application, the court shall have power, if an application is made under this section by that person or by the personal representative of the deceased, to vary or discharge that periodical payments order or to revive the operation of any provision thereof which has been suspended under section 31 of that Act [of 1973 or Part 11 of that Schedule].

(2) In exercising the powers conferred by this section the court shall have regard to all the circumstances of the case, including any order which the court proposes to make under section 2 or section 5 of this Act and any change (whether resulting from the death of the deceased or otherwise) in any of the matters to which the court was required to have regard when making the secured periodical payments order.

(3) The powers exercisable by the court under this section in relation to an order shall be exercisable also in relation to any instrument executed in pursuance of the order.

AMENDMENTS

Words in s 16(1) inserted by Civil Partnership Act 2004, ss 71, 263(2), Sch 4 para 23(a); Civil Partnership Act 2004 (Commencement No 2) Order 2005 (SI 2005/3175), art 2(1), Sch 1

Words in s 16(1) inserted by Civil Partnership Act 2004, ss 71, 263(2), Sch 4 para 23(b); Civil Partnership Act 2004 (Commencement No 2) Order 2005 (SI 2005/3175), art 2(1), Sch 1

17 Variation and revocation of maintenance agreements.

(1) Where an application for an order under section 2 of this Act is made to the court by any person who was at the time of the death of the deceased entitled to payments from the deceased under a maintenance agreement which provided for the continuation of payments under the agreement after the death of the deceased,

then, in the proceedings on that application, the court shall have power, if an application is made under this section by that person or by the personal representative of the deceased, to vary or revoke that agreement.
(2) In exercising the powers conferred by this section the court shall have regard to all the circumstances of the case, including any order which the court proposes to make under section 2 or section 5 of this Act and any change (whether resulting from the death of the deceased or otherwise) in any of the circumstances in the light of which the agreement was made.
(3) If a maintenance agreement is varied by the court under this section the like consequences shall ensue as if the variation had been made immediately before the death of the deceased by agreement between the parties and for valuable consideration.
(4) In this section "maintenance agreement", in relation to a deceased person, means any agreement made, whether in writing or not and whether before or after the commencement of this Act, by the deceased with any person with whom he [formed a marriage or civil partnership], being an agreement which contained provisions governing the rights and liabilities towards one another when living separately of the parties to that marriage [or of the civil partners](whether or not the marriage [or civil partnership] has been dissolved or annulled) in respect of the making or securing of payments or the disposition or use of any property, including such rights and liabilities with respect to the maintenance or education of any child, whether or not a child of the deceased or a person who was treated by the deceased as a child of the family in relation to that marriage [or civil partnership].

AMENDMENTS

Words in s 17(4) substituted by Civil Partnership Act 2004, ss 71, 263(2), Sch 4 para 24(a), (b), (c); Civil Partnership Act 2004 (Commencement No 2) Order 2005 (SI 2005/3175), art 2(1), Sch 1

18 Availability of court's powers under this Act in applications under ss 31 and 36 of the Matrimonial Causes Act 1973.

(1) Where—

(a) a person against whom a secured periodical payments order was made under the Matrimonial Causes Act 1973 has died and an application is made under section 31(6) of that Act for the variation or discharge of that order or for the revival of the operation of any provision thereof which has been suspended, or
(b) a party to a maintenance agreement within the meaning of section 34 of that Act has died, the agreement being one which provides for the continuation of payments thereunder after the death of one of the parties, and an application is made under section 36(1) of that Act for the alteration of the agreement under section 35 thereof,

the court shall have power to direct that the application made under the said section 31(6) or 36(1) shall be deemed to have been accompanied by an application for an order under section 2 of this Act.

(2) Where the court gives a direction under subsection (1) above it shall have power, in the proceedings on the application under the said section 31(6) or 36(1), to make any order which the court would have had power to make under the provisions of this Act if the application under the said section 31(6) or 36(1), as the case may be, had been made jointly with an application for an order under the said section 2; and the court shall have power to give such consequential directions as may be necessary for enabling the court to exercise any of the powers available to the court under this Act in the case of an application for an order under section 2.

(3) Where an order made under section 15(1) of this Act is in force with respect to a party to a marriage, the court shall not give a direction under subsection (1) above with respect to any application made under the said section 31(6) or 36(1) by that party on the death of the other party.

[18A Availability of court's powers under this Act in applications under paragraphs 60 and 73 of Schedule 5 to the Civil Partnership Act 2004.

(1) Where—

(a) a person against whom a secured periodical payments order was made under Schedule 5 to the Civil Partnership Act 2004 has died and an application is made under paragraph 60 of that Schedule for the variation or discharge of that order or for the revival of the operation of any suspended provision of the order, or

(b) a party to a maintenance agreement within the meaning of Part 13 of that Schedule has died, the agreement being one which provides for the continuation of payments under the agreement after the death of one of the parties, and an application is made under paragraph 73 of that Schedule for the alteration of the agreement under paragraph 69 of that Schedule,

the court shall have power to direct that the application made under paragraph 60 or 73 of that Schedule shall be deemed to have been accompanied by an application for an order under section 2 of this Act.

(2) Where the court gives a direction under subsection (1) above it shall have power, in the proceedings on the application under paragraph 60 or 73 of that Schedule, to make any order which the court would have had power to make under the provisions of this Act if the application under that paragraph had been made jointly with an application for an order under section 2 of this Act; and the court

shall have power to give such consequential directions as may be necessary for enabling the court to exercise any of the powers available to the court under this Act in the case of an application for an order under section 2.

(3) Where an order made under section 15ZA(1) of this Act is in force with respect to a civil partner, the court shall not give a direction under subsection (1) above with respect to any application made under paragraph 60 or 73 of that Schedule by that civil partner on the death of the other civil partner.]

AMENDMENTS

Section 18A inserted by Civil Partnership Act 2004, ss 71, 263(2), Sch 4 para 25; Civil Partnership Act 2004 (Commencement No 2) Order 2005 (SI 2005/3175), art 2(1), Sch 1

19 Effect, duration and form of orders.

(1) Where an order is made under section 2 of this Act then for all purposes, including the purposes of the enactments relating to capital transfer tax, the will or the law relating to intestacy, or both the will and the law relating to intestacy, as the case may be, shall have effect and be deemed to have had effect as from the deceased's death subject to the provisions of the order.

(2) Any order made under section 2 or 5 of this Act in favour of—

- (a) an applicant who was the [former spouse or former civil partner] of the deceased, or
- (b) an applicant who was the husband or wife of the deceased in a case where the marriage with the deceased was the subject of a [judicial separation order] and at the date of death [the order] was in force and the separation was continuing, [or
- (c) an applicant who was the civil partner of the deceased in a case where, at the date of death, a separation order under Chapter 2 of Part 2 of the Civil Partnership Act 2004 was in force in relation to their civil partnership and the separation was continuing,]

shall, in so far as it provides for the making of periodical payments, cease to have effect [on the formation by the applicant of a subsequent marriage or civil partnership, except in relation to any arrears due under the order on the date of the formation of the subsequent marriage or civil partnership.]

(3) A copy of every order made under this Act [other than an order made under section 15(1) [or 15ZA(1)] of this Act] shall be sent to the principal registry of the Family Division for entry and filing, and a memorandum of the order shall be endorsed on, or permanently annexed to, the probate or letters of administration under which the estate is being administered.

AMENDMENTS

Words in s 19(2)(a) substituted by Civil Partnership Act 2004, ss 71, 263(2), Sch 4 para 26(2); Civil Partnership Act 2004 (Commencement No 2) Order 2005 (SI 2005/3175), art 2(1), Sch 1

Words in s 19(2)(b) substituted by Divorce, Dissolution and Separation Act 2020, s 8(1), (8), Sch para 44(6)(a), (b); Divorce, Dissolution and Separation Act 2020 (Commencement) Regulations 2022 (SI 2022/283), reg 2

Section 19(2)(c) and preceding word inserted by Civil Partnership Act 2004, ss 71, 263(2), Sch 4 para 26(3); Civil Partnership Act 2004 (Commencement No 2) Order 2005 (SI 2005/3175), art 2(1), Sch 1

Words in s 19(2) substituted by Civil Partnership Act 2004, ss 71, 263(2), Sch 4 para 26(4); Civil Partnership Act 2004 (Commencement No 2) Order 2005 (SI 2005/3175), art 2(1), Sch 1

Words in s 19(3) inserted by Administration of Justice Act 1982, s 52

Words in s 19(3) inserted by Civil Partnership Act 2004, ss 71, 263(2), Sch 4 para 26(5); Civil Partnership Act 2004 (Commencement No 2) Order 2005 (SI 2005/3175), art 2(1), Sch 1

20 Provisions as to personal representatives.

(1) The provisions of this Act shall not render the personal representative of a deceased person liable for having distributed any part of the estate of the deceased, after the end of the period of six months from the date on which representation with respect to the estate of the deceased is first taken out, on the ground that he ought to have taken into account the possibility—

(a) that the court might permit the making of an application for an order under section 2 of this Act after the end of that period, or

(b) that, where an order has been made under the said section 2, the court might exercise in relation thereto the powers conferred on it by section 6 of this Act,

but this subsection shall not prejudice any power to recover, by reason of the making of an order under this Act, any part of the estate so distributed.

(2) Where the personal representative of a deceased person pays any sum directed by an order under section 5 of this Act to be paid out of the deceased's net estate, he shall not be under any liability by reason of that estate not being sufficient to make the payment, unless at the time of making the payment he has reasonable cause to believe that the estate is not sufficient.

(3) Where a deceased person entered into a contract by which he agreed to leave by his will any sum of money or other property to any person or by which he agreed that a sum of money or other property would be paid or transferred to any person out of his estate, then, if the personal representative of the deceased has reason to believe that the deceased entered into the contract with the intention of defeating an application for financial provision under this Act, he may, notwithstanding anything in that contract, postpone the payment of that sum of

money or the transfer of that property until the expiration of the period of six months from the date on which representation with respect to the estate of the deceased is first taken out or, if during that period an application is made for an order under section 2 of this Act, until the determination of the proceedings on that application.

21 ...

Amendments

Section 21 repealed by Civil Evidence Act 1995, s 15(2), Sch 2; Civil Evidence Act 1995 (Commencement No 1) Order 1996 (SI 1996/3217), art 2

22 ...

Amendments

Section 22 repealed by Administration of Justice Act 1982, s 75, Sch 9 Pt I

[23 Determination of date on which representation was first taken out.
(1) The following are to be left out of account when considering for the purposes of this Act when representation with respect to the estate of a deceased person was first taken out—

(a) a grant limited to settled land or to trust property,
(b) any other grant that does not permit any of the estate to be distributed,
(c) a grant limited to real estate or to personal estate, unless a grant limited to the remainder of the estate has previously been made or is made at the same time,
(d) a grant, or its equivalent, made outside the United Kingdom (but see subsection (2) below).

(2) A grant sealed under section 2 of the Colonial Probates Act 1892 counts as a grant made in the United Kingdom for the purposes of this section, but is to be taken as dated on the date of sealing.]

Amendments

Section 23 substituted by Inheritance and Trustees' Powers Act 2014, s 12(2), Sch 3 para 2 (with s 12(4)); Inheritance and Trustees' Powers Act 2014 (Commencement) Order 2014 (SI 2014/2039), art 2

24 Effect of this Act on s 46(1)(vi) of Administration of Estates Act 1925.
Section 46(1)(vi) of the Administration of Estates Act 1925, in so far as it provides for the devolution of property on the Crown, the Duchy of Lancaster or the Duke of Cornwall as bona vacantia, shall have effect subject to the provisions of this Act.

25 Interpretation.

(1) In this Act—

"beneficiary", in relation to the estate of a deceased person, means—

(a) a person who under the will of the deceased or under the law relating to intestacy is beneficially interested in the estate or would be so interested if an order had not been made under this Act, and
(b) a person who has received any sum of money or other property which by virtue of section 8(1) or 8(2) of this Act is treated as part of the net estate of the deceased or would have received that sum or other property if an order had not been made under this Act;

"child" includes an illegitimate child and a child en ventre sa mere at the death of the deceased;
"the court" means [unless the context otherwise requires] the High Court, or where [the county] court has jurisdiction by virtue of section [25 of the County Courts Act 1984], [the county] court;

["former civil partner" means a person whose civil partnership with the deceased was during the lifetime of the deceased either—

(a) dissolved or annulled by an order made under the law of any part of the British Islands, or
(b) dissolved or annulled in any country or territory outside the British Islands by a dissolution or annulment which is entitled to be recognised as valid by the law of England and Wales;]

[["former spouse"] means a person whose marriage with the deceased was during the lifetime of the deceased either—

(a) dissolved or annulled by a [divorce order or nullity of marriage order made, or a decree of divorce or of nullity of marriage granted,] under the law of any part of the British Islands, or
(b) dissolved or annulled in any country or territory outside the British Islands by a divorce or annulment which is entitled to be recognised as valid by the law of England and Wales;]

"net estate", in relation to a deceased person, means:—

(a) all property of which the deceased had power to dispose by his will (otherwise than by virtue of a special power of appointment) less the amount of his funeral, testamentary and administration expenses, debts and liabilities, including any capital transfer tax payable out of his estate on his death;

(b) any property in respect of which the deceased held a general power of appointment (not being a power exercisable by will) which has not been exercised;

(c) any sum of money or other property which is treated for the purposes of this Act as part of the net estate of the deceased by virtue of section 8(1) or (2) of this Act;

(d) any property which is treated for the purposes of this Act as part of the net estate of the deceased by virtue of an order made under section 9 of the Act;

(e) any sum of money or other property which is, by reason of a disposition or contract made by the deceased, ordered under section 10 or 11 of this Act to be provided for the purpose of the making of financial provision under this Act;

"property" includes any chose in action;

"reasonable financial provision" has the meaning assigned to it by section 1 of this Act;

"valuable consideration" does not include marriage or a promise of marriage;

"will" includes codicil.

(2) For the purposes of paragraph (a) of the definition of "net estate" in subsection (1) above a person who is not of full age and capacity shall be treated as having power to dispose by will of all property of which he would have had power to dispose by will if he had been of full age and capacity.

(3) Any reference in this Act to provision out of the net estate of a deceased person includes a reference to provision extending to the whole of that estate.

(4) For the purposes of this Act any reference to a [spouse,] wife or husband shall be treated as including a reference to a person who in good faith entered into a void marriage with the deceased unless either—

(a) the marriage of the deceased and that person was dissolved or annulled during the lifetime of the deceased and the dissolution or annulment is recognised by the law of England and Wales, or

(b) that person has during the lifetime of the deceased [formed a subsequent marriage or civil partnership].

[(4A) For the purposes of this Act any reference to a civil partner shall be treated as including a reference to a person who in good faith formed a void civil partnership with the deceased unless either—

(a) the civil partnership between the deceased and that person was dissolved or annulled during the lifetime of the deceased and the dissolution or annulment is recognised by the law of England and Wales, or
(b) that person has during the lifetime of the deceased formed a subsequent civil partnership or marriage.

(5) Any reference in this Act to the formation of, or to a person who has formed, a subsequent marriage or civil partnership includes (as the case may be) a reference to the formation of, or to a person who has formed, a marriage or civil partnership which is by law void or voidable.
(5A) The formation of a marriage or civil partnership shall be treated for the purposes of this Act as the formation of a subsequent marriage or civil partnership, in relation to either of the spouses or civil partners, notwithstanding that the previous marriage or civil partnership of that spouse or civil partner was void or voidable.]
[(5B) In sections 1(2), 3(2), 14, 15 and 19(2)—

(a) a reference to a divorce order includes a decree of divorce,
(b) a reference to a nullity of marriage order includes a decree of nullity of marriage;
(c) a reference to a judicial separation order includes a decree of judicial separation;
(d) a reference to making includes granting;
(e) a reference to an order being made final includes a decree being made absolute.]

(6) Any reference in this Act to an order or decree made under the Matrimonial Causes Act 1973 or under any section of that Act shall be construed as including a reference to an order or decree which is deemed to have been made under that Act or under that section thereof, as the case may be.
[(6A) Any reference in this Act to an order made under, or under any provision of, the Civil Partnership Act 2004 shall be construed as including a reference to anything which is deemed to be an order made (as the case may be) under that Act or provision.]
(7) Any reference in this Act to any enactment is a reference to that enactment as amended by or under any subsequent enactment.

AMENDMENTS

Words in s 25(1) inserted by Matrimonial and Family Proceedings Act 1984, s 8(2)

Words in s 25(1) substituted by Crime and Courts Act 2013, s 61(3), Sch 9 para 92(a); Crime and Courts Act 2013 (Family Court: Transitional and Saving Provision) Order 2014 (SI 2014/956), art 2(c) (with art 3) (with transitional provisions and savings in Crime and Courts Act 2013 (Family Court: Transitional and Saving Provision) Order 2014 (SI 2014/956), arts 3–11)

Words in s 25(1) substituted by Crime and Courts Act 2013, s 61(3), Sch 9 para 92(b); Crime and Courts Act 2013 (Commencement No 10 and Transitional Provision) Order 2014 (SI 2014/954), art 2(c) (with art 3) (with transitional provisions and savings in Crime and Courts Act 2013 (Family Court: Transitional and Saving Provision) Order 2014 (SI 2014/956), arts 3–11)

Section 25(1): definition of "former civil partner" inserted by Civil Partnership Act 2004, ss 71, 263(2), Sch 4 para 27(3); Civil Partnership Act 2004 (Commencement No 2) Order 2005 (SI 2005/3175), art 2(1), Sch 1

Section 25(1): Definition substituted by Matrimonial and Family Proceedings Act 1984, s 25(2)

Section 25(1): definition of ""former husband" or "former wife"" becomes definition of "former spouse" by virtue of Civil Partnership Act 2004, ss 71, 263(2), Sch 4 para 27(2); Civil Partnership Act 2004 (Commencement No 2) Order 2005 (SI 2005/3175), art 2(1), Sch 1

Words in s 25(1) substituted by Divorce, Dissolution and Separation Act 2020, s 8(1), (8), Sch para 44(7)(a); Divorce, Dissolution and Separation Act 2020 (Commencement) Regulations 2022 (SI 2022/283), reg 2

Word in s 25(4) inserted by Civil Partnership Act 2004, ss 71, 263(2), Sch 4 para 27(4)(a); Civil Partnership Act 2004 (Commencement No 2) Order 2005 (SI 2005/3175), art 2(1), Sch 1

Words in s 25(4)(b) inserted by Civil Partnership Act 2004, ss 71, 263(2), Sch 4 para 27(4)(b); Civil Partnership Act 2004 (Commencement No 2) Order 2005 (SI 2005/3175), art 2(1), Sch 1

Section 25(4A)–(5A) substituted for s 25(5) by Civil Partnership Act 2004, ss 71, 263(2), Sch 4 para 27(5); Civil Partnership Act 2004 (Commencement No 2) Order 2005 (SI 2005/3175), art 2(1), Sch 1

Section 25(5B) inserted by Divorce, Dissolution and Separation Act 2020, s 8(1), (8), Sch para 44(7)(b); Divorce, Dissolution and Separation Act 2020 (Commencement) Regulations 2022 (SI 2022/283), reg 2

Section 25(6A) inserted by Civil Partnership Act 2004, ss 71, 263(2), Sch 4 para 27(6); Civil Partnership Act 2004 (Commencement No 2) Order 2005 (SI 2005/3175), art 2(1), Sch 1

26 Consequential amendments, repeals and transitional provisions

(1) ...

(2) Subject to the provisions of this section, the enactments specified in the Schedule to this Act are hereby repealed to the extent specified in the third column of the Schedule; and in paragraph 5(2) of Schedule 2 to the Matrimonial Causes Act 1973 for the words "that Act" there shall be substituted the words "the Matrimonial Causes Act 1965."

(3) The repeal of the said enactments shall not affect their operation in relation to any application made thereunder (whether before or after the commencement of this Act) with reference to the death of any person who died before the commencement of this Act.

(4) Without prejudice to the provisions of section 38 of the Interpretation Act 1889 (which relates to the effect of repeals) nothing in any repeal made by this

Act shall affect any order made or direction given under any enactment repealed by this Act, and, subject to the provisions of this Act, every such order or direction (other than an order made under section 4A of the Inheritance Family Provision Act 1938 or section 28A of the Matrimonial Causes Act 1965) shall, if it is in force at the commencement of this Act or is made by virtue of subsection (3) above, continue in force as if it had been made under section 2(1)(a) of this Act, and for the purposes of section 6(7) of this Act the court in exercising its powers under that section in relation to an order continued in force by this subsection shall be required to have regard to any change in any of the circumstances to which the court would have been required to have regard when making that order if the order had been made with reference to the death of any person who died after the commencement of this Act.

AMENDMENTS

Section 26(1) repealed by Crime and Courts Act 2013, s 61(3), Sch 11 para 210 Table; Crime and Courts Act 2013 (Commencement No 10 and Transitional Provision) Order 2014 (SI 2014/954), art 2(e) (with art 3) (with transitional provisions and savings in Crime and Courts Act 2013 (Family Court: Transitional and Saving Provision) Order 2014 (SI 2014/956), arts 3–11)

27 Short title, commencement and extent.

(1) This Act may be cited as the Inheritance (Provision for Family and Dependants) Act 1975.

(2) This Act does not extend to Scotland or Northern Ireland.

(3) This Act shall come into force on 1st April 1976.

SCHEDULE Enactments Repealed

Chapter	Short Title	Extent of Repeal
1938 c 72	The Inheritance (Family Provision) Act 1938	The whole Act.
1952 c 64	The Intestates' Estates Act 1952	Section 7 and Schedule 3.
1965 c 72	The Matrimonial Causes Act 1965	Section 26 to 28(A) and section 25(4) and (5) as applied by section 28(2).
1966 c 35	The Family Provision Act 1966	The whole Act, except section 1 and subsections (1) and (3) of section 10.
1969 c 46	The Family Law Reform Act 1969	Sections 5(1) and 18.
1970 c 31	The Administration of Justice Act 1970	In Schedule 2, paragraph 16.
1970 c 33	The Law Reform (Miscellaneous Provisions) Act 1970	Section 6.
1970 c 45	The Matrimonial Proceedings and Property Act 1970	Section 36.
1971 c 23	The Courts Act 1971	Section 45(1)(a).
1973 c 18	The Matrimonial Causes Act 1973	In section 50, in subsection (1)(a) the words from "and sections 26" to the end of the paragraph, in subsection (1)(d) the words "or sections 26 to 28A of the Matrimonial Causes Act 1965" and in subsection (2)(a) the words "or under section 26 or 27 of the Matrimonial Causes Act 1965". In Schedule 2, paragraph 5(1) and in paragraph 12 the words "(a) sections 26 to 28A of the Matrimonial Causes Act 1965".
1975 c 7	The Finance Act 1975	In Schedule 12, paragraph 6.

A9 CIVIL PROCEDURE RULES PART 57 – PROBATE AND INHERITANCE, EXTRACT

Contents of this Part

Scope of this Part and definitions

57.1

(1) This Part contains rules about—

(a) probate claims;
(b) claims for the rectification of wills;
(c) claims and applications to—

(i) substitute another person for a personal representative; or
(ii) remove a personal representative;

(d) claims under the Inheritance (Provision for Family Dependants) Act 1975.

(2) In this Part:

(a) 'probate claim' means a claim for—

(i) the grant of probate of the will, or letters of administration of the estate, of a deceased person;
(ii) the revocation of such a grant; or
(iii) a decree pronouncing for or against the validity of an alleged will;

not being a claim which is non-contentious (or common form) probate business;
(Section 128 of the Senior Courts Act 1981 defines non-contentious (or common form) probate business.)

(b) 'relevant office' means—

(i) in the case of High Court proceedings in a Chancery district registry, that registry;
(ii) in the case of any other High Court proceedings, Chancery Chambers at the Royal Courts of Justice, Strand, London, WC2A 2LL; and
(iii) in the case of County Court proceedings, the office of the County Court hearing centre in question;

(c) 'testamentary document' means a will, a draft of a will, written instructions for a will made by or at the request of, or under the instructions of, the testator, and any document purporting to be evidence of the contents, or to be a copy, of a will which is alleged to have been lost or destroyed;
(d) 'will' includes a codicil.

I PROBATE CLAIMS

General

57.2

(1) This Section contains rules about probate claims.
(2) Probate claims in the High Court are assigned to the Chancery Division.
(3) Probate claims in the County Court must only be started by sending the claim to, or making the claim at—

(a) a County Court hearing centre where there is also a Chancery district registry; or
(b) the County Court at Central London.

(4) All probate claims are allocated to the multi-track.

How to start a probate claim
57.3 A probate claim must be commenced—

(a) in the relevant office; and
(b) using the procedure in Part 7.

Acknowledgment of Service and Defence
57.4

(1) A defendant who is served with a claim form must file an acknowledgment of service.

(2) Subject to paragraph (3), the period for filing an acknowledgment of service is—

(a) if the defendant is served with a claim form which states that particulars of claim are to follow, 28 days after service of the particulars of claim; and
(b) in any other case, 28 days after service of the claim form.

(3) If the claim form is served out of the jurisdiction under rule 6.32 or 6.33, the period for filing an acknowledgment of service is 14 days longer than the relevant period specified in rule 6.35 or Practice Direction 6B.

(4) Rule 15(4) (which provides the period for filing a defence) applies as if the words 'under Part 10' were omitted from rule 15.4(1)(b).

Lodging of testamentary documents and filing of evidence about testamentary documents
57.5

(1) Any testamentary document of the deceased person in the possession or control of any party must be lodged with the court.

(2) Unless the court directs otherwise, the testamentary documents must be lodged in the relevant office—

(a) by the claimant when the claim form is issued; and
(b) by a defendant when he acknowledges service.

(3) The claimant and every defendant who acknowledges service of the claim form must in written evidence—

(a) describe any testamentary document of the deceased of which he has any knowledge or, if he does not know of any such testamentary document, state that fact, and
(b) if any testamentary document of which he has knowledge is not in his possession or under his control, give the name and address of the person

in whose possession or under whose control it is or, if he does not know the name or address of that person, state that fact.

(A specimen form for the written evidence about testamentary documents is annexed to Practice Direction 57.)

(4) Unless the court directs otherwise, the written evidence required by paragraph (3) must be filed in the relevant office—

(a) by the claimant, when the claim form is issued; and
(b) by a defendant when he acknowledges service.

(5) Except with the permission of the court, a party shall not be allowed to inspect the testamentary documents or written evidence lodged or filed by any other party until he himself has lodged his testamentary documents and filed his evidence.

(6) The provisions of paragraphs (2) and (4) may be modified by a practice direction under this Part.

Revocation of existing grant

57.6

(1) In a probate claim which seeks the revocation of a grant of probate or letters of administration every person who is entitled, or claims to be entitled, to administer the estate under that grant must be made a party to the claim.

(2) If the claimant is the person to whom the grant was made, he must lodge the probate or letters of administration in the relevant office when the claim form is issued.

(3) If a defendant has the probate or letters of administration under his control, he must lodge it in the relevant office when he acknowledges service.

(4) Paragraphs (2) and (3) do not apply where the grant has already been lodged at the court, which in this paragraph includes the Principal Registry of the Family Division or a district probate registry.

Contents of statements of case

57.7

(1) The claim form must contain a statement of the nature of the interest of the claimant and of each defendant in the estate.

(2) If a party disputes another party's interest in the estate he must state this in his statement of case and set out his reasons.

(3) Any party who contends that at the time when a will was executed the testator did not know of and approve its contents must give particulars of the facts and matters relied on.

(4) Any party who wishes to contend that—

(a) a will was not duly executed;
(b) at the time of the execution of a will the testator lacked testamentary capacity; or
(c) the execution of a will was obtained by undue influence or fraud,

must set out the contention specifically and give particulars of the facts and matters relied on.

(5)

(a) A defendant may give notice in his defence that he does not raise any positive case, but insists on the will being proved in solemn form and, for that purpose, will cross-examine the witnesses who attested the will.
(b) If a defendant gives such a notice, the court will not make an order for costs against him unless it considers that there was no reasonable ground for opposing the will.

Counterclaim

57.8

(1) A defendant who contends that he has any claim or is entitled to any remedy relating to the grant of probate of the will, or letters of administration of the estate, of the deceased person must serve a counterclaim making that contention.

(2) If the claimant fails to serve particulars of claim within the time allowed, the defendant may, with the permission of the court, serve a counterclaim and the probate claim shall then proceed as if the counterclaim were the particulars of claim.

Probate counterclaim in other proceedings

57.9

(1) In this rule 'probate counterclaim' means a counterclaim in any claim other than a probate claim by which the defendant claims any such remedy as is mentioned in rule 57.1(2)(a).

(2) Subject to the following paragraphs of this rule, this Part shall apply with the necessary modifications to a probate counterclaim as it applies to a probate claim.

(3) A probate counterclaim must contain a statement of the nature of the interest of each of the parties in the estate of the deceased to which the probate counterclaim relates.

(4) Unless an application notice is issued within 7 days after the service of a probate counterclaim for an order under rule 3.1(2)(e) or 3.4 for the probate counterclaim to be dealt with in separate proceedings or to be struck out, and the application is granted, the court shall order the transfer of the proceedings to either—

(a) the Chancery Division (if it is not already assigned to that Division) and to either the Royal Courts of Justice or a Chancery district registry (if it is not already proceeding in one of those places); or
(b) if the County Court has jurisdiction, to a County Court hearing centre where there is also a Chancery district registry or the County Court at Central London.

(5) If an order is made that a probate counterclaim be dealt with in separate proceedings, the order shall order the transfer of the probate counterclaim as required under paragraph (4).

Failure to acknowledge service or to file a defence
57.10
(1) A default judgment cannot be obtained in a probate claim and rule 10.2 and Part 12 do not apply.
(2) If any of several defendants fails to acknowledge service the claimant may—

(a) after the time for acknowledging service has expired; and
(b) upon filing written evidence of service of the claim form and (if no particulars of claim were contained in or served with the claim form) the particulars of claim on that defendant;

proceed with the probate claim as if that defendant had acknowledged service.
(3) If no defendant acknowledges service or files a defence then, unless on the application of the claimant the court orders the claim to be discontinued, the claimant may, after the time for acknowledging service or for filing a defence (as the case may be) has expired, apply to the court for an order that the claim is to proceed to trial.
(4) When making an application under paragraph (3) the claimant must file written evidence of service of the claim form and (if no particulars of claim were contained in or served with the claim form) the particulars of claim on each of the defendants.
(5) Where the court makes an order under paragraph (3), it may direct that the claim be tried on written evidence.

Discontinuance and dismissal
57.11
(1) Part 38 does not apply to probate claims.

(2) At any stage of a probate claim the court, on the application of the claimant or of any defendant who has acknowledged service, may order that—

(a) the claim be discontinued or dismissed on such terms as to costs or otherwise as it thinks just; and
(b) a grant of probate of the will, or letters of administration of the estate, of the deceased person be made to the person entitled to the grant.

II RECTIFICATION OF WILLS

Rectification of Wills
57.12

(1) This Section contains rules about claims for the rectification of a will.
(Section 20 of the Administration of Justice Act 1982 provides for rectification of a will. Additional provisions are contained in rule 55 of the Non-Contentious Probate Rules 1987.)
(2) Every personal representative of the estate shall be joined as a party.
(3) Practice Direction 57 makes provision for lodging the grant of probate or letters of administration with the will annexed in a claim under this Section.

III SUBSTITUTION AND REMOVAL OF PERSONAL REPRESENTATIVES

Substitution and Removal of Personal Representatives
57.13

(1) This Section contains rules about claims and applications for substitution or removal of a personal representative.
(2) Claims under this Section must be brought in the High Court and are assigned to the Chancery Division.
(Section 50 of the Administration of Justice Act 1985 gives the High Court power to appoint a substitute for, or to remove, a personal representative.)
(3) Every personal representative of the estate shall be joined as a party.
(4) Practice Direction 57 makes provision for lodging the grant of probate or letters of administration in a claim under this Section.
(5) If substitution or removal of a personal representative is sought by application in existing proceedings, this rule shall apply with references to claims being read as if they referred to applications.

IV CLAIMS UNDER THE INHERITANCE (PROVISION FOR FAMILY AND DEPENDANTS) ACT 1975

Scope of this section

57.14 This Section contains rules about claims under the Inheritance (Provision for Family and Dependants) Act 1975 ('the Act').

Proceedings in the High Court

57.15

(1) Proceedings in the High Court under the Act shall be issued in either—

(a) the Chancery Division; or
(b) the Family Division.

(2) The Civil Procedure Rules apply to proceedings under the Act which are brought in the Family Division, except that the provisions of the Family Procedure Rules 2010 relating to the drawing up and service of orders apply instead of the provisions in Part 40 and Practice Direction 40B.

Procedure for claims under section 1 of the Act

57.16

(1) A claim under section 1 of the Act must be made by issuing a claim form in accordance with Part 8.
(2) Rule 8.3 (acknowledgment of service) and rule 8.5 (filing and serving written evidence) apply as modified by paragraphs (3) to (5) of this rule.
(3) The written evidence filed and served by the claimant with the claim form must, except in the circumstances specified in paragraph (3A), have exhibited to it an official copy of—

(a) the grant of probate or letters of administration in respect of the deceased's estate; and
(b) every testamentary document in respect of which probate or letters of administration were granted.

(3A) Where no grant has been obtained, the claimant may make a claim without naming a defendant and may apply for directions as to the representation of the estate. The written evidence must—

(a) explain the reasons why it has not been possible for a grant to be obtained;
(b) be accompanied by the original or a copy (if either is available) of the will or other testamentary document in respect of which probate or letters of administration are to be granted; and

(c) contain the following information, so far as known to the claimant—

  (i) brief details of the property comprised in the estate, with an approximate estimate of its capital value and any income that is received from it;
  (ii) brief details of the liabilities of the estate;
  (iii) the names and addresses of the persons who are in possession of the documents relating to the estate; and
  (iv) the names of the beneficiaries and their respective interests in the estate.

(3B) Where a claim is made in accordance with paragraph (3A), the court may give directions as to the parties to the claim and as to the representation of the estate either on the claimant's application or on its own initiative.
(Section 4 of the 1975 Act as amended confirms that nothing prevents the making of an application under the Act before representation with respect to the estate of the deceased person is taken out.)
(4) Subject to paragraph (4A), the time within which a defendant must file and serve—

(a) an acknowledgment of service; and
(b) any written evidence,

is not more than 21 days after service of the claim form on him.
(4A) If the claim form is served out of the jurisdiction under rule 6.32 or 6.33, the period for filing an acknowledgment of service and any written evidence is 7 days longer than the relevant period specified in rule 6.35 or Practice Direction 6B.
(5) A defendant who is a personal representative of the deceased must file and serve written evidence, which must include the information required by Practice Direction 57.

A10 CIVIL PROCEDURE RULES PRACTICE DIRECTION 57 – PROBATE (THIS PRACTICE DIRECTION SUPPLEMENTS CPR PART 57)

Contents of this Practice Direction

I PROBATE CLAIMS

General

1.1

This Section of this practice direction applies to contentious probate claims.

1.2

The rules and procedure relating to non-contentious probate proceedings (also known as 'common form') are the Non-Contentious Probate Rules 1987 as amended.

How to start a probate claim

2.1

A claim form and all subsequent court documents relating to a probate claim must be marked at the top 'In the estate of [*name*] deceased (Probate)'.

2.2

The claim form must be issued out of—

(1) Chancery Chambers at the Royal Courts of Justice; or
(2) one of the Chancery district registries; or
(3) if the claim is suitable to be heard in the County Court—

  (a) a County Court hearing centre in a place where there is also a Chancery district registry; or
  (b) the County Court at Central London.

There are Chancery district registries at Birmingham, Bristol, Caernarfon, Cardiff, Leeds, Liverpool, Manchester, Mold, Newcastle upon Tyne and Preston.

(Section 32 of the County Courts Act 1984 identifies which probate claims may be heard in the County Court.)

2.3

When the claim form is issued, the relevant office will send a notice to Leeds District Probate Registry, Coronet House, Queen Street, Leeds, LS1 2BA, DX 26451 Leeds (Park Square), telephone 0113 243 1505, requesting that all testamentary documents, grants of representation and other relevant documents currently held at any probate registry are sent to the relevant office.

2.4

The commencement of a probate claim will, unless a court otherwise directs, prevent any grant of probate or letters of administration being made until the probate claim has been disposed of.

(Rule 45 of the Non-Contentious Probate Rules 1987 makes provision for notice of the probate claim to be given, and section 117 of the Senior Courts Act 1981 for the grant of letters of administration pending the determination of a probate claim. Paragraph 8 of this practice direction makes provision about an application for such a grant.)

Testamentary documents and evidence about testamentary documents

3.1

Unless the court orders otherwise, if a testamentary document is held by the court (whether it was lodged by a party or it was previously held at a probate registry) when the claim has been disposed of the court will send it to the Leeds District Probate Registry.

3.2

The written evidence about testamentary documents required by this Part—

(1) should be in the form annexed to this practice direction; and
(2) must be signed by the party personally and not by his solicitor or other representative (except that if the party is a child or protected party the written evidence must be signed by his litigation friend).

3.3

In a case in which there is urgent need to commence a probate claim (for example, in order to be able to apply immediately for the appointment of an administrator pending the determination of the claim) and it is not possible for the claimant to lodge the testamentary documents or to file the evidence about testamentary documents in the relevant office at the same time as the claim form is to be issued, the court may direct that the claimant shall be allowed to issue the claim form upon his giving an undertaking to the court to lodge the documents and file the evidence within such time as the court shall specify.

Case management

4

In giving case management directions in a probate claim the court will give consideration to the questions—

(1) whether any person who may be affected by the claim and who is not joined as a party should be joined as a party or given notice of the claim, whether under rule 19.8A or otherwise; and
(2) whether to make a representation order under rule 19.6 or Rule 19.7.

Summary judgment

5.1

If an order pronouncing for a will in solemn form is sought on an application for summary judgment, the evidence in support of the application must include written evidence proving due execution of the will.

5.2
If a defendant has given notice in his defence under rule 57.7(5) that he raises no positive case but—

(1) he insists that the will be proved in solemn form; and
(2) for that purpose he will cross-examine the witnesses who attested the will;

any application by the claimant for summary judgment is subject to the right of that defendant to require those witnesses to attend court for cross-examination.

Settlement of a probate claim
6.1
If at any time the parties agree to settle a probate claim, the court may—

(1) order the trial of the claim on written evidence, which will lead to a grant in solemn form;
(2) order that the claim be discontinued or dismissed under Rule 57.11, which will lead to a grant in common form; or
(3) pronounce for or against the validity of one or more wills under section 49 of the Administration of Justice Act 1985.

(For a form of order which is also applicable to discontinuance and which may be adapted as appropriate, see Practice Form No. CH38.)

(Section 49 of the Administration of Justice Act 1985 permits a probate claim to be compromised without a trial if every 'relevant beneficiary', as defined in that section, has consented to the proposed order. It is only available in the High Court.)

6.2
Applications under section 49 of the Administration of Justice Act 1985 may be heard by a master or district judge and must be supported by written evidence identifying the relevant beneficiaries and exhibiting the written consent of each of them. The written evidence of testamentary documents required by rule 57.5 will still be necessary.

Application for an order to bring in a will, etc.
7.1
Any party applying for an order under section 122 of the Senior Courts Act 1981 ('the 1981 Act') must serve the application notice on the person against whom the order is sought.

(Section 122 of the 1981 Act empowers the court to order a person to attend court for examination, and to answer questions and bring in documents, if there are reasonable grounds for believing that such person has knowledge of a testamentary document. Rule 50(1) of the Non-Contentious Probate Rules 1987 makes similar provision where a probate claim has not been commenced.)

7.2
An application for the issue of a witness summons under section 123 of the 1981 Act—

(1) may be made without notice; and
(2) must be supported by written evidence setting out the grounds of the application.

(Section 123 of the 1981 Act empowers the court, where it appears that any person has in his possession, custody or power a testamentary document, to issue a witness summons ordering such person to bring in that document. Rule 50(2) of the Non-Contentious Probate Rules makes similar provision where a probate claim has not been commenced.)

7.3
An application under section 122 or 123 of the 1981 Act should be made to a master or district judge.

7.4
A person against whom a witness summons is issued under section 123 of the 1981 Act who denies that the testamentary document referred to in the witness summons is in his possession or under his control may file written evidence to that effect.

Administration pending the determination of a probate claim

8.1
An application under section 117 of the Senior Courts Act 1981 for an order for the grant of administration pending the determination of a probate claim should be made by application notice in the probate claim.

8.2
If an order for a grant of administration is made under section 117 of the 1981 Act—

(1) Rules 69.4 to 69.7 shall apply as if the administrator were a receiver appointed by the court;

(2) if the court allows the administrator remuneration under rule 69.7, it may make an order under section 117(3) of the 1981 Act assigning the remuneration out of the estate of the deceased; and

(3) every application relating to the conduct of the administration shall be made by application notice in the probate claim.

8.3

An order under section 117 may be made by a master or district judge.

8.4

If an order is made under section 117 an application for the grant of letters of administration should be made to the Principal Registry of the Family Division, First Avenue House, 42–49 High Holborn, London WC1V 6NP.

8.5

The appointment of an administrator to whom letters of administration are granted following an order under section 117 will cease automatically when a final order in the probate claim is made but will continue pending any appeal.

II RECTIFICATION OF WILLS

Scope of this Section

9

This Section of this practice direction applies to claims for the rectification of a will.

Lodging the grant

10.1

If the claimant is the person to whom the grant was made in respect of the will of which rectification is sought, he must, unless the court orders otherwise, lodge the probate or letters of administration with the will annexed with the court when the claim form is issued.

10.2

If a defendant has the probate or letters of administration in his possession or under his control, he must, unless the court orders otherwise, lodge it in the relevant office within 14 days after the service of the claim form on him.

Orders

11

A copy of every order made for the rectification of a will shall be sent to the Principal Registry of the Family Division for filing, and a memorandum of the order shall be endorsed on, or permanently annexed to, the grant under which the estate is administered.

III SUBSTITUTION AND REMOVAL OF PERSONAL REPRESENTATIVES

Scope of this Section

12

This Section of this practice direction applies to claims and applications for substitution or removal of a personal representative. If substitution or removal of a personal representative is sought by application in existing proceedings, this Section shall apply with references to the claim, claim form and claimant being read as if they referred to the application, application notice and applicant respectively.

Starting the claim

13.1

The claim form must be accompanied by—

(1) either—

(a) a sealed or certified copy of the grant of probate or letters of administration, or

(b) where the claim is to substitute or remove an executor and is made before a grant of probate has been issued, the original or, if the original is not available, a copy of the will; and

(2) written evidence containing the grounds of the claim and the following information so far as it is known to the claimant—

(a) brief details of the property comprised in the estate, with an approximate estimate of its capital value and any income that is received from it;

(b) brief details of the liabilities of the estate;

(c) the names and addresses of the persons who are in possession of the documents relating to the estate;

(d) the names of the beneficiaries and their respective interests in the estate; and

(e) the name, address and occupation of any proposed substituted personal representative.

13.2

If the claim is for the appointment of a substituted personal representative, the claim form must be accompanied by—

(1) a signed or (in the case of the Public Trustee or a corporation) sealed consent to act; and
(2) written evidence as to the fitness of the proposed substituted personal representative, if an individual, to act.

Production of the grant

14.1

On the hearing of the claim the personal representative must produce to the Court the grant of representation to the deceased's estate.

14.2

If an order is made substituting or removing the personal representative, the grant (together with a sealed copy of the order) must be sent to and remain in the custody of the Principal Registry of the Family Division until a memorandum of the order has been endorsed on or permanently annexed to the grant.

14.3

Where the claim is to substitute or remove an executor and the claim is made before a grant of probate has been issued, paragraphs 14.1 and 14.2 do not apply. Where in such a case an order is made substituting or removing an executor a sealed copy of the order must be sent to the Principal Registry of the Family Division where it will be recorded and retained pending any application for a grant. An order sent to the Principal Registry in accordance with this paragraph must be accompanied by a note of the full name and date of death of the deceased, if it is not apparent on the face of the order.

IV CLAIMS UNDER THE INHERITANCE (PROVISION FOR FAMILY AND DEPENDANTS) ACT 1975

Acknowledgment of service by personal representative – rule 57.16(4)

15

Where a defendant who is a personal representative wishes to remain neutral in relation to the claim, and agrees to abide by any decision which the court may make, he should state this in Section A of the acknowledgment of service form.

Written evidence of personal representative – rule 57.16(5)

16

The written evidence filed by a defendant who is a personal representative must state to the best of that person's ability—

(1) full details of the value of the deceased's net estate, as defined in section 25(1) of the Act;

(2) the person or classes of persons beneficially interested in the estate, and—

 (a) the names and (unless they are parties to the claim) addresses of all living beneficiaries; and
 (b) the value of their interests in the estate so far as they are known.

(3) whether any living beneficiary (and if so, naming him) is a child or a person who lacks capacity (within the meaning of the Mental Capacity Act 2005); and
(4) any facts which might affect the exercise of the court's powers under the Act.

Separate representation of claimants
17
If a claim is made jointly by two or more claimants, and it later appears that any of the claimants have a conflict of interests—

(1) any claimant may choose to be represented at any hearing by separate solicitors or counsel, or may appear in person; and
(2) if the court considers that claimants who are represented by the same solicitors or counsel ought to be separately represented, it may adjourn the application until they are.

Production of the grant
18.1
On the hearing of a claim the personal representative must produce to the court the original grant of representation to the deceased's estate.

18.2
If the court makes an order under the Act, the original grant (together with a sealed copy of the order) must be sent to the Principal Registry of the Family Division for a memorandum of the order to be endorsed on or permanently annexed to the grant in accordance with section 19(3) of the Act.

18.3
Every final order embodying terms of compromise made in proceedings under the Act, whether made with or without a hearing, must contain a direction that a memorandum of the order shall be endorsed on or permanently annexed to the probate or letters of administration and a copy of the order shall be sent to the Principal Registry of the Family Division with the relevant grant of probate or letters of administration for endorsement.

ANNEX

A form of witness statement or affidavit about testamentary documents

(CPR rule 57.5)

(Title of the claim)

I [name and address] the claimant/defendant in this claim state [on oath] that I have no knowledge of any document—

(i) being or purported to be or having the form or effect of a will or codicil of [name of deceased] whose estate is the subject of this claim;

(ii) being or purporting to be a draft or written instructions for any such will or codicil made by or at the request of or under the instructions of the deceased;

(iii) being or purporting to be evidence of the contents or a copy of any such will or codicil which is alleged to have been lost or destroyed,

except ... [describe any testamentary document of the deceased, and if any such document is not in your control, give the name and address of the person who you believe has possession or control of it, or state that you do not know the name and address of that person] ...

[I believe that the facts stated in this witness statement are true. I understand that proceedings for contempt of court may be brought against anyone who makes, or causes to be made, a false statement in a document verified by a statement of truth without an honest belief in its truth.] [or jurat for affidavit]

(NOTE: 'testamentary document' is defined in CPR rule 57.1)

Updated: Saturday, 1 October 2022

A11 ACTAPS PRACTICE GUIDANCE FOR THE RESOLUTION OF PROBATE AND TRUST DISPUTES (ACTAPS CODE)[1]

Paragraph 4 of the Practice Direction on Protocols has been substantially amended. It states that 'in cases not covered by any protocol, the court will expect the parties to act reasonably in exchanging information and documents relevant to their claim and in trying to avoid the necessity for the start of proceedings'.

Moreover, with effect from 1 April 2003, the 30th update to the CPR imposes on all parties to a dispute (whatever its nature) an obligation to comply with specified procedures designed to avoid litigation commencing.

Practitioners will no doubt remember the dicta of the Court of Appeal in *Carlson v Townsend* [2001] 3 All ER 663 where it stated the use of the protocol was not limited to fast track cases. The spirit if not the letter of the protocol was equally appropriate to some higher value claims. In accordance with the aims of the civil justice reforms, the courts expected to see the spirit of reasonable pre-action behaviour applied in all cases regardless of the existence of a specific protocol.

The Association of Contentious Trust & Probate Specialists 'ACTAPS' and the Trust Law Committee have, as many practitioners will be aware, given much thought to the possibility that a special Pre-Action Protocol ought to be developed for disputes within their area of expertise. Indeed a draft has for some time been on the ACTAPS website (www.actaps.com) and has since been the subject of extensive discussions with representatives of the judiciary concerned.

It is now clear that no special protocol will be adopted, despite a recognition that the draft contains useful elements. It will be seen that it deals in particular with the following matters:

(a) appointment of a representative to act on behalf of beneficiaries who cannot be ascertained or traced;
(b) requirement for a letter of claim setting out the basis of claim;
(c) early disclosure of documents;
(d) use of joint experts where possible;
(e) a joint letter of request for medical records;
(f) a joint *Larke v Nugus* letter; and
(g) a joint letter requesting details of deceased's capacity.

---

1 The ACTAPS Code is reproduced by kind permission of the Association of Contentious Trust and Probate Specialists (Henry Frydenson, Frydenson & Co, Chair ACTAPS, Central Court, 25 Southampton Buildings, London, WC2A 1AL).

In these circumstances the committee of ACTAPS has concluded that it would be useful to encourage members to have regard to The ACTAPS Code as a means of developing best practices in areas where special problems may arise, for example the need to have representatives for persons who cannot speak for themselves in a context where others may feel that mediation would be desirable.

It is understood that the judges who have considered The ACTAPS Code have expressed no concerns that it is out of line with the CPR objectives or that to follow its principles would give rise to unnecessary problems in practice. In particular it is thought that CPR Rule 19.7(3)(b) gives the necessary scope for securing the appointment of representatives of those who are absent, unborn, or members of a large class, as well before as after the commencement of proceedings.

It is also hoped that in the context of probate issues the common difficulty of medical practitioners considering that they may as a matter of professional confidence be restricted in releasing records can be overcome by joint application (and following discussions between ACTAPS and the BMA the latter has confirmed that its future guidance will facilitate disclosure in accordance with The ACTAPS Code). The ACTAPS Code contains an outline for such a letter.

In these circumstances it is suggested that practitioners in the areas of trust and probate law should seek to follow the approaches indicated in The ACTAPS Code, approved by the Trust Law Committee and ACTAPS, on the basis that it may serve to amplify the basic principles of the general protocols and indicate considered methods of carrying the objectives of the general protocols into effect in areas which may be found to give rise to special difficulties with which the general protocols do not grapple. In putting forward this suggestion the committee of ACTAPS believes that it has the support of all who have been concerned to consider the draft protocol; the rejection of the proposal that it be adopted as a special protocol owes nothing (so far as is known) to any perception of defects and merely reflects the belief that the public interest is best served by seeking, where possible, to avoid specific protocols and to develop best practices in areas where general protocols have to be supplemented to meet the needs of special situations.

With that in mind the committee of ACTAPS encourages members and other users to help move the search for best practices forward by commenting on any defects, inadequacies or other difficulties which may be found to arise in carrying the terms of The ACTAPS Code into effect. Please make any such comments to the ACTAPS Chairman's or the ACTAPS Secretary's e-mail address.

Practitioners will wish to bear in mind the need for trustees and executors to consider the adequacy of their powers to enter into any particular course of conduct and the possibility that they may need eg Beddoes type directions if they propose a course of conduct to which their beneficiaries might wish to raise objection (as for example where the trustees wish voluntarily to disclose confidential documents to third parties) or which may involve material burdens of costs (as for example the institution of a lengthy mediation). But of course in circumstances where the aim is to explore ways of reaching agreement or otherwise saving costs any necessary order might be expected to be forthcoming (within the appropriate limits) without difficulty on the basis that the Court would be being asked to facilitate a course of action essentially in accordance with the overriding objective.

1. Introduction

The Scope of The Code

1.1 This Code is intended to apply to disputes about:

- the devolution and administration of estates of deceased persons
- the devolution and administration of trust funds ('probate and trust disputes'). It is not intended to displace other protocols if in the circumstances of the case they can be seen to be more appropriate.

The main types of disputes within the ambit of this Code can be expected to be:

- challenges to the validity of a will, for example on grounds of want of capacity or knowledge and approval, undue influence or forgery
- claims under the Inheritance (Provision for Family and Dependants) Act 1975 ('the Inheritance Act')
- actions for the removal of an administrator or executor or trustee or the appointment of a judicial trustee
- actions for the rectification of a will or other document
- disputes as to the meanings of provisions in a will or a trust
- administration actions
- allegations of breach of trust.

The ACTAPS Code may also apply to certain types of dispute where the provisions of a trust or the devolution of an estate are of the essence, for example where a claimant seeks in the alternative to set aside or overturn a trust or to take advantage of rights under a trust.

The Code has two aims; to encourage the resolution of disputes without hostile litigation; and even where litigation may be necessary to ensure that it is simplified as far as possible by maximizing the scope for the exchange of relevant information before the litigation process has commenced.

The Code is in general terms unlikely to be appropriate for disputes which involve:

- disputes as to the rights appertaining under rules of forced heirships under the law of some foreign jurisdiction
- the need for emergency injunctions
- (except in so far as concerns pre-action exchange of information) the need for a binding precedent or a declaration by the Court as to the true construction of some trust instrument or testamentary disposition.

The Code is formed in general terms to cover the broad range of trust and probate disputes; but it is recognised that the appropriate investigations and exchange of information will vary according to the circumstances of the dispute. However one of its primary purposes is to provide for a special feature of disputes in this area, namely that there may be beneficiaries who cannot speak for themselves but whose interests must be protected.

1.2 In cases where the express terms of The Code is not appropriate parties will be expected to follow the spirit of The Code and seek to achieve its aims so far as practicable in the particular case.

1.3 It is also to be borne in mind that there are certain cases in which a trust or probate dispute seeks to fulfil some non-contentious purpose, as for example where a question of difficulty is identified to which the parties are agreed that the best solution lies in inviting the Court to approve constructive proposals by way of compromise or where the objective is simply to find the cheapest way of protecting trustees or personal representatives against the risks involved in the existence of some theoretical doubt. In such cases The Code is unlikely to have any role to play.

1.4 One of the principal features of trust and probate disputes is that they may affect the interests of persons not of full capacity, as yet unborn or unascertained, or interested as members of a large class of persons who have similar beneficial interests. The Code is thus designed to make express provision for the need to find mechanisms that assist despite the absence of such persons (providing in particular an expedited process for Court approval of agreements reached in mediation). It is thus wrong in principle to regard a dispute as not amenable to the use of The Code just because there are persons concerned who cannot speak for themselves.

2. Principal guidelines

Parties

2.1 The parties to the probate or trust dispute will usually be trustees (or personal representatives or persons claiming to be entitled as such) and beneficiaries of the trust or estate who are of full capacity, though The Code is designed also to be capable of being used in exterior/third party disputes where appropriate.

2.2 In the case where interests of unascertained persons, minors, unborns, mentally incapacitated persons or members of a large class (such that it is not appropriate for all members of the class to be made parties to the dispute) will be affected, the procedure to be adopted will be an application to the Court (see Annex A) whether or not a claim has yet been instituted before the Court.

Status of Letters of Claim and Response

2.3 A letter of claim or of response is not intended to have the same status as pleadings. Matters may come to light as a result of investigation after the letter of claim has been sent or after the defendant has responded. These investigations could result in the pleaded case of a party differing in some respects from the case outlined in that party's letter of claim or response. It would not be consistent with the spirit of The Code for a party to complain about this difference provided that there was no indication of any intention to mislead.

Disclosure of Documents

2.4 The aim of the early disclosure of documents by the defendant is not to encourage 'fishing expeditions' by the claimant, but to promote an early exchange of relevant information to help in clarifying or resolving issues in dispute. The claimant's solicitors can assist by identifying in the letter of claim or in a subsequent letter the particular documents or categories of documents which they consider are relevant, and by providing copies of these where appropriate.

2.5 All documents are disclosed on the basis that they are not to be disclosed to third parties (other than legal advisers) or used for any purpose other than the resolution of the dispute, unless otherwise agreed in writing or permitted by the court.

Experts

2.6 Expert evidence appropriate to probate and trust disputes may include in particular medical evidence, handwriting evidence, valuation evidence, tax-related or actuarial evidence.

2.7 The Code encourages joint selection of, and access to, experts. However, it maintains the flexibility for each party to obtain their own expert's report. It is for the court to decide whether the costs of more than one expert's report should be recoverable.

Costs

2.8 Where The Code provides for the initial cost of obtaining information or reports to be borne by one party, it shall not restrict the court's discretion in relation to ultimate liability for such costs.

Negotiations/Mediation

2.9 Parties and their legal representatives are encouraged to enter into discussions and/or negotiations prior to starting proceedings. The parties should bear in mind that the courts increasingly take the view that litigation should be a last resort, and that claims should not be issued prematurely when a settlement is in reasonable prospect. Mediation of probate and trust disputes may assist in achieving a compromise, particularly in relation to disputes between family members. The form of the mediation will be set out in the mediation agreement between the mediator and the parties.

2.10 Mediation can be used to try to achieve a compromise whenever negotiation is appropriate and can be used at any stage in a trust dispute. Typically mediation may be considered:

- (i) before proceedings have commenced but once the issues are fairly well defined and the parties affected by them are known;
- (ii) even after proceedings have commenced and the statements of case have been served so that the parties have a better appreciation of the issues;
- (iii) at any critical stage in the litigation such as after disclosure of documents, exchange of experts' reports, exchange of witness statements and in the lead up to the trial.

The parties should seek to conclude a mediation within 42 days of the appointment of the mediator.

2.11 Since mediation negotiations are treated by the Courts as without prejudice, points disclosed during an attempt to reach a settlement will be confidential between the parties and cannot be used as evidence in subsequent Court proceedings unless expressly agreed by the party who made the disclosure. The mediator will not divulge information without consent. Also he will not pass on such information to outside parties or act for either party to the dispute in subsequent proceedings.

2.12 A settlement reached pursuant to a mediation should be recorded in writing and signed by the parties or their authorised representative. In probate and trust disputes, if and insofar as the subject matter of the dispute requires the sanction and approval of the Court, any agreement achieved as a result of the mediation should be expressed to be subject to the approval of the Court.

2.13 In a probate or trust dispute where the position of the Inland Revenue may have some bearing on any compromise solution which may be reached, any agreement may be made conditional upon indications of the Inland Revenue's position or adjourned to enable clarification of its position to be sought.

3. The Code

Letters of Claim

3.1 The Claimant shall send a letter of claim to each of the deceased's personal representatives or to the trustees, as the case may be and, unless it is impractical (e.g. because there is a large class of beneficiaries or the beneficiaries are minors) to each beneficiary or potential beneficiary of the estate or trust fund likely to be adversely affected by the claim (referred to as 'the proposed Defendants'), as soon as sufficient information is available to substantiate a realistic claim which the Claimant has decided he is prepared to pursue.

3.2 The letter shall contain a clear summary of the claim and the facts upon which it is based and state the remedy sought by the claimant.

3.3 Solicitors are recommended to use a standard format for the claim letter. A sample letter is set out at Annex B; this can be amended to suit the particular case.

3.4 In claims under the Inheritance Act the claimant should give details to the best of his ability of the matters set out in Section 3 of the Inheritance Act as relevant to the exercise of the Court's discretion (see Annex B).

3.5 Copies of documents in the claimant's possession which he wishes to rely upon or which any other party is likely to wish to rely upon should be enclosed with the letter of claim. Examples of documents likely to be relevant in different types of dispute are set out at Annex C. These lists are not exhaustive. The letter of claim may specify classes of document considered relevant for early disclosure by the proposed defendants.

Letter of Response

3.6 Each of the proposed defendants should respond to the letter of claim within 21 days stating whether he admits or denies the claim, responding in outline to the matters of fact relied upon by the claimant and setting out any particular matters of fact upon which he relies. If a proposed defendant intends to make an answering claim on his own behalf, the letter of response should contain the same information and documents as a letter of claim in relation to the Part 20 claim. If a proposed defendant is unable to respond within the time limit on any particular matter, the letter of response should give the reasons for the absence of a full response and state when it will be available.

3.7 In claims under the Inheritance Act each proposed defendant should give details to the best of his ability of the matters set out in Section 3 of the Inheritance Act as relevant to the exercise of the Court's discretion (and set out in Annex B).

3.8 Copies of documents in the proposed defendant's possession which he wishes to rely upon or which any other party is likely to wish to rely upon should be enclosed with the letter of response. Examples of relevant documents in relation to different categories of disputes are set out at Annex C. These lists are not exhaustive.

Documents

3.9 In relation to the documents in Annex C, the personal representatives of the deceased (including executors named in the last alleged will of the deceased) or trustees as appropriate should provide copies of such documents (if available) to a party requesting a copy within 14 days of the date of a letter of request (or such other reasonable time as may be agreed between the parties) or, if a copy is only available from a third party with the consent of the personal representatives or trustees, provide to the party making the request written authority to the third party to provide a copy of the document to that party.

3.10 Trustees or personal representatives should not be inhibited from making full disclosure by the absence of litigation.

Applications for documents or information in control of third parties

3.11 In a probate dispute the release of medical notes may cast much light on the likely outcome and it should be assumed for the purposes of The Code that they ought to be disclosed at the outset absent special reason.

3.12 If so requested in writing by any party all parties shall (in the absence of good reason to withhold the relevant items) within 14 days of any such request (or such longer period as shall reasonably be agreed):

(1) Sign and return to the party making the request, a joint application for the provision of copies of the deceased's medical notes or social worker's reports to all parties. The notes and/or reports should be sent separately and directly to each party. A specimen joint application is at Annex D.
(2) Sign, and return to the party making the request, a joint application for a statement by the solicitor who prepared the will of the deceased setting out all the circumstances leading up to the preparation and making of the will. A specimen joint application is at Annex E.

3.13 The party making the request for a joint application for information or documents from a third party shall:

(1) Submit it to the third party within 7 days of receipt of the joint application completed by the other parties.
(2) on receipt of the information or documents from the third party check that they have been received by all other parties and, if not, provide them with copies within 7 days of receipt.

3.14 In cases where the mental capacity of a deceased at the date of a testamentary instrument is in issue, the party seeking to uphold the testamentary instrument should obtain a report as to the deceased's mental capacity from his GP as soon as possible after the issue is identified and send it to all other parties within 7 days of receipt. A specimen letter of request is at Annex F.

Experts

3.15 Parties should consider the use of jointly instructed experts so far as possible. Accordingly before any prospective party (the first party) instructs an expert he should (unless of the opinion that another party will want to instruct his own expert) give the other (second) party a list of the name(s) of one or more experts in the relevant discipline whom he considers are suitable to instruct.

3.16 Within 14 days the second party may indicate an objection to one or more of such experts and suggest alternatives. The first party should then instruct a mutually acceptable expert.

3.17 If an expert to be jointly instructed is not agreed, the parties may then instruct experts of their own choice. It would be for the court to decide subsequently, if proceedings are issued, whether either party had acted unreasonably. No party shall be entitled to instruct an expert proposed in a list of experts for joint instructions until it is clear that joint instructions cannot be agreed and thereafter the party who submitted the list of experts shall be entitled to nominate one of the experts on this list as his own chosen expert and no other party shall instruct any expert named on the list until such nomination has taken place.

3.18 If the second party does not object to an expert nominated, he shall not be entitled to rely on his own expert evidence within that particular discipline unless:

(1) the court so directs, or
(2) the first party's expert report has been amended and the first party is not prepared to disclose the original report.

3.19 Either party may send to the expert written questions on the report, relevant to the issues, via the first party's solicitors. The expert should send answers to the question separately and directly to each party.

3.20 The cost of the report from an agreed expert will usually be paid by the party first proposing that a joint expert be instructed. The costs of the expert replying to questions will usually be borne by the party asking the questions. The ultimate liability for costs will be determined by the Court.

ANNEX A

REPRESENTATION IN ESTATE OR TRUST DISPUTES OF INTERESTED PERSONS WHO CANNOT BE ASCERTAINED ETC.

(1) In any estate or trust dispute concerning:-

(a) property comprised in an estate or subject to a trust or alleged to be subject to a trust; or

(b) the construction of a written instrument; or

(c) a situation where the interests of beneficiaries may require separate representation

the Court, if satisfied that it is expedient to do so, and that one or more of the conditions specified in paragraph (2) are satisfied, may appoint one or more persons to represent any person (including a person under a disability, a minor or an unborn person) or class who is or may be interested (whether presently or for any future, contingent or unascertained interest) in or affected by the dispute.

(2) The conditions for the exercise of the power conferred by paragraph (1) are as follows:-

(a) that the person, the class or some member of the class cannot be ascertained or cannot be readily ascertained, or is not of full capacity; or

(b) that the person, the class or some member of the class, though ascertained, cannot be found; or

(c) that, though the person or the class and members thereof can be ascertained and found, it appears to the Court expedient (regard being had to all the circumstances, including the amount at stake and the degree of difficulty of the point to be determined) to exercise the power for the purposes of saving expense or for any other reason.

(3) Where, in any case to which paragraph 1 applies, the Court exercises the power conferred by that paragraph, a judgment or order of the Court given or made when the person or persons appointed in exercise of that power are before the Court shall be binding on the person or class represented by the person or persons so appointed.

(4) Where, in any such case, a compromise is proposed and some of the persons who are interested in, or who may be affected by the compromise have not been consulted (including persons under a disability, minors or unborn or unascertained persons) but

(a) there is some other person in the same interest before the Court who assents to the compromise or on whose behalf the Court sanctions the compromise; or

(b) the absent persons are represented by a person appointed under paragraph (1) who so assents, the Court, if satisfied that the compromise will be for the benefit of the absent persons and that it is expedient to exercise this power, may approve the compromise and order that it shall be binding on absent persons, and they shall be bound accordingly except where the order has been obtained by fraud or non-disclosure of material facts.

ANNEX B

To Defendant

Dear

Re:

The estate of [name of deceased] The Settlement made by [Settlor] on [date]

We are instructed on behalf of [claimant] [give details of relief sought eg to seek reasonable provision out of the estate of the above-named deceased; to set aside probate of the will of the above-named deceased dated [date]; to seek a declaration that upon a proper construction of the above settlement our client is entitled to ...]

The basis of our clients claim is: [brief outline]

The facts upon which our client relies are as follows:- [set out material facts with sufficient clarity and detail for the proposed defendants to make a preliminary assessment of the claim]

The details of matters to which the Court would have regard under Section 3 of the Inheritance (Provision for Family and Dependants) Act 1975 insofar as they are known to our client are:-

(a) Financial resources and needs of claimant;

(b) Financial resources and needs of any other claimant;

(c) Financial resources and needs of beneficiaries;

(d) Obligations and responsibilities of deceased towards claimants and beneficiaries;

(e) Size and nature of estate;

(f) Disabilities of claimants and beneficiaries;

(g) Any other matter; and if claimant spouse or co-habitee,

(h) age of claimant, length of marriage/co-habitation and contribution to family welfare.

We enclose the following documents which are relevant to the claim:- [list documents]

In accordance with The ACTAPS Code for probate and trust disputes, we look forward to receiving a letter of response, enclosing the documents in your possession and relevant to the claim within [21] days. We believe that the following documents relevant to the claim are likely to be in your possession:- (list documents)

Pursuant to The ACTAPS Code as [personal representatives of the deceased/trustees of the settlement] we invite you to furnish us within 14 days of the date of this letter with copies of the following documents or written authority, in the form enclosed, to obtain copies of such document(s):- [list asterisked documents required]

We have also sent a letter of claim to (name and address) and a copy of that letter is enclosed.

Yours faithfully

ANNEX C

All documents upon which you rely or upon which the other party is likely to wish to rely including but not limited to the following categories:

1. In disputes in which the assets of an estate/trust fund or the financial resources of an individual are relevant; eg claims under the Inheritance Act, breach of trust claims:

   - The Inland Revenue Account and any Corrective Account;
   - A schedule of the capital assets (with values, estimated where appropriate) and income of the estate, trust fund or individual as appropriate;
   - Trust or Estate Accounts.

2. In disputes in which the mental capacity or medical condition of an individual is relevant, eg challenges to testamentary capacity, Inheritance Act claims where disability is alleged:

   - A copy of the medical records of the individual or, if appropriate, the written authority of the personal representatives of a deceased to obtain his medical records together with an office copy of the grant of probate or letters of administration or other proof of their status.

3. In disputes as to the validity, construction or rectification of a will or other testamentary instrument of the deceased:

   - A statement setting out details of any testamentary script (now in CPR called testamentary document) within the knowledge of the claimant or proposed defendant and details of the name and address of the person who, to the best of his knowledge, has possession or control of such script.

Nb1: The provision of the statement in 3 above is of vital importance to all parties in a dispute since it ensures that the correct testamentary documents are being considered. This will prevent the problem of a dispute over a later testamentary document being allowed to overshadow the existence of an intermediate testamentary document which would be upheld if the later testamentary document fails.

Also it helps identify the correct parties to the existing disputes.

Nb2: Following from Nb1 above, it is most important that the fullest and most exhaustive search for all testamentary documents is made. Accordingly while the following list is not exhaustive it is incumbent upon all parties to check:-

(i) with all known solicitors of the deceased as to the existence of a testamentary document;

(ii) with all attesting witnesses to testamentary documents as to the existence of testamentary documents;

(iii) with all named executors of testamentary documents as to the existence of testamentary documents;

(iv) with immediate family members (brothers, sisters, parents and children of the deceased) as to the existence of testamentary documents.

Nb3: Definition of Testamentary Script (now in CPR called Testamentary document)

A will, a draft of a will, written instructions for a will made by or at the request of, or under the instructions of, the testator, and any document purporting to be evidence of the contents, or to be a copy, of a will which is alleged to have been lost or destroyed. The word 'will' includes a codicil.

ANNEX D

JOINT APPLICATION FOR MEDICAL NOTES OR SOCIAL WORKER'S REPORTS

To: The medical records officer/social services

Dear Sir

Re: (Name) Deceased of (address), (date of birth)

We the undersigned Messrs (firm's name) (ref) of (firm's address), Solicitors for (the Executors named in the Will of the late (deceased's name) of (deceased's address) who died on (date of death) and we, the undersigned Messrs (firm's name) of (firm's address), Solicitors for parties interested in his/her estate, hereby authorise you to forward [a full set of copies of the deceased's Medical Records] [all social workers reports and notes relating to the deceased] to each of the aforementioned firms.

We confirm that we will be responsible for your reasonable photocopying charges and your invoice in this regard should be sent to (firm's name) and marked for the attention of (ref).

Dated [ ] 20[ ]

Signed [ ]

Signed [ ]

ANNEX E

JOINT APPLICATION LETTER TO SOLICITORS WHO PREPARED WILL REQUESTING LARKE v NUGUS STATEMENT

Dear Sirs

[Name of Deceased] deceased

We, the undersigned Messrs (firm's name) (ref) of (firm's address), solicitors for the Executors named in the Will of (deceased's name) of (deceased's address) and we, the undersigned Messrs (firm's name) (ref) of (firm's address), solicitors for parties interested in his/her estate regret to inform you that (deceased's name) died on (date of death).

We understand that you drafted the deceased's last will dated [ ].

You may be aware that in 1959 the Law Society recommended that in circumstances such as this the testator's solicitor should make available a statement of his or her evidence regarding instructions for the preparation and execution of the will and surrounding circumstances. This recommendation was endorsed by the Court of Appeal on 21st February 1979 in *Larke v Nugus*.

The practice is also recommended at paragraph 24.02 of the Law Society's *Guide to the Professional Conduct of Solicitors*, 7th edition (page 387).

Accordingly, we hereby request and authorise you to forward to each of the aforementioned firms statements from all appropriate members of your firm on the following points:

- How long had you known the deceased?
- Who introduced you to the deceased?
- On what date did you receive instructions from the deceased?
- Did you receive instructions by letter? If so, please provide copies of any correspondence.
- If instructions were taken at a meeting, please provide copies of your contemporaneous notes of the meeting including an indication of where the meeting took place and who else was present at the meeting.
- How were the instructions expressed?
- What indication did the deceased give to you that he knew he was making a will?
- Were you informed or otherwise aware of any medical history of the deceased that might bear upon the issue of his capacity?
- Did the deceased exhibit any signs of confusion or loss of memory? If so, please give details.

- To what extent were earlier wills discussed and what attempts were made to discuss departures from his earlier will-making pattern? What reasons, if any, did the testator give for making any such departures?
- When the will had been drafted, how were the provisions of the will explained to the deceased?
- Who, apart from the attesting witnesses, was present at the execution of the will? Where, when and how did this take place?
- Please provide copies of any other documents relating to your instructions for the preparation and execution of the will and surrounding circumstances or confirm that you have no objection to us inspecting your relevant file(s) on reasonable notice.

We confirm that we will be responsible for your reasonable photocopying charges in this connection and your invoice in this regard should be sent to (each firm's name etc) and marked for the attention of (each firm's ref.).

Dated this [ ] day of [ ] 20[ ]

Signed [ ]

Signed [ ]

ANNEX F

LETTER TO DECEASED'S GP REQUESTING REPORT AS TO MENTAL CAPACITY

To: Deceased's GP

Dear Dr [ ]

Re: (Name) Deceased of (address), (date of birth)

We the undersigned Messrs (firm's name) (ref) of (firm's address) are Solicitors for (the Executors named in the Will of the late (deceased's name) of (deceased's address) who died on (date of death)) and we, the undersigned Messrs (firm's name) of (firm's address), are Solicitors for parties interested in his/her estate.

We enclose a photocopy of the deceased's last Will. The clauses in the Will which cause particular concern are (clause numbers).

The question of the deceased's mental capacity at the time of the making of his/her last Will dated has now been raised.

The test of testamentary capacity remains that established in the case of *Banks -v- Goodfellow* where it was said:-

> 'It is essential that a testator (1) shall understand the nature of the act and its effects; (2) shall understand the extent of the property of which he is disposing; and (3) shall be able to comprehend and appreciate the claims to which he ought to give effect, and; with a view to the latter object, (4) that no disorder of mind shall poison his affections, pervert his sense of right or pervert the exercise of his natural faculties; (5) that no insane delusions shall influence his mind in disposing of his property and bring about a disposal of it which if his mind had been sound, would not have been made.' (We have added numbers for convenience).

(Set out the nature of the Estate if complex).

We would therefore be grateful if you would kindly provide us with a report setting out:-

1. Your medical qualifications and your experience in assessing mental states and capacity.
2. For how long you were the deceased's GP, how well you knew the deceased and a summary of his/her medical condition, insofar as it may have bearing upon the deceased's mental capacity.
3. Your findings as to the deceased's mental capacity at and around the time of the date of his/her last will.

4. Please also deal with any mental disorder from which the deceased may have been suffering at the relevant time, and any medication which could have affected his/her capacity as detailed above.

5. Please also consider any issues of vulnerability or suggestibility at or around the date of the deceased's last Will.

We confirm that we will be responsible for your reasonable fees in the preparation of your report which we look forward to receiving as soon as possible.

Dated this [ ] day of [ ] 20[ ]

Signed [ ] (ref:)

Signed [ ] (ref:)

Index

References are to page numbers. Abbreviations have the same meanings as in the text.